The Holy Koran

An Interpretive Translation from Classical Arabic into Contemporary English

Translated by

Mohamed K. Jasser

Acacia Publishing, Inc.

Acacia Publishing, Inc.
1366 E Thomas Rd., Suite 305
Phoenix, AZ 85014

ISBN 978-0-9814629-1-2
LCCN 2008920531

Published by Acacia Publishing, Inc.
Phoenix, Arizona
www.acaciapublishing.com

for Karim Holdings, LLC

Printed and Bound in the United States of America

INTRODUCTION

This translation of the Koran differs from other available English translations, in numerous respects. Most, if not all, available translations use old Arabic interpretations of the Koran as a source for the meaning of words and sentences. In effect, they are translations of those old interpretations rather than translations of the actual text of the Koran.

The Koran was revealed in the Arabic language, a very complicated language, as the language was used at the time the revelations occurred. The Koran text should actually speak for itself, to those who are familiar with classical Arabic. Interpretations written hundreds of years ago have nothing to recommend them as having high degrees of accuracy or correctness. Most of these old interpretations were heavily influenced by opinions or conclusions of others, and derived heavily from Hadith (*defined as the collected comments, sayings, and actions of the Prophet, Mohammed*). These importations frequently appear to be incompatible with the actual text, and appear to be attempts at overriding the apparent meaning of the text by using the prestige and influence of the Prophet himself and by employing sayings attributed to him.

Hadith was collected 300 years after the death of Mohammed, relying on a very unreliable method of transmission, which is the word of mouth, with individuals relaying the sayings to each other, over hundreds of years.

The Koran is one of the best preserved books in history, and unlike Hadith, it was put down in writing while the Prophet was still alive. None of it depended on the memory or the truthfulness of anyone. Basic to Islamic theology, the Koran contains a promise from God, that the accuracy of the text of the Book shall be preserved and guaranteed accurate by God himself: *"We have revealed the Mention (the words of the Book as they are read) and We shall preserve it"* (Chapter 5, verse 9). It is interesting that the Arabic word used in that verse to refer to the Koran, which was translated as the "Mention," is one of the names of the Koran, but it is a word that attributes higher importance to the way the text and the words are read rather than to the way they are interpreted. In Arabic that implies variability of the meaning.

It is basic to Islamic belief that the Koran was revealed for all times and all ages. That by itself excludes fixed interpretations over all times and all ages. It is actually an indication of a certain degree of fluidity and variability of meaning. So although the text is fixed, the interpretation is variable – Principle of the fixation of the text and fluidity of the meaning. In the Koran it is actually stated: *"Some of it is clear and some of it is ambiguous"* (Chapter 3, verse 7).

In many places, in the Koran, there are pointed indications that the correct interpretation of many parts of the Koran will not be clear to all people at certain times. Emphasis on the way words are said or pronounced rather than their apparent meaning is so strong that it was included in an admonishment to the Prophet himself, and it carries the clear implication, that even Mohammed himself is not necessarily guaranteed to find the correct meaning for everything in the Book: *"Do not move your tongue with the words fast. We are responsible for putting it together, and the way it should be read. As you recite it, pay more attention to the way you read it. The meaning is our responsibility"* (Chapter 75, verses 16, 17, 18 and 19).

This makes such perfect logic with the concept of "for all times and all ages," that it actually indicates that the Koran will become fully and accurately understood only on the Day of Judgement, and that the principle of fixation of the text and the fluidity of the meaning is the only thing that makes sense. This also reveals the fallacy of resorting to, or translating from, interpretations written hundreds of years earlier, or using Hadith to interpret the Koran.

Interpretation of the Koran belongs to anyone who feels qualified to do it. Interpretations can be right in many things and wrong in some. The guide should be the language, logic, and measuring the Koran against itself, such as noting the use of certain words in one place and comparing it with the way they are used in other places. The Koran recognizes no hierarchy for accepted interpretations. The Koran clearly states: *"No clergy in Islam."*

Those who interpret the Koran correctly shall be rewarded by God, and those who do it incorrectly shall be punished by Him, and those who are incapable of interpretation, will have to depend on the work of others, and then make a judgement on their own.

In translation, which is interpretation in a language other than Arabic, there is a need for the work to be original, based strictly on language, logic, knowledge in classical Arabic, and the basic principles of Islamic theology.

In this work, the Koran was translated, or interpreted in English, based on the same criteria declared in the Koran itself. For the parts that are clear and straightforward, the translation is relatively simple, and hopefully clear. The parts that appear to be unclear and ambiguous, words were checked for their meaning and use at the time the Koran was revealed. Frequently the Koran was checked against itself. Certain words appear unclear in some locations and the lack of clarity was found to be related to interpretations. Better logic and clarity are possible to achieve by resorting to the way the words are used in different locations, and where different interpretations appear, and thus the translation would be different.

Many of the social, cultural, and environmental factors in the traditional Arab community over the years played a major role in misguiding interpretations away from the original text.

The Arabic word meaning "clean" was interpreted always in its simplest and most common usage, in a nation of desert dwellers, where everything relates to water and the importance of it in their lives. The traditional interpretation of a statement in the Koran is: *"It (the Koran) can be touched only by those who are clean."* It is a strictly ritual and simplistic interpretation. Those who want to hold or touch the Koran have to be clean. They need to resort to cleaning themselves with water, or actually perform ablution prior to holding it -- a ritualistic rule that makes little sense. Why not say "Do not touch it or hold it in your hand unless you clean yourself first"! The way it was worded sounds more like a challenge than a prohibition. When the two Arabic words "clean" and "touch" are researched for their use in the Koran, it is found that they are used, far more frequently, in their metaphorical meaning than the simplistic one. The Arabic word for "touch" is used far more frequently in a different way: "touched by God's favor," "touched by a calamity," "touched by the Devil." And the word "clean" is used to mean "ready" or "receptive." So the cleanliness intended is that of the heart, and not necessarily that of the body. The interpretation, and thus the translation of that verse should be: *"Its correct meaning can be reached only by those who are receptive to it."*

Along the same lines, in the 4th chapter it says in the Koran using traditional interpretation: "They ask you about the menses, say it is harmful." The old Arabic word for "harmful" was used, at that time, to mean "painful." It is obvious that the right meaning is "painful," and not "harmful." So instead of an ill-informed sexist statement, the correct interpretation is a factual and scientifically correct statement. Following that verse, there is another statement addressing men, in regard to menstruation. Again, if the traditional interpretation is used: "Do not go near them (*women*) until they are clean," it would create the clear implication that menstruating women are unclean. In effect, the true meaning, and thus the interpretation should be: *"Do not approach them until they are receptive to you." Clean is used in the Koran to indicate meanings other than simple cleanliness. Many prophets chosen by God are said to be cleansed by Him, which clearly indicates being made more open-minded and receptive.*

Another example of erroneous interpretation because of difference in times and places is the following:

"If you are able to penetrate through the layers of heaven and the regions of the earth, go ahead. You shall not succeed until you find a source for a great power" (Chapter 55, verse 23).

At this time and age, this verse requires no interpretation, but if one looks it up in the famous interpretation by Ibn Kathier, which is a thousand years old, it reads: *"You cannot run away from God and his dominance over you. He can find you anywhere."*

Moslems have been taught for years in Islamic schools and universities that Mohammed, the Prophet of Islam, was illiterate. A shamefully fallacious fabrication, that was all related to misguided interpretation of a word in the Koran, which became gradually, in more recent Arabic, to mean illiterate. But in pre-Islamic Arabic, the word "Oummee" was used to mean the equivalent of the word "gentile" in English today, meaning "non-Jewish" or "non-Hebrew." Christians and Jews in Arabia at that time were better educated than the pagan Arabs. Thus the word "oummee" or "gentile" started to be used in a derogatory fashion to mean those who are uneducated. The word in the Koran was used describing Mohammed, to remind him and others that he was the first Prophet chosen by God to be of non-Hebrew or non-Jewish origin.

Mohammed came from the most distinguished tribe in Arabia (*Kouraish*) and the most distinguished family in Kouraish (*Bni Hashem*). Kouraish is a tribe that sponsored a competition in Arabic poetry yearly, with the wining pieces getting hung on the walls of the Kaaba (*the House of Abraham*), the most sacred building in Arabia. This was a tribe in which education and ability in language was held in high esteem. Is it anything but ridiculous to even imagine that the man chosen to lead, and make an impact that changed the world, was illiterate.

The chapter revealed first in the Koran, during the first contact between Gabriel and Mohammed states: *"Read in the name of God who created humans from a clot. Read in the name of your Lord. He taught humans to write with a pen. He taught them what they did not know."* It requires feeble-mindedness to believe that God's first contact with an illiterate person will concentrate on reading and writing.

It is easy to see how erroneous it was to interpret the Arabic word "oummee," to mean illiterate, and how much better it would fit in the following verse for the interpretation and the translation to be "gentile." In Chapter 62, verse 2: *"He (God) is the One who sent an apostle to the gentiles, reciting to them his verses, purifying them, and providing them with the Book and wisdom, for prior to that, they were clearly misguided."* Replacing the word "gentiles" with "illiterates" in the above verse will have the clear meaning of Mohammed being the Apostle sent to the illiterates, which would be unquestionably erroneous.

Status of Hadith:

As already mentioned, in this work, Hadith was avoided as a source to support the interpretive translation of the Koran, but it is useful to explain further why. Unlike the Koran, Hadith was not written down during the life of the Prophet, or at anytime soon thereafter. It was collected by several individuals three hundred years later, principally by a man with the name of Boukhari, his student Moslem, and a few others. These were collected by transmission through word of mouth, over many years, from one individual to another. A system was used for evaluating the correctness and validity that depended mainly on studying the reputation of the transmitters. Little consideration was given to the fact that people tend to relay things more like the way they understood them, than by using the exact words they heard, even with the best of intentions. In one of those so-called "verified" sayings, the Prophet himself was quoted as discouraging his companions from writing or recording his sayings because he was very concerned about having them become confused with the Koran. Very conveniently, another Hadith was found that contradicted that.

The first four caliphs after the death of Mohammed, who were his four closest companions, spent huge amounts of their time supervising the collection of the written Koran to have it put correctly in one volume, and confirm that absolutely correct copies were reproduced. None of the four closest companions to the Prophet lifted a finger to do anything in regard to Hadith.

A few principles have been agreed upon as a given, over the years in regard to Hadith:

1. No Hadith can be accepted as true or validated if it contradicts anything in the Koran.

2. Anything in Hadith, even when validated, is strictly optional and nonobligatory when it cannot be found in the Koran.

A validated Hadith even describes a man putting a question to the Prophet, asking: "What would happen to me if I followed everything that was decreed in the Koran by God, but did not follow any of your Sounna (*example*) or your Hadith," and the Prophet's answer was: "If I enter heaven, you shall." This is the framework in which Hadith or Sounna was supposed to work when Hadith was first collected. A status that does not even come close to the status of the Koran. Most Moslems, some grudgingly, agree with this framework, yet many of them start showing hesitation when it appears to be challenging a lot of their long-held beliefs and traditions.

In Islamic schools they teach that illicit sexual activity between consenting adults is called fornication when it occurs between unmarried individuals, and adultery when it occurs among those who are married, but with those other than their spouses. They are also told that the penalty for fornication is one hundred lashes with a whip, and that the penalty for adultery is stoning, which is a death penalty, and in effect a horrible death. If one searches the Koran, no penalty of stoning is found anywhere, and neither will one find a distinction between fornication and adultery. The penalty of 100 lashes is specified for both, after a set of conditions is satisfied for the proof necessary, that is practically impossible to satisfy.

Execution of individuals charged with adultery in many Islamic countries has no basis in the Koran whatsoever.

A top cleric in Egypt, who was president of the famous "Azhar Islamic University," made a statement recently, saying that 60% of Islamic Shariaa (or Law) comes from Hadith. This is the same individual who excused suicidal homicide missions and female circumcision.

The Prophet in his "farewell speech" recited one of the last and then, most recently revealed, verses of the Koran: *"Today I have completed your religion for you, and finished my blessings upon you, and approved Islam as your religion."* The words "finished" and "completed" are words that are absolute, and are always and uniformly 100%. It is a verse that would cause the cleric's statement to be rejected, as false, right off hand. *He also must have neglected to familiarize himself with the 60% he was talking about.*

Relayed by Moslem, the Prophet said:

"He who kills himself with a steel knife, will be an eternal resident of hell, and will have that weapon in his hand, thrusting it in his abdomen, over and over; and he who kills himself by drinking poison, shall be sipping that poison in the fire of hell where he will stay forever. And he who kills himself by jumping off the edge of a mountain will forever continue to fall in the fire of hell and stay there."

The non-existence of special circumstances or justifications for suicide is relayed in Hadith by both Boukhari and Moslem: *"None of you should long for death, nor should you pray for it before it comes, because when it arrives, it will terminate all your good deeds.*

In the Koran it is said: *"Do not ever throw yourselves into a certain death."*

Also from the Koran: *"Do not kill a soul which God forbade."*

"He who kills an innocent person, shall be put in the hands of the victim's next of kin" (Chapter 17, verse 33).

"Those who kill a human are unbelievers" (Chapter 80, verse 17).

There is absolutely nothing in the Koran or Hadith that gives recognition to anything as savage, mutilating, and monstrous as female circumcision.

Moslems need to find in Hadith what is appropriate and fits perfectly with the word of God in the Koran. *For Islam is the Koran and the Koran is Islam.*

Attitude towards other religions:

Support for any form of Islamic extremism cannot be found in the Koran. The draconian laws and regulations enforced by the Wahabis (*a fanatical sect dominant in Saudi Arabia*) have little valid foundation in Islamic theology. One such shameful concept is that Christians and Jews cannot enter the cities of Mecca and Madina in Arabia. It is quite appropriate to use validated Hadith, besides the Koran, to defeat concepts advocated by people who abuse and misuse Hadith the most.

Relayed by Boukhari and Moslem: *"Of all mankind I am closest to Jesus Christ. All prophets are brothers even when they are from different mothers, but Jesus is special, because there are no other prophets between him and me."*

Also relayed by Boukhari: *"The Prophet, upon witnessing the Jews in Madina observing a fast on the day of Ashura. He asked them about the significance of that day they are observing. They told him it was the day of their delivery, along with Moses, from the pharaoh. The Prophet said: We are just as close to that, and have as much reason to observe it as you are, and started fasting on that day every year, and recommended to others to do so."*

The Prophet also said to one of his companions: *"You have two qualities which God loves, one is mildness and the other is toleration."*

The Wahabis and similarly inclined Moslems will argue that those Christians and Jews were different theologically from those of today. This is a fallacious claim because the same Koran that called them people of the book, also recognized that Christians call Jesus the son of God, and admonished them for that. The Christians who lived in

Arabia and the Christian King who ruled Ethiopia were the ones who provided refuge to many persecuted Moslems, and many companions of the Prophet. All of these Christians did believe that Jesus was the son of God.

Wahabis and similarly inclined Moslems even argue, just as shamefully, that Moslems cannot take Christians and Jews as friends; another flagrant misinterpretation of the Koran. The Arabic word "awliaa" was knowingly and intentionally misinterpreted. This word never meant friend, nor has it ever been used as such. It can mean a sponsor, a mentor, or a guardian, and can even be used to describe God as He relates to humans. It is never a word that implies equality as friendship does.

A whole chapter in the Koran was devoted to the strong disappointment felt by the Prophet Mohammed and the Moslems about the war that occurred between the Byzantines (*Christians*) and the Zoroastrians, and ended up with a Zoroastrian victory. Chapter 30, which is called "the Byzantines," contained reassurances to the Moslems that the war was not yet over and that the final victory shall be for the Christians, which is what eventually occurred. So not only were the Moslems close to the Christians, they were actually allies.

Islam and War:

"When you fight in the cause of God, only fight those who are fighting you, and do not ever be aggressors" (Chapter 2, verse 190).

This is an area where, over the years, a bizarre, though probably unintended, alliance occurred between Islamic fanaticism and the anti-Islamic orientalism; each pumping a new life into the other. The orientalist intellectuals drew a picture of a huge monster by the name of Islam, and the Islamic fanatics continuously provide for them evidence that the monster does, in fact, exist. In this effectively defaming collaboration, the truth started to matter less and less. The Moslem fanatics interpret the Koran the way it suits them, and what they cannot find in the Koran they can easily find a way to attribute to Hadith and have a good chance of finding it there; for although much of Hadith may be valid, a lot of it is probably manufactured. A hierarchy of clerics that was not supposed to exist in Islam developed gradually, providing self-serving distortion of the Koran, and much of the manufactured Hadith.

The western intellectual orientalists took a very clever and deceptive attitude in the middle of all of that. It does not matter what is in the Koran, when Moslems believe it to be different, and Islamic traditions interpret it otherwise. That was a very unfortunate attitude. It was self-serving to preserve the façade of correctness of their long-held opinions, instead of playing a positive role in bringing the fanatic views to the test of reality, and assisting in cultivating the only solution to Islamic fanaticism (*the so-called Islamism*), by pulling the rug from under the fanatics and exposing the bankruptcy and fallaciousness of their views. The solution has to include discrediting the fanatics from within the folds of Islamic theology, based on facts and not demagoguery.

The basic concepts held in western circles about the warlike attitudes of Islam are just simply erroneous. The Islamic empire, and many Islamic countries, engaged in wars and acts of aggression and occupation that were simply expansionist. Those Islamic powers were no different from western colonial powers in trying to put a moral face on their acts of aggression and expansion. How is the Islamic occupation of Spain any different from the British occupation of India? The British, in one eighth of the time, left more Christians in India than the Moslem empire left Moslems in Spain. When Moslem control over Spain fell, Spain was left, basically, a Christian country. If conversion to Islam was achieved by the sword, 620 years of Islamic rule in Spain were certainly enough to achieve that. Yet the few Moslems left in Spain were all subjected to the courts of inquisition and forcibly converted. The Indian subcontinent (*including India and Pakistan*) contains the largest concentration of Moslems in the world, yet the subcontinent never came under Islamic administrative or political rule. The Jews who lived 600 years under Islamic rule found the Moslem rulers of Spain far more tolerant than their previous or subsequent Christian rulers. Jewish history books describe that period as the Golden Age. The only wars in history that fit perfectly the definition of a "holy war" were the crusades, when the Christian kings of Europe attacked the Middle East with the declared intention of defeating Islam and Moslems.

For Islam to be spread by the sword, there has to be somewhere in the Koran a place where war was ordered or encouraged for the purpose of conversion, yet this does not exist. In many places in the

Koran there is the obvious recognition that there will always be multiple religions.

"Those who believed, the Jews, the Sabaeans, the Christians, the Zoroastrians, and the pagans, God shall deal with them on the Day of Judgement. God is cognizant of all things" (Chapter 22, verse 17).

Furthermore, in the Koran, conditions set for a justifiable war could not be any clearer.

- It has to be defensive.
- Against those who declare war because of religion.
- Against those who also because of religion, unjustly force Moslems out of their homes and confiscate their property.

"Permission is given to fight for those who are victims of aggression and God is capable of providing them with victory. This is especially true if they were forced out of their homes, for no reason but believing in God. If it was not for God using some against the others, many monasteries, synagogues, and mosques, where the name of God is mentioned in prayers, will be destroyed. God will grant victory to those who work for Him. He is powerful and exalted" (Chapter 22, verses 39 and 40).

In the Koran, no animosities based on religion are countenanced.

"God may will that you have friendship and goodwill between you and those who were your enemies. God is Capable, Forgiving and Merciful. God does not forbid you from befriending those who did not fight you because of your religion, and did not force you out of your homes. You can be friendly and fair with them, and God loves those who are fair. God does forbid you to befriend those who fought you because of your religion, and forced you out of your homes, and supported others in doing so. Those who befriend them are transgressors" (Chapter 60, verses 7, 8, 9).

The Koran does not contain a single statement that encourages or orders war for the purpose of conversion.

"You are but a reminder. You have no control over them" (Chapter 88, verse 21, and 22).

Virgins in Heaven:

This is rather a ridiculous subject. There is not a single verse in the Koran that promises a soul entering heaven anything different from others there, regardless of the reason for their being in heaven. The so-called virgins are in reality angels, dedicated to providing service to dwellers of Heaven. They are both males and females. The services they provide are care services and not sexual. The Koran talks about their purity to emphasize their total devotion to service, and any sexual implications occur only in the minds of those who are sexually repressed. This is to be distinguished from the mention of spouses in heaven who are supposed to be whoever the person wants or imagines them to be. They could be the same spouses the dwellers of heaven had in the first life, recreated as virgins, if that is their wish. Spouses in heaven are totally devoted to each other and possess no inclination to anyone else.

The so called 72 virgins on TV programs notwithstanding, Chapter 56, verses 15 to 25 say:

"They shall be reclining on comfortable beds, opposite each other. Served by young boy servants, who are immortalized in their service. With cups and pots and glasses of wine, which does not give them a headache or impair their judgement. They will get fruits of their choice, and bird meat of the kind they desire.

They will have beautiful and slender spouses, who are like well-preserved pearls. As a reward for their good deeds."

To be noted is that each person has one spouse, and spouses in heaven are characterized by being attracted only to one another.

In verses 35, 36, and 37 in the same chapter: *"Their spouses of choice will be recreated to be virgins, and they shall be faithful to each other and interested only in each other."* And in Chapter 55, verse 55, the spouses of heaven are described as: *"Finding no one in heaven better than their spouses."*

This is certainly not the description of a sexual orgy with 72 virgins — a shameful nonsense, suited for stupid suicidal fanatics, and hungry press with nothing to do.

The concept of Jihad:

In the Koran, and thus in Islam, the concept of "holy war" does not exist. The word Jihad does not mean war, it means struggle. If one dies while struggling to make a living for one's family, that would be considered death for a worthy cause, and deserving of reward in heaven. The concept of martyrdom also does not exist in Islam. The closest Arabic word in meaning to martyr is "shaheed," a word derived from the Arabic word that means witness. This is so important, because no one can make himself a martyr. It is God witnessing the circumstances of the death that makes it a worthy cause or not, and thus deserving of reward or not. That certainly does not include death having been planned as a certain outcome of the action that led to it. *Expectation of a chance for survival is an absolute requirement for the death not to become a suicide, which is punishable by eternal hell. The intention is what controls the result.*

"No soul is to die, unless permitted by God. A preordained event, timed by Him" (Chapter 3, verse 145).

Again, the idea of war to produce belief or conversion is never permitted in the Koran. The Koran admonishes: *"You have been given certain signs by your Lord, one who sees does so for one's self, and those who are blinded, I am not their keeper."* Also in support of free choice in Islam, the Koran says: *"The truth is from your Lord. One who wants to believe, can do so, and one who does not can deny."*

Furthermore, addressed to Mohammed: *"The unbelievers who extend their hand to you in peace, God gives you no authority over them."*

Logic and Reason vs. Fanatacism and Self-serving Interpretations:

If one believes in God as the Supreme being that Moslems, Christians and Jews believe Him to be, it's a great blasphemy to attribute to Him human qualities such as forgetfulness, lack of intention, or meanings in His words that go beyond what is being said, unintended actions or unintended lack of action. When God does not mention something, then by necessity He felt it did not need to be mentioned or should not be mentioned. When humans fabricate things like "Fatwa" or rulings on certain things that do not exist in the Koran, they are in effect usurping God's authority, which is a great sin. God's Book is all inclusive, and for all times and places. The word "Fatwa" does not exist in the Koran, and such authority was not given to anyone, not even the Prophet himself. *"O' Prophet why do you forbid what I permitted?"* (Chapter 66, verse 1) This was about a rule in the Koran that no man can marry a woman who used to be wedded to his son. The Prophet simply extended that to adopted sons, and he was reprimanded for that. In effect, he was being told by God: "If I did not mention adopted sons, it automatically means they are not included." The clear implication is that anything not specifically forbidden by God is automatically permitted, and even the Prophet himself cannot make additions, not to mention the so-called "Fatwas" by insignificant others.

Another subject of great deal of abuse is the so-called *"cancelled verses."* Everything in the Koran is revealed by God, including where a verse falls in sequence, punctuation, and sequence of chapters, and their headings. Some verses were cancelled by revelation, and replaced with other verses. It is absolute nonsense and fabrication that verses present in the Koran as it stands have been cancelled. God said in the Koran: *"We will not cancel a verse or cause it to be forgotten without replacing it with a verse that is the same or better. Did you not know that God is capable of everything?"* The word "replaced" is not "cancelled and left there." Every verse in the Koran is intended to be there, for all times and all ages.

When God states in the 4th chapter, verse 43: *"Do not ever aproach prayer while you are drunk. You should wait until you can understand what you are saying"* that verse means exactly what it says. There are Moslems who may drink although it is strongly discouraged (*not absolutely forbidden*), and may want to pray, and that verse is for them. There is a difference between *"forbidden"* which is absolute, and *"strongly discouraged."* The Koran is a reference for classical Arabic, and no stupid manipulations can change the meaning of Arabic words.

An example of absolute forbiddance: *"It is forbidden that you should eat the flesh of the dead, blood, the meat of the pig, and that of any animal that was consecrated to anyone other than God"* (Chapter 2, verse 173).

An example of strong discouragement that was embedded in relativity: *"People who believe, wine, gambling, idols, and games of chance, are abominations invented by the devil; avoid them"* (Chapter 5, verse 90).

"They ask you about wine and gambling, say: There is a great harm in both and some benefit. But their harm is far greater than their benefit" (Chapter 2, verse 219).

Another huge controversy created by fanaticism and longstanding Arab antifeminism is the issue of the cover for women. Again penetration by the enemy through their land to attack the Moslem city. During the attack, Bni Kouraiza not only allowed an attack through their territory, they actually joined it. As the pagans lost, Bni Kouraiza were attacked and destroyed. That was called the War of the Ditch.

Following that, the strength of the Moslems reached a point that they could enter Mecca without a drop of blood being shed. Peace was negotiated between the Prophet and the leader of the pagan Kouraish, Abou Soufian. The city surrendered to the Moslem army with an agreed-upon written declaration that was posted on the walls of Mecca stating: "Those who stay in their homes and close their doors are safe. Those who enter the great mosque (*around the Kabaa*) are safe, and those who seek the protection of the house of Abou Soufian (*the negotiator*) will also be safe."

After that Moslems controlled Arabia. Force was not used to convert non-Moslems, but rather to make sure that those who adopted Islam remained safe.

Final note:

This work is based on a long-standing knowledge of the Koran and classical Arabic. It is not sanctioned by any authority, nor is it officially approved by anyone. It is a labor of love, a labor of faith and a labor of conviction.

The spellings of certain words differ from that adopted by certain Islamic conventions in recent years. The reason is a strong disagreement with these adopted spellings, for they tend to violate the rules of pronunciation for both English and Arabic. The English spelling of the word "Moslem" that is closest to the Arabic origin is certainly not "Muslim." For in English, a word that starts with "MUS-" will most likely be pronounced similar to the way it is pronounced in the word "MUST". The last three letters of the Arabic word are far closer in pronunciation to "-lem" than to "-lim". It was felt that the spelling of "Moslem" though not perfect has at least the advantage of higher familiarity and length of time used. Whenever possible, the use of an "o" or an "ou" was favored over a single "U", for a "U", in English is practically never pronounced the way it is intended to be pronounced in Arabic unless it is in short words that end with an "e".

Because I have studied in England, certain peculiarities of British grammar and spelling appear throughout the text, for example the spelling of "judgement" and the forms of "worship". Certain grammatical conventions have been implemented to conform to the nature of the text. Statements made by God are not marked off by quotation marks, while statements made by humans are so marked. Seemingly unusual capitalization generally denotes that a term refers to God (for example, "He") or a quality of God (for example, "Exalted and Wise"). Two exceptions are the terms "Apostle" and "Prophet," which are capitalized only when referring to a specific apostle or prophet, such as Moses or Mohammed.

Mohamed K. Jasser

THE OPENING (1)

In the name of God, most merciful, and most beneficent. (1)

Thanks to God, Lord of the Universe. (2)

The Beneficent and Merciful. (3)

Owner of the Day of Judgement. (4)

It is You we worship and on You we rely. (5)

Guide us through to the straight path. (6)

The path of those you have favored and away from the path of those who incurred your wrath, and the path of the misguided. (7)

THE COW (2)

In the Name of God, Most Merciful, and Most Beneficent.

Alef, Lam, Meem. (1)

This Book is not to be doubted. It is a guide to the righteous. (2)

Those who have faith in the untold future are steadfast in prayer and spend in charity some of what We gave them, (3)

and those who believe in what was revealed to you and to those who came before you, and who are certain of the life to come, (4)

These are rightly guided by their God and they are the triumphant. (5)

As for the unbelievers, it is the same to them whether you warn them or not. They will not believe. (6)

It is as if God has put a seal on their hearts, their hearing, and their eyesight, and a painful torture awaits them. (7)

Among the people are those who say: "We believe in God and in the Last Day" and they are insincere. (8)

While they intend to deceive God and those who believe, they deceive none but themselves and they do not know it. (9)

There is illness in their heart and God made them more ill. They shall have excruciating torture for their lies. (10)

If one tells them: "Do not corrupt the earth," they answer: "We are none but reformers." (11)

They are the corrupters, but they do not know it. (12)

And if they were asked to believe like the rest of the believers, they respond: "Shall we believe like the fools do?" It is they who are the fools but they do not know it. (13)

When they meet those who believe they say: "We believe," but when they are back alone with their Devils, they say: "We are with you, we were only mocking." (14)

God will mock them and let them blunder further in their misguided reign. (15)

Those are the ones who traded being guided for being lost. Their trade was a loss and they will not find the right path. (16)

Their example is that of a man who kindled a fire, and as soon as it illuminated what was around him God extinguished it, and left him blind in the dark. (17)

Deaf, dumb and blind, they shall never find the right path. (18)

Or like the example of those who, in the middle of a storm with thunder and lightning, would thrust their fingers in their ears in fear of death from lightning; and God will confound the unbelievers. (19)

Lightning almost went with their eyesight. When it flashed they walked and when it darkened they stood. If God wished he could take away their hearing and eyesight; God is capable of all deeds. (20)

People, worship your Lord who created you and those before you so that you may be pious. (21)

He who made the earth your bed and the sky a dome over you, and brought water down from heaven and produced the fruits for your sustenance, do not knowingly set up peers for Him. (22)

If you are in doubt of what we sent down to Our Servant, We challenge you to produce one chapter, and you can use your own Gods to assist you if you are truthful. (23)

You shall not be able to reproduce it; so keep yourself out of the fire whose fuel is people and stone, prepared for the unbelievers. (24)

Convey the good tidings to those who have good faith and do good work. Theirs shall be gardens watered by flowing rivers, and whenever they are served the fruits, they say: "This is what we used to receive before." They will be served what they enjoyed before. They shall have chaste and faithful spouses and they will live there eternally. (25)

God is not reluctant to make an example of a mosquito or a larger creature, and those who are believers know that it is the true word from their Lord, but the unbelievers ask why God wanted to mislead many, while leading many others. God does not mislead but the evildoers. (26)

Those who break their covenant with God after they made it, and disrupt what God wanted connected and spread evil in the land, these are the losers. (27)

How can you deny God when you were dead and He resurrected you? Then He will let you die and resurrect you again, and to Him you shall always return. (28)

He is the One who created what is on earth then ascended to heaven and made it in seven layers, and He is the One who has knowledge of all things. (29)

When your Lord said to the Angels: I am creating on earth a deputy, they asked: "Why would You put there someone who will corrupt it and shed blood on it when we have always sung your praise and sanctified Your Name?" and He said: I know what you do not know. (30)

And He taught Adam all the names and then introduced him to the Angels and asked them: Tell Me the names of these things if you are right. (31)

They said: "The glory is yours, we never knew but what you taught us. You are the All-knowing and the Wise." (32)

He said: Adam, tell them the names and when he did, He said: Did I not tell you that I know the future of the Heavens and Earth and I know what you reveal and what you hide? (33)

When We told the Angels to kneel in front of Adam, they all did except for the Devil who refused and became arrogant and joined the unbelievers. (34)

We said to Adam: You and your wife dwell in Paradise and eat of its fruits to your heart's content, anywhere you wish, except for this tree. Stay away from it or you are a transgressor. (35)

The Devil misled them and got them out of where they were and We said: Descend to earth where you will be enemies to each other, and there your sustenance and dwelling will be for a while. (36)

Adam then learned prayer from his Lord Who then forgave him. He is the Forgiving and the Merciful. (37)

We said: Go down all of you, and when Our guidance is revealed, those who accept it have nothing to fear or be sorry for. (38)

But those who disbelieve Our verses shall become possessors of hell and in it they shall be immortalized. (39)

Children of Israel, remember the blessings I have bestowed upon you, and uphold your covenant with Me and I shall uphold mine with you, and it is Me you should fear. (40)

Believe in what I revealed which is confirmation of your own Scriptures, and do not be the first to deny it, and sell My verses for a cheap price. To Me your loyalty belongs. (41)

Do not confound truth with falsehood while knowingly hiding the truth. (42)

Attend to your prayers and pay the alms-tax and prostrate yourselves along with others. (43)

You admonish others to be righteous and forget yourselves while you read the Scriptures, do you have no sense? (44)

Rely on patience and prayers which may prove to be difficult disciplines, but not for the devout, (45)

who know they will meet their Lord and that to Him they shall return. (46)

Children of Israel, remember the blessing I have bestowed upon you and that I have favored you over the rest of the world. (47)

Have fear of the day when a soul cannot benefit another nor be allowed to intercede for another, nor will a ransom be accepted from any; none will find supporters. (48)

We saved you from the Pharaoh's people, who were torturing you, slaying your sons while sparing your daughters; this was undoubtedly a great trial from Your Lord. (49)

We split the sea to save you and We drowned the Pharaoh's people while you watched. (50)

While We convened with Moses for forty nights, in his absence you took up the calf to worship, and thus did evil. (51)

Then We forgave you; is that not a reason to be thankful? (52)

We gave Moses the Scriptures and the distinction between right and wrong so that you may be rightly guided. (53)

When Moses said to his people: "You have wronged yourselves when you took up the calf; repent to your Creator and kill the culprits. This will be best for you in His eyes and He will forgive you, He is the Forgiving and the Merciful." (54)

And when you said to Moses: "We shall not believe until we see God openly," a thunderbolt struck you while you were looking. (55)

And We resurrected you after you were dead so you may be thankful. (56)

We caused the clouds to cast a shadow over you, and sent down to you the manna and quails (food from heaven) and told you: "Eat of the good things we have given you." Indeed, they did not wrong Us but wronged themselves. (57)

When We said: Enter this town and eat where you wish to your hearts' content, but enter through the gates reverently prostrating yourselves and repenting; your sins shall be forgiven and abundance shall be bestowed on the doers of good. (58)

The evildoers perverted Our words and We sent them a scourge from heaven, as punishment for their misdeeds. (59)

When Moses requested water for his people We said: Hit the rock with your staff and twelve springs exploded from the rock and each tribe knew where their drinking place was. Eat and drink from what God bestowed, and do not be wicked and corrupt the earth. (60)

To Moses, you said: "We shall not tolerate this unchanging diet, ask your Lord to give us some of the produce of the earth, green herbs and cucumbers; corn, lentils, and onions." He answered: "Would you exchange that which is good with what is worse? Go back to Egypt where you shall find all that you asked for." Humiliation and misery was theirs to have, and they incurred the wrath of God since they disbelieved God's verses and killed many a prophet without a reason. A deserved punishment for their disobedience and transgression. (61)

The believers, the Jews, the Christians and the Sabaens who believe in God and the Last Day and do good works will have their reward with their Lord and they need not be afraid or sad. (62)

We made a covenant with you, and raised the Mount over you. Take what We gave you forcefully and keep in mind its content so you may keep your piety intact. (63)

Even after all that, you still abandoned your obligations and if it was not for God's favor to you and mercy upon you, you would have been lost. (64)

You know those among you who violated the Sabbath, and We made them disgraced apes. (65)

We made their ending an example for those who lived with them and those who lived later and an appropriate reminder for those who are pious. (66)

When Moses said to his people: "God orders you to slay a cow," they replied: "Are you making fun of us?" and Moses answered: "God forbids that I should be such a fool." (67)

They said: "Call on your Lord to tell us what kind of a cow is it?" and Moses said: "He tells you it is neither an old cow nor a very young one but in between, and do what you are told." (68)

They said: "Call on your Lord to tell us what color is it?" and Moses answered: "He tells you it is of yellow color that is pleasing to the eye." (69)

They said: "Call on your Lord to tell us which cow is it because all cows look the same to us, and if God is willing we shall find it." (70)

Moses replied: "Your Lord says it is a cow that is not worn out by plowing the earth or watering the fields; it is intact without a blemish." "Now we can find it" they said and they slew the cow when they almost succeeded in evading compliance. (71)

When you slew a man and then had a falling out among you because of him, God brought out what you were hiding. (72)

We said: Strike parts of the corpse with each other and God restored the dead to life and showed you His signs so that you may think. (73)

Yet after all of that, your hearts became as hard as rock if not harder, because some rock split to give origin to rivers and other rock cracked giving outlet to water and springs and some rock simply rolled down and fell in fear of God, and God is never oblivious to what you do. (74)

Do you then hope that they will believe you when some of you have heard the Word of God and then changed it after fully understanding it, and doing it knowingly? (75)

If they meet those who believe they say: "We believe," and when they are with each other they say: "How would you tell them about what God has given you so they may argue with you in front of God using it?" Do you not have sense? (76)

Do they not know that God knows what they conceal and what they reveal? (77)

Among them are illiterate individuals who are ignorant of the Scriptures and know nothing about it but lies and fantasies. (78)

Cursed are those who write Scriptures of their own composition, in their own hands, then they say: "This came from God," to buy with it cheap benefits. They are cursed and their hands are cursed and cursed are their gains. (79)

They declare: "We shall be touched by fire in Hell but a few days" and you should ask: "Did God give you such a promise? Because if He did He shall keep it; or are you saying for God things you have no knowledge of?" (80)

It is those who commit sin and their sins bring them down, those are the heirs to Hell, and in it they shall be immortalized. (81)

And those who believe in God and do good work are the heirs to paradise, and in it they shall be immortalized. (82)

We made a covenant with the Israelites. We said: "Worship only God, and be kind to your parents and your relatives and the orphans and the destitute, speak to other people nicely, and pray to God and pay the alms-tax." Only a few of them complied and the rest did not heed. (83)

And when We made a covenant with you not to shed blood and not to force others out of their homes. To this you consented and witnessed. (84)

Yet you killed each other, and one group of you turned the others out of their homes while aligning yourselves with others against them, with sin and hatred in your hearts. Then they are brought to you as captives, and you should have ransomed them, since it was forbidden that you push them out to start with. How do you believe in some of the book while you disbelieve the rest of it? Those of you who behave as such shall be rewarded with disgrace in this life, and then on the Day of Judgement they shall be dealt the worst of torture, and God is never oblivious to what you do. (85)

Those are the ones who traded the next world for this one; they will not get a reprieve from torture and they will not be aided. (86)

We gave Moses the Scriptures and sent several Prophets after him; We gave Jesus, Son of Mary veritable signs and strengthened him with the Holy Spirit. Are you, then, every time a prophet is sent with a message you do not favor, going to become arrogant? Some of them you will deny while the others you will murder. (87)

They claim their hearts are sealed, but God has cursed them in their unbelief, and there are very few things they believe in. (88)

And when they get a Book from God which confirms what they have in their own Scriptures, and about which they frequently boasted to the unbelievers, they deny it; the curse of God will befall the unbelievers. (89)

Evil is that for which they traded their souls, when they questioned God's wisdom in His choice of who should be the receiver of His bounty among His servants. This way they incurred God's wrath anew, over the wrath they have already incurred, and to the unbelievers there will be a humiliating torture. (90)

If they were asked to believe in what God revealed, they say: "We will believe in what was revealed to us," and they deny what was revealed since, even though it corroborates what was revealed to them. Say: "Why did you kill God's prophets before, if you are believers?" (91)

Moses has brought you veritable signs and yet you worshiped the calf in his absence and adopted evil. (92)

When We made a covenant with you and raised the mount over you and instructed you to take what We gave you, with strength in your hearts, you stated: "We hear but disobey." They took the calf into their heart with their disbelief. Say: "Evil is what disbelief gets you if you are believers." (93)

Say: "If you claim that God's paradise is for you and for you alone, then you must be wishing death if you are truthful." (94)

They will never wish that, because they know what they have done, and God is most knowledgeable with the evildoers. (95)

You will find them clinging to life more than anyone else, and among the unbelievers are some who wish they survive a thousand years. The years will not keep them from Our certain torture. God is always cognizant of what they do. (96)

Say: "He who was inimical to Gabriel, when he revealed the Koran, with God's sanction, to you, confirming what was revealed before; light, guidance and good tidings to the believers." (97)

He who is enemy to God, His Angels, His Prophets, Gabriel or Michael shall count on God being the Enemy of the unbelievers. (98)

We brought you verses with veritable signs. These will be denied only by the corrupted. (99)

Every time We make a covenant a group of them reject it. Most of them are not believers. (100)

When they were sent a Prophet from God who confirmed what they had, a group of the people of the book turned their back on God's Book as if they knew nothing. (101)

They accepted what the devils told of Solomon's Kingdom. Solomon was not an unbeliever but the devils were. They were teaching people witchcraft and that which was revealed to the two Angels at Babylon, Harut and Marut. Yet the two Angels never instructed anyone without warning them beforehand: "We have been sent to tempt you, do not renounce your faith." From these two, men could learn ways by which discord can be created between a husband and wife. They can do harm to no one by what they have learned, except that which God chooses to permit. These men learned what cannot profit them; yet they knew well that he who engages in their trade will never be a part of the life to come. Evil is that for which they sold their souls, if they knew it. (102)

Had they believed in God and kept themselves from evil it would have been far better for them if they only knew it. (103)

Believers, do not say to Our prophet: "Look upon us (*Ra'ina*)" but rather say: "Look at us (*inzourna*)" and listen (*these are words that sound innocent but used intentionally to imply insulting meaning*). The unbelievers shall have excruciating torture. (104)

The unbelievers among People of the Book and the pagans did not like God favoring you with His bounty, but God favors with His mercy whomever He wishes. He is the Great Benefactor. (105)

We will not cancel a verse or cause it to be forgotten without replacing it with a verse that is the same or better. Did you not know that God is capable of everything? (106)

Did you not know that God has the kingdom of heaven and earth, and except for Him, you have no defender or sponsor? (107)

Do you want to ask your Prophet what Moses was asked before? But remember that those who substitute faith with blasphemy have lost the straight path. (108)

Some of the People of the Book wish they could return you to disbelief, after you have adopted the faith, out of envy, and in their own behalf, after they have already found the truth. Forgive and forget until God makes known His wishes. God is capable of everything. (109)

Attend to your prayers and give the alms-tax, and whatever good you do for yourself you will find it with God. God is mindful of all your actions. (110)

They said: "No one will go to heaven but the Jews and the Christians." These are their fantasies; tell them to produce their proof if they are truthful. (111)

He who turns his face to God in complete surrender and does good works shall receive his Lord's reward, and he and others like him will have no fears or regrets. (112)

The Jews say the Christians are misguided and the Christians say the Jews are misguided, and they are both reading the same book. The pagans say the same of both. God shall adjudicate between them, in whatever they continue to remonstrate over, on the Day of Judgement. (113)

Those who interfere with the mentioning of God's name in His Mosques and work for their destruction instead of entering them with fear in their hearts, they shall be disgraced on earth, and on the Day of Judgement they shall have great torture. (114)

To God belongs the east and the west and anywhere you turn, you face God. God is everywhere and knows everything. (115)

They say God has begotten a son. His are all that the earth and heavens contain and all are accountable to Him. (116)

The Creator of the Heavens and Earth; all He needs to say is: "Be," and it is. (117)

The ignorant said: "If God will only talk to us or give us one of His signs." Other people before them said the same, and their hearts were similar. We brought the signs to people who have faith. (118)

We sent you to proclaim the truth and be a deliverer of warning; you shall not bear responsibility for the owners of Hell. (119)

The Jews and Christians will not like you until you follow their faith. Say to them: "To follow God's Guidance is to be guided," but if you were to follow their fancies, after the knowledge that was bestowed upon you, you will have from God no sponsorship or help. (120)

Those to whom we gave the Book, and who read it the way it should be read, are the ones who believe in it. Those who deny it are the losers. (121)

Children of Israel, remember my bounty which I bestowed upon you, and that I gave you preference over the rest of the world. (122)

Be mindful of the Day when no soul can stand for another and no appeal or intercession will be accepted for any, and none will be aided. (123)

When His Lord put Abraham to the test with certain commandments and Abraham complied, He said: I am appointing you a leader to mankind, and when Abraham asked: "What of my descendants?" God said: My covenant does not include the tyrants. (124)

We made the House a resort and a sanctuary to all of mankind, who used the house of Abraham as a place for prayer. We ordered Abraham and Ishmael to keep My House clean for those who walk around it, meditate or retreat in it, and those who kneel and prostrate themselves. (125)

When Abraham said: "Lord, make this town a safe haven and give those who believe, of its people, your bounty of fruits. Give it to those who believe in God and the Last Day." He (God) said: But as to those who do not believe, I shall let them enjoy it for a while; then a torture by fire shall be their end, and there is the worst of all fates. (126)

After Abraham and Ishmael built the House up from its foundation, they said: "Lord, to you we dedicate this House, accept it from us you hear all and you are the all-knowing."(127)

Lord, help us surrender to you, and help our descendants make a nation that surrenders to you. Show us how to worship you, and forgive us. You are most Forgiving and Merciful. (128)

Lord, send them (our descendants) a prophet from among them, reading to them your verses, and teaching them your Book and wisdom, and help purify them of sin; you are the Exalted and the Wise. (129)

Those who turn away from the faith of Abraham have corrupted souls. We chose him in this life; and in the next life, he is one of the righteous. (130)

When his Lord asked him to surrender himself to God, he said: "I surrendered to the Lord of the Universe." (131)

Abraham and Jacob admonished their children: "God has chosen the faith for you; do not die without having surrendered yourselves to Him." (132)

Were you present when death came to Jacob? He said to his children: "Whom will you worship after my death?" They answered: "We will worship your God and the God of your fathers; Abraham, Ishmael, and Isaac; the One God, to whom we shall surrender ourselves." (133)

That was a nation that is gone; they were responsible for what they did, and you are responsible for what you do; you are not answerable for them. (134)

They say: "Accept Christianity or Judaism and you shall be on the right path;" say: "We believe in the faith of Abraham, the upright faith; he was not an idolworshiper (*pagan*)." (135)

Say: "We believe in God and in what was revealed to us, and what was revealed to Abraham, Ishmael, Isaac, Jacob and the tribes, and in what was revealed to Moses and Jesus and the other Prophets from their Lord; we do not discriminate among them, and to God we are in complete surrender." (136)

If they adopt your faith, they shall be on the right path; but if they reject it, they shall be divided and they shall have their hands full, and in disarray. God hears and knows all. (137)

We shall adopt God's color and what better color to adopt? Him we shall worship. (138)

Say: "You argue with us about God and He is our Lord and Yours. You shall answer for your works, and we shall answer for ours, and to Him we shall remain faithful." (139)

Do you allege that Abraham, Ishmael, Isaac, Jacob and the tribes were Jews or Christians? Then say: "Who knows better, you or God?" Who can be deeper in wickedness than a witness who hides a testimony that was made available to him from God? God is never oblivious to what you do. (140)

That is a nation no longer; to them is what their deeds earned and to you is what your deeds earn. You are not answerable to what they were doing. (141)

The impertinent among the people will ask what made them change the direction to which they pray (*Quiblah*) from what it was before. Say: "To God belongs the east and the west, and He guides whomever He wishes to the right path." (142)

We made you a moderate nation so that you may serve as witnesses on other nations, while the apostle will be a witness on you. We decreed the Quiblah you were praying towards only to find out who are the Apostle's true followers, as opposed to those who will renounce him. It was indeed a challenge, except for those who God has guided. God would have never wasted your faith, and with people He is always Compassionate and Merciful. (143)

Many times We have seen you turning your face towards heaven and we decided to turn you in a direction that will please you. So turn your face towards the Sacred Mosque, and wherever you are turn your faces towards it. Those who were given the Scriptures know that it is the right order from their Lord and God is never oblivious to what they do. (144)

Whatever proof you give, to those who received the Scriptures, they will not follow your direction, (*Quiblah*) and neither will you follow theirs, and none will follow the other. If you follow their fancies after the knowledge that God conferred upon you, you will be among the transgressors. (145)

Those to whom we gave the Scriptures know them the way they know their own children, and some of them conceal the truth while they know. (146)

What is right is from your Lord; do not ever equivocate. (147)

For each there is a direction to which one is devoted; choose the good wherever you are, for God will bring you all back, and God is capable of all things. (148)

In whatever direction you depart turn your face towards the Sacred Mosque; it is the right thing ordered by your Lord and God is not oblivious to what you do. (149)

In whatever direction you depart, turn your face towards the Sacred Mosque and wherever you are turn your faces towards it so that others could not criticize you, except for those among them who are transgressors. Do not fear them but fear Me. I shall complete the bounty I have bestowed upon you so that you may be guided, (150)

just as I sent you an Apostle from among you who recites Our revelations to you, purifies you, and teaches you the Book and wisdom and what you did not know. (151)

Remember Me and I shall remember you and be thankful to Me and do not disbelieve. (152)

You who believe, rely on patience and on prayer; God is with those who are patient. (153)

Do not say that those who die in the way of God are dead. They are alive but you cannot sense it. (154)

We shall afflict you with fear, hunger and shortages in property, men and crops. Convey good tidings to those who are patient. (155)

Those who are faced with adversity will always say: "We belong to God and to Him we shall return." (156)

Such are the men to whom God's blessing and mercy belong, and those are the rightly-guided. (157)

Safa and Marwa are symbolic of God, and whoever is on pilgrimage (Haj) or visiting (Oumra) should not hesitate to walk around them; and those who volunteer to do it, should know that God is Grateful and Knowing. (158)

Those who conceal the signs and guidance we made available to the people in the Scriptures shall be cursed by God and by all who curse (159)

except for those who repent and make amends. Those I shall forgive; I am the Forgiving and Merciful. (160)

Those who unbelieve and die unbelievers, shall be cursed by God, the angels and all the people. (161)

In it they shall be immortalized. Their torture shall be unrelenting, and they will not be looked upon. (162)

Your God is One; None other than Him; the Compassionate and Merciful. (163)

In the creation of heaven and earth, and in the alternation of day and night, and in the ships that sail the oceans in the service of man, and in what God brings down from the sky that revives the earth and livens it with all creatures, and in the travel of wind and clouds, between the sky and the earth, are signs for men who have sense. (164)

Yet there are those who worship idols instead of God. They love them similar to the love of God; but those who believe are far more devoted to God. If only the transgressors could see the power of God and the power of his torture. His torture is excruciating indeed. (165)

When the leaders will deny their followers and the bonds that now holds them together fall apart, (166)

those who followed those leaders will say: "If we could ever do it again we would deny them the way they denied us." This is the way God shows them their deeds. They shall be overtaken by remorse, but from hell they shall not depart. (167)

People, eat of what is permitted to you on this earth and enjoy it, and do not follow the steps of the Devil, he is your clearest enemy. (168)

He directs you towards evil and indecency, and tempts you to say, of God, what you do not know. (169)

When they are asked to follow what God has revealed, they said: "We will follow what our forefathers have been following." Even when their forefathers had no sense, and were not rightly guided! (170)

Preaching to the unbelievers is like calling on animals. All you hear is shouting and crying. Deaf, dumb and blind; they have no sense. (171)

You people who believe, eat of the good that God has given you, and be thankful to God, if it is Him that you worship. (172)

It is forbidden that you eat the flesh of the dead, blood, the meat of the pig, and the meat of any animal that was consecrated in the name of any one other than God. Whoever was constrained and ate with neither willfulness nor deliberation shall incur no guilt. God is Forgiving and Merciful. (173)

Those who conceal what God has revealed in the Scriptures buy with it little value. They will not eat in their bellies but fire. God shall not talk to them on the Day of Judgement. He will not purify them and they shall meet with an excruciating torture. (174)

They have traded being lost for being guided, and torture for forgiveness. Let them find out how tolerant they will be of hellfire. (175)

God has revealed the Scriptures rightly, but those who remonstrate over it are deeply divided. (176)

Righteousness is not acquired by turning your faces to the east or to the west. The righteous believe in God, the Last Day, the Angels, the Books, and the apostles, and contribute of their possessions to their relatives, to the orphans, to the destitute, to the homeless, to the beggars and for the purpose of liberating slaves. They are the ones who pray and pay the alms-tax and fulfill their promises when they make them. They are patient in the face of adversity, hardship and despair of war. These are the true believers and the righteous. (177)

You who believe, God has decreed justice for killing. A free man for a free man, a slave for a slave; and a female for a female. He who is forgiven by his brother shall be prosecuted fairly and required to pay fair compensation. This is commutation from your Lord. Transgressors shall face excruciating torture. (178)

As to you, men of intellect, in justice resides the essence of your lives, so that you can be righteous. (179)

It is decreed that when one of you is to die, he shall bequeath his property equitably to his parents and relatives. This is so that you can be righteous. (180)

Those who change a will after they hear it, shall bear the full responsibility for the sin. God hears all and is All-knowing. (181)

He who knows of an error or an injustice on the part of a testator in regard to a will, and brings about a restoration shall incur no sin; God is Forgiving and Merciful. (182)

Believers, fasting has been decreed for you the same way it has been for people before you, so that you can be righteous. (183)

For a defined number of days, you are to fast; but those who are ill or are travelling, a few days can be postponed. For those who can afford it there is a ransom of feeding a poor man. Those who volunteer, it is better for them, but if you fast it is better for you, if you only knew it. (184)

The month of Ramadan is the month when the Koran was revealed, guidance for the people and a clear distinction between good and evil. He who sees the start of the month shall fast, and whoever is ill or travelling shall postpone a few days. God wants ease for you and not hardship, so you may fulfill your obligations; recognize My guidance to you, and be thankful. (185)

If My worshipers ask about Me, I am near, and I answer the prayers of those who pray; thus they should respond to Me and believe in Me if they are wisely guided. (186)

It is lawful for you to have relations with your wives on the nights of fasting; they are comforting to you as you are to them. God knew you were committing deception on yourselves, so He relented towards you and forgave you. You may approach them and seek what God permitted from them. Also eat and drink until there is enough light to distinguish a white thread from a black one in early morning. Then continue the fast until nightfall. Do not go near your wives when you are retreating for prayers in the mosques. These are the boundaries set by God; do not cross them. God reveals His verses to people so that they can become righteous. (187)

Do not ever take each others' property through illegal means or try to use property to bribe judges so that the property of some people can be usurped through evil means with full knowledge on your part. (188)

They ask you about the lunar months, say: "These are timing devices for people and for pilgrimage." Righteousness is in piety and in entering homes from their front and not their back door. To be righteous, fear God so you may succeed. (189)

Fight in the way of God those who fight you and never be the aggressor. God does not like aggressors. (190)

Kill them anywhere you find them and push them out from where they pushed you out. Rioting is worse than killing. Do not kill them in the Sacred Mosque until they fight you in it. If they fought you in it, kill them. This is the consequence for unbelieving. (191)

If they desist, God is Forgiving and Merciful. (192)

Fight them to prevent rioting and establish God's religion. If they desist, no aggression is permitted, except against the evildoers. (193)

A sacred month for a sacred month; even the sacred are subject to just retaliation. Those who attack you, attack them the way they attacked you. Be righteous and know that God is with the righteous. (194)

Spend of your fortune in the way of God and do not endanger your lives unwisely. Be charitable; God loves those who are charitable. (195)

Complete a pilgrimage and a visit for God. If you cannot you should send such offerings as you may afford, and do not shave your heads until the offering reaches its destination. Those who are ill and cannot shave their heads should pay a ransom such as fasting, charity or sacrifice. When safe, and for whoever continues a visit into pilgrimage, shall send offerings from what he can afford, and if he cannot he shall fast three days during the pilgrimage, and seven days upon his return; a total of ten. This is for those whose families are not present at the Holy Mosque. Have fear of God and know that His retribution is stern indeed. (196)

Pilgrimage is decreed in a certain month and those on pilgrimage should refrain from sexual relations, indecency or arguments; and whatever good you do God knows it. Provide for yourself and the best of provisions is righteousness. You people of intellect, be righteous. (197)

It is not wrong for you to seek your Lord's bounty, and after you come down from Arafat, remember God as you approach the sacred structure. Remember that He guided you, and before Him you were lost. (198)

Then depart from where pilgrims depart and implore forgiveness of God; God is Forgiving and Merciful. (199)

After you have fulfilled your sacred duties, remember God the way you remember your forefathers, if not with greater reverence. Some people say: "Lord, give us abundance in this world," and those shall have no role in the life to come. (200)

And some say: "Lord, give us what is good in this life and the life to come and protect us from the fire of Hell." (201)

They shall be rewarded for their deeds. God's reckoning is quite prompt. (202)

Remember God for a few appointed days. He who leaves after two days shall incur no sin. Nor is it wrong to stay longer. Be fearful of God and know that for Him you shall all be assembled. (203)

Some men in this life will talk pleasingly and ask God to witness what is in their heart, while in reality they are bitter enemies. (204)

When away from you, their effort is toward corruption on this earth and the destruction of crops and the young. God does not like corruption. (205)

If they are asked to fear God, they are overtaken by their pride in evil. Their destination is Hell; a suitable resting place indeed. (206)

Among the people are those who will sell themselves in pursuit of God's approval and God is Merciful with His worshipers. (207)

You who believe, enter the safety of submission, all of you, and do not follow the footsteps of the Devil; he is your clearest enemy. (208)

If you slip after the clear evidence was made known to you, then remember that God is Mighty and Wise. (209)

Are they going to wait until God comes to them through the shadows of the clouds, with the angels, to judge them? By that time it will be too late. All matters will eventually go to God. (210)

Ask the children of Israel how many a veritable sign we brought them. He who changes God's bounty after he gets it should remember that God's punishment is severe. (211)

For the unbelievers this life is full of enjoyment and attractions. They even mock those who believed and the righteous. Those are above them (*the unbelievers*) on the Day of Judgement. God provides His bounty to whom He wishes without measure. (212)

Once people were one nation and God sent them the Prophets bringing them good tidings and warnings, and sent with them the Scriptures, establishing the right basis for judgement on disputes among people. None disputed them except for those who received the signs and then denied them because of envy among them. God leads to the right path those who believed in the right that others disputed. God will lead whomever He wants to the straight path. (213)

Do you think you will enter Paradise without going through what those who came before you went through? They have been touched with wretchedness and adversity and were heavily shaken until the apostle and those who believed with him said: "When shall we be blessed with God's help and become triumphant?" God's triumph is quite near. (214)

They ask you how should they spend in charity, say: "Spend God's bounty on your parents, your relatives, the orphans, the destitute and the homeless; and whatever good you do God will know it." (215)

Fighting is ordained for you even though you may dislike it. Many times you may dislike things that are good for you while you may like things that are evil. God knows and you do not. (216)

They ask you about fighting during the sacred month, say: "This is a grave violation of God's rulings and disbelief in Him, but the Sacred Mosque and the forcible ejection of worshipers from it is far more important to God. Instigation of rioting is worse than carnage. They will continue to fight you until they succeed in converting you back from your religion. Those of you who convert and die, shall die unbelievers. Their endeavors shall fail in this life and in the life to come. They are the owners of hell and in it they shall be immortalized." (217)

Those who believed and those who immigrated and struggled in the way of God; they are the ones who are entitled to ask for God's mercy. God is Forgiving and Merciful. (218)

They ask you about wine and gambling, say: "There is great harm in both and some benefit, but their harm is far greater than their benefit," and they ask you about what they should spend in charity, say: 'What you can spare." This is the way God makes the verses known to you so that you may think (219)

of this life and the next. They question you in regard to the orphans, say: "To deal with them justly is what is right, and if their affairs are intermingled with yours be mindful of the fact that they are your brothers." God knows those who are corrupt and those who are straight. If God chooses He can afflict you. God is Mighty and Wise. (220)

You should not marry unbelieving women until they believe. A believing slave is better than an unbelieving free woman even if you like her. You should not marry an unbeliever until she believes. A believing slave is better than an unbelieving freeman even if you like him. They will be inviting you to Hell while God invites you to Paradise and to forgiveness by His bidding. He reveals His verses to people so they may remember. (221)

They ask you about menses, say: "It is painful. Leave women alone during menstruation and do not go near them until they are willing to receive you. Then you can have relations with them from where God has sanctioned." God loves those who stay away from sin and who remain clean. (222)

Your women are where your children are formed. Approach your women as you please, provide for yourselves with good work, fear God and know that you will be facing Him and give good tidings to the believers. (223)

Do not make God the subject of your swearing, and if you do good, fear God, and make peace among people, God will hear and have knowledge. (224)

God will not punish you for unintended swearing but He will hold you to what is in your heart. God is Forgiving and Tolerant. (225)

Those who declare their wives divorced, their wives shall wait four months. If they change their mind God is Forgiving and Merciful. (226)

If they insist on divorce, God hears all and knows all. (227)

Divorced women must wait and keep their chastity until three menstrual periods have passed. It is forbidden for them to hide any pregnancy they may have, from their husbands, if they believe in God and the Last Day. Their husbands have a higher priority if they wanted them back, and wanted reconciliation. Women, in justice, shall have rights similar to those exercised over them, although men do have a step higher in priority. God is Exalted and Wise. (228)

A woman can be divorced twice only. After that, she is either kept with dignity or released with honor. It is forbidden that you take away from them anything you have given them, unless you both willingly feel that certain gifts cannot be utilized within the limits set by God; then the wife can choose to ransom herself, for not having remained within God's borders. Do not ever cross the limits set by God. Those who do are transgressors. (229)

Once divorced for the third time, a woman cannot remarry her husband until she is wedded to another man. Then if she is divorced, she and her previous husband, can be wedded again, if they are both willing to remain within the limits, revealed by God, to people who have knowledge. (230)

If you divorce women, and after they finish their waiting period, either keep them gracefully or let them go with honor. Do not hold on to them out of spite, and he who does is a transgressor and will only hurt himself. Do not ever take God's verses lightly and remember God's bounty which He has bestowed on you, and that He sent to you the Koran and wisdom and lectured you. Fear God and know that He is Knowledgeable of all things. (231)

If you divorce your women and they come to the end of their waiting period, do not stand in their way if they have come to an agreement to marry. This is an admonishment to those of you who believe in God and the Last Day. It is much healthier and cleaner for you this way. God knows and you do not. (232)

Mothers are entitled to breast-feed their children two full years. If they wish to finish it, the father is then responsible for their support and their clothing, cheerfully. No one is encumbered beyond his endurance. Neither a mother should suffer on account of her child, nor a father should suffer on account of his child. The same obligations pass on to the father's heir. If both father and mother by mutual agreement and consultation choose to wean the child, they shall incur no sin. Nor should it be an offence for you to hire a nurse to nurse your child, provided you pay her and abide by your promise to her; proportional to usage. Fear God and know that God sees what you do. (233)

Widows shall keep themselves chaste for four months and ten days following the death of their husbands. After their waiting period is over, they shall incur no sin by doing whatever they shall wish with themselves so long as it is decent, and God is Knowledgeable with what you do. (234)

It shall not be an offence for you to propose marriage to widowed women or to have feelings for them in your hearts. God knows that you shall think of them; but do not make secret promises to them unless you intend them to be truthful and honorable, and do not move towards finalizing the marriage until the waiting period is completed. Know that God knows what is in your heart. Fear Him and know that he is Forgiving and Tolerant. (235)

It shall not be sinful for you to divorce your women before you touch them or before any dowry is settled. Provide for them, in such an event, with fairness, the rich man according to what he can afford and the poor man according to what he can afford. This is binding on the righteous of men. (236)

If you divorce them before you touch them but after a definite dowry is set, then upon divorce pay them half of what was set; unless they forgive you or you are forgiven by whoever presided over the marriage contract. If you forgive, it is closer to piety. Do not forget to show kindness to each other. God observes all that you do. (237)

Attend to your prayers on time, including the middle prayer, and stand up for God in total devotion. (238)

If you become fearful while walking or riding and then come to safety, remember God and remember how He taught you what you did not know. (239)

Those of you who die shall provide in their will enough support for their wives to be able to stay in their homes without having to leave for at least a year. If they choose to leave, and decently, do with themselves whatever they want to do, it shall be no offence for you; God is Exalted and Wise. (240)

Divorced women shall also have reasonable provisions, which is an absolute requirement for the righteous. (241)

This is the way God reveals to you His verses so that you may understand. (242)

Did you not see the example of those who fled their homes, in the thousands, out of fear of death, and God ordered them dead, then He resurrected them? God bestows His bounty on people, but most people do not say thanks. (243)

Fight in the way of God and know that God Hears all and Knows all. (244)

Those who make loans to God charitably, He makes it back to them many times over. God provides with shortage or abundance. To Him you shall return. (245)

Did you not see what the leaders of the Children of Israel did to one of their prophets after Moses? They said: "Appoint for us a king and we shall fight in the cause of God." He said: "And what if you refuse to fight, after you are ordered to do so?" They said: "Why would we not fight when we have been driven out of our homes along with our children?" When fighting was ordained for them, they all backed out except very few. God has knowledge of the evildoers. (246)

Their Prophet said: "God has appointed Saul as king over you," and they said: "Why should he be king? We are more deserving than he is; besides the fact that he has no money." The Prophet said: "God chose him over you, and increased him in knowledge and physical ability." God gives His sovereignty to whomever He wishes, God is Immense and Knowledgeable. (247)

Their Prophet also said: "As a sign of His sovereignty you will see the ark and in it tranquility from your Lord and relics remaining from the houses of Moses and Aaron, carried by the angels. It will be a sign for you if you are believers." (248)

When Saul marched out with his army, he said to them: "God is putting you to the test at a river we shall pass. He who drinks from it is not with me, and he who does not, is. Except for those who satisfy themselves with only a sip that does not exceed what fills the hollow of your hands." Most of them drank from it, except a few. After he passed it with those who believed, they said: "We cannot stand up to Goliath and his warriors," but those of them who were mindful of eventually meeting God, said: "Many a small group become victorious over larger groups with God's permission." God is with those who hold their grounds. (249)

When Goliath and his army appeared, they said: "God, inspire us with steadfastness and courage and grant us victory over the unbelievers." (250)

They defeated them, and David killed Goliath, and God gave him sovereignty and wisdom, and taught him what He wished. If it was not for the fact that God uses some people to divert the evil that may come from other people, there would have been a lot of corruption on earth, but God is the Benefactor for all of the world. (251)

These are God's verses which We recite to you in righteousness, and you are one of the apostles. (252)

These are the Prophets. We favored some of them over the others. Some of them spoke to God, and God elevated some of them a certain number of steps. We gave Jesus, the son of Mary, veritable signs, and fortified him with the Holy Spirit. If God so desired, people who came afterwards would not have fought with each other, after they received the signs, but they did split apart. Some of them believed and some of them disbelieved. If God wished they would not have split, but God does what He wishes. (253)

People who believe, spend of the bounty that God bestowed upon you before a day comes when there is no sale, fellowship or intercession. The unbelievers are the evildoers. (254)

God is the only God, no God but Him, He is alive and always alert. He is never overtaken by drowsiness or sleep; to Him belong the Heavens and the Earth. No one will intercede before Him without His permission. He knows what is in between their hands, and what hides behind them. No one is in possession of any of His knowledge, except for what He permits. His sovereignty extends over all of the heavens and the earth, and their preservation is well within His means. He is Supreme and Mighty. (255)

There is no compulsion in religion. Being guided has become distinct from being lost, and those who reject evil and believe in God have gotten their hand firmly on the most reliable handle which will never fail them. God Hears all and is very Knowledgeable. (256)

God sponsors those who believed. He will take them out from the dark into the light. The unbelievers are sponsored by the Devil. He is taking them from the light to the dark. They are the owners of Hell and in it they shall be immortalized. (257)

Did you not see the one who tried to argue with Abraham about his Lord, because God gave him the kingdom? When Abraham said: "My God has the power over life and death," the king said: "I do, too." Then Abraham said: "My Lord brings the sun up from the east; can you bring it up from the west?" And the unbeliever was confounded. God provides no guidance to evildoers. (258)

Or take the example of the one who passed a village empty of all signs of life and said: "Who can resurrect this after death?" God put him to death for a hundred years, then resurrected him, then he was asked: "How long have you been away?" He answered: "A day or so." He (*God*) said: "No, you were away for a hundred years. Look at your food and drink, which has not rotted, and look at the bones of your donkey. We shall make you a sign for people. Look at the bones how they are spread. Then we shall cover them with flesh." After he saw that, he said: "I know God is capable of all things." (259)

When Abraham said: "My Lord, show me how you resurrect the dead," God said: Did you not believe? and Abraham replied: "Yes, but I want more comfort in my heart." God said: Take four birds; cut them to pieces, then spread those pieces over several mountains. Then call them and they will come to you in a hurry; and know that God is Exalted and Wise. (260)

The example of those who spend their money in the way of God is the same as a grain, growing and producing seven ears, each carrying a hundred grains. God will multiply to whomever He wishes. God is Immense and Knowledgeable. (261)

Those who spend their money in the way of God, and then do not hold the subjects of their charity beholden to them or do others any harm, they shall be rewarded by their Lord and they shall never be afraid or unhappy. (262)

A nice word followed by forgiveness is better than charity followed by harm and God is Wealthy and Tolerant. (263)

People who believe, do not cancel out your charity by holding people beholden to you, and doing harm. He who spends his money to acquire favor among people, and does not believe in God and the Final Day, his example is like a rock covered with dust; then hit with a rainstorm leaving it washed out and bare. They gain nothing from what they spend, and God will provide no guidance to unbelieving people. (264)

The example of those who spend their money seeking God's approval is like a garden, hit with rain and yielded double its usual production. Even when no heavy rain falls on it, it will at least be watered with a light dew. God will see all that you do. (265)

Does one of you wish to have a paradise with dates and grapes and under it flowing rivers, while loaded with all fruits; and then be hit with old age and weak descendants, and then be afflicted with a storm and fire which burns and destroys everything? This is how God reveals His verses to you so that you may think. (266)

People who believe, spend of the good you earn, and of what We make the earth produce for you. Do not spend that which is worthless or which you would have accepted, only reluctantly, if it was offered to you. God is Wealthy and Not-in-Need. (267)

The Devil promises you poverty, and guides you to indecency, while God promises you forgiveness in addition to His bounty. God is Immense and Knowledgeable. (268)

He gives wisdom to whomever He wishes, and he who is granted wisdom has been granted a lot of good, yet only men of intellect even realize that. (269)

Everything you spend in charity or you are promised in goodness, God knows about it. Evildoers have no supporters. (270)

If you give in charity openly, that is fine, and if you give the poor secretly, that is better for you. God will forgive your sins, and He is quite Knowledgeable with what you do. (271)

Their guidance is not your responsibility. God provides guidance to whomever He wishes and whatever you spend for the good is for your own good. Spend only to please God, and whatever you spend is for your own good and refrain from evil. (272)

The righteous poor are so busy advocating the cause of God that they are left no time to travel seeking to make a living. Those who do not know them think they are rich because of their pride; you know them by their demeanor, and they never beg. Whatever you spend for the good, God will know about. (273)

Those who spend their money in charity, night and day, in secret and openly, shall have their reward from their Lord and they shall not be fearful or sad. (274)

Those who benefited from usury shall stand before God shaking, like those who have been touched by the Devil. This is because they said: "Selling is like usury, and God has permitted selling and forbade usury." Those who are lectured by their Lord and they stop will not be punished for what passed, but those who repeat are the owners of hell and in it they shall be immortalized. (275)

God has cursed usury and blessed charity and God does not like the unbelieving sinners. (276)

Those who believe, do good works, pray and pay the alms-tax, shall have their reward with their Lord, they shall not be fearful or sad. (277)

People who believe, fear God and drop whatever you are still practicing of usury if you are true believers. (278)

If you do not, war will be declared on you by God and His apostle. If you repent, you can have your capital back; and you will neither abuse nor be abused. (279)

If your debtor is in trouble grant him an extension until he can discharge his debt to you, and if you forgive his debt as an alms-tax payment it shall be better for you, if you knew. (280)

Fear the day when you will go back to God, and every soul has to deal with what it has done and none will be dealt with unfairly. (281)

You who believe, if you loaned each other money for a defined period, write it down. Have the contract between you recorded by a just third party. No one shall refuse to write, the way God has taught him. The writing should be dictated by he who will owe the debt. He should fear God and never dictate any less than what he will owe. If the debtor was of weak reputation or health, or unable to dictate, the dictation shall then be done by his legal guardian. Use two witnesses from among your men, and if not two men, then a man and two women. If one of them makes a mistake, the other will correct her. Witnesses shall not decline when asked to testify. Do not decline to write debts be they large or small, and include the date of payment. This is better for you and easier to witness and less likely to be confused later, unless you have an ongoing business between you, then it shall not be an offence not to write it down. Use witnesses if you sell each other. No recorder or witness shall be harmed, and to harm them is sinful. Fear God and God will teach you, He is Knowledgeable of all things. (282)

If you were traveling, and you could not find a recorder then you can resort to a delivered collateral. If you choose to trust each other, he who is trusted better deliver on his trust and be fearful of God. Do not ever withhold testimony, and those who do are committing a grave sin in their heart, and God is Knowledgeable with what you do. (283)

To God belongs what is in the heavens and on earth. Whether you declare what is in your heart or hide it, God will hold you responsible for it. He will forgive whomever He wishes and torture whomever He wishes and God is Capable of all things. (284)

The Apostle believed in what his Lord revealed to him and each of the believers believed in God, His angels, His books, and His Apostles. We do not discriminate among any of His Apostles, and they said we heard and obeyed. We seek your forgiveness our Lord, and we are destined to you. (285)

God does not ask of a soul what is beyond its ability. To each soul what it earns and on each the consequences of what it commits. God, do not punish us if we forgot or erred. God, do not hold over us the burdens You have held over those who came before us. Lord, do not make us bear what we are not capable of bearing. Pardon us, forgive us and be merciful with us. You are Our Guardian. help us prevail over the unbelieving people. (286)

THE IMRANS (The Family of Imran)(3)

In the Name of God, Most Merciful and Most Beneficent.

Alef Lam Meem. (1)

God; there is no God but Him; the living and the ever-lasting God. (2)

He has revealed the Book to you, confirming what was revealed before. He also revealed the Torah and the Gospel. (3)

To guide men, He also revealed the distinguisher (*the part of the Koran that distinguishes between right and wrong*). Those who still disbelieve His verses shall have severe torture, and God is Exalted and Revengeful. (4)

Nothing in heaven or on earth will escape His attention. (5)

He is the One who shapes you in the womb however He wishes. There is no God but Him, the Exalted and the Wise. (6)

He is the One who revealed the Koran to you. Some of it are verses that are precise in meaning, and represent the foundation of the Book (*mother of the Book*). Other parts of it are ambiguous. Those whose hearts are misguided will emphasize the ambiguity so as to create dissension and misinterpret it their own way. Only God knows the exact interpretation. Those who are well rooted in knowledge will say: "We believe; it is all from our Lord;" but only those with intellect will realize that. (7)

God, do not let our hearts go astray after You have guided us. Grant us mercy from Your generosity; You are the ultimate Giver. (8)

Our Lord, You are the One bringing the People together, on a day that is not to be doubted. God never misses an appointment. (9)

The unbelievers shall find that their fortunes and their children will be of no benefit to them and they themselves will be fuel for the Fire. (10)

The Pharaoh and his family and many who came before him denied Our verses and God made sure that their sins caught up with them, and God's penalty is severe. (11)

Say to the unbelievers: "You shall be defeated and then ushered into Hell, a miserable place for rest." (12)

There was a good example for you in the two groups that met in war, one group fighting in the cause of God and the other an unbelieving group. The believers with their own eyes saw their own number to be twice what it actually was. God will aid with His victory whomever He wishes, and in it there shall be a lesson for those with vision. (13)

Men are enticed by desires that include women and children, and heaps over heaps of gold and silver, thoroughbred horses, cattle and land for cultivation. These are the enjoyments of this life, while God has the final good end. (14)

Say: "I shall bring you tidings of far better reward for those who are righteous, from their Lord: blooming Paradise with flowing rivers underneath, and with faithful spouses and a bliss from God. God sees what all His worshipers do." (15)

They are the ones who say: "Our Lord, we believed. Forgive our sins and protect us from the torture of fire, (16)

including the patient, the truthful, the modest, the charitable, and those who seek forgiveness with their early morning prayer." (17)

God bore witness that there is no other God but Him. So did the angels and those who have been given a lot of knowledge. He is the Enactor of justice. No God but Him; Exalted and Wise. (18)

The religion of God is Islam. Those who were given the Scriptures split among themselves after they received the knowledge, and with deliberate mischief. Among them are even people who denied God's verses and God's reckoning is quite quick. (19)

If they argue with you, say: "I have totally surrendered myself to God," and invite people of the Book and the gentiles to follow your example. If they refuse, remember that your job is limited to delivering the message. God has all worshipers in sight. (20)

Those who deny Our verses and kill the apostles out of wickedness, and kill those among the people who are suing for justice; you can foretell for them excruciating torture. (21)

Those are the ones whose endeavors shall fail in this life and the life thereafter and they will have no supporters. (22)

Consider those who have received a portion of the Scriptures then when called to follow the word of God, some of them turned their backs and refused. (23)

They say: "Fire will not touch us but a few days." They started, in their religion, believing their own lies. (24)

How would they do when We assemble them on a day which is not to be doubted, and when every soul has to provide an accounting for what it has earned, and none will be wronged? (25)

Say: "God, the Owner of all sovereignty, You dispense sovereignty to whomever You wish and take it away from whomever You wish. You honor whomever You want and disgrace whomever You want. Abundance is in Your Hand, and You are capable of all things. (26)

You cause the night to pass into the day and the day into the night. You extract the living out of the dead, and the dead out of the living, and give abundantly to whomever You wish with no accounting." (27)

Believers do not take unbelievers as sponsors in preference to believers. Those who do cannot hope for anything from God; unless you have to do it for self-preservation. God warns you of Himself, and with Him is your destiny. (28)

Whether you conceal what is in your heart or declare it, God knows about it, and knows what is in the heavens and on the earth, and God is Capable of all things. (29)

The day will come when every soul will want the good it has done very close; but the evil, it will wish it was very far away. God will warn you of Himself. God is merciful with His worshipers. (30)

Say: "If you love God, follow me and God will love you, and forgive your sins. God is Forgiving and Merciful." (31)

Say: "Obey God and His Apostle, and should they decline, God does not like the unbelievers." (32)

God has favored Adam, Noah, the family of Abraham and the family of Imran over the rest of His creation. (33)

They were descendants of one another; God hears all and is all Knowledgeable. (34)

The wife of Imran said: "God, I am pledging what I have in my belly dedicated to You. Accept it from me, You are the One who Hears and Knows." (35)

When she delivered, she said: "God I have delivered a female and God knows better what I delivered. Males and females are not the same. I named her Mary. I entrust her and her descendants to Your protection from the condemned Devil." (36)

Her Lord accepted her well, and nurtured her well and entrusted her to the care of Zechariah and whenever Zechariah visited her in the Shrine he found her well supplied with food. He said: "Mary, where do you get this from?" She replied: "It is from God. He gives to whomever He wishes without accounting." (37)

Zechariah beseeched his Lord: "Lord, grant me from Your blessings a good family of descendants, You are the listener to all prayers." (38)

The angels called him while he was praying at the Shrine and said: "We bring you from God the good tidings of the coming of John, who shall reaffirm the word of God. He shall be a Master, Pure, and a prophet among the righteous." (39)

He said: "God, how would I get a child? I am old and my wife is barren." The angel said: "God does what He wants." (40)

"Lord," he said: "Select a token for me," and God said: Yours is not to speak to anyone for three days, except for sign communication, and remember your Lord a lot and repeat His name in the morning and evening. (41)

The angels said: "O' Mary, God has selected you, purified you and favored you over the women of the world. (42)

O' Mary, devote yourself to your Lord, kneel and prostrate yourself with others who do." (43)

This is a description of what is little known, We relay to you since you were not there when lots were cast to decide who takes charge of Mary and then they fought over it. (44)

The angels said: "O' Mary, God brings you good tidings with a word from Him; his name is Jesus, son of Mary, a man of status in this life and the life to come and one of those closest to God. (45)

He talks to people from the crib and preaches to them as a middle aged man, and is one of the righteous." (46)

She said: "My Lord, how would I have a child and I have never been touched by a human?" He said: God creates whatever He wishes; whatever He wants done, all He needs to do is say: Be, and it is. (47)

God will teach him the Scripture, wisdom, the Torah and the Gospe1. (48)

He is an apostle to the Children of Israel to say: "I brought you a sign from your Lord; I will create for you the likeness of a bird from clay, then I will blow in it and make it a bird with God's permission, and with His permission, I will give sight to the blind, heal the leper and raise the dead, and I will tell you what you eat and what you hoard in your homes, and in all of that there are signs for you if you are believers. (49)

It confirms what I have between my hands in the Torah. I am to relax some of what was forbidden to you and bring you verses from your Lord; fear your God and obey. (50)

God is my Lord and your Lord, worship Him; this is the straight path." (51)

When Jesus felt disbelief on their part, He asked: "Who will support me in the cause of God?" The disciples said: "We are the supporters of God, we believe in God and bear witness that we are surrendered to Him. (52)

Our Lord, we believe in what you revealed and we followed the Apostle, list us among your witnesses." (53)

They deceived and God deceived them. God is the best deceiver. (54)

God said: O' Jesus, I am letting you die and elevating you to Me and purifying you from those who disbelieved, and making those who followed you superior to those who unbelieved until the Day of Judgement and then to Me you will all return and I will be the judge on what you had disagreement on. (55)

Those who disbelieved I will torment them severely in this life and the life thereafter, and they will have no supporters. (56)

But those who believe and do good work, God will reward them properly. God does not like the evildoers. (57)

These revelations are recited to you as forms of wise admonition. (58)

The example of Jesus is like the example of Adam. He created him from dust, then said to him: Be, and he was. (59)

This is the truth from your Lord; do not be one of those who waver. (60)

If they argue with you (*about Jesus*) after all the knowledge you have received, tell them: "Why do you not call over our children, and your children, and our wives and your wives, and ourselves and yourselves, and let's call God's damnation on the liars?" (61)

This was the true story, and there is only but one God, and God is Exalted and Wise. (62)

If they refuse, God is Knowledgeable of the corrupters. (63)

Say: "People of the Book, let us come to an agreement between us. We will both worship none but God, and will associate no one with Him, and we will not set up each other in a position of divinity next to God." If they refuse, say: "Be witnesses that we are Moslems." (64)

People of the Book, why do you argue about Abraham, when the Torah and the Gospel came only after him, do you not have sense? (65)

There you were, arguing about things you know something about. Why do you argue with things you know nothing about? God knows and you do not. (66)

Abraham was neither a Jew, nor was he a Christian, but rather a strict Moslem; neither was he an idolater. (67)

Those who have a claim on Abraham are those who followed him; this Prophet (*Mohammed*) and those who believe. God is the Master of the believers. (68)

A faction of the people of the Book wish that they could misguide you, but they misguide none but themselves, and they do not know it. (69)

People of the Book, why do you deny God's revelations when you know them to be true? (70)

People of the Book, why do you take what you know to be right and dress it to seem wrong and conceal what is right while you know it? (71)

A group of the people of the Book said: "Believe in what the believers believe in, in the morning, and deny it at night, so as to shake your faith." (72)

Trust only those who adopt your entire religion. Say: "Guidance is God's guidance, and no one will be given the like of what you were given, nor is anyone likely to argue with you about it in front of God. Bounty is in God's hands. He gives it to whomever He wishes. God is Vast and Knowledgeable. (73)

He selects for His mercy whomever He wishes, and God is the Great Benefactor." (74)

Among people of the Book are some who if trusted with a large sum they will return it to you intact; and among them are those who when trusted with a coin will not return it to you unless you stay on top of them, since they say they have no obligation to be honest with someone who is not one of them. They attribute lies to God while they very well know it. (75)

Those who fulfill their obligations and fear God know that God loves the righteous. (76)

Those who sell their faith in God and swear falsely for a cheap price, shall have no moral standing on the Last Day, and God will not consider them on the Day of Judgement, and He will not purify them, and for them there shall be excruciating torture. (77)

Among them are a group who bring some parts of the Scriptures on their tongues in such a way as to make it sound like it is from the Scriptures when it is not. They say it is from God and it is not. They fabricate lies in the name of God knowingly. (78)

No man who was given God's Scriptures, wisdom and prophethood will say to men: "Be my worshipers instead of God." He will rather say: "Be devoted worshipers to God, as He taught you the Scriptures that you have been studying." (79)

Nor would such a man encourage you to adopt the angels and the prophets as Gods. How would he lead you into disbelief after you have become Moslems? (80)

God has made a covenant with the prophets: With what I have brought you, in Scriptures and wisdom, would you promise that when an apostle comes to you, confirming what you already have, you will believe in him and support him, and agree to make a solid promise on that with Me? They said: "We will." God said: Bear witness on that and I shall bear witness with you. (81)

Those who decline after that are the evildoers. (82)

Do they seek a religion other than God's religion, when all that is in the heavens and on the earth has surrendered to Him willingly or forcibly, and to Him they will all return? (83)

Say: "We believe in God and what He revealed to us, and what He revealed to Abraham, Ishmael, Isaac, Jacob and the tribes, and what was revealed to Moses, Jesus, and the Prophets, from their Lord; we make no distinction among them, and we are to Him surrendered." (84)

He who seeks a religion other than Islam, it will not be accepted from him, and on the Day of Judgement he will be a loser. (85)

How would God guide those who disbelieve after they declared their belief and after they bore witness that the apostle was right, and after they were in receipt of veritable signs? God does not guide the evildoers. (86)

Those have their punishment as a curse from God, the angels and all of the people. (87)

They shall be immortalized in Hell, with no reprieve from torture or any further consideration, (88) except for those who repent and afterwards do good works. God is Forgiving and Merciful. (89)

Those who disbelieved after they believed and then reached new heights in their disbelief, their repentance shall not be accepted, and those are the misguided. (90)

Those who disbelieve and die unbelievers, they will not be able to ransom themselves with the whole earth full of gold, and for those an excruciating pain is waiting. They shall have no supporters. (91)

You shall not attain true righteousness until you spend from what you like to have yourself. Whatever you spend, God is in full knowledge of. (92)

All food was allowed the Israelites except that which they disallowed themselves, until the revelation of the Torah. Say: "Bring the Torah and read it, if you are truthful." (93)

Then whoever lies about God, he will be among the transgressors. (94)

Say: "God has declared the truth; follow the faith of Abraham, the straight faith; he was not an idolater." (95)

The first shrine ever built for man was placed in Mecca, blessing and guidance to the world. (96)

In it there are veritable signs, the residence of Abraham, and whoever enters it is safe, and people owe God a pilgrimage to it; whoever has a way of doing it. As to those who disbelieve, God is in no need of them, or of the rest of the world. (97)

Say: "People of the Book why do you disbelieve God's verses when God is witness to whatever you do?" (98)

Say: "People of the Book, why do you obstruct the way of others to God, and seek to make their way crooked when it is quite straight and you know it to be? God is never oblivious to what you do." (99)

People who believe, if you obey those who were given the Scriptures, they will send you back after you believed to being an unbeliever. (100)

And how could you not believe while you are hearing God's verses recited to you, and in your midst is His Apostle! And whoever is steadfast in holding to God, he shall be guided to the straight path. (101)

People who believe, fear God the way He should be feared, and die only as Moslems. (102)

And hold on all of you to God's rope, and do not pull apart, and remember God's bounty to you, as He brought you together after you were enemies and created warmth between your hearts and with His blessing you became brothers; and after you were on the very edge of a hole that leads to Hell, He saved you from it. This is how God reveals His verses to you so that you may be guided. (103)

Let a nation evolve from you that will advocate righteousness, strive for fairness and stand up against evil; and such will be triumphant. (104)

Do not be like those who pulled apart and became divided after they were given veritable signs. Those shall have great torture. (105)

The day when some faces are whitened and other faces are blackened, those who disbelieved after belief shall be the ones whose faces are blackened. Taste the torture for your disbelief. (106)

Those whose faces are whitened shall be in God's mercy immortalized. (107)

These are God's verses. We recite to you rightly as God wants no injustice to befall your world. (108)

To God belongs what is in heaven and on earth and to God all matters shall return. (109)

You were the best nation introduced to mankind; You promote kindness and charity, denounce evildoing and believe in God. If People of the Book believed it would have been better for them; some of them are believers but most of them are corrupted. (110)

They will not be able to harm you but little, and if they fight you, they shall turn their back and run and they will not be victorious. (111)

They are destined to humiliation wherever they go, unless they receive help from God and from other people, but they shall get none but God's displeasure. They have also been humbled as a result of their disbelief in God's revelations and their killing of the prophets unjustly. What befalls them will be the result of their disobedience and transgression. (112)

Not all people of the Book are the same. Among them are thriving nations that recite God's verses throughout the night, while prostrated. (113)

They believe in God and the Last Day and promote charity and kindness while denouncing evildoing; they hasten to charity and they are among the righteous. (114)

The benefit of whatever good they do will not be denied to them and God has full knowledge of righteous men. (115)

Those who disbelieve, their riches and their children shall not provide them with any redemption from God. They are the owners of Hell and in it they shall be immortalized. (116)

The funds they spend in this world are like a freezing wind that hits a cultivated field that belongs to people who wronged themselves and laid it to waste. God has not wronged them, but they wronged themselves. (117)

People who believe do not surround yourselves with those who are not of you, because they carry no great love for you. Their disdain of you is frequently on their tongues and what is in their hearts is even worse than what is on their tongues. God reveals His verses to you so you may find reason. (118)

You like them but they do not like you, and while you believe in the entire revelations, they will say they believe when they meet with you, but when they are with each other they bite the tips of their own fingers from their anger. Say: "Die from anger. God knows what you hide in your chest." (119)

If good befalls you it disappoints them, while harm that touches you gives them comfort. If you are patient and righteous their wickedness will not hurt you in anyway, and God has complete awareness of what they do. (120)

You remember when you left your family at an early hour to assign your men their battle positions and God hears and knows everything. (121)

Two groups on your side were about to fail, but God was their sponsor, and on God the believers shall depend. (122)

In Badr, God granted you victory when you were the favored to lose; fear God and be thankful. (123)

Say to the believers: "Is it not enough that God descended three thousand angels to help you?" (124)

Yes, if you hold your ground and fear God, and they attack you, God will reinforce you with five thousand angels splendidly equipped. (125)

God brings you such good tidings so as to bring comfort to your hearts. Victory comes from no one but God, the Exalted and the Wise. (126)

God may cut the flank of the unbelievers, put them to flight or have them totally defeated. (127)

It is not a concern of yours if God forgave them or dealt punishment to them; they are transgressors. (128)

To God belongs what is in heavens and on earth. He forgives whomever He wants and punishes whomever He wants. God is Forgiving and Merciful. (129)

People who believe, do not use usury to double your wealth many times over and fear God so you can succeed. (130)

Fear the fire that is readied for the unbelievers. (131)

Obey God and the Apostle so that you may receive mercy. (132)

And hurry to forgiveness from your Lord and to a paradise that is as wide as the heavens and the earth, readied for those who are righteous. (133)

Those who spend in charity when prosperous or when afflicted with calamity, and those who control their anger and forgive their fellow humans. God loves those who are charitable. (134)

And those who, when they commit a sin and wrong themselves, remember God, and beseech Him to forgive their sins; and who else forgives sins but God? They do not persist in their sinful behavior knowingly. (135)

Those will have their reward from their Lord; gardens under which rivers are flowing. In it they shall be immortalized; a suitable reward for hard workers. (136)

Before you there were many examples; roam the world and see how those who disbelieved ended. (137)

These are signs for people, guidance and admonishment to those who are righteous. (138)

Do not despair and do not be sad and you shall triumph if you are believers. (139)

If you have suffered a setback, but so did your enemy. These are afflictions that We alternate between people so God may test those who believed, and create martyrs among them. God does not like the transgressors. (140)

God shall test the faithful and annihilate the unbelievers. (141)

Did you think you would enter paradise without God ascertaining who among you have fought for Him and who are those who held their ground? (142)

You were wishing death before you came to meet it. How do you feel after you did?(143)

Mohammed is but an Apostle, before whom many apostles have come and gone. Are you going to turn away from guidance if he died or got killed? If you do, you shall not affect God. God shall reward the thankful. (144)

No one dies without God's permission; a predetermined eventuality. Those who seek this life's rewards, We shall give them some of it, and those who seek the rewards of the next life, we shall give them some of it also. We shall reward the thankful. (145)

Many apostles have fought with armies of the faithful on their side, and they neither wavered nor weakened in face of what afflicted them, while fighting in the way of God, nor did they ever yield ground. God loves those who hold their ground. (146)

They only said: "God, forgive our sins, and our excesses and help us hold our positions steadfast and grant us victory over the unbelievers." (147)

God rewarded them in this life and then even more highly in the life to come. God loves those who are charitable. (148)

O' people who believe, if you obey those who disbelieved, they shall take you back and change you to losers. (149)

It is God who is your sponsor and He is the best of all allies. (150)

We shall throw terror into the hearts of the unbelievers, because they assigned to God partners without His sanction. Their shelter shall be the Fire; a dismal resting place for the transgressors. (151)

God has fulfilled His pledge to you when you prevailed by His permission. Then you failed, and feuded with each other and disobeyed after you were shown the way and brought within sight of what you wished for. Some of you wish for the rewards of this world, while others wish for the rewards of the life to come. He allowed you to face defeat so He can test you. Then He forgave you. God is the benefactor of believers. (152)

Remember when you descended the hill with the Apostle calling on you from your rear to hold on to your positions? God thus rewarded you with one sorrow to replace another (*that of defeat to replace missing a share of the spoils*), so as not to worry about what you missed or what befell you. (153)

Then after sorrow He granted you tranquility. Slumber overtook some while others became victims of their own thoughts. They started thinking wrongly of God. They started saying: "What have we got to do with this?" Say: "Everything belongs to God." But they hide what they do not tell you. They say: "If we had an interest in this we would not have been killed." Say: "If you stayed in your homes, those who are destined to be killed shall die. It was God's will to test your faith, and steadfastness. God knows what is in your chests." (154)

Those of you who retreated when the two armies met, have been made vulnerable to inducements from the Devil, because of evil they have committed. God has forgiven them. He is Forgiving and Tolerant. (155)

O' people who believe, do not be like the unbelievers who say if their brothers travel or go to war and die, had they stayed with us they would not have died or been killed. God will make them regret their words. God is the One who makes life and takes it away, and God sees what you do. (156)

For one to be killed in the way of God or die with His forgiveness and mercy is far better than anything others accumulate. (157)

If you ever die or get killed, to God you shall finally be assembled. (158)

It was through mercy from God that you were lenient with them. If you were obnoxious and had a hard heart, they would have deserted you. Forgive them, ask for their forgiveness, and consult with them on matters of interest to them. If you decide, count on God's help; God loves those who count on His help. (159)

If God is your ally no one can defeat you, and if His support is withdrawn from you, on whose support can you count? It is on God's help that the believers will count. (160)

No Prophet will defraud his people, because those who do will bring the product of their fraud with them on the Day of Judgement. Then every soul shall be paid in full for what it has earned, and none will be wronged. (161)

Can a man who strives to please God be compared to one who incurs God's wrath? His home shall be Hell; a miserable destination. (162)

All have different standings in the eyes of God and God sees what they do. (163)

It is God's special favor to the believers when He sent an Apostle from among them, reciting God's verses to them, purifying them, and teaching them the Book and wisdom after they were totally misguided. (164)

When a disaster befalls you after you have inflicted twice as much harm on the other side, you ask: "How did we get this?" Say: "It was your own fault, God is Capable of all things." (165)

What befell you the day the two armies met was with God's sanction, intended to test the believers. (166)

The hypocrites, when asked to fight in the way of God, they said: "If we knew how to fight we would have surely been with you." On that day they were closer to disbelief than to being believers.

Their mouths said what was not in their hearts. God is more Knowledgeable with what they hide. (167)

These were the men, who as they sat, they said of their brothers: "If they obeyed us they would not have been killed." Say to them: "Why, then, you cannot protect yourselves from death if you are truthful?"(168)

Do not ever believe that those who are killed in the way of God are dead. They are alive and thriving with their Lord, (169)

rejoicing in what God gave them from His bounty and receiving good tidings from those they left behind. They shall have no worries, nor shall they ever be sad. (170)

They shall have the good tidings of God's bounty and favor. God will never forgo the believers' earned reward. (171)

The ones who responded to God and the Apostle after they suffered defeat, and then continued to do good, and to be righteous men, shall be greatly rewarded. (172)

They are the ones who, when told the enemy is approaching with a great force be fearful of him (*the enemy*), they became more tenacious in their belief and said: "We are in the hands of God and with Him is the best of all destinies." (173)

Their fortunes turned with the grace of God and His favor. No harm touched them, and they enjoyed God's favor. God's favor is great indeed. (174)

The Devil induces his followers to fear him. Do not fear him, but fear Me if you are believers. (175)

Do not let those who easily unbelieve make you sad. They shall not affect God at all. God shall give them no chance on the Day of Judgement, and great torture awaits them. (176)

Those who substitute disbelief for belief shall do no harm to God and excruciating torture awaits them. (177)

The unbelievers should not think that We prolong their days for their own good. They are rather given an opportunity to increase in wickedness and awaiting them is a humiliating torture. (178)

It is not God's intention to leave the believers in their present status until the good is totally separated from the bad, nor is it God's intention to make knowledge of the future known to you. But God may favor with such a knowledge whomever He chooses from among His apostles. Believe in God and in His apostles and if you believe and become righteous people, you shall be greatly rewarded. (179)

Those misers who hoard God's bounty should never believe it is good for them. It shall become an evil they carry around their necks on the Day of Judgement. God is the final inheritor of the heavens and the earth and He is knowledgeable with what you do. (180)

God has heard those who said: "God is poor and we are rich." We shall record what they said, add to it their unjust killing of apostles. Then We will say: Taste the torture of Fire. (181)

This is what you have done to yourselves. God does not wrong His subjects. (182)

There were those who said: "God has made a covenant with us, that we do not believe an apostle until he bring us down an offering that can be consumed by fire." Say: "You had apostles who brought you veritable signs in addition to what you said. Why did you kill them? If you are truthful." (183)

If they denied you, they have denied apostles before you who brought them veritable signs, the Psalms and guidance-giving Scriptures. (184)

Every soul shall taste death. You shall receive your worth only on the Day of Judgement. He who is spared the fire and enters paradise has truly won. This life is nothing but a fleeting arrogance. (185)

You shall be hurt in yourselves and your possessions and you shall hear painful words from those who received the Scriptures before you and the unbelievers. If you are steadfast and righteous you will prevail. (186)

God made a covenant with those who received the Scriptures to reveal them to the entire world and not conceal them. They turned their back on that covenant and sold it for a cheap price. Shame on them for what they got. (187)

Those who are proud of their misdeeds and those who like to get credit for what they have not done; they shall escape the torture. Excruciating torture awaits them. (188)

To God belong the heavens and the earth, and God is Capable of all things. (189)

In the creation of the heavens and the earth, and the alternation of the night and day, are examples for those who have intellect. (190)

Those are the ones who mention God when they are up and down and while lying on their sides, and they are the ones who contemplate the creation of the heavens and the earth. They say: "Our Lord, you have not created all of this without a purpose. We glorify You; protect us from the torture of Fire. (191)

Our Lord, Those who You humiliate by entering the Fire shall be shamed, and the wrongdoers have no allies. (192)

God, we have heard the caller, calling people to believe in the Lord. We believed our Lord; forgive us our sins, and purify us from our misdeeds and then help us die with the righteous. (193)

Our Lord, give us what You promised us through your apostles and let us not be sad on the Day of Judgement. You never miss an appointment."(194)

Their Lord responded to them: I never waste the good works of anyone of you, male or female. You are both from each other. Those who immigrated, or were forced out of their homes and were hurt while striving in My way and who fought and got killed; I shall forgive their sins, and enter them into Gardens, watered from below by rivers. A reward from God. God has the best of rewards. (195)

Do not be misled by the apparent success of the unbelievers on the land. (196)

A little enjoyment, then their home is Hell; a miserable resting place. (197)

But those who fear their Lord, theirs are gardens with flowing rivers, immortalized in it; a guest-house from God. God has a special bounty for the righteous. (198)

Among People of the Book are those who believe in what was revealed to you and revealed to them. They are pious and do not sell God's verses for a cheap price. They will have their reward with their Lord. God's accounting is quick. (199)

O' people who believe, be steadfast, patient and hold your ground and fear God so you may succeed. (200)

WOMEN (4)

In the Name of God, Most Merciful, and Most Beneficent.

O' People, be mindful of God who created you from a single soul, then from it He created its mate, and from them He created many men and women. Be mindful of God in whose name you swear to one another, and be respectful of the mothers from whose wombs you were born. God is watchful of what you do. (1)

Give orphans the property that rightfully belongs to them. Do not ever try to exchange what is good and valuable in their property with other things which are worthless, nor do you ever embezzle their property and add it to yours. Such would be a grave sin. (2)

If you become afraid of not being honorable with female orphans, you should marry whoever you like, even two, three or four; unless you cannot be fair, and then you marry only one. You can even marry a slave girl that belongs to you. That is far better for you than being dishonorable. (3)

Give women their dowry as a free gift; but if they, willingly and of their own accord, make some of it available to you, it shall not be sinful for you to make use of that, with Our blessing. (4)

Do not give the incompetent the property that God has put you in charge of. Only provide for them, clothe them and be absolutely kind to them. (5)

Take care of the orphans in your charge until they are old enough to be married. Then if you believe they have become responsible, pay their money to them without wasting any of it. Those who are not in need, it is better if they do not charge the orphan's estate for their labor. Those who are in need can pay themselves fairly. When you transfer their property back to them, make sure you have witnesses. God does have complete account of what you do. (6)

To men shall belong a share of what their parents or relatives leave, and to women shall belong a share of what their parents or relatives leave. Whether it is big or small, they shall have a definite share of it. (7)

If, at the division of an inheritance, relatives, orphans and the destitute are present, give them some of it, and be kind to them. (8)

Let those who would worry if they die and left dependents behind, remember that while they are taking care of the interest of orphans left behind by others, let them fear God and provide for their charges sage advice. (9)

Those who usurp the property of the orphans unjustly shall swallow fire in their bellies and shall become fuel for the great fire. (10)

God trusts you as to your children's inheritance. For the male, twice the share of the female. If there are more than two girls, they shall inherit two thirds of the total inheritance. If there is one female, she will inherit one half of her father's inheritance. The parents shall inherit one sixth each, if he has children. If he does not have children, the deceased will be inherited by his parents. His mother shall have one third. If the deceased has brothers and sisters, his mother shall inherit one sixth after his debts are paid and any legacies he may have bequeathed. It is not up to you to decide whether your children or your parents are closer or more helpful to you, this is God's Law and God is Knowledgeable and Wise. (11)

You will inherit half of what your deceased wives leave if they have no children. If they have children you will inherit one fourth, after legacies they bequeath or debts they leave are paid. Your wives shall inherit one fourth of what you leave if you have no children, and one eighth of what you leave if you have children, after any legacies you bequeath or debts you leave are paid. If a man was to be inherited by a distant descendent or a woman and has a brother or a sister, they shall each have one sixth. If his siblings are more than two, they shall all share one third, after any legacy he bequeathed or debts he left are paid, without any prejudice to the rights of the heirs. It is God's law, and God is Knowledgeable and Tolerant. (12)

These are the limits established by God, and he who obeys God and His apostle shall enter gardens watered by rivers from below, immortalized in it, and that is the great prize. (13)

He who disobeys God and His apostle and trespasses beyond the set limits of God; he shall enter a Fire, immortalized in it forever and a humiliating torture awaits him. (14)

Those among your wives who commit indecency, and after their offence is substantiated by four witnesses, you can restrict them to their homes until they die or God finds another way for them. (15)

If two men among you commit indecency, they will have to pay a price for doing it. If they repent and correct their ways, leave them alone; God is Forgiving and Merciful. (16)

God is Forgiving for those who commit evil out of ignorance then turn to Him in repentance fast. God is Knowledgeable and Wise. (17)

Repentance is not for those who commit evil until they are near death and then they try to repent, nor is it available to those who die unbelievers. We have excruciating torture waiting for them. (18)

O' People who believe, it is unlawful for you to try to inherit women forcibly nor should you try to put pressure on them to give back to you what you have already given to them, unless they commit a clear evil. Treat them kindly, since even if you dislike them, God may put a lot of good in things you may dislike. (19)

If you ever decide to replace one spouse for another do not try to take back any amount of money you have given her. Would you want to earn something that is an injustice and a grave sin? (20)

How can you take it back after you have lived together and made a strict contract with each other? (21)

Do not ever wed women who were wedded to your fathers, except for what has already occurred prior to this. This was an evil, indecent and misguided practice. (22)

You are forbidden marriage to your mothers, daughters, sisters, your paternal and maternal aunts, the daughters of your brothers and sisters, the women who breast-fed you and their daughters, the mothers of your wives, and the daughters of your wives after your marriage to their mothers had been consummated. If the marriage had not been consummated, you can marry their daughters with no sin attached. You cannot also marry the wives of your own begotten sons, nor can you marry two sisters at the same time, except for what may have occurred prior to this, and God is Forgiving and Merciful. (23)

You are also forbidden to take in marriage married women, unless you own them. You can marry any other woman so long as you approach them honorably, be ready to spend your money for acquiring their hand in marriage, and not through fornication. You have to pay their dowry as ordered in regard to any enjoyment you derive from the marriage; although, between you, and without coercion you can agree to any terms, after your duty towards them and any agreements you have already made, have been fulfilled. God is Knowledgeable and Wise. (24)

If you are unable to marry free chaste women, you can choose to marry believing slave girls. God knows the status of who you own. You can marry those slave girls only with their families' permission, and pay them their dowry and do not take them through fornication or cohabitation, and after they marry, if they commit adultery, their punishment is only half of what is deserving for free women. These are the rules for those who are afraid of committing sin, but those who can endure; it is better for you if you refrain, and God is Forgiving and Merciful. (25)

God wishes to show you the way and guide you using the example of those who preceded you. He wants to forgive you and God is Knowledgeable and Wise. (26)

God wants to forgive you while those who follow their own desire would like to see you deviate badly. (27)

God wants to make things easier for you. Humans are created weak. (28)

O' people who believe, do not usurp each other's property unjustly unless such occurs in the course of normal trade and with mutual agreement, and do not kill yourselves. God is Merciful with you. (29)

He who does such things unjustly and with deliberate transgression, We shall light fire under him; which is quite easy for God. (30)

If you avoid the worst of what has been forbidden to you, We shall forgive your sins and steer you through an honorable entrance to heaven. (31)

Do not envy others for what God has favored some of you over the rest. Men deserve a reward for their labor and women deserve a reward for their labor. Do ask God to bestow His favors on you; God has knowledge of all things. (32)

We have decreed inheritance rights for the heirs, from whatever is left from every parent and relative. So did We decree the rightfulness of certain bequests and promises made to others. Deliver to all, their fair shares; God is a witness to all transactions. (33)

Men are in a position of authority over women in as much as God has favored them with certain capabilities, and in as much as they spend their money on maintaining women. Good righteous women are dignified and keep covered what God kept covered (*and different*) of their anatomy. Those who you have reason to fear their deviation, reason with them, punish them by refusing to have relations with them, and some you may have to get going on their way. Once the deviation is corrected, do not ever take advantage of them; God is Supreme and Exalted. (34)

If a split between a man and his wife is imminent, seek arbiters from his and her families. If they wish reconciliation God will help them get back together; God is Knowledgeable and Wise. (35)

Worship God and do not assign associates to Him. Be kind to your parents and also be kind to your relatives, the orphans and the destitute. Be kind to your close and distant neighbors, to your fellow travelers and to the homeless. Be kind to any slaves you may own; God does not like those who are arrogant and boastful. (36)

Nor does God like those who are misers and encourage others to be misers like them, and hoard what God had bestowed upon them of His bounty. We have reserved for the unbelievers a humiliating torture. (37)

The same ending will also afflict those who spend their money simply to impress other people, and those who do not believe in God or the Last Day, and those who take the Devil as a close friend; a miserable friendship indeed. (38)

Would they not have been better off if they had believed in God and the Last Day, and spent from what God has given them and realized that God has always been aware of them? (39)

God does not wrong anyone a hair; and for the good you do He will reward you many times over and add a huge bonus. (40)

How is it going to be when We bring a witness from each nation and We bring you as a witness on the witnesses? (41)

That will be the day when those who unbelieved or disobeyed the Apostle will wish they can disappear under the earth, and will not be able to hide a word from God. (42)

O' people who believe, do not ever go near prayer while you are drunk. You should wait until you can understand what you are saying. You should not approach prayer following sexual activity until you wash yourselves all over, unless you were travelling. If you were ill or travelling, and have engaged in sexual activity or relieved yourselves through the rectum, and water was not available, you ought to perform "*TIAMUM*"; where you seek clean dust and rub your faces and hands with it. God is Forgiving and Tolerant. (43)

Did you not see those to whom some of the Scriptures were given, how they bargained to be lost and now they want the same lack of guidance for you? (44)

God knows your enemies better than you do. God is the only sponsor and ally you need. (45)

Some Jews have engaged in changing the place and sequence of words. They say: "We heard and disobeyed instead of saying we heard and obeyed." They say: "Watch for us (*Raina*) instead of look at us (*Inzurna*)," thus twisting their tongues with different but similar sounding words, so they can ridicule the religion. If they had used the right words, it would have been better for them and more upright; God has cursed them for their disbelief. They believe but very little. (46)

O' people of the Book, believe in what we revealed which is confirming what you already have, before we obliterate faces and turn them backwards, or curse them the way we cursed the Sabbath-breakers before them. What God orders shall be executed. (47)

God shall not forgive associating others with him, but may forgive any lesser sin to whomever He wishes; and whoever associates others with God has committed a grave sin. (48)

Look at those who keep on promoting themselves. God promotes whomever He wishes and none will be wronged a hair. (49)

See how they fabricate things about God; such is a grave sin. (50)

See those who received some of the Scriptures; they believe in idols and false gods and then they say to the unbelievers that they are better than the believers. (51)

Those are the ones whom God has cursed; and those who are cursed by God shall find no supporters. (52)

If they get a share in the kingdom, they will not give other people a speck of dust. (53)

They envy people for what God has bestowed upon them. We gave the descendants of Abraham the Scriptures and wisdom and permitted them to have a great kingdom. (54)

Some of them believed and others rejected the revelation. Hell will have plenty of fuel. (55)

Those who unbelieved our verses, we shall light fire under them and every time their skins are gone, we shall replace them with new skin so they can taste again the torture. God is Exalted and Wise. (56)

Those who believed and did good work, we shall enter them into gardens watered from below by flowing rivers, immortalized in them forever; and in it they shall have purified spouses, and they shall continue to live in a shaded bliss. (57)

It is God's decree that you should turn back what you are entrusted with to its original owners on demand; and if you sit in judgement on others that you act with justice. God steers you towards being morally noble. God hears all and sees all. (58)

O' People who believe, obey God and the Apostle, and those who are justly in a position of authority; and if you have a dispute take it back to God and the Apostle, if you believe in God and the Last Day. This is better for you, and will permit you to be seen in a better light. (59)

Did you not see those who claim they believe in you, and in what was revealed to you, and what was revealed before you; yet they want to take their disputes to the Devil, when they were clearly ordered not to believe in him. The Devil was about to mislead them far off. (60)

If they were invited to what was revealed by God to the Apostle, the hypocrites shall refuse and shrink away from you. (61)

Then if they become afflicted with a calamity, brought on to them by what their own hands earned, they will come to you taking one oath over another, saying they intended nothing but good and success. (62)

God knows well what is in their hearts. Be careful with them, lecture to them and bring out what is inside them with eloquent speech. (63)

We never sent an apostle not to be obeyed, with God's permission; and if after they wronged themselves they came to you and asked for God's forgiveness, and you asked forgiveness for them, they would have found God Forgiving and Merciful. (64)

By God's name, they will not be believers until they come to you with their disputes and put you in judgement, then they will have no problem in abiding by your judgement and totally surrender to it. (65)

If We had asked them to risk their lives or leave their homes, only a few of them would have. If they did what they were asked, it would have been better for them, and it would have strengthened their faith. (66)

We would have greatly rewarded them, (67)

and guided them to the straight path. (68)

Those who obey God. and the apostle; they are the ones who will enjoy God's bounty and will have the company of the prophets, the saints, the martyrs, the righteous, and the best company that could be had. (69)

A favor from God and God is most Knowledgeable. (70)

O' People who believe, be cautious. Those in the front should be the most reliable or you should be all together. (71)

Some of you may slow down. If a calamity befell you, they will say: "God has favored us by not taking us as martyrs." (72)

But if you succeed they will act as if they were not your friends, and say: "If we were with them we would have shared in the success." (73)

Let the fighting be for those who are willing to exchange this life for the life next. He who fights for God, whether he wins or gets killed, he shall be rewarded greatly. (74)

How would you not fight for God and for the weak of the men, women and children, who say: "Our Lord, deliver us from this village with its ruthless people. Provide for us a leader and give us an ally." (75)

Those who believe fight for God, and the unbelievers fight for the Devil. Fight the Devil's followers; the Devil's wickedness has always been weak. (76)

Did you not see those to whom it was said: "Refrain from sin, establish prayers and pay the alms-tax;" but when they were ordered to fight, they appeared to fear people as much or more than God. They said: "Our Lord, why did You order us to fight and did not give us a little more time in this life?" Say: "This life is little and the next life is better for the righteous and none will be wronged a hair." (77)

Anywhere you are, death will catch up with you, even if you stayed in fortified towers. If good befell them, they say this is from God, and when afflicted with bad they say this is from you (*the Prophet*). Say it is all from God. How is it that those people have a problem understanding what is being said to them? (78)

Whatever befalls you, if it is good, it is from God and if it is bad blame yourselves. We sent the people an apostle, and God shall be the witness. (79)

Whoever obeys the Apostle, he obeys God, and those who do not, you are not their keeper. (80)

To you they talk obedience, and after they leave you, some of them talk differently. God has record of what they hide. Ignore them and depend on God. He is all you need to rely on. (81)

Do they not contemplate the Koran? If it was from someone other than God they would have found it full with discrepancies. (82)

If they learn of a rumor that concerns fear for safety they propagate it. If they had passed it to the Apostle or the people in authority, they would have had a chance to check its validity. If it was not for God's favor to you, and His mercy upon you, all but a few of you would have followed the Devil. (83)

Fight in the way of God and do not coerce anyone but yourself and motivate the believers so that God may limit the ruthlessness of the unbelievers. God is much stronger and more revengeful. (84)

He who intercedes to do good shall receive a part of the reward, and he who intercedes to do bad, shall get a part of the blame. God will account for everything. (85)

If you are greeted, answer with a better greeting or equal to it. With God you shall have to account for everything. (86)

God, the only God, will assemble you on the Day of Judgement, which is never to be doubted; and who is more truthful than God? (87)

How did you manage to split into two groups over the hypocrites, when God has already rejected them over their deeds? Do you want to guide those who God Has misguided? He who is misguided by God will never find the right path. (88)

The hypocrites wish you disbelieve the way they did, so you may become equalized. Do not adopt sponsors from among them until they migrate in the way of God. If they betray you, take them and kill them wherever you find them and never take one of them as a sponsor or an ally. (89)

Excluded are those who take refuge among people with whom you have an executed treaty, or those who come to you because their hearts do not permit them to fight against you or against their own people. You should realize that if God wished it they would have been fighting you. So if they leave you alone and offer you peace, God has left you nothing on them. (90)

You will find some who try to have peace with you and with their people, but every chance they have, they participate in acts of subversion against you. So if they do not stay away from you and keep absolute peace, take them and kill them anywhere you. find them. These We give you over them absolute authority. (91)

It is forbidden for a believer to kill another believer, except by accident. He who kills another believer by mistake, shall free a believing slave and pay ransom to his family, unless they choose to have it given away in charity. If the deceased is a believer from an opposing people with whom you are at war, then also freeing a believing slave is needed. If the people of the deceased have a treaty with you then paying ransom to his family and freeing a believing slave are both necessary. He who cannot find a way to do the foregoing will have to fast two months in succession to seek God's forgiveness. God is Knowledgeable and Wise. (92)

He who kills a believer with premeditation, his penalty shall be hell; immortalized in it forever, with God's wrath and curse on him forever; and awaiting him is a great torture. (93)

O' People who believe, if you go fighting for God, be discerning and never say to those who are offering you peace, "you are not believers," intending to get a chance at the spoils of war. God has much more valuable rewards. These were your old ways, but now God has favored you with His guidance, so show consideration to others; God is Knowledgeable with what you do. (94)

Those of the believers who stay behind during war cannot be equal to those who struggle in the way of God, endangering themselves and their property. They are a step higher than those who stayed behind unless staying behind was necessitated by physical impediment. God will favor those who struggled over those who stayed behind by a huge reward. (95)

It is His classification, His forgiveness and His mercy. God is Forgiving and Merciful. (96)

Those that the angels carry after their death, having made peace with evildoing, the angels will ask: "What were you doing?" Their answer will be: "We were too weak and persecuted to do any different." The angels will ask: "Was not God's earth large enough for you to immigrate?" Their home shall be hell; a miserable destiny, (97)

except for those persecuted men, women and children who have no way out regardless of how they try. (98)

Those may be forgiven by God. God is Forgiving and Tolerant. (99)

He who migrates in the way of God shall find on earth refuges and opportunities; and he who leaves his home to fight for God and His apostle, and death catches up with him, his reward from God will already be deserved. God is Forgiving and Merciful. (100)

If you are traveling in God's mission and fear attack, it is not sinful for you to shorten your prayers. The unbelievers are your most evident enemies. (101)

If at war and it is time to lead them in prayer, let a group of them pray with you while the others take up their arms and stand as guards in your rear. Then those who prayed will take the arms and stand guard, while those who have not prayed join you in prayers. All should be watchful for themselves and their weapons. The unbelievers would like nothing more than to see you neglect your weapons and your equipment, so they can attack you. If you become afflicted with heavy rain or illness it is not wrong for you to put down your weapons while keeping your guard. God has prepared for the unbelievers a humiliating torture. (102)

If you are finished with prayers, continue to mention God while you are up, down or on your sides. Once you feel safer, resume prayers. Prayers have been decreed for the believers in specified times. (103)

Continue to seek your enemy unrelentingly. If you are suffering, so are they, but you can hope from God what they could never hope for. God is Knowledgeable and Wise. (104)

We revealed the Book to you so that you may make judgements among people based on what God has taught you. Do not spend time remonstrating with failures. (105)

Ask for God's forgiveness. God is Forgiving and Merciful. (106)

Do not intercede for those who betrayed their own souls. God does not like traitors or wrongdoers. (107)

They seek a disguise from men, but they have no disguise from God. He is with them when they secretly say what He does not like. God is aware of what they do. (108)

If you argue for them in this life, who will argue for them on the Day of Judgement? Who is going to be their representative then? (109)

He who commits evil or wrongs himself then asks for God's forgiveness shall find God Forgiving and Merciful. (110)

He who commits sin, commits it against himself. God is Knowledgeable and Wise. (111)

He who commits sin and then lets an innocent person take blame for it, has committed an injustice and a prominent transgression. (112)

If it was not for God's favor on you and His mercy, a group of them was about ready to mislead you. They mislead none but themselves, and they will not hurt you in any way. God has revealed to you the Book and wisdom, and taught you what you did not know. God's favor on you has been tremendous. (113)

There is no value in much of their advice, except for those who recommend charity and kindness or intercession in favor of peace among people. Those who do these things strictly seeking God's pleasure shall be greatly rewarded. (114)

He who splits from the Apostle after guidance has been fully revealed to him and follows a path different from the believers; he shall get what he is asking for. We shall light him up in Hell; a miserable destiny. (115)

God does not forgive associating others with Him, but does forgive lessor sins, to whomever He wishes. One who associates others with God has been misguided too far. (116)

Some pagans pray to females; they are in reality praying to the rebellious Devil himself. (117)

The Devil was cursed by God, and he promised: "I shall take a big toll among Your worshipers." (118)

"I shall mislead them and entice them into sinful desires. I shall order them to split the ears of cattle and tamper with God's creation." He who takes the Devil as sponsor has suffered a huge loss. (119)

He promises them and entices them; but the Devil can deliver nothing but empty arrogance. (120)

These will have Hell for a home, and will find it inescapable. (121)

Those who believed and did good works We shall enter them into Gardens, watered from below by flowing rivers; immortalized in it forever; a true promise from God. Whose promise is more truthful than His promise? (122)

It shall not be in accordance with your wishes nor the wishes of those who received the Scriptures. He who commits evil shall find it and he shall have no sponsors or allies other than God. (123)

Those believers who do good works, men or women, shall enter Paradise and shall not be wronged a hair. (124)

Who is more religious than he who surrenders himself to God willingly and follows the pure faith of Abraham? God has befriended Abraham. (125)

To God belongs what is in heavens and on earth. God is in control of all things. (126)

They ask you about women, say: "God's decrees in regard to them are already in the Book." Such as the orphan women who do not receive what belongs to them, and those you wish to marry. Already covered also is the handling of the weak of children, and the need to deal with the orphans with justice. Whatever you do good, God will have knowledge of it. (127)

If a woman feared her husband's deviation or neglect she would not be wrong in asking for conciliation; for conciliation is best. Humans have some inclination to greed; but if you are charitable and righteous God will have full knowledge of what you do. (128)

You will not be able to deal with your wives equally, though try you may. Never let yourself totally gravitate towards one, while discarding the other like a used utensil. If you reform and do what is right you will find God Forgiving and Merciful. (129)

If the spouses separate, God will provide assistance to both out of His own vast resources. God is Vast and Wise. (130)

To God belongs what is in heavens and on earth. We exhorted those who got the Scriptures before you, and you, to fear God; and if you disbelieve, God has what is in heavens and on earth. God is wealthy and to Him thankfulness should be directed. (131)

To God belongs what is in heavens and on earth, with Him as sponsor you need no one else. (132)

If it is His wish, He can obliterate all of you and replace you with other men. He is Capable of all that. (133)

Those who seek the rewards of this life should know that God holds the key to all rewards, those of this life and the one next. God hears all and sees all. (134)

O' People who believe, always bear true witness, even against yourselves, your parents or your relatives. Whether the concerned individuals are rich or poor they are more God's responsibility than yours. Do not follow your emotions; and whether you are truthful, or deviate from the truth, or decline to testify, God will have full knowledge of what you do. (135)

O' People who believe, believe in God, in His apostle and the Book that was revealed to His apostle, and the Book that was revealed before. He who disbelieves God, His angels, His Books, His apostles, and the Last Day has gone astray very far. (136)

Those who believed then disbelieved, then believed, then disbelieved again, then increased in their disbelief; God will never forgive them nor will He show them the right path, ever. (137)

As for the hypocrites; you can predict for them excruciating torture. (138)

Those who adopt unbelievers as sponsors, in preference to believers, seeking some of their glory, should remember that all glory belongs to God. (139)

God has decreed in the Book that if you ever hear God's verses being disbelieved or mocked by a certain group, you are never to join them or sit with them, until they engage in a different subject. If you do, you become like them. Remember that God will get all the unbelievers and the hypocrites in Hell together as one group. (140)

They watch your fortunes very closely, and if God granted you success they will claim to have been with you. If the unbelievers get the upper hand, they will say to them: "We helped fend the believers off for you." God shall have the final judgement on them, on the Day of Judgement, and He will not let the unbelievers have the believers at a disadvantage. (141)

The hypocrites are trying to deceive God and He had them deceived; if they get up to pray, they do it with laziness to deceive people while in reality they do not mention God but very little. (142)

They keep on wavering, neither on this side nor on the other; he who tries to deceive God will never find the way. (143)

O' People who believe, do not take the unbelievers as sponsors, in preference to the believers; do you want to provide God with clear evidence against yourselves? (144)

The place for the hypocrites is the lowest level of Hell, and they shall find no ally. (145)

Except for those who repent and reform and adhere to God's line and become faithful to their religion; these will be with the believers, and God shall give the believers a great reward. (146)

God has no interest in torturing you if you believe and you are thankful. God is Grateful and Knowledgeable. (147)

God does not like the public utterance of harsh words or criticism unless it comes from people who were wronged. God Hears, and God Knows. (148)

If you declare the good or keep it hidden, or if you refrain from evil, God will always be capable of forgiveness. (149)

Those who unbelieve in God and His apostles, they try to discriminate between His apostles, and say: "We believe some and disbelieve others, and try to find middle ground between belief and disbelief." (150)

These are the true unbelievers. We have prepared for the unbelievers humiliating torture. (151)

The believers are those who believe in God, and His apostles and do not discriminate against any of them; they shall have their reward, and God is Forgiving and Merciful. (152)

As to people of the Book asking you to bring them a Book from heaven; they asked more of Moses; they wanted to see God outright, and the thunderbolt took them with their evildoing. Then they took up the calf after veritable signs were brought to them. We still forgave that, and gave Moses a great kingdom. (153)

We raised the Mount over them, and said: "Enter through the door and prostrate yourselves," and took their covenant not to violate the Sabbath. (154)

They broke their covenant, disbelieved Our verses, and killed prophets unjustly. They said: "Our hearts are sealed." In effect, God has stamped their hearts with their disbelief. They do not believe but very little. (155)

In their disbelief they invented disgraceful falsehoods about Mary. (156)

They claimed we killed Jesus, son of Mary, the Apostle of God. They neither killed him nor did they crucify him; they thought they did. The disagreement between them is a demonstration of their doubt. They have no direct knowledge; it is all presumption on their part. They never knew they killed him for sure. (157)

God has elevated him to His presence; God is Exalted, and Wise. (158)

Some people of the Book never believed in him before his death and on the Day of Judgement he shall be a witness on them. (159)

Because of their transgressions, and their practice of putting obstacles in the way of others to God, certain things were forbidden to the Jews after they were permitted previously. (160)

It is because of the fact that they took up usury although it was forbidden, and their usurping of other people's money unjustly. We have prepared for the unbelievers excruciating torture. (161)

Some of them, who are well established in knowledge and the believers who believe in what was revealed to you and what was revealed before you; those who hold prayers and pay the alms-tax and those who believe in God and the Last Day; they shall receive their great reward. (162)

We have made revelations to you like we made them to Noah, and other Prophets after him. We also made revelations to Abraham, Ishmael, Isaac, Jacob and the tribes in addition to Jesus, Job, Jonah, Aaron and Solomon. To David we revealed the Psalms. (163)

There are apostles We told about before and some We have not. God talked to Moses in person. (164)

Apostles who brought good tidings and warnings, so that people will have no excuses later. God is Exalted and Wise. (165)

God will certify what He has revealed to you, of His knowledge and so will the angels. God needs no other witnesses. (166)

Those who unbelieved and rejected the path decreed by God, have strayed far away in misguidance. (167)

Those who disbelieved and wronged others, God will not forgive them, nor shall He show them the way; (168)

except for the way to Hell, and in it they shall be immortalized forever, which is easy for God. (169)

O' People, an apostle came to you with what is right from your Lord. Believe; it is better for you. If you disbelieve, to God belongs what is in heaven and on earth, and God is Knowledgeable and Wise. (170)

O' People of the Book, do not be transgressors in your own religion and say only the truth about God. Jesus, son of Mary is but an Apostle of God, and His word which He transmitted to Mary through His angel. Believe in God and His apostles and do not say three. If you refrain from that it is better for you. God is One God, the Glorious; how could He have a son when to Him belongs what is in heaven and on earth? God is the only sponsor. (171)

The Messiah never denied being God's servant, neither did the closest of the angels. Those who refrain from worshiping Him and become arrogant shall all be assembled to Him. (172)

But those who believed and did good works shall be paid in full and some more. As to those who declined and became arrogant; they shall receive excruciating torture, and shall find no sponsor or ally other than God. (173)

O' People, You received proof from your Lord, and We revealed to you a distinguishing light. (174)

Those who believed in God and adhered to His line, He shall enter them into His mercy and favor, and shall guide them to the straight path. (175)

They ask you about inheritance of the childless; say: "If a man died childless and he has a sister, his sister shall inherit one half. If a childless woman dies, her brother inherits all. If a childless man dies and has two sisters; they inherit two thirds. A childless man or woman who dies leaving sisters and brothers; they will inherit, with the brothers receiving twice the share of the sisters." God shows you the way so you may not err. God is Knowledgeable of all things. (176)

THE TABLE (5)

In the Name of God, Most Merciful, and Most Beneficent.

People who believe, abide by the contracts you make. It is lawful for you to eat all of the wild of cattle, but it is forbidden that you engage in hunting while you are on pilgrimage; God decrees as He wishes. (1)

Believers, do not ever violate the symbols of God's legislation nor the sanctity of the sacred month. Do not interfere with the signs on cattle indicating assignment as offerings, nor with ornaments intended for identification during the sacred month, nor with anyone seeking the sacred house for God's blessing. Once the sacred month is over you can go back to hunting. Do not be led by your hatred to those who did interfere with your pilgrimage to the sacred house, and collaborate on the goodness and piety and not on sin and transgression. Be mindful of God; He deals severe punishment. (2)

You are forbidden from eating the flesh of dead animals, spilled blood, the flesh of the pig, and flesh of any animal sacrificed in dedication to some one other than God. You are also forbidden the flesh of animals that are strangled, beaten, had fallen or had been gored to death; or those that are fed upon, as a prey, by a lion, unless you happen to purify it by delivering the final killing strike yourself, or animals that were killed as sacrifices to idols. You are also forbidden to decide by consulting the Three Arrows. It is a corrupt vicious practice. The unbelievers have given up trying to vanquish your religion, do not fear them. Today I have completed your religion and finished my favor to you. I have certified my choice of Islam as a religion for you. He who is constrained by extreme hunger and has to eat from what God has forbidden with no intention of sin will find God Forgiving and Merciful. (3)

They ask you what is permissible for them to eat, say: "That which God has told you you can eat, and you may teach birds of prey or dogs so that they may hunt for you. Eat of what they catch for you after you mention the name of God over it, and be mindful of God, His reckoning may be fast in coming." (4)

God made it lawful for you to eat all of the good things. Food of people of the Book is lawful for you to eat, as is your food to them. Lawful to you are the uncorrupted believing women and the uncorrupted women of the Book, provided that you pay their dowries and do not just cohabit or live with them in sin. Those who disbelieve after believing; their efforts are to fail and on the Day of Judgement they are losers. (5)

People who believe, when you get up to pray, wash your hands up to the elbows and wipe with water your heads and wash your legs down to the heels, and if you have had sexual relations you will have to wash and clean yourselves, and if you were sick or traveling or you had to relieve yourselves through the rectum or you had sexual relations and did not find water you can seek purification (or tiamum) using clean earth dust, wiping your faces and hands with it. God intends no inconvenience for you but He intends to purify you, complete His blessings to you, so that you may be thankful. (6)

Remember God's favor to you and the covenant He made with you, and your declaration of acknowledgment and obedience. Be mindful of God; He has knowledge of what is in your hearts. (7)

People who believe, stand up for guidance provided to you and be witnesses for justice. Your hatred for others should not interfere with your duty to do justice. Justice is closer to piety, be mindful of God. He is Knowledgeable with what you do. (8)

God has promised those who believed and did good works that for them there is forgiveness and great rewards. (9)

Those who disbelieved and denied our verses, they are the owners of Hell. (10)

People who believe, remember God's favor to you, when He restrained the hands of those who intended to harm you. Be mindful of God. It is on God that the believers can rely. (11)

God made a covenant with the people of Israel, and then raised among them twelve chieftains, and God said: I am with you, if you stand up in prayer, pay the alms-tax and believe in my apostles and supported them and did good for God. Then I shall forgive your transgressions and enter you gardens with rivers flowing under them. Those who disbelieve after that shall be missing the straight path. (12)

In as far as they violated their covenant We cursed them and We hardened their hearts. They changed the words and its sequence in their books and forgot some of what they were reminded of; you will continue to see betrayal on the part of many of them except a few. Pardon them and forgive them; God loves the righteous. (13)

Those who said: "We are Christian," We made a covenant with them, but they forgot some of what We reminded them of, and because of which We instigated among them animosity and hatred which will last to the Day of Judgement. God will inform them on what they were doing. (14)

People of the Book, Our apostle has come to you revealing a lot of what you were hiding of your Scriptures, and forgiving you for a lot. You have from God light and a veritable Book. (15)

With it God shows those who follow His favor the path to peace and takes them out of darkness to the light by His permission and guides them through to the straight path. (16)

Unbelieving are those who say God is Jesus, the son of Mary. Say: "Who can interfere with God if He chose to annihilate Jesus the son of Mary, his mother and all of those on earth?" To God belongs all that is in heaven and on earth and what is in between. He creates whatever He wishes and God is Capable of all things. (17)

The Jews and Christians said: "We are the children of God and His favorites;" say: "Why would He then inflict torture on you for your sins?" You are none but humans among those He created. He forgives whomever He wishes and tortures whomever He wishes. To God belongs the kingdom of heavens and earth and what is in between and destiny is to Him. (18)

People of the Book, Our apostle has come to you after a long period with many other apostles so that you cannot say we have received no good tidings or warnings. You have received both, good tidings and warnings. God is Capable of all things. (19)

Remember the words of Moses to his people: "Remember God's favor to you and blessings upon you as He created prophets among you and made you kings and bestowed upon you what He bestowed upon none on earth." (20)

Moses said: "Enter the Holy land which God has allotted to you and do not run away and become losers." (21)

They said: "Moses. It is the dwelling of ruthless people, we shall not enter it until they leave it, and if they do not, we are not going in." (22)

Two God-fearing men, who God has favored said: "Enter upon them through the main door, and if you do, you shall be victorious, and rely on God if you are believers. " (23)

They said to Moses: "We shall not enter it so long as they are in it. You and your God go and fight, we shall be sitting here." (24)

Moses said: "God, I have none but myself and my brother, separate us from the transgressors." (25)

God said: The land will be forbidden to them for forty years. They shall be lost and homeless on earth, do not be sorry for the transgressors. (26)

Tell them the true story of the two sons of Adam. They both made offerings to God. The offerings of one were accepted while those of the other were not. With his offerings rejected he (*Cain*) said to his brother: "I shall kill you." His brother said: "Offerings are accepted from the righteous. (27)

If you extended your hand to kill me, I shall not extend my hand to kill you since I fear God, Lord of the universe. (28)

I would rather see you kill me and acquire your sins and mine, and become one of the owners of hell; a fitting punishment for the transgressors." (29)

He (*Cain*) followed his whim, and killed his brother and became one of the losers. (30)

God sent a crow who started digging the earth to show him how to bury the bare corpse of his brother. "Alas," he said to himself, "am I not even as good as this crow to know that I need to bury the nakedness of my brother, thus becoming repentant?" (31)

That was the reason why We ordained to the People of Israel that he who kills a human being, except in punishment for murder, an evil contribution to corruption on earth, shall be considered as if he killed all of mankind, while he who saves a life shall be considered as if he saved the life of all mankind. Our apostles continued to bring them veritable guidance, yet many of them continue to spread excessive evil in the land. (32)

Those who raise arms against God and His apostle and strive to spread evil and corruption in the land shall be killed or crucified and as punishment their arms and legs can be amputated on opposite sides, or they may be banished from the land. They shall be put to shame in this world, and in the next, a great torture awaits them. (33)

Except for those who repent before they are brought under control by other means; and know that God is Forgiving and Merciful. (34)

People who believe, be mindful of God, seek his favor, and struggle in His behalf so that you may succeed. (35)

If the unbelievers owned all that is on earth, and tried to use it to ransom themselves from the torture of the Day of Judgement, it shall not be accepted from them, and awaiting them is an excruciating torture. (36)

They will want to get out of the fire, and from it they will have no exit and for them the torture is permanent. (37)

The thieves, male or female, deserve to have their hands amputated in punishment for their ill-begotten gains, a shame inflicted by God. God is Exalted and Wise. (38)

He who repents after transgressing and mends his ways, God will forgive him. God is Forgiving and Merciful. (39)

Did you not know that to God belongs the kingdom of heaven and the earth? He tortures whomever He wants and forgives whomever He wants and God is Capable of all things. (40)

Apostle, do not be bothered by those who are fast to disbelieve among those who believed by their words without believing through their hearts or by the Jews who listen to the fabrications of others while they change the place and sequence of words (*in the Scriptures*) away from its true meaning, intending it to mean the opposite. They say to each other: "If you are given what you want take it, and if not, beware. He who wants to subvert the word of God can expect none from Him." These are the ones that God refused to purify their hearts. They shall be put to shame in this world and in the next awaits them great torture. (41)

They listen to lies and profit from illegality. If they seek your judgement, judge for them, or avoid them. If you avoid them, they shall not bother you, and if you judge for them judge judiciously, God loves the judicious. (42)

How would they use your judgement when they have the Torah and in it is the judgement of God, from which they deviated later? These are not believers. (43)

We sent the Torah and in it guidance and light. With it the prophets who surrendered to God shall judge the Jews, the rabbis and the priests on the Book of God which was entrusted to them and they were made witnesses on it. Do not fear people but fear Me and do not exchange my verses for a cheap price, and those who do not judge based on what God has ordered are the unbelievers. (44)

In the Torah we decreed a life for a life, an eye for an eye, a nose for a nose, an ear for an ear, a tooth for a tooth, and a wound for an equal wound. If one charitably refrains from retaliation it shall earn rewards for him, and those who do not judge by what God decreed are the transgressors. (45)

We followed them by Jesus, the son of Mary, reaffirming the Torah and We gave him the Gospel and in it there is guidance and light, confirming the Torah that he already has, in addition to guidance and lecturing to the righteous. (46)

People of the Gospel have to make judgements based on what God has sent in it. Those whose judgement is not based on God's decree are transgressors. (47)

To you We sent the Book, confirming the books before it and standing watchfully over them. Make your judgement based on God's revelations to you and do not follow their fancies and deviate from the truth revealed to you. To each of you we enacted a law and made a curriculum. If such was the desire of God, he would have easily made you one nation. But He chose to test you with what He provided for you. Compete with each other in doing good, because to Him you shall all return, and then He shall tell you about your differences. (48)

Make judgements among them based on God's revelations and do not follow their whims. Be careful not to let them pressure you into deviating away from what God has revealed to you, and if they do not accept your judgement you have to realize that God may be wanting to catch them with some of their sins, and many people are sinners. (49)

Is it judgement by pagan laws that they are seeking? Who is a better judge than God for those who are faithful? (50)

People who believe do not take the Jews or Christian as sponsors. They should sponsor each other, and whoever chooses their sponsorship becomes one of them, and God shall not guide the transgressors. (51)

Those who have weakness in their hearts apply for their sponsorship, thinking that their fortunes may turn, but when God leads the faithful to victory and they supervene, those who made the secret choices shall end up in regret. (52)

And those who believed will ask them, what happened to those who swore in the name of God to be with you. Their plans have failed and they have become losers. (53)

People who believe, those of you who renounce their religion, God will replace them with others who love God and God loves them. They are humble with the believers and strong with the unbelievers; they struggle in the way of God without fear of blame. These are favors from God granted to whomever God wishes, and God is Vast and Knowledgeable. (54)

Your sponsors are God, the Apostle and the believers who hold their prayers and pay the alms-tax while kneeling to God in worship. (55)

Those who take God, the Apostle and the believers as their sponsors shall find themselves with God's victorious party. (56)

People who believe, do not take those of the people of the Book and the unbelievers who treated your religion with sarcasm and lack of seriousness as sponsors, and be mindful of God if you were believers. (57)

They have even taken your call to prayers sarcastically and not seriously because they are people who lack sense. (58)

People of the Book, do you hold it against us that we believed in God and in what He revealed to us, and in what He revealed before us, while most of you are transgressors? (59)

Shall I tell you of instances deserving of worse punishment from God? These are those that God has cursed, and got angry with and made them into monkeys and pigs and followers of the Devil, and those who worship idols. These are in an even worse position as they deviated further away from the straight path. (60)

Some come to you and say: "We believe," and they were unbelievers when they came in and when they left. God is more knowledgeable of what they are hiding. (61)

Many of them are fast to engage in transgression and aggression, and make use of ill-begotten gains; cursed are their efforts. (62)

Why did their rabbis and priests did not warn them against their transgressions and their use of ill-begotten gains? Cursed are the things they were doing. (63)

The Jews said that God's hands are tied (*God is stingy*). Their hands are the ones that are tied and they are cursed because of what they said. God's hands are open, He spends as He wishes. What was revealed to you by God will increase the arrogance and disbelief in many of them. We created animosity and hatred between them till the Day of Judgement. Every time they light up the torch of war God puts it out. They try to spread corruption in the land. God does not like those who spread corruption. (64)

If people of the Book believed, and became mindful of God, We would have forgiven their sins and entered them the blessed gardens. (65)

And if they had obeyed what was in the Torah and the Gospel and what God has revealed to them they would have received Our blessings from above and below. Among them are many good people but also many who are wrongdoers. (66)

Apostle, convey what was revealed to you from your God. If you do not, the message will fail. God will protect you from all people. God will not provide guidance to the unbelievers. (67)

People of the Book, you have nothing until you obey the Torah and the Gospel and what was revealed to you from your Lord. What God has revealed to you will increase the arrogance and the disbelief of many of them. Do not let the unbelievers bother you. (68)

The believers, the Jews, the Sabeaens, and the Christians who believed in God and the Last Day and did good works have nothing to fear and shall not be sad. (69)

We have made a covenant with the people of Israel and we sent them Apostles. Whenever an apostle brings them what their hearts do not desire some they deny and some they kill. (70)

They thought they were immune from harm, so they became deaf and blind. Nevertheless God even forgave them, but many of them again became deaf and blind. God sees what they do. (71)

Unbelieving are those who say God is Jesus, the son of Mary. Jesus said to the people of Israel: "Worship God, my Lord and your Lord. He who worships anyone with God shall be forbidden entry to paradise and his destiny is hell, and transgressors shall have no supporters." (72)

Unbelieving are those who say God is one of three. There is none but one God. And if they do not refrain, the unbelievers among them shall be touched by an excruciating torture. (73)

They had better repent and ask God for forgiveness. God is Forgiving and Merciful. (74)

Jesus, the son of Mary is but an Apostle like many apostles who were long gone before him. His mother was a believing woman and they both ate of the food provided on this earth. Look at how We revealed Our verses to them and look at how they still misbehave. (75)

Say: "How would you worship anyone but God? Would you worship someone who can do you neither good nor harm, while God is the one who listens and is Knowledgeable?" (76)

Say: "People of the Book, do not ignore the bounds of your religion and do not follow the whims of people who went astray and led many astray with them and they all missed the straight path." (77)

Cursed were those who disbelieved of the people of Israel, pronounced by David and Jesus, son of Mary, because of their disobedience and their transgression. (78)

They never refrained from evils they were doing. Evildoing were their deeds. (79)

Many of them sponsor the unbelievers and provide aid to them. Evil is what they do, and when God becomes resentful of them they shall become immortalized in torture. (80)

If they were believers in God and the Prophet and what was revealed to him, they would not have provided aid and sponsorship to the unbelievers, but many of them are transgressors. (81)

You shall find that the strongest in animosity to the believers are among the Jews and the unbelievers, while the nearest in affection to them are those who call themselves Christians, because among them are priests and monks who stay away from arrogance. (82)

When they hear what was revealed to the Apostle their eyes become flooded with tears as they recognize the truth in it. They say: "God, we are believers, include us with the witnesses. (83)

How could we not believe in God and what was revealed to us of the truth and then hope that our Lord include us with the righteous people?" (84)

God rewarded them on what they said with gardens under which rivers flow and in it they shall be immortalized. This is the reward for the righteous. (85)

And those who disbelieved and denied our verses; they shall be the owners of Hell. (86)

People who believe, do not forbid the good things that God has allowed you and do not transgress; God does not like the transgressors. (87)

Eat from what God has granted you of what is good and lawful, and be mindful of God in whom you believe. (88)

God will not hold against you the inadvertent oaths that you may take, but He will hold you to any oath you take seriously, and if you ever violate that, you shall repent and seek forgiveness by feeding ten hungry and poor men, the equivalent of the average you feed your family, or dress them the same way, or, alternatively, you can liberate a slave. If not possible and as a last resort you may fast three days in repentance for your violated oath if you made it. God shows you the way through His verses, so that you may be grateful. (89)

People who believe, wine, gambling, idols, and the choice arrows are abominations invented by the Devil; avoid them. (90)

The Devil wants to instigate animosity and hatred among you, by the use of wine and gambling. He also wants to divert you away from remembering God and your prayers. Will you desist? (91)

Obey God and obey the Apostle and be careful, and if you err know that the Apostle is obligated only to give clear warning. (92)

Those who believe and do good works shall have nothing to fear, and those who are righteous and do good works, and believe and those who are righteous, believe and are charitable shall have nothing to worry about in what they earn. God loves those who are charitable. (93)

In hunting God shall test you in what you may take by your hands or by your spears, to find who fears Him with no one watching Him. Those who transgress shall get excruciating torture. (94)

People who believe, do not kill game while on pilgrimage, and one who does kill game intentionally, such a person's repentance shall include the sacrifice of an equivalent domestic animal as food for the poor while visiting the Kaaba or feeding the equivalent to the hungry poor, and if not possible fasting shall be resorted to, to achieve some appreciation of the gravity of the violation. God shall forgive past deeds, but those who repeat the deed shall receive God's retaliation. God is the Exalted Retaliator. (95)

God has made lawful for you all that you may catch from the sea to eat and enjoy while traveling, but hunting on land is not allowed while you are on pilgrimage. Be mindful of God to whom you will eventually be assembled. (96)

God has specified the sacred House for the people to visit, He also declared the sacred Month and allowed the marking bracelets used on animals during that month, so that you may know that God knows all that is in heaven and on earth, and God is Knowledgeable of all things. (97)

You need to know that God can deliver severe punishment and He is also Forgiving and Merciful. (98)

The Apostle has only to warn you, and God knows what you declare and what you hide. (99)

Evil and good can never be equal, even when you are enticed by the availability of the evil. Those who have knowledge, be mindful of God so that you may succeed. (100)

People who believe, do not ask about things that will misguide you if revealed to you. Those who did that when the Koran was revealed have already been forgiven. God is Forgiving and Tolerant. (101)

People before you have asked about these things and then ended up denying them. (102)

God does not approve of those camels that the pagans dedicated to their Gods and their devils and left them with their milk unused (*bahiera*) or untied (*Saeiba*) unconnected (*wasiela*) and exempted from loading and carrying (*hamm*). Those who disbelieve attribute to God what God had nothing to do with, and most of them have no sense. (103)

When they are invited to what God has revealed to the Apostle, they say they have to adhere to the way of their fathers, even when their fathers knew nothing and were misguided. (104)

People who believe, your main responsibility is to yourselves. Those who remain misguided cannot hurt you after God has guided you. To God you shall return, and He shall inform you of how well you have done. (105)

People who believe, if you feel you are close to death, let your last will and testament be witnessed by two honest men of your acquaintances or two others if you are traveling. The two witnesses, after praying, shall swear by the name of God that they will not sell their testimony for any price. The witnesses can even be relatives. They will promise never to hide what they witnessed or otherwise they shall be transgressors. (106)

If it needs to be, even those who are beneficiaries can be witnesses. They shall take an oath to testify to the truth, and not deviate or they will be transgressors. (107)

They may be more reluctant to have their testimony under oath be contradicted by others. Be mindful of God and listen carefully, God shall not guide people who are wrongdoers. (108)

God will gather the Apostles one day and ask them: "How was your revelation received?" And they shall answer: "We have no knowledge; it is You who has knowledge of all that is hidden." (109)

God said: Jesus, son of Mary, remember how I favored you and favored your mother and supported you with the Holy Spirit. You talked to people while still in the crib and as a fully grown man. I taught you the Books and wisdom and the Torah and the Gospel and with My permission you were able to take the likeness of a bird and then by My leave you were able to breath life into it thus becoming a real bird. By My leave you healed the blind and the leper and were able to bring the dead back to life. I have held back the people of Israel away from you when they accused you of practicing sorcery as you presented to them what was revealed to you. (110)

I have also ordered the disciples to believe in me and my Apostle. They said: "We believe and be a witness to our surrender." (111)

The disciples said: "Jesus, son of Mary, can you ask your Lord to send down for us a table spread from heaven?" and Jesus said: "Be mindful of God if you are believers." (112)

They said: "We like to eat from it and remove any doubt in our hearts and enjoy the comfort of witnessing the truth you brought us." (113)

Jesus, son of Mary said: "Our Lord, send us a table spread of food from heaven, and it shall be a feast and celebration for those who came before us and will come after us. A solid proof from You and a declaration of Your favor; you are the best giver." (114)

God said: I shall send down what you ask, but whoever disbelieves after that I shall torture him like no one has been tortured of all people. (115)

And God said: Jesus, son of Mary, did you ask people to install you and your mother as gods, like God? and Jesus said: "How can I pretend to something I am not, and if I did You would have known it, since You know all that is in my soul, when I do not know what is in Yours. You are the One who has knowledge of what is hidden. (116)

I never said to them anything but what you ordered me, which is to worship God, my Lord and yours and I was a witness on them while I was with them. Since I died by Your leave, You are the watcher over them and You are the witness to everything. (117)

If You torture them, they are Your subjects and if You forgive them You are Exalted and Wise." (118)

God said: This shall be the day when the honest shall benefit from their honesty, because theirs shall be Gardens, under which rivers are flowing, immortalized in it for ever. God is satisfied with them and they are happy with Him, and there is the final reward. (119)

To God belong the heavens and the earth and what is on them. He is Capable of all things. (120)

CATTLE (6)

In the Name of God, Most Merciful, and Most Beneficent.

Be thankful to God who created the heavens and the earth, and made the darkness and the light, yet those who disbelieved their God try to install equivalents to Him. (1)

He who created you from mud then gave you a span of life that He pre-decided, yet you continue to doubt without justification. (2)

He is the God, in the heavens and on earth, He knows what you declare and what you hide, and knows what you do. (3)

Every one of God's verses that was revealed to them they deny. (4)

They denied the truth after it was revealed to them. They shall receive the news on what they were being sarcastic about. (5)

Did they not see how many generations We annihilated before you, even after they were more established than you are? We sent on them steady rains and we made rivers flow from under them and We annihilated them with what they sinned and then We replaced them by other generations. (6)

Even if we had sent you a Book already transcribed with a pen on paper, so they can touch it, those who disbelieve will say it is nothing but clear magic. (7)

They ask why an angel was not sent to him, but even if We had sent an angel, it would not have solved the problem, and they would still be questioning. (8)

We would have had to make the angel look like a man, and they would have been even more confused. (9)

Some have tried to make fun out of my apostles before and they ended up being afflicted with the curse of what they were making fun of. (10)

Say to them: "Go and travel on the earth and see how did those who disbelieved their apostles ended up." (11)

Ask to whom belongs what is in heavens and on earth. To God, who committed Himself to mercy and promised to gather you the day of resurrection without a doubt. Those who will lose themselves are those who do not believe. (12)

To him belongs those who take there rest during the day and those who take their rest at night. He hears all and has Knowledge of all. (13)

Say: "How can I take anyone but God as a sponsor?" The benefactor of the heavens and the earth, who feeds and is not fed; say: "I was ordered to be the first Moslem." Do not be among the unbelievers. (14)

Say: "If I disobeyed my Lord, I am afraid of the torture of a great day." (15)

He who is spared that day will have been granted mercy, and that is the real victory. (16)

If God inflicted harm on you, you shall find no relief from it, and if He blessed you with His favor, remember that He is Capable of all things. (17)

He is dominant over His subjects, He is the Wise and the Knowledgeable. (18)

Say: "Who is a bigger witness between me and you but God Himself? He revealed this Koran to me so that I can warn you." To whomever asks you to declare other Gods with God, say: "I will not. God is the one and only God and I have no responsibility for your disbelief." (19)

Those to whom we revealed the Book know it the way they know their children, and those who disbelieved have lost themselves. (20)

Transgressors are those who manufacture lies about God and deny His verses. The transgressors will not succeed. (21)

The day We gather them all, We shall ask the Idolaters: Where are your idols that you were worshiping? (22)

And as if they have done nothing they shall say: "We have never worshiped idols." (23)

Look at how they will lie even to themselves and they shall find that their idols cannot help them. (24)

Even if some of them appear to be listening to you, We have covered their hearts with veils so that they do not understand what they hear. Even if they see each verse they will not believe. They will argue with you and claim that this is nothing but the myth of the old and gone generations. (25)

They forbid it to themselves and to others. They shall destroy none but themselves, but they do not realize it. (26)

If you were to watch as they are brought to the fire, they will say we wish we can be back and have a chance to refrain from denying our Lord's verses and be able to join those who believed. (27)

They have seen the truth that they were hiding before, and if they were brought back they will not have straightened out. They are nothing but liars. (28)

Before, they said: "All we have is this life and there will be no resurrection." (29)

When they face their Lord He shall ask them: Is this not the truth of what you knew? and they will say: "Yes, our Lord." Their Lord will say: Go ahead and taste the torture deserved by your disbelief. (30)

Those who denied that they will meet God have lost. When the Day of Judgement catches up with them suddenly, and they say: "Alas, we have lost the opportunity." They will continue to carry their sins on their backs. Pure evil are their burdens. (31)

The life in this world is nothing but play and games. The next life is better for those who remain mindful of God. Do you not have sense? (32)

We know that what they say saddens you. They are not disbelieving you, but the transgressors are disbelieving God's verses. (33)

Apostles have been disbelieved before you. They endured the disbelief and the hurt until We granted them triumph. Nothing can change the words of God, you have already heard about many of those apostles. (34)

If their denial became hard for you to bear, then why do you not seek a tunnel under the earth or a ladder to heaven so you may bring them some thing they will believe? If God wishes He will unify them in guidance. Do not be ignorant. (35)

Only those who hear will respond. The dead God will resurrect and to hHim they shall return. (36)

They said: "Maybe if God sent him a sign, the situation may be different." Say: "God is capable of sending a sign, but most of them do not know." (37)

All the animals that roam the earth and all the birds that fly in the sky are formed in comunities like your own. We have left nothing out from the Book, and they shall all be assembled to God. (38)

Those who denied Our verses are deaf and mute in the dark. He who God wishes to be lost will be lost, and he who God wishes to guide will find the right path. (39)

If you were suddenly hit by a calamity from God or the Day of Judgement catches up with you, will you call anyone for help but God if you are truthful? (40)

It is Him you will call, and if He wishes He shall relieve you and then you will forget what you were associating with God. (41)

We sent apostles to nations before you, and We afflicted them with calamities and misfortunes so that they may humble themselves and ask for forgiveness. (42)

They would have humbled themselves when Our might hit them except for the fact that their hearts were hardened by the Devil who convinced them with the appropriateness of what they were doing. (43)

When they forgot what they were reminded with, We gave them all that their hearts desire until they were overwhelmed with joy, and then they were hit with Our might suddenly which left them in total despair. (44)

So God eliminated the influence of the transgressing people. Thanks to God, Lord of the universe. (45)

Say: "If God took away your sight and your hearing and sealed off your heart, would anyone other than God be able to give them back to you?" See how clear are the verses We reveal to you and yet they manage to turn away. (46)

Say: "Be watchful for the torture of God because it may come to you very suddenly or openly." God does not destroy but the people who are transgressors. (47)

We send the apostles only as carriers of good tidings and warnings. Those who believe and straighten themselves they have nothing to fear and they shall not be sad. (48)

Those who deny Our verses shall be touched by torture as a punishment for their evildoing. (49)

Say: "I do not tell you I am in possession of God's treasures, nor do I claim to see into the future, nor do I claim to be an angel. I follow what is being revealed to me." Say: "Is a blind man ever the equal of a seeing man; do you not think?" (50)

Give warning to those who are afraid of being assembled to their Lord, when they have no one to sponsor them or plead for them other than Him so that they remain mindful of Him. (51)

Do not send away those who pray to God morning and evening asking for His mercy. You do not answer for them and they do not answer for you. If you send them away, you will be a transgressor. (52)

We used some of them to test the others. They will say to each other: "Are those the ones that God has chosen among us. Is God not more knowledgeable about who are the ones that are more thankful?" (53)

When those who believe in our revelations come to you say: "Peace be upon you. Your Lord has committed Himself to mercy.

Whoever among you commits a sin out of ignorance and then repents and corrects his ways, shall find God Forgiving and Merciful." (54)

Our verses are thus intended to make clear the error of the ways of the transgressors. (55)

Say: "I have been forbidden to worship the Gods you advocate instead of God and if I follow your whims I will be lost and I will never be among the guided." (56)

Say: "I am perfectly clear about my Lord who you deny. I have no way of hastening the arrival at a settlement between you and me. The final judgement is for God; He is the best of judges." (57)

Say: "If I had the power to push for a prompt settlement, I would have. God has best knowledge of who are the transgressors. (58)

He has the only key to kowledge of the future. He has knowledge of all that the sea and land contain. No leaf falls down from a tree without His leave and no seed lies in the dark cracks of the earth, those that are damp and those that are dry, without His design. (59)

It is He who puts you to sleep at night knowing full well what you have done during the day, then lets you rise up in the morning to continue your specifically allotted span of life, then He will let you know of what you have done. (60)

He has power over His subjects. He sends angels that watch over you, and collect your souls when the exact time comes. (61)

Then you return to God, your real sponsor, and who has the final word, and with Him occurs the most swift of reckoning. (62)

Who rescues you from the peril of land and sea, you beseech Him secretly saying that if you were rescued you will be among the thankful?" (63)

Say: "God rescues you from all kinds of calamities and yet you continue to disbelieve." (64)

Say: "He is capable of sending you tortures that can come at you from above and from below. He can divide you into opposing factions and set the might of one party against the other." Observe how We designed the verses so that they may understand. (65)

Your people denied it, and it is the truth. Say: "I am not your keeper." (66)

The time will come when every thing you have been warned of will come true, and you shall see it. (67)

If you come upon those who are engaging in the distortion of Our verses, stay away from them until the engage in a different subject. Be mindful of the Devil who may induce you to forget the evildoing they are engaged in. Do not sit and participate with the transgressors. (68)

Those who are believers are not accountable for their sins, but We say that as a reminder for you to be mindful of God and guard yourself against evil. (69)

Avoid those who take their faith lightly, and are more concerned with what is in this life. Point out to them that their souls may be overwhelmed by their sins. They need to be reminded that without God they have no sponsor or interceder. If they try to ransom themselves, their ransom shall not be accepted. Their drink shall be boiling water, and excruciating torture awaits them because of their disbelief. (70)

Say: "How do we worship anyone but God? How do we worship those who are incapable of doing us good or bad? How do we go back after God has guided us, thus becoming like those who were seduced by the devils, wandering lost while their friends are trying to call them back to the right path. Say: "God's guidance is the right guidance, and to the Lord of the universe we shall surrender ourselves." (71)

Rise to your prayer, and be mindful of God. To Him you shall be assembled. (72)

He is the One who created the heavens and the earth, and whenever He says be it will become. What He says is the truth and to Him belongs the kingdom, the day the trumpet is sounded. He has knowledge of the obvious and the unseen and He is the Wise and the most Knowledgeable. (73)

Tell them about Abraham when he said to his father Azar: "You adopted idols as God's; I see you and your people to be greatly misguided." (74)

This is how We showed Abraham the kingdom of the heavens and the earth, and he became a believer. (75)

As the darkness of the night drew over Abraham he saw a star. He said: "Could that be my God?" And then when the star faded he said: "My God cannot fade." (76)

Then when he saw the moon shining he said: "That must be my God" and then when it faded, he said: "If my God did not guide me I shall be among the people who are lost." (77)

Then when he saw the sun rising he said: "That must be my God because it is bigger," then after sunset he said to his people: "I shall take no responsibility for your disbelief. (78)

I am turning my face towards the One who created the heavens and the earth. I shall live a righteous life and I shall not be among the unbelievers." (79)

When his people argued with him, Abraham said: "How do you argue with me after God has guided me? I am not afraid of what you believe in. Nothing can touch me unless God lets it. His power of knowledge includes everything, remember that. (80)

How can I be afraid of what you worship when you are not afraid of your disbelief in God and in what He revealed and with all His power over you? Which side has the better reason to feel safe, if you know anything?" (81)

Those who believe and then do not burden their belief with any transgression, they shall be safe and they are the guided. (82)

This was the strength of argument that we gave to Abraham over his people. Those We favor we shall elevate to whatever level We wish, your Lord is Knowledgeable and Wise. (83)

We gave Abraham Isaac and Jacob and we gave them guidance the way we guided Noah before them. Among his descendents were David, Solomon, Job and Joseph and Moses and Aaron; thus We reward the righteous. (84)

Zacharia, John, Jesus and Elias all were straight and God-fearing men. (85)

And Ishmael, Elisha, Jonah and Lot, each We favored over the rest of the world. (86)

Many of their fathers, descendents, brothers and sisters We elevated above others and guided them to the right path. (87)

This was the guidance of God extended to whomever He wishes. If they had disbelieved it would have been withdrawn from them, and they will have surely failed. (88)

These are the ones We gave the wisdom, the Books, and the prophethoods. If their people deny the faith We shall entrust with it others who do not deny it. (89)

Say: "Those are the men who God has guided, and we shall follow their lead." Say: "I do not ask you to compensate for that, but it is rather a reminder for all mankind." (90)

They have failed to see the might of God in its true light when they say: "God has not revealed to mankind anything." Say: "Who revealed the Book which Moses has brought you, containing light and guidance for the people?" You wrote it on different pages, you show some of it and you hide many, after you were taught many things that your fathers never knew. Say to them: "It is God who revealed all that" and then leave them and let them play their games. (91)

This is a blessed Book, and We revealed it confirming the Books that came before it so that the Mother of Cities and its surroundings are warned, and so will the warning reach those who believe in it and in the Last Day and those who are persevering in their prayers. (92)

Transgressors are those who lie about God, when they claim that things were revealed to them and it was not, or those who say: "I will reveal similar to what God has revealed." Just imagine the transgressors as they are overtaken by death how the angels will be demanding with outstretched hands to receive their souls. Now taste the humiliation of torture in punishment for what you said about God untruthfully, while you were too arrogant to accept His verses. (93)

You shall come to us individually like we created you the first time. You will come to us, leaving behind all that we bestowed upon you and all that you thought will intercede for you, such as your gods and idols. You will be cut off from all and you shall not find any of what you used to believe in and claim. (94)

God who splits the seeds and reveal their nuclei, and generates life from death and death from life. This is God; how can you deny Him? (95)

He is the one who turns on the light of the sunrise and the one who made the night for rest and the light of the sun and the moon come in exact timing. (96)

He gave you the stars to use in finding direction in the dark of the sea and land. We detailed the verses for those who can understand. (97)

It is God who created you from one human being, and ordained for you a dwelling and a resting site. We detailed the verses to those who can comprehend. (98)

He brings down water from the sky and causes plants and everything green to grow with it. Then from it, seed and grain are accumulated. From the pollen of the palm trees clusters of dates are formed. Gardens of grapes olives and all kinds of pomegranates are formed. Look at all of these fruits and how they ripen and you shall find signs for those who believe. (99)

They made members of the jinn-kind and their descendents His equals and they gave Him sons, and daughters, without His knowledge, the almighty, Who is above and far from their fabrications. (100)

The designer of the heavens and the earth; how could He have a child when He never had a mate? He created everything, and has knowledge of all things. (101)

This is God, your Lord. There is no God but Him. He created every thing. Worship Him, for He has control over all things. (102)

No eyesight can see Him, but He controls all sights. He is the Merciful and His expertise extends to all things. (103)

Your Lord provided you with signs you can see. He who sees, the benefit will come to him, and he who is blind will suffer the consequences. I am not your keeper. (104)

We composed the verses in such a way so that it becomes clear to the knowledgeable that you studied with someone else (*and that it is not originating from you*). (105)

Follow what was revealed to you by your Lord who you have no other god but Him, and pay no attention to the unbelievers. (106)

If God wished they would not have disbelieved, and We would not have made you a witness over them. You are not their keeper. (107)

Do not abuse their gods to which they pray, excluding God. If you do you will be inviting them to abuse God in retaliation without intending to. To every nation We describe what needs to be done. To God they shall all return, and He shall inform them of what they were doing. (108)

They (*Moslems*) swore strongly, in the name of God, that if signs were given to the unbelievers they shall believe in it. Say: "God is capable of giving them many signs. But when are you going to realize that even if true signs were given to them they shall not believe?" (109)

We shall confuse their hearts and their vision for not believing the first time, not to mention letting them blunder further in their transgression. (110)

If We brought the angels down to them caused the dead to speak to them and brought back all who lived before them, they shall not believe unless it was God's wish for them to do so, but most of them are ignorant of the truth. (111)

We made an enemy for every prophet. The devils of both humans and jinn collaborate and inspire each other with pleasing words that feed each other's arrogance. If it was the will of God that they do not do that, they would have not. Shun them and their lies. (112)

Such is intended so that it will be picked up by the unbelievers to encourage further the deception that is already in their hearts and lead them to commit what they are committing in misdeeds. (113)

Say: "How can I seek judgement from anyone but God when He was the One who sent us the the Book with its details?" Those who received the Book know that it is revealed by God and that it contains the truth. Do not join those who are sinful in doubt. (114)

The words of your Lord were fulfilled in truth and justice. There is no change to His words. He hears all and has knowledge of all. (115)

If you follow most people on earth, they shall make you deviate from the true path of God. They follow only their suspicions, and do nothing but lie. (116)

Your Lord knows better who are the misguided and who are the guided. (117)

Eat of what the name of God has been mentioned on if you truly believe in God's verses. (118)

Why should you not eat of what had the name of God mentioned over it, when He has fully explained to you what has been forbidden for you to eat, unless you have been constrained. Many make mistakes guided by their whims and out of ignorance. Your Lord knows who are the transgressors. (119)

Refrain from sin openly and secretly. Those who commit sin shall be punished for what they committed. (120)

Do not eat of what has not had the name of God mentioned over it. It is impious to do so. The devils inspire the people they sponsor to argue with you. If you obey them you will disbelieve. (121)

Is there anything in common between two men, one who was dead and we brought him to life and provided him with a light which he uses to walk among people, and another who is in the dark and shall never leave it? This is how the sinful acts of the unbelievers seem reasonable to them. (122)

This is how in each town we installed its most prominent criminals to plot. They plot against none but themselves, but they do not know it. (123)

If they were given a verse from God they will say: "We shall not believe until we receive all that the messengers of God received." God knows more about who to entrust with His message. Those criminals shall be humiliated, and they shall be afflicted with great torture for their transgressions. (124)

Whomever God chooses to guide He shall introduce comfort in his chest that accompanies his belief in Islam, while those He wishes to misguide the faith shall cause tightness in their chest, similar to the tightness pruduced by ascending high in the sky. That is the abomination that shall afflict the unbelievers. (125)

This is the straight path of your Lord which He detailed in His verses to people who are mindful of Him. (126)

They are granted the House of Peace with their Lord. He is their sponsor in all that they did. (127)

When they are all assembled in front of God He will say: You members of the jinn-kind you have enticed too many of the humankind. The humans they sponsored shall say "Our Lord, we have actually enjoyed the company of each other, until the end of the term you have pre-assigned for us." He will say: The Hell-fire is your home, and in it you shall be immortalized as long it is the wish of God. Your Lord is Wise and Knowledgeable. (128)

This is how We make some transgressors the sponsors for other transgressors as punishment for their deeds. (129)

O' Jinn-kind and mankind, did you not have apostles among you telling My verses to you, and warn you about meeting this day? They said they shall be witnesses on themselves, and later they were seduced by the life on earth, and witnesses on themselves they shall become, as they were unbelievers. (130)

Your Lord will not destroy villages unjustly while the people are oblivious to what is happening. (131)

Each of them is ranked based on His deeds. Your Lord is never unaware of what they do. (132)

Your Lord, whose resources are plentiful and His attitude is merciful, if He wished He can replace you with others, the same way you were created as a descendent of others. (133)

What you were promised shall come, and you will not be able to change it. (134)

Say: My people, do what you can to secure your place and I shall certainly do my share. You shall find out who will be the winner of the ultimate reward. The transgressors shall not succeed. (135)

They assigned a share of what they grew in cultivation and cattle to God. They claimed a part was for God and another part for their gods. Whatever the share of their gods was it never made its way to God, but God's share always made it to their gods. Their judgement was evil. (136)

The Idols they worship have caused many pagans to kill their own children (*as sacrifices*). This has caused them confusion and uncertainty in their own faith. If God willed, they would not have been able to do that. Stay away from them and from what they do. (137)

They say: "These cattle and these crops are forbidden to anyone to eat from except by our permission;" as they claim. They define animals that cannot be used for riding. And some cattle they proclaimed unfit for the mention of the name of God. They lied in His name and He shall punish them for their lies. (138)

They claimed that the offspring of some cattle are allowed for consumption by their males but not by their females, but if they were stillborn they were allowed for both. He shall punish them for their fabrications, He is Wise and Knowledgeable. (139)

Losers are those who killed their own children out of foolishness and ignorance and forbade what God has allowed falsifying God's wishes. They were misguided and they shall never find the way. (140)

He is the one who created gardens of shrubs and upright trees, such as palm trees and other plants that produce food including olives and pomegranates. Some of those plants are similar and some are not. Eat the fruits when it ripens, and handle it conservatively on the day of harvest. Do not waste it. He does not like those who are wasteful. (141)

Some of the cattle are for carrying and some of their derivatives are used for your bed and cover. Eat of what God has bestowed upon you, and do not follow the steps of the Devil; he is your unquestionable enemy. (142)

Of eight pairs of cattle, one pair of sheep and one pair of goats, what is forbidden? The two males or the two females, or is it the fetuses in the wombs of the two females? Tell me of your knowledge if you are truthful. (143).

A pair of camels and a pair of cows. Tell me, is it the two females or the two males that are forbidden or is it the fetuses in the wombs of both females? Were you present when God instructed you on such things? No one is a bigger transgressor than the one who lies about

God to mislead those who are uninformed. God will never guide the transgressors. (144)

Say: "I do not find in what was revealed to me any sanctions against eating except when it is the flesh of a carcass, spilled blood, or the meat of the pig, for it is abominable." It is also impious to partake in the meat of what is consecrated under a name other than God unless you are constrained to do so without intending a violation or a transgression. Your Lord is Forgiving and Merciful. (145)

We forbade to the Jews all animals with single non-split hoofs. We also forbade to them the fat of cattle and sheep, except for that located on their backs. They were also forbidden their intestines and any parts of them that get mixed with their bones. This was punishment for their misdeeds. We always do what We promise. (146)

If they denied you, say: "Your Lord has a vast capacity for mercy, but the criminals shall never be spared His might." (147)

Those who associate idols with God say: "We would not have made associates for Him if He did not wish that. Our fathers would not have done that either." Their ancestors made the same argument until they tasted the impact of Our might. Say: "If you have any actual knowledge other than mere suspicions, bring it out for all to see. You are doing nothing but lying." (148)

Say: "Only God can bring arguments that cannot be defeated. If He wished He would have guided all of you." (149)

Say: "Bring your witnesses who are able to testify that God forbade this or that." Do not participate with them, nor should you follow the whims of those who denied Our verses, and do not believe in the Last Day, and adopt equals to their Lord. (150)

Say: "Come to me and listen to the recital of what your Lord has forbidden. Do not associate others with Him, and honor your parents. Do not kill your offspring out of fear of poverty; We shall provide for you and them. Refrain from indecency in public and in secret, and do not ever take a life, which God has forbidden, unless it is done following full adjudication. These are His admonishments to you so that you may learn." (151)

Do not go near the assets of orphans, unless you want to add to them, until they reach maturity. Observe strict honesty in weights and measurements in your dealings. We never require anyone to perform above his ability. If you spoke, be fair even if it is against a relative. Make good your promises in front of God. These are His admonishments to you, so that you may remember. (152)

This is my straight path, follow it, in preference to all others. These others shall separate you from His path. These are His admonishments to you so that you may remain righteous. (153)

We revealed the Book to Moses, completed in the best way, with details for everything with guidance and mercy, so that they may believe in their eventual meeting with their Lord. (154)

This is a Book We revealed with Our blessing. Follow it, and be righteous, so you may receive mercy. (155)

So that you do not say: "The Scriptures have been revealed to two people before, and we have no knowledge of what they received." (156)

Nor will you be able to say: "If what was revealed to them was revealed to us instead, we would have been better guided than they were." You have received veritable sign from your Lord, guidance and mercy. Those transgressors who deny God's verses and turn away from them. Those who dare to turn away from our verses shall be afflicted with torture in punishment for turning away. (157)

Are they looking for the angels to come to them from your Lord or certain signs from Him? By then believing will not benefit those who did not believe before, nor did they earn prior credit in righteousness. Say to them: "Go ahead and wait, He shall be waiting for you." (158)

Those who break their religion into different sects and followings, you have nothing to do with them. They will end up with God and He shall deal with them. (159)

He who does good shall be rewarded ten times for his good deeds, and he who does evil shall be punished equal to it. None will be unfairly judged. (160)

Say: "My Lord Has guided me to the straight path. A most valuable religion, following in the path of Abraham, who was truly faithful, and never associated others with God." (161)

Say: "My prayers and my worship, my life and my death are for God, Lord of the Universe. (162)

He never had an associate, He ordered me to do so, and I am the first Moslem (*who surrendered to His wish*)." (163)

Say: "Would I seek some one other than God as my Lord?" He is the Lord of all things." A soul shall earn good only for its own benefit. No soul shall answer for the guilt of another. Then to your Lord you shall return, and He shall provide the final settlements for your disputes. (164)

He is the one who permitted you to inherit the earth. He permitted some of you to preside over others in order to test your behavior in what He has given you. Your Lord provides swift punishment while He is Forgiving and Merciful. (165)

THE HEIGHTS (7)

In the Name of God, Most Merciful, and Most Beneficent.

Alef Lam Meem Sad. (1)

This Book was revealed to you. Let there be no trepidation in your heart about admonishing others as to what came in it, and reminding those who believe of its contents. (2)

Follow what was revealed to you by your Lord, and do not assume sponsors besides Him; but you seldom heed the warnings. (3)

How many a village did we annihilate while its people were asleep during the night or drowsy during the day? (4)

Only when they felt Our wrath did they say: "We have been wicked people." (5)

We shall question those to whom the messages were sent, and We shall question the messengers. (6)

We shall tell them of what they have done, and they will find We have not been absent. (7)

The weighing of good deeds on that Day is the true weighing; and those who carry the heaviest loads are the successful. (8)

Those who carry the light loads have gotten themselves lost, as they denied Our verses. (9)

We have established you on earth and created a living for you on it. Seldom do you give thanks. (10)

We created you and gave you your human form, then We said to the angels: "Kneel for Adam." They all knelt, except for the Devil, who was not among those who knelt. (11)

God said: What prevented you from kneeling? He said: "I am better than him. You created me from fire, while you created him from mud." (12)

He (God) said: You are hereby banned from Paradise. There is no place in it for your despicable pride. (13)

The Devil said: "Give me a reprieve until the Day of Judgement." (14)

God said: You are reprieved. (15)

"Just like you caused me to sin, I shall be waiting for those who are following your straight path. (16)

I shall come at them from the front and from the back, and from the right and from the left, and you shall find that most of them are ungrateful." (17)

Leave, said God, a detestable outcast. I shall fill hell with you and those who follow you. (18)

And you, Adam, dwell in paradise, you and your wife, and eat from wherever you wish except for this tree. Stay away from it or you shall be a transgressor. (19)

The Devil got to them and pointed out their nakedness, of which they were not aware. He also told them: "Your Lord forbade you the tree so that you do not become an angel and thus immortal." (20)

He promised them he will give them good advice. (21)

When they tasted the fruit from the tree, they suddenly perceived their own nakedness and started trying to cover themselves with leaves from Paradise. Their Lord called upon them: Did I not forbid you to eat from that tree, and did I not tell you that the Devil is your most obvious enemy? (22)

They said: "Our Lord, we betrayed our own soul. If You do not forgive us and have mercy on us, we shall be losers." (23)

He (*God*) said: You and the Devil both shall descend to earth, and you shall be each other's enemies. On earth you shall have residence and enjoyment for a while. (24)

He (*God*) said: Earth is where you shall live and die and from where you shall come back out. (25)

Children of Adam, We gave you clothes to cover your nakedness, along with feathers for decoration; but the dress of piety is best for you. These are from God's verses, so they may remember. (26)

Children of Adam, do not let the Devil seduce you like he did your parents before you. He took away their covers and made them see their own nakedness. The Devil and his tribe can see you from where you cannot see them. We made the devils sponsors for the unbelievers. (27)

If they commit an indecency, they say: "That is what we found our fathers doing. God has ordered us to do that." Say: "God does not order indecency. Do you say of God things you do not know?" (28)

Say: "My Lord has ordered justice. Turn to Him when you pray in any mosque and beseech Him while you are faithful to Him in your belief. The way you started is the way you will return." (29)

Some He has led to the right path and some He has justly let go astray since they took the devils as their sponsors while they pretend to be on the right path. (30)

Children of Adam, wear your best to the mosque, and eat and drink without excess. He does not like those who spend to excess. (31)

Say: "Who forbade you to dress well and eat well from God's bounty which he granted to those who believe in this life and it is theirs exclusively in the next life?" This is how we detail our verses to those who understand. (32)

God forbade indecency, whether overt or covert. He also forbade oppression and injustice, and indulging in what He has not authorized, and for anyone to say of Him what he does not know. (33)

For the life of every nation, there is a fixed length of time. When their final day comes, they cannot delay it or advance it one hour. (34)

Children of Adam, as apostles come among you, telling my verses to you; whoever among you heeds the message and mends his ways, he shall have nothing to fear and shall have no reason to be sad. (35)

Those who denied Our verses and acted arrogantly, shall be the owners of hell, and in it they shall be immortalized. (36)

Who is more misguided than one who lies about God and denies His verses? These individuals will get what is promised to them in this Book. Then when they die, and our angels come to pick up their souls, they are asked: "What of the claims they made in their denial of God?" They will admit they went astray and that they were unbelievers. (37)

God will say: Enter into hell full of nations of men and jinn who came before you. Every nation entering will curse the nation who preceded it in entry. The last arriving will point to those preceding saying: "Our Lord these are the ones who led us astray; let them have twice the torture." You will all have twice the torture but you do not know it. (38)

The earlier entries will say to the last: "You are no better than us; do have the torture you really deserve." (39)

Those who denied our verses and arrogantly scorned our revelations, the doors to heaven shall remain closed for them and they shall not enter paradise until the camel passes through the eye of a needle, and this is how we punish the criminals. (40)

Their beds are in hell and layers of fire are their cover. This is how we reward the transgressors. (41)

As to those who believed and did good work, God never requires a soul to do that which it is not capable of doing. They are the owners of heaven and in it they shall be immortalized. (42)

We have removed all vindictiveness from their hearts. Rivers shall be flowing right below their feet and they said: "Thanks to God who guided us. We would have never been guided if it was not for His guidance. Our Lord's apostles brought us none but the truth." They were told: "Here is Paradise; you have inherited it because of what you have done." (43)

Owners of heaven called the owners of hell. They said: "We have found that what our Lord promised us was the truth. Did you find what your Lord promised you to be the truth?" They said: "Yes." An announcer among them declared: "The curse of God shall befall the transgressors." (44)

They are the ones who try to hinder access to the path of God, attempting to misguide, and they disbelieve in the Last Day. (45)

Between them stands a screen, and up on the heights are men who distinguish the residents of heaven from those of hell by their features. They will welcome and salute the owners of heaven. They have not entered heaven but they desire it. (46)

When their gaze meets the owners of Hell, they say: "Our Lord, do not include us with the transgressors." (47)

The men on the heights will call men they recognize by their features and ask: "How did you benefit from your alliance with each other and your collective arrogance?" (48)

Those you swore will not be touched by God's mercy, they were told: "Enter Paradise, you shall have nothing to fear and you shall not be sad." (49)

Owners of Hell shall call the owners of Heaven: "Will you divert to us some of your excess water and some of what God has bestowed upon you?" They will answer: "God has denied that to the unbelievers." (50)

Those who took their religion as a subject of jest and play and were seduced by the life on earth; today We shall forget them like they forgot meeting this day, while they were denying Our verses. (51)

We brought them a Book and directed its details towards knowledge and guidance and mercy to those who believe. (52)

Do they contemplate its interpretation? The day when the final interpretation comes, those who forgot it before shall say: "Our Lord's apostles brought us the truth. Are we going to have someone who will intercede for us and get us forgiveness, or will we be returned with an opportunity to do different from our deeds before?" They have lost themselves, and they are trapped by their own lies. (53)

Your Lord is God, who created the heavens and the earth in six days. Then He settled on the throne. After He brings the darkness of the night, He has it followed closely by the light of the day. The sun, the moon and the stars are under His complete control. To Him belongs creation and control. Blessed be God, Lord of the universe. (54)

Beseech God humbly and privately. God does not like those who are aggressively boastful. (55)

Do not go back and spread corruption after reform and ask for God's aid out of fear of His wrath and desire for His bounty. God's mercy is always close to the righteous. (56)

He is the One who sends the winds to bring good tidings of His mercy, to be followed by heavy clouds loaded with rain driven towards a dead town with water brought down producing crops. This is how We resurrect the dead so that you may remember. (57)

In the land of good crops these are produced by His permission. From wicked lands only little and the useless is produced. We bring the informative verses to those who are thankful. (58)

We sent Noah to his people, and he said: "My people worship God, you have no God other than Him. I am afraid for you from the torture of a colossal day." (59)

The leaders of his people said: "We see that you are nothing but totally misguided." (60)

He said: "My people, I am anything but misguided. I am an apostle sent by the Lord of the universe. (61)

I am relaying the message of my Lord to you. I am advising you and I know of God that which you do not know." (62)

Do you not find it unusual that a reminder from your God is coming to you through a man among you, so that you may shield yourselves from evil and then God may be merciful with you? (63)

They still denied him and We saved him and those with him in the ark and We drowned those who denied Our verses; they were people blind to the truth. (64)

To the people of Aad, We sent to them Houd from among them. He said to his people: worship God, you have no other God but Him, will you not shield yourself with righteousness. (65)

The unbelieving leaders of his people said: "We see that you are suffering from a case of impertinence and we suspect you of being a liar." (66)

He said: "My people, I am not impertinent but rather an apostle sent by the Lord of the universe. (67)

I am delivering to you a message from my Lord and I am giving you a faithful advice. (68)

Do you find it unusual that a reminder comes to you through a man among you, as a warning to remember that you were made the heirs of the people of Noah and were granted more powers than other men? Keep the favors of God alive in your minds so you may succeed. (69)

Are you coming to us so that we may worship God alone and forget the gods worshiped by our fathers, and threaten us with the wrath of God? Bring down His wrath if you are truly truthful." (70)

He said: "You have already earned God's wrath and punishment. You argue with me about gods that you and your fathers named yourselves and which God has never sanctioned. You wait and I will be waiting with you." (71)

We saved him and those who stood with him as an act of mercy from Us and We removed all traces of those who denied our verses and were never believers. (72)

To Thamoud we sent to them from among them Saleh. He said: "My people worship God; you have no God but Him. Your Lord has sent you a sign: this female camel is God's camel; leave her to feed on her own in God's land and never touch her or you shall be touched by God's excruciating torture. (73)

Remember that God let you be the heirs to Aad and let you preside over the earthbuilding palaces on its meadows and carving homes inside the rocks of its mountains. Keep in mind God's bounty to you and do not spread corruption in the land. (74)

The leaders of his people who were arrogant started asking those who believed and followed him: "Are you certain that Saleh is sent by his Lord?" And they responded: "In what he was sent with, we are believers." (75)

The arrogant people said to them: "And we are disbelieving what you believe." (76)

They killed the camel and defied their Lord's orders and said to Saleh: "Bring on us the punishment you promised if you are the messenger." (77)

They were taken by the shaking (*earthquake*) which left them on their faces motionless, the following morning. (78)

He left them, saying: "My people, I have conveyed the massage to you from my Lord and gave you good advice. But you have no love for people who advise you." (79)

And Lot said to his people: "How do you permit yourselves to commit indecent acts committed by none in the world before you?" (80)

You lust after men in preference to women. You are truly perverted. (81)

The answer of his people was: "Get them out of our village. They are trying to purify themselves." (82)

We saved him and his people, except for his wife who remained adherent to her people's ways. (83)

They were hit with a rain. You should have seen what was the final destiny of criminals. (84)

To Midian We sent to them Shoaib from among them. He said: "My people, worship God, you have no other God than Him. Your

Lord has sent you a veritable sign: Be very conscientious in all measures and weights. Do not cheat people out of their properties, nor are you to spread corruption in the land, after it was reformed. This is better for you if you were believers. (85)

Do not sit at every street corner threatening people to strip them of their possessions or to deflect them away from the path of God after they believed with the intention of misguiding them. Remember when you were few and God made you many, and contemplate the destiny of those who did spread corruption in the past. (86)

If some of you have become believers in what was sent to me and others did not, be patient until it is time for God to be the final arbiter between us. He is the best of all arbitrators." (87)

The leaders of his people who became arrogant said to him: "We shall send you and the people who believed with you out of our village, unless you go back to believing in our religion." He said: "Would you force us to do that? (88)

If we go back to your religion after God rescued us we will be lying to God. We shall not change unless it is God's wish. God has knowledge that includes everything. On our Lord we shall rely. Lord, help us remove the obstacles between us and our people in justice. You are the best of all peacemakers." (89)

The unbelieving leaders of his people said: "If you follow Shoaib you shall be the losers." (90)

They were taken by the shaking (*earthquake*) which left them motionless on the floor of their homes in the morning. (91)

Those who denied Shoaib might have as well not even lived there. Those that denied him were the losers. (92)

He left and said: "My people, I have conveyed to you the message of my Lord, and gave advice to you. How can I grieve for the unbelievers?" (93)

We never sent a prophet to a village until we tested its people with adversity and prosperity so that they may become more humble. (94)

Then when we change their fortunes to prosperity and they increased in number and fortune, they say this is nothing but a natural cycle of the good and bad in life which happened the same way to our forefathers. Then we take them suddenly when they are unaware. (95)

If the people of those villages believed and stayed away from sin We would have opened for them the doors of our blessings and bounty on the earth and in heaven, but they lie and we take them with what they commit. (96)

Did the people of those villages feel they can be secure from Our revenge which finally over-took them in their homes as they slept. (97)

Did the people of those villages feel they can be secure from Our might which hit them in the morning as they play? (98)

They believed they can be out of God's reach and vengefulness. Only the losers acquire such sense of security. (99)

Is it not obvious to the generation that inherits the earth after the previous occupants are gone that if We choose to We can inflict upon them the punishment for their sins, seal their hearts closed and leave them totally unable to comprehend? (100)

We tell you the stories of these villages whose prophets brought them veritable signs, and still they would not believe, encumbered by their previous denials, and this is how God seals the hearts of the unbelievers. (101)

We found most of them to be unfaithful to their own covenants, and the majority of them are doers of evil. (102)

After these prophets we sent Moses with Our signs to the Pharaoh and his people. They paid no heed to it, and look how the corrupted ended up. (103)

Moses said: "O' Pharaoh, I am an Apostle from the Lord of the universe. (104)

I am obligated to say nothing about God but the truth. I brought veritable signs from the Lord, let the people of Israel go with me." (105)

The Pharaoh said: "If you brought a sign show it to us if you are truthful." (106)

Moses threw his staff and it became an obvious snake. (107)

Then Moses drew his hand out from under his robe and it came out solid white for all to see. (108)

The elders of Pharaoh's people said: "This is obviously a great magic. (109)

He is obviously seeking to take over your kingdom; what do you want us to do?" (110)

They said: "Just hold him and his brother until we send out messengers to different cities. (111)

They shall bring you the best magicians there are." (112)

The magicians said to the Pharaoh: "We hope to be richly rewarded if we are victorious." (113)

He said: "Yes, and you shall also have position and influence." (114)

They said to Moses: "Are you going to start or shall we?" (115)

They threw a show of magic that drew admiration and respect from the audience. (116)

We told Moses to throw down his staff, which canceled all the deceiving magic they came up with. (117)

The truth was revealed and their conniving failed. (118)

They were defeated and shown to be small. (119)

The magicians fell, prostrated, (120)

and said: "We believe in Lord of the universe, (121)

Lord of Moses and Aaron." (122)

The Pharaoh said: "You dared declare your belief in Him without my permission. This appears to be a conspiracy to get my people out of their city, and you shall find out. (123)

I shall have an arm and a leg amputated on alternate sides of each of you. And then I shall have you all crucified." (124)

They said: "We have to go back to our Lord anyway. (125)

You are only retaliating because we believed in the veritable signs that came to us from our Lord. But He gave us patience and He shall make sure that we die in a state of complete surrender to Him." (126)

The elders of Pharaoh's people said to him: "Are you going to let Moses and his people free to spread corruption in the land and abandon you and your gods?" The Pharaoh said: "We shall kill their sons and spare their daughters and we shall subjugate them." (127)

Moses said to his people: "Depend on God and be patient. The land belongs to God and He shall have it inherited by whomever He wishes among His subjects, and the final reward is for those who shield themselves from evil." (128)

The people of Moses said to him: "We have been hurt before you came to us and after." Moses said: "Why do you not hope that God shall annihilate your enemy and choose you as the heirs for the earth after He looks at your deeds?" (129)

We afflicted people of the Pharaoh with famine, shortages and drought so that they may be reminded. (130)

But the good they ascribed to themselves, and the shortages they blamed on Moses and his people. The responsibility for their misfortunes was with God, but little did they know. (131)

They said: "Whatever you send our way that is intended to put us under a spell of magic shall not make us believe in you." (132)

We sent on them the flood, locusts, lice, the frogs and the blood; detailed and veritable signs, yet they were arrogant and people afflicted with criminality. (133)

And finally when they had the plague they said: "O' Moses, pray to God for us, using your credit with Him to deliver us from the plague, and we shall believe in you, and let the people of Israel leave with you." (134)

As soon as We lifted the plague they went back on their promise. (135)

We retaliated against them and drowned them in the sea as they denied Our signs and ignored them. (136)

We let the people they took advantage of to become the heirs on earth, in the east and the west which we have blessed, and thus

God's gracious promise to the people of Israel was fulfilled as a reward for their patience. We destroyed all of the achievement of Pharaoh and his people including the throne. (137)

And as We got the people of Israel across the sea, they came upon people worshiping their idols. They said: "Moses, get us gods like their gods." He said: "You are ignorant people. (138)

What those idolaters follow is doomed and all of their works lead to nothing. (139)

Do you expect me to participate in getting you a god other than God, when He favored you over all the rest of men? (140)

He saved you from the people of the Pharaoh, persecuting and torturing you while killing your sons and sparing your women. Surely that was a severe enough trial from your Lord." (141)

We promised Moses that we will talk to him in thirty nights and then we added ten. And as his appointment with his Lord was confirmed in forty nights, Moses said to his brother Aaron: "Be in my place with my people and keep the peace among them and do not be misled by the corrupted." (142)

When Moses appeared for Our date and his Lord talked to him he said: "Lord, let me see you." He said: You will not see Me, but look towards the mountain, and if it stays in place, then you may see Me. Then when God revealed Himself to the mountain, the mountain was pulverized into fine dust, and Moses fell unconscious. When he woke up he said: "Glory is to you. To you I repent and I am the first of all believers." (143)

God said: Moses, I chose you in preference to all others to deliver my message and my words. Take what I gave you and be among the grateful. (144)

We wrote for him on the tablets detailed advice for everything. Take it strongly, and order your people to emulate the best of it. I will show you the home where evildoers end. (145)

I shall keep away my signs from those who are arrogant on earth without justification. Every sign they see they deny. And if they are shown the path to wisdom they shun it, and when they find the path to sin they follow it. This is a natural outcome of denying Our verses and remaining ignorant of it. (146)

Those who denied Our verses and the Last Day, their work shall fail and their reward shall be quite fitting for their actions. (147)

In Moses' absence, his people adopted a golden calf they made from their own jewelry. It was hollow and echoed noise back. They never saw that it cannot talk to them nor could it guide them. They adopted the calf and became transgressors. (148)

But as they realized what they had done and so that they have sinned they said: "If our Lord did not have mercy upon us and forgive us we shall be losers." (149)

Then Moses returned to his people, angry and regretful, and he said: "You should be absolutely ashamed of what you did in my absence. Are you trying to bring God's vengeance on you even earlier?" He threw the tablets and took his brother's head in his hand, pulling him towards him, and said: "Son of my mother, these people are taking advantage of me and they are about to kill me. Please do not let my enemies gloat over my misfortune, and save me from finding myself among the transgressors." (150)

He said: "God forgive me and my brother, and let us enter under the wing of your mercy. You are the most Merciful." (151)

Those who adopted the calf shall face the fury of the Lord, and they shall be disgraced in this life. This is the penalty for blasphemy. (152)

Those who commit sin but repent and believe in God after that, they shall find God Forgiving and Merciful. (153)

When Moses' anger subsided, he took back the tablet which had inscribed on it a promise of guidance and mercy for those who have fear of their Lord. (154)

Moses then chose seventy men of his people for their appointment with God. And when the shaking (earthquake) overtook them He said: "Lord, if you wanted to destroy them, you would have done that a long time ago, but will you destroy us for what a few impertinent people among us did? I am certain it is a test designed by You to mislead whomever you wished and guide whomever you wished. You are our sponsor. Forgive us, and have mercy upon us. You are the best of forgivers. (155)

Send to us what is good in this life and the one coming next. We shall all return to you." God said: With my torture I shall afflict whomever I wish. My mercy can include anything. It shall be had by those who protect themselves from evil, pay the alms and those who believe our verses. (156)

Those who will follow the Apostle (*the gentile prophet*), who they will find described in the Torah and the Gospel; He shall order them to do the good and refrain from what is evil. He shall allow them what is good and disallow what is harmful. He will relieve their burdens and take away the chains that shackle them. Those who will believe in Him, support Him and stand up for Him, and be guided by the light that is revealed to him. Those are the ones who will succeed. (157)

Say: "O' people, I am the messenger of God to you all. He is the one who is the Owner of the heavens and the earth, no other God but Him, He creates life and ordains death. Believe in God and His

Apostle, the gentile prophet, who believes in God and His words and follow him so that you may be guided." (158)

Among the people of Moses was a nation that was guided by the truth and ruled with justice. (159)

We divided them into twelve tribes, each a nation. And when they came to Moses asking for water, We told him to hit the rock with his staff and twelve springs sprang out, one for each tribe, and each learned where their drinking place is. We sent clouds casting protective shades over them and gave them manna and quails for food, and said: "Eat of the goodness we bestowed upon you." Eventually they did us no wrong but they rather wronged themselves. (160)

When We told them: "Live in this village, eat from wherever you want, beg for forgiveness and enter the doors prostrating yourselves humbly. Then we shall forgive your sins, and reward those who are doing good." (161)

Some of them knowingly changed the words and made it different from what we revealed. We sent on them a plague from heaven as punishment for their transgression. (162)

Ask them about the village overlooking the sea, who started cheating and violating their Sabbath, and the fish started appearing only on the Sabbath and disappear the rest of the week. This is how we punished them for their violations. (163)

When one of their nations asked another: "Why do you warn people who God shall destroy and severely torture?" They said: "We do it so that we do not share any blame with them and because we hope they may eventually protect themselves from evil." (164)

When the evildoers paid no attention We saved those who were giving warning to them, and then We inflicted severe torture on the transgressors as punishment for their sins. (165)

When they persisted further they were transformed to pathetic apes. (166)

If your God wished He would have sent to them those who will persecute them until the Day of Judgement. Your God's punishment can be very swift. He is Forgiving and Merciful. (167)

We dispersed them as different nations on the face of the earth. Some of them were righteous and some of them were less than that. We tested them with the good and the bad so they may get back to the straight path. (168)

After them came descendents who inherited the Scripture, but they gave up the struggle to spread righteousness in favor of benefiting from what is available to them in this life. They said: "We shall be forgiven our sins," and persisted in their erring ways. Did they not agree to the covenant that came with the Book, when they promised to say nothing other than the truth of God, and to study the Book? The Last Day will bring only the good to the righteous. Do you not have common sense? (169)

Those who adhere to the dictates of the Book and persevere in their prayers should keep in mind that We never neglect to reward the righteous. (170)

We extended the mountain so much over them, to protect them with its shade, that they thought it will fall over them. Take that which We have given to you with determination, and be mindful of its content so that you may keep away from evil. (171)

The descendents of the children of Adam (*humans*) were derived from their loins, and then we made them witnesses on themselves when We asked them: "Am I not your Lord?" And they answered: "Yes, You are." On the Day of Judgement you'd better not act oblivious to your testimony. (172)

You might also say: "It is our fathers who disbelieved before us, and we are merely their descendents. Are you going to destroy the descendents for what their evil-doing fathers did?" (173)

Thus we detail Our verses to them to give them a chance to return to the straight path. (174)

Tell them of the example of the man to whom We granted our verses and then he was snatched away by the Devil and ended up among the misguided. (175)

If We desired, We would have elevated him by the signs We gave him, but he chose his destiny in favor of earthly whims. He became like the dog who pants with an extended tongue whether you move towards him or away from him. The same example applies to those who denied Our verses. Tell them of these examples; they may start to think. (176)

A bad example is provided by those who denied our verses, and ended up hurting themselves the most. (177)

Those who are guided by God are the ones who are truly guided, and those who are misled are the real losers. (178)

We have destined for Hell many of the men and jinn. Those of them who appear to have hearts that are closed shut to understanding, eyes that are blind to vision and ears that are deaf to warning. They are like animals and even less. They are truly oblivious. (179)

To God belong all the good names; use them to call on Him and ignore those who sin by misusing his names. They shall be punished appropriately for their misdeeds. (180)

Among the nations We created are those who guide to the truth and rule with justice. (181)

As for those who deny our verses, We shall lead them gradually to ruin in ways they will never anticipate. (182)

Though I may show them tolerance for a while, My final plans for them are solid. (183)

Do they not realize that the Apostle, their compatriot, is not mad, but rather a messenger with a very clear warning? (184)

Do they not look at the kingdom of the heavens and the earth, and all that life created? Do they not consider that their final day may be drawing near and that they may never have a chance again at believing in anything? (185)

Those who are misguided by God shall never be guided. He shall let them sink deeper in their transgression. (186)

They ask you about the Hour (*Day of Judgement*) and when is it coming. Say: "That knowledge is only possessed by my Lord, and will not reveal it until it is time for it. It shall involve the Heavens and the Earth, and shall come upon you only suddenly." They ask you as if you have any knowledge of it. Say: "Knowledge of it rests solely with God." Most people remain ignorant of this. (187)

Say: "I have no power to help or hurt myself except in as much as God wishes. If I have knowledge of the future, I would have known how to increase the good in it, and totally avoid evil. I can only deliver warning or good tidings to people who believe." (188)

He is the One who created all of one soul and created from it its mate, so as to find comfort in her, and as he laid down with her, she conceived, and the conception started light and easy and then became heavier and harder." They called on their Lord: "Bestow upon us a good child and we shall be truly grateful." (189)

As the good child was granted, they set up associates for God in return for His grant to them. God is far superior above their ungrateful lack of belief. (190)

They associate with God what cannot create anything similar to their own creation. (191)

Their idols cannot intercede for them, nor could they intercede for themselves. (192)

When you invite them to guidance they do not follow whether you invite them or remain silent. (193)

Those you plead to besides God are only like you. Plead to them and let them answer you if you are truthful. (194)

Do they have legs to walk on, or do they have hands to crush with, or do they have eyes to see with or ears to hear with? Say: "Call for the aid of your gods and plot against me and spare me no time or trick." (195)

My sponsor is God, who revealed the Book to me. He is the sponsor of the righteous. (196)

Those you plead with, other than Him, cannot give you support nor can they provide support for themselves. (197)

If you invite them to guidance they shall not hear, and you shall see them look at you without seeing you. (198)

Resort to forgiveness, and direct towards justice and keep your distance from the ignorant. (199)

If the temptation of the Devil is tempting you, seek refuge in God. He hears you and He is most Knowledgeable. (200)

Those who seek God to insulate themselves from evil should always remember their shield when the temptation of the Devil reaches them, and they will see the way. (201)

Some of their brothers may continue to try to misguide them, and may never cease. (202)

If you do not recite verses to them they may say to you: "Did you stop making them?" Say: "I follow what is revealed to me from my Lord." This is revelation from your Lord, guidance, and mercy for those who believe. (203)

When the Koran is recited, listen to it and be silent so that you may deserve mercy. (204)

And deep within you be mindful of your Lord, revere Him and have fear of Him, in thought rather than by declaration, and as you come and go and do not be negligent. (205)

Those who are on the side of your Lord, possess no arrogance as they worship Him, glorify Him and prostrate themselves before Him. (206)

THE SPOILS (8)

They ask you about the spoils, say: "The spoils belong to God and His Messenger." Adhere to righteousness before God, improve relationships among yourselves, and obey God and His Apostle, if you are believers. (1)

The true believers are those whose hearts shake with fear upon mentioning the name of God, and if His verses are recited to them their belief even increases, and on their Lord they depend. (2)

They rise up in prayers, and spend in the way of God from what we granted them. (3)

These are the true believers. They have achieved high ranks with their Lord, in addition to mercy and being blessed with plenty. (4)

As your Lord asked you to leave your house and travel to fight for righteousness, some of the believers left quite reluctantly. (5)

They argue with you about subjects in which the right has already been revealed. They behaved like they were being driven to a certain death as they watch. (6)

God promised you victory against the stronger one of both groups, but you wanted to take on the group that was not armed. But God wants the right prevail with His word and wanted to wipe out the tracks of the unbelievers. (7)

The right shall prevail and the wrong shall be defeated in spite of the criminals. (8)

You pleaded for help from your Lord, and He responded. I am sending you a thousand angels of different ranks. (9)

God is sending them, for your support, as good tidings, so as to reassure your hearts. Victory does come from God. God is Exalted and Wise. (10)

And as drowsiness came to you with the feeling of comfort, He brought down rain over you from heaven to purify your souls and wash away from your hearts the impurities left by the Devil so as to strengthen your hearts and stabilize your feet in place. (11)

Your Lord addressed the angels, saying: I am with you stabilize the believers. I shall introduce terror to the hearts of the unbelievers; aim for their necks and their joints. (12)

They have challenged God and His Apostle. He who challenges God and the Apostle shall find God's punishment severe. (13)

Let them taste it, and then the torture of the hellfire awaits the unbelievers. (14)

People who believe, if you meet the advance of the forces of the unbelievers do not ever turn and run. (15)

Those who turn their backs and run, except when it is done as a tactic, or to rejoin with other fighters, shall end with the wrath of God, and the hellfire shall be his home; a very poor final home indeed. (16)

You did not kill them, but God killed them. It was not you who threw the dust in their faces, but it was God who threw it. He shall richly reward the believers; God Hears and Knows. (17)

God shall frustrate the connivance of the unbelievers. (18)

If you (*the unbelievers*) are seeking a final resolution to your conflict with the believers then you do have one now. If you desist it is better for you. If you come back We will come back. Your numbers will not help you, and God will always be with the believers. (19)

People who believe, obey God and His apostle, and never run away from Him after you heard His message. (20)

Do not be like those who say: "We heard" but show no sign of comprehension. (21)

The worst of God's creatures are those who are deaf and dumb. They do not comprehend. (22)

If God wished the good for them, He would have let them hear. But even if they hear they shall turn away in refusal. (23)

People who believe, respond to God and the Apostle if he called upon you to what will put new life in you, and know that God stands between you and your inner desires. To Him you shall be assembled. (24)

Beware of a riot that does not only afflict the transgressors, and know that God's punishment is most severe. (25)

Remember how you were persecuted on this earth, afraid of other people actually pulling you apart. He gave you refuge, supported you to victory, and bestowed upon you all that is good, so that you may be thankful. (26)

People who believe, do not betray God and the Apostle, nor betray what was entrusted to you knowingly. (27)

Remember that your property and your children can represent seduction for you, and God has the greatest reward. (28)

People who believe, if you follow the rule of God, He shall provide you with criteria to separate the good from the evil. He shall cleanse away your infractions, and forgive your sins. God's bounty is great. (29)

When the unbelievers conspired to confine you, kill you or drive you away, they conspired and plotted and so did God. His plots always work the best. (30)

When Our verses were recited to them, they said: "We heard this before and if we want we can say things like it. It is only the myth of the old." (31)

They said: "God, if this is the truth from you, cause the sky to rain stones over us, or send us a great torture." (32)

God will not afflict them with such things while you are among them, nor shall He torture them if they repent. (33)

But they will receive punishment for interfering with the access to the Sacred Mosque. They have never been the keepers of the Mosque, for His keepers are only the righteous. But most of them are ignorant. (34)

Their prayers at the House were nothing but a farce and an obstruction. Taste the torture in punishment for your disbelief. (35)

The unbelievers spend their money to deflect people away from the path of God. They shall spend it, and then it will become a source for constant regret, for they shall be defeated, and the unbelievers shall be assembled in hell. (36)

God shall separate those who are wicked from those who are righteous. The wicked shall be heaped on top of each other, and then disposed of in the hellfire, and those are the true losers. (37)

Say to the unbelievers: If they desist We shall forgive what they have already committed in deals. The years of their elders are already gone. If they persist on causing riots against the believers then fight them until God's religion is supreme. If they desist God shall be watchful over what they do. (39)

But if they persist in their animosity, be assured that God is your sponsor. He is the best sponsor and the best supporter. (40)

Know that of the spoils you earn, one fifth belongs to God, the Apostle, your relatives, the orphans and the miserable poor. Believe in God and what We have revealed to our servant. The day the right was separated from the wrong, the same day the two armies met. God is Capable of all things. (41)

You ended on the near side of the valley and the unbelievers on the far side of the valley and the caravan in the middle. Considering the difference in numbers, if it was an appointment between you and them you would not have shown up. But God executed an order that was inevitable; to destroy those who were destroyed after everything was made clear to them and to let the others survive also after everything was revealed to them. God hears all and knows all. (42)

In your sleep, God showed them to you as a few. If you had seen them as many as they really were, you would have failed and quarreled among yourselves, but God saved the day. He knows what is inside the chest of all men. (43)

As you met with them, God made them seem little in your eyes and made you seem little in their eyes, the outcome that he destined will come out fulfilled. To God everything shall return. (44)

People who believe, if you face the enemy hold your grounds, and be mindful of God all the way through, so that you may succeed. (45)

Obey God and His Apostle and do not quarrel with each other for then you may fail as a consequence of losing your resolve. Remain patient; God is with those who are patient. (46)

Do not be like those who left their homes only because of arrogance and to show off to others. They actually try to deflect others away from the path of God. God is fully aware of what they are doing. (47)

The Devil has made their actions seem good to them, and told them that no one can defeat them and that he shall be with them. Then when the two armies were within eyesight from each other, he turned around and ran, saying: "I have nothing to do with you. I see what you cannot see. I am afraid of God, and His punishment is extremely severe." (48)

The hypocrites and the cowards shall say they were all deceived by their religion. He who depends on God shall find God Exalted and Wise. (49)

If you see the unbelievers die and the angels are carrying away their souls as they hit their faces and their rear ends. Taste the torture of fire. (50)

You earned this with what you have done; God is never unfair to His servants. (51)

Like what happened to the Pharaoh's people and those before them, when they denied God's signs and God took them for their sins. God's punishment is most severe. (52)

God shall not withdraw a gift He had bestowed upon a people until they change what is inside them. God hears all and knows all. (53)

Just like the people of the Pharaoh and those before them who denied the signs of their Lord. We destroyed them by their sins, and drowned the people of the pharaoh. They were all transgressors. (54)

The lowest creatures in the eye of God are those who are unbelievers and have no faith. (55)

Those with whom you have made treaties and yet they break it every time. They have no scruples. (56)

If you capture them in war, punish them more than their followers, so that they will have something to remember. (57)

If you become afraid of betrayal on the part of an ally, break your treaty with them and attack them. God does not like those who are treacherous. (58)

Let the unbelievers not think that they can escape from Us. They cannot do that. (59)

Prepare for the enemy as much force and equipment as you can, so as to put the fear in the hearts of the enemies of God and your enemies, and others that you may not know but God knows. Any spending you make in the way of God shall be repaid to you and you shall not be treated unjustly. (60)

If they opt for peace choose the same and depend on God for He hears all and knows all. (61)

If they intend to deceive you with their move towards peace you have to depend on God for He is the one who supported you with victory and supported the believers with you. (62)

He brought the hearts of the believers together, and you would not have been able to bring their hearts together even if you had spent all of the money on earth, but God did bring them together. He is Exalted and Wise. (63)

Prophet, all you need is God and the believers who follow you. (64)

Prophet, you have to induce the believers to fight. Twenty steadfast believers can defeat two hundred and a hundred can defeat a thousand of the unbelievers because they are people who are confused. (65)

Even if God were to lighten your burden because of weakness He may detect in you, a hundred of you who are steadfast should still be able to defeat two hundred of the unbelievers, and a thousand of you should still be able to defeat two thousand unbelievers, with God's permission, and God is with those who are steadfast. (66)

Prophets were not allowed to take prisoners of war until they have complete control of the Land. You (*the believers*) want the benefits of this life and God wants for you those of the next one. God is Exalted and Wise. (67)

If it was not for a prior decree from God, you would have received a great torture for what you took in ransom. (68)

So make use of whatever you have gained this time with no sanctions attached, and be mindful of God, God is Forgiving and Merciful. (69)

Prophet, say to the prisoners under your control that if God finds the goodness in your hearts He shall compensate you for what was taken away from you in war, and will forgive you. God is Forgiving and Merciful. (70)

But if they betray you, remember that they have betrayed God before, and God has caused you to defeat them. God is Knowledgeable and Wise. (71)

Those who have believed, left their homes and struggled with their property and with themselves in the way of God, and those who provided them with shelter and aid, both sponsor each other, but those believers who have not had to immigrate you are not obligated to sponsor them until they find it necessary to immigrate. But if they seek your support in a conflict over their religion, you will have to give them support, unless the conflict is between them and those who may have a treaty with you. God is always aware of what you do. (72)

The unbelievers support each other. If you did not do the same there will be great disturbances and corruption in the Land. (73)

Those who believed, immigrated and struggled in the way of God, and those who provided shelter and support for them, are the true believers, and a large forgiveness and bounty awaits them. (74)

Those who believed and immigrated later, and struggled along-side you, those are worthy of full sponsorship by you, even if the presence of kinship does provide a high priority for your support, in the Book of God. God has Knowledge of all things. (75)

REPENTANCE (9)

Amnesty from God and the Apostle was granted to those unbelievers with whom you made an agreement. (1)

Go out unafraid in the land for four months and know that you cannot run away from God and God shall humiliate the unbelievers. (2)

On the day of the great pilgrimage a proclamation shall come from God and His Apostle: The contractual obligation of God and His Apostle to the unbelievers will thereby finish. If you repent it is better for you, but if you persist know that you cannot escape God. You can promise the unbelievers that an excruciating torture awaits them. (3)

Those of the unbelievers who have signed treaties with you and did not violate them, did not provide support for any of your enemies, and fully abided by their commitment to you, then by all means keep your commitment to them until it expires. God loves those who do not violate their promises. (4)

But once the amnesty period is over, fight the unbelievers anywhere you find them, arrest them and be prepared for them at every corner. If they repent, stood up in prayer and paid the alms-tax then let them go, God is Forgiving and Merciful. (5)

If an unbeliever requests an asylum with you, grant it to him so he may have a chance of hearing the word of God. But then deliver him to a safe place and get rid of him. They are people who know little. (6)

The unbelievers have no credibility with God or with His Apostle. As to those who made the treaty with you at the Sacred Mosque, honor your agreement with them so long as they honor it with you. God loves those who abide by what they promise. (7)

If they ever had the upper hand over you they would not honor any agreements or promises. They try to assure you with a sweet tongue, but in their hearts they reject you. They are all doers of evil. (8)

They sold God's verses for a cheap price and deflected people away from His path. Evil was what they did. (9)

They will not honor their commitments or their promises with the believers, and they are the transgressors. (10)

If they repent and stand up in prayers and pay the alms-tax they become your brothers in religion. We detail the verses for those who have knowledge. (11)

If they violate their treaties with you, and attack your religion, fight the leaders of disbelief, for you cannot turn your back to them and they must desist. (12)

Will you not fight people who violated their oath with you and were about to try to force the Apostle out from among you and they were the ones who started the animosity towards you? Are you afraid of them when it is God of whom you should be afraid of, if you are believers? (13)

Fight them and God shall make their punishment at your hands, and shall defeat them and bring you victory against them, and the spirit of the believers shall be revitalized. (14)

The anger in their heart shall clear. God shall forgive whomever He wishes. God is Knowledgeable and Wise. (15)

Did you think you can be abandoned or that God is unaware of those among you who struggled and fought, and served no one but God, His Apostle and the believers with devotion? God is always aware of what you do. (16)

The associaters (*idol worshipers*) are ill-suited to build God's Mosques for they are self-proclaimed unbelievers. Their efforts shall fail, and in hell they shall be immortalized. (17)

Building mosques is appropriate for those who believe in God and the Last Day, stand in prayer, pay the alms-tax and fear none but God. Those are among the guided. (18)

Do you consider providing water to thirsty pilgrims to drink while visiting the Sacred Mosque, is equivalent in its value to believing in God, the Last Day, and struggling in the way of God? In the eyes of God these are not equal. God does not guide the transgressors. (19)

Those who believed, immigrated, struggled in the way of God with their property and themselves are higher in rank in the eyes of God, and they are the winners. (20)

Their Lord sends them good tidings of mercy from Him, a bliss and gardens in which they will have everlasting happiness, (21)

immortalized in it forever. God is in possession of the greatest reward. (22)

People who believe, do not sponsor your parents, your sisters and brothers if they favored disbelief over believing. Those who sponsor them are transgressors. (23)

If your attachment to parents, to your children, to your friends, to your spouses, to your tribe, or the importance of moneys you have earned or a trade you are engaged in that you may fear will fail, have a higher priority to you than God and His Apostle, and the struggle in the way of God, then you are going to have to watch for the Day of God's final decree. God shall not guide the transgressors. (24)

God has caused you to triumph on many occasions, including the day of Hounain, when you were so proud of yourselves, and you liked your high numbers, which eventually did nothing for you, and the earth became small for you with all its size, and you started running away. (25)

Then God brought down his tranquility upon the Apostle and the believers, and brought down soldiers you never saw, and punished the unbelievers, which was what was deserving for the unbelievers. (26)

After such an incident God may forgive those He wishes. He is the Forgiving and Merciful. (27)

People who believe, the associaters (*associate idols with God*) are but an abomination. They shall not be permitted near the Sacred Mosque after this year. Do not be concerned about loss of commerce for God shall replace it out of His own bounty, if He so wishes. God is Knowledgeable and Wise. (28)

Of the people of the Book, fight only those who do not believe in God or the Last Day, and do not forbid what God and His apostle have forbidden, and do not adhere to the true faith until they agree willingly to pay the submission-tax and are completely docile. (29)

The Jews said: "Ezra is the son of God" and the Christians said: "Christ is the son of God." These are their own allegations which seem to mirror sayings of unbelievers of years before. God shall nullify and expose these lies whenever they are made. (30)

They associated some of their Rabbis and Monks and Christ, son of Mary, with God in their worship of God, when they were ordered to worship God and God alone, who is Exalted far higher over what they associate with Him. (31)

They would like to extinguish the light of God, but God will see that His light will achieve its purpose, whether the unbelievers like it or not. (32)

He is the One who sent His Apostle with guidance and the religion of truth to prevail over all religions, whether the unbelievers like it or not. (33)

People who believe, some of the Rabbis and Monks defraud other people of their money and possessions and deflect others away from the path of God. As to those who hoard gold and silver and do not spend it in the way of God, predict for them excruciating torture. (34)

It (*the gold and silver*) will become hot in the hellfire and then it will fall over their foreheads, their sides and their backs. This is what you hoarded as a prize for yourselves; now get a taste of your own prize. (35)

The number of months in a year are twelve, as decreed by God since the day He created the heavens and the earth. Of those twelve months, four are sacred. Do not violate these months' sacredness or you will be transgressing against yourselves. You can never-the-less fight the associaters throughout the year, the same way they fight you throughout the year, and know that God is with the righteous. (36)

The act of postponement of the sacred months is an act of disbelief testifying to the misguidedness of the unbelievers. One year they allow it and the next year they forbid it, in their attempts to allow what God forbade and to forbid what He allowed. They admired their own misdeeds, but God does not guide the unbelieving people. (37)

People who believe, how is it that when you are mobilized to fight in the way of God, you seem to be taking your time about going? Are you satisfied with this life in preference to the next? Whatever you have in this life is nothing compared to the next. (38)

If you do not promptly mobilize, He shall excruciatingly torture you, and replace you with another nation. You do not make any difference to Him and God is Capable of all things. (39)

If you do not support him, (*the Apostle*) God has supported him. The unbelievers chased him out. He found himself with his companion (*Abu-Bakker*) hiding in the cave, and he said: "Do not worry; God is with us." God extended His protection to him and supported him with unseen soldiers. He made the word of the unbelievers the lowest and the word of God the highest. God is Exalted and Wise. (40)

Mobilize yourselves, whether you have little or too much responsibilities. Struggle with your properties and yourselves. This is better for you if you only knew. (41)

If the battles were close or the trip was short they would have followed you, but they find it difficult to go the distance. They will swear, using God's name that they will go with you if they could. They are destroying themselves, and God knows they are liars. (42)

God has forgiven you for the mistake you made when you granted them an excuse before it was clear to you who was telling the truth and who were the liars. (43)

Those who believe in God and the Last Day will not ask you for an excuse from fighting using their property or using themselves. God is aware of the righteous. (44)

Those who ask you to excuse them are the ones who do not believe in God and the Last Day, and have doubts in their hearts, and it is because of their doubt that they hesitate. (45)

If they truly wanted to go, they would have prepared for their trip a lot better. But God hated to see them go, so He made it easier for them to hesitate, and said: Go ahead and sit with the rest who are sitting. (46)

If they go with you they shall only add confusion to your ranks. They would have weakened your enthusiasm, and produced discord among you; for among you are some who may be liable to listen to them. God is well aware of the transgressors. (47)

They have sought discord before among you and managed to turn situations against you, until the truth came out, and the wishes of God prevailed in spite of them. (48)

Some of them claimed that they applied for an excuse to stay behind in order to avoid being tempted (by the women of the enemy) and sin against themselves. They have already done that. Hell shall engulf the unbelievers. (49)

If your campaign succeeds they will be unhappy, but if you fail they will say we have been cautious, and they will turn away feeling happier. (50)

Say: "Nothing will touch us except that which God has destined for us. He is our Sponsor, and on God the believers shall rely." (51)

Say: "Are you waiting for anything to happen to us except success or death as martyrs? We are waiting for you to be hit with the torture of God, or directly at our hands. So go ahead and wait and we shall be waiting with you." (52)

Say: "It will do you no good if you spent money willingly or unwillingly. God will not accept it from you, for you are wrong-doing people." (53)

The benefit from their spending will not reach them for they disbelieved in God and His Apostle. They pray only lazily and spend their money only reluctantly. (54)

Do not admire their money or their children. God shall use both to torture them in this life, and then they shall die unbelievers. (55)

They swear in the name of God that they are believers like you. They are not, but they are afraid of you. (56)

If they can find a shelter, a cave or a protection that can protect them from you, they would have ran to it without hesitation. (57)

Some of them criticize you in regard to the way the alm-taxes are distributed. If they get a portion of it they will be contented, and if they do not, they get resentful. (58)

They should have been contented with what God and His Apostle gave them and said: "We are satisfied with what God has given us from His bounty, and from His Apostle, and to God's wish we submit." (59)

The Alms are for the poor, the destitute, those who work on collecting them, to ransom believing prisoners and to help pay the indebtedness of those who are deserving of help, to provide assistance for new believers, for the homeless and in whatever the way of God dictate. It is imposed by God, and God is Knowledgeable and Wise. (60)

There are those who try to hurt the Prophet by saying he believes all that is said to him, say: "He believes in what is good; he has faith in God and has faith in the believers. He is a blessing for the believers among you, and those who hurt the Apostle of God shall have excruciating torture." (61)

They swear using the name of God to satisfy most of you. God and His Apostle are more deserving of being satisfied if they are believers. (62)

Did they not know that one who disputes God and His Apostle shall be the owner of the hellfire, immortalized in it, and that shall be a great disgrace? (63)

The hypocrites say among themselves (sarcastically) that they are afraid of a revelation that will make public what is in their heart. Say: "Go ahead and be sarcastic. God shall bring out what you are afraid of." (64)

If you ask them about it they will say: "We were only playing and joking." Say: "Have you been using God, His verses, and His Apostle to have fun?" (65)

Do not apologize; you have disbelieved after believing, and even if We forgive some of you, the others will be tortured for they are evildoers. (66)

The hypocrites, men and women; they derive from each other. They advocate what is evil and deflect what is good. They hold their purse-strings shut tight. They forgot God and God has forgotten them. The hypocrites are transgressors. (67)

God promised the hypocrites, men and women, and the unbelievers the hellfire, immortalized in it. It is all they can look forward to. They have earned the curse of God, and they shall have unrelenting torture. (68)

Like people before you, who were stronger and richer and had more numerous children, they enjoyed their earthly possessions, and you enjoy your earthly possessions like them. You also engage in useless talk and in practices similar to theirs. Their efforts have failed in this life and the life to come. They are the losers. (69)

Did they not hear of those that disappeared before you? The people of Noah, Aad, and Thamoud; also of the people of Abraham, and the people of Madian, and those of the destroyed cities. Their Apostles brought them verifiable signs from Him. God would not have been unjust with them, yet they were unjust with themselves. The believers, men and women, sponsor each other. They advocate good deeds and denounce evildoing, they rise up in prayer and pay the alms-tax. They obey God and His Apostle. They are the ones who will receive God's mercy, God is Exalted and Wise. (70)

The believers of men and women have been promised gardens watered by flowing rivers. In it they shall be immortalized. Their dwellings will be blessed, in the gardens of Eden, with God's gift. Such is the truly great prize. (72)

Prophet, wage war against the unbelievers and the hypocrites, and deal with them decisively. Their dwelling is hell, the worst of all destinies. (73)

They deny it, but they did utter words of blasphemy after they believed. They conspired and yet they failed. They never had a reason to be resentful while God and His Apostle enriched them from God's bounty. If they repent that will be better for them, but if they persist they shall receive God's excruciating torture, in this life and the next, and on this earth they shall find no sponsor or supporter. (74)

Some of them have promised God that if they were included in His bounty they shall believe and be among the righteous. (75)

Upon receiving His bounty then they became more solicitous, and turned their backs on what they promised. (76)

God caused hypocrisy to dominate their heart until the day they meet with Him and face their unkept promises and their lies. (77)

Did they not know that God knows their secret longings and aspirations? God has Knowledge of all that is hidden. (78)

Those who mock the believers who contribute all they have in charity or those who give what they can, God shall mock them and an excruciating torture awaits them. (79)

Whether you ask forgiveness for them or not, and even if you ask for forgiveness for them seventy times God shall not forgive them for they denied God and His Apostle and God shall provide no guidance for the corrupted. (80)

Those who the Apostle of God left behind were glad they stayed. They were not willing to struggle for God using themselves or their possessions. They said to others: "Do not go, it is going to be very hot out there." You should say: "Hellfire is much hotter, if they had any sense." (81)

They shall laugh a little and cry a lot; a punishment for what they did. (82)

If God created another occasion in which you were to leave, (fighting in the way of God) and they seek your permission to go out with you, say: "You shall not accompany me ever, and you shall never fight an enemy on my side. You elected to sit the first time, so stay behind with those who stayed." (83)

Do not pray on any of their dead, nor visit their graves. They denied God and His Apostle and died unbelievers. (84)

Do not admire their riches or their children. God intends to torture them in this life and then let them die unbelievers. (85)

And if in a chapter in the Book God revealed that you should believe in God and fight for Him and alongside His Apostle, those with a status among them will ask you to excuse them and to be among those who stay behind. (86)

They were satisfied to be among the sitters. Their hearts are stamped with disbelief and little do they understand. (87)

But the Apostle and the believers struggled with their possessions and with themselves. They will be the receivers of His bounty and they are the ones who will succeed. (88)

God has prepared for them gardens, with rivers flowing underneath, immortalized in them, and that is the great prize. (89)

Then came the Arab tribesmen applying for their own excuses to stay behind in addition to those who stayed behind having denied God and His apostle. Those of them who disbelieved shall face an excruciating torture. (90)

No stigma shall be attached to the weak, the infirm or to those who have no way to support the war effort to stay behind if they are truly sincere in their loyalty to God and His Apostle and God is Forgiving and Merciful. (91)

Nor there shall be any sin attached to those who come to you asking for a ride due to their inability to walk and when told that rides were not available they returned with tears in their eyes, distressed over their inability to spend in support of the effort. (92)

The questioning shall fall on those who are rich, and yet come to you for exemptions to stay behind. God has stamped their heart shut; for they know little. (93)

On your return they shall come apologizing. Say to them: "Do not apologize. We shall not trust you. God has kept us informed of your actions. God and His Apostle shall continue to watch you, and when you are returned to Him, He who has full knowledge of all that is hidden and all that is seen, He shall inform you of all that you have done." (94)

Upon your return they shall invoke the name of God to please you and convince you to forgive them. Stay away from them. They are abominable, and their eventual dwelling is hell; their punishment for their evil deeds. (95)

They will swear to you to gain your acceptance, and if you accept them God will not accept those who are corrupted. (96)

The Arab tribesmen (*Bedouins*) are usually stronger in the depth of their unbelief and in their propensity for hypocrisy and the likelihood of ignoring the boundaries of God's revelations. God is Knowledgeable and Wise. (97)

Some of the Arab Bedouin tribesmen look upon the alms-tax as a fine and lurk there waiting for a disaster to befall you. Misfortune will only befall them. God responds and is always aware. (98)

Some Bedouin tribesmen believe in God and the Last Day and look upon what they spend in the way of God as the means to get closer to God and to earn the prayers of the apostle, and closer to God they shall be brought. He shall enter them under the wing of His mercy. God is Forgiving and Merciful. (99)

As to the early believers who immigrated to uphold their faith along with those who sponsored and supported them and then those who followed their example; they are the ones who pleased God and God pleased them. He prepared for them gardens watered by flowing rivers, immortalized in it forever, and that is the greatest prize. (100)

Of the tribesmen around you and even among some of the dwellers of Madina there are hypocrites of long standing; you do not know them but We do. They shall feel the torture twice before they return to us on the Day of Judgement for the greatest torture of all. (101)

Others have admitted their sins and carry a mixed bag of good and evil doings. They may be forgiven by God. God is Forgiving and Merciful. (102)

Take of their moneys a portion for charity that will help clean them and purify them and earn them your prayers, for your prayers shall be their security blanket. God hears all and has Knowledge of all. (103)

Did they not know that God is the one who has to accept repentance from all his worshipers and is the receiver of all of their charities, and God is Forgiving and Merciful? (104)

Say: "Do the good work and it shall be seen by God, His Apostle and the believers. Then you shall return to Him, He who has all knowledge of what is hidden and what is seen. He shall tell you of what you have been doing." (105)

The fate of some will remain on the balance until the very end. God my inflict torture on them or He may forgive them. God is Knowledgeable and Wise. (106)

And those who put up a mosque with the intention of causing harm and spreading hatred among the believers out of their own disbelief and in support of those who fought against God and His Apostle before. Then they swore that they never intended anything but good and claimed God as a witness. They are nothing but liars. (107)

Do not raise prayers in it ever, for a mosque that was built from the outset on a foundation of piety is far more deserving of your rise to prayers, and because in it there are men who yearn to become purified. God loves those who are purified. (108)

Who is better? One who builds on a foundation of piety and God's pleasure or the one who builds at the edge of a depression which then slides in the hellfire? God does not provide guidance for the transgressors. (109)

What they build will remain a source of weakness and hesitation in their hearts until their hearts are hearts no more. God is Knowledgeable and Wise. (110)

God has purchased from the believers themselves and their possessions, and the price is paradise. If they fought, and got killed, it is theirs a promised rightful possession, so promised in the Torah, the Gospel and the Koran. One who fulfils his promise to God, let him receive the good tidings of a great bargain, and there is the greatest triumph. (111)

To the repentant worshipers, the thankful wanderers, the kneeling and the prostrated; to those who promote good and discourage evil, and to those who adhere to the limits imposed by God; bring good tidings. They are the believers. (112)

The Apostles and the believers are not to seek forgiveness for the associators even if they were their relatives after they know them to be the owners of Hell. (113)

Abraham prayed for his father's forgiveness only because of a promise he previously made to him. When it became clear to Abraham that he was an enemy of God, he dissociated himself from him. Nevertheless, Abraham was tender and forbearing. (114)

God was never to misguide a people after he guided them until He makes clear to them what to avoid. God is Knowledgeable of all things. (115)

To God belongs the kingdom of the heavens and the earth. He creates and takes life away, and in His stead you can seek no sponsorship or support. (116)

God looked with favor at the Apostle, those who immigrated (*the immigrants*) and those who sponsored them (*the sponsors*) who followed Him at a time of extreme hardship and although the hearts of some of them have nearly swerved, He forgave them, and was to them Caring and Merciful. (117)

God was also merciful with the three who stayed behind rather than fight. And as the vastness of the earth became too narrow for their existence and their very souls were in a tight squeeze they became convinced that there is no refuge from God but Him, and as they repented He forgave them. God is Forgiving and Merciful. (118)

People who believe, fear God and be among the truthful. (119)

People of Medina and its surrounding tribes should have never considered staying behind and away from supporting the Apostle of God and favoring themselves over Him, for no thirst, exhaustion, or hunger they may suffer for God, nor will any step they take that may anger the unbelievers, nor any injury they may receive, will fail to earn them the record of a good deed with God. God will never overlook the reward for the doers of good. (120)

They will not spend any amount, large or small, in the cause of God, nor will they cross a valley for Him, that will not earn them a reward from God that is not superior to what they extended. (121)

Yet, the believers need not all be mobilized. If a portion of each group is mobilized and the Apostle was staying behind, those who remain stay with him and continue their education and keep up with the new revelations so as to teach their fellow believers upon their return home from battle, to keep them informed. (122)

People who believe, fight the unbelievers who surround you and impress them with your toughness, and know that God is with those who fear Him. (123)

As new chapters of the Book are revealed, some will ask whose faith is increased with this. Those who are believers will increase their faith as they rejoice. (124)

But those who harbor sickness in their hearts, the uncleanliness of their thoughts will increase and they shall die unbelievers. (125)

Do they not see that every year they are put to the test once or twice and yet they neither repent nor do they remember? (126)

And as a new chapter is revealed they look at each other then they look to find out if they are being observed, then they look away. God turned their hearts away for they are people who cannot understand. (127)

You (*the Arabs*) were sent an Apostle who is one of you. He values what is valuable to you and is anxious to protect you. And with the believers he is caring and gentle. (128)

If they decline, say: "To God I shall turn. There is no God but Him. On Him I shall rely. He is the Lord of the Supreme Throne." (129)

JONAH (10)

In the Name of God, Most Merciful, and Most Beneficent.

Alef Lam Raah (*A, L, & R*). (1)

These are the verses of the sage Book. Is it so strange to people that We sent our revelation to a man from among them and exhorted him to warn the people and bring good tidings to those who believed? Tell them of the priority they have with God by their early belief, while the unbelievers said: "This is obviously nothing but the work of magic." (2)

Your Lord who in six days created the heavens and the earth, and then mounted His throne is the One in charge of things. No one can intercede on your behalf without His permission. He is God, your Lord. Worship Him, and you better take heed. (3)

It is God's true promise that to Him you shall all return. He started the creation and He shall call it back, so He can reward those who believed, did good works and acted with justice. Those who disbelieved shall get their drinks from hell and excruciating torture awaits them for their lack of belief. (4)

He produced the sun's brightness and the moon's luminescence and sequenced them in such a rhythm that will help you keep track of the years and learn arithmetic. These were only created to reveal the truth, and He detailed His verses for those who comprehend. (5)

The sequencing of the night and day, and the creation of what is in heaven and on earth are signs for righteous men. (6)

Those who do not yearn to meet Us and have grown comfortable and contented with this life and became oblivious to Our verses. (7)

Those are the ones who will have hell for a home in punishment for their deeds. (8)

Those who believed and did good works, God will advance them further in faith. They shall have rivers flowing beneath them in the gardens of His blessings. (9)

In it their prayers shall glorify God, and their greetings shall symbolize the peace they enjoy, and their ultimate offerings shall be thankfulness to God, Lord of the universe. (10)

If God advanced to people adversity the same speed they would like to receive His bounty their fate would have been sealed long ago. Give warning to those who are not looking forward to meeting Us. They are blinded by their own transgressions. (11)

As man is afflicted with harm, he calls upon Us, while sitting or standing to come to his aid. Then when We lift his affliction he acts as if he never called upon Us to relieve the harm that touched him. Such is the way the transgressors fail to perceive their excesses. (12)

We have annihilated many a generation before them for their transgressions when they did not believe and were punished as criminals. (13)

We replaced them on this earth with you after they were gone and We shall see how you do. (14)

As our veritable verses are recited to those who are not looking forward to meeting Us, they demanded: "Bring us another Koran or change it." Say: "How can I change it on my own, I have done nothing but follow what was revealed to me. If I disobeyed my Lord I will be terrified of the torture of the Great Day." (15)

Say: "If God so desired I would have never recited it to you, and you would have never known it existed. I have spent a lifetime among you before it was revealed; do you not have any sense?" (16)

Those who transgress by fabricating what God has never said or denying his verses shall fail, for criminals never prevail. (17)

They worship what cannot hurt them or help them instead of God. They claim that their idols will intercede for them with God. Say: "Are you trying to inform God of something He does not know in the heavens or on earth?" The glory is His and He shall be exalted over those who associate others with God and what they associate with Him. (18)

At one time, all the people were one nation. Then they split and if it was not for a prior determination by your Lord, He would have permanently settled their differences long ago. (19)

They ask: "Why has God not given him a sign?" Say to them: "Only God knows what will happen in the future, so wait and I will be waiting with you." (20)

If We granted people mercy after a calamity that afflicted them, they soon start subverting our verses. Tell them that God's subversion is much faster. Our Apostles are keeping a record of your subversion. (21)

He is the one who guides you over land and in the sea. As they went aboard a ship and had a gentle wind that enhanced their progress they were happy. Then as the wind turned into a storm and the waves came at them from every direction, and they thought they were finished, they prayed to God in earnest: "If you save us from this we shall always be among the grateful." (22)

When He saved them they still went on spreading corruption on earth, and swaying away from what is right. People, your transgressions bring harm to you first. This life's joys and possessions are fleeting. To Us you shall all return and We will then face you with what you have been doing. (23)

Life on this earth is exemplified by the water We bring down from the sky which stimulates the growth of plants of which man and animals eat. And as the earth becomes dressed in luxuriant and decorated covering, and its owners are getting ready to reap the harvest, Our curse comes at night or during the day. It lays the harvest to waste and make it like it never was. Thus We detail the verses to those who think. (24)

God invites you to the house of peace. He guides whomever He wants to the straight path. (25)

Those who did good works many times over, their faces shall not show signs of want or shame. They are the owners of paradise and in it they shall be immortalized. (26)

Those who commit evil shall find an evil act for an evil act. They shall show signs of weakness and shame. No one can provide them with a refuge from God. Their faces shall appear like they were masked with pieces of the night's darkness. They are the owners of hell and in it they shall be immortalized. (27)

The day We assemble them all We shall say to those who associate others with God, your place is with your associates, and as they got together, the associates asked: "How did you worship us?" (28)

God is a witness between us and you. He knows we were not aware of your worship. (29)

On that day each soul answers for itself. To God they shall return. They shall be abandoned by those they associated with God out of utter falsehoods. (30)

Say: "Who grants you His bounty by what He brings down from the sky and up from the earth? The One Who holds the power of hearing and sight and the one who brings the living from the dead and the dead from the living and who manages all things." They shall say: "God" and you say: "Why do you not adhere to righteousness?" (31)

This is your True God and the only alternative to the truth is to be misguided. How can you consider anyone but Him? (32)

The word of your Lord is realized on the transgressors for they are not believers. (33)

Ask: "Who of your associates can start the creation and then bring it back again?" Say: "Only God can start the creation and then bring it back again. How could you go so far astray?" (34)

Ask: who of your associates provide guidance towards the truth. Say that He who provides guidance is far more deserving of following than the one who is lost until he is guided. What kind of judgement do you have. (35)

Most of them only follow their suspicions and suspicions are no substitute for belief and God knows what they are doing. (36)

The Koran could not have been brought by anyone but God. It confirms what has been revealed before. The details in the Book are beyond doubt those of the Lord of the Universe. (37)

When they say he made it up, say: "Why do you not come up with one chapter like it and have help from whoever you want except God, if what you are saying is true?" (38)

They deny everything that they have no knowledge of, even when the truth is revealed to them. People before them also denied the truth, and look at how the transgressors ended. (39)

Some of them believe in the Book and some of them do not. Your Lord has more knowledge of the corrupted. (40)

If they deny you, tell them: "I shall be responsible for what I do, and you shall be responsible for what you do. You shall bear no guilt for me and I shall bear no guilt for you." (41)

Some of them hear you and you make them hear even if they were deaf and dumb. (42)

Some of them look at you as if you were capable of making them see you even if they were blind. (43)

God does not persecute anyone. Men bring persecution on themselves. (44)

The day they are assembled it will seem to them like they have been away for only an hour of the day. They start recognizing each other, and losers are those who denied the day they meet God, and remained among the misguided. (45)

We may let you witness some of what We shall do to them, or We may let you die before that occurs. To Us they shall all return and God shall be a witness to everything they did. (46)

To every nation God sent an Apostle. Their Apostle shall rule among them with justice and none will be persecuted. (47)

They say: "When will the promise be fulfilled if you are telling the truth?" (48)

Say: "I cannot even do myself good or bad unless God so decrees. For each nation there is a set ending, and when it comes they cannot bring it earlier or postpone it by even an hour." (49)

Say to them: "How does it matter if God's torture that awaits them comes to them at night or during the day? Why are the sinners in a hurry to get there?" (50)

Then as the day comes you will believe in it for sure. and then you will wonder why you were in a hurry to get to it. (51)

To the transgressors it will be said: "Taste the immortal torture. You are receiving punishment only for what you deserve." (52)

They ask you if it is the truth, say: "By my Lord it is the truth and you shall not succeed in evading it." (53)

Each soul that transgressed will give up all the earth and what is on it, if it was hers to ransom itself. They started repenting privately as they witnessed the torture. They shall be judged fairly without being wronged. (54)

To God belongs what is in heavens and on earth. His promise is the truth, but most of them do not know. (55)

He gives you life and decrees your death and to Him you shall return. (56)

People, you have received an advice from your Lord. It will heal you inside and provide you with guidance and mercy for the believers. (57)

It is God's bounty and His mercy what shall bring them happiness and not the earthly possessions they keep on hoarding. (58)

Did you see how God blessed you with his bounty and you, on your own made some of it allowed and some is not? Did God permit you to do that or are you transgressing in the name of God? (59)

Those who lie in the name of God have not entered the Day of Judgement in their consideration. People are indebted to God, but most of them do not show gratefulness. (60)

Whatever is occupying you, and whatever part of the Koran you read and whatever action you take, We shall be witnesses on you as you engage in it. Even a speck of sand does not escape your Lord's attention, on earth or in heaven, and not even smaller or larger things. It is all recorded verifiably. (61)

Those whom God has sponsored shall have nothing to fear and they shall not be sad. (62)

They are the ones who believed and became righteous. (63)

They shall have good tidings of their destiny in this life and the one coming next. The word of God is unchangeable, and their lies the greatest triumph. (64)

Do not let their uttering upset you. Glorified is God above all, He is Listening and Knowledgeable. (65)

To God belongs all that is in heavens and on earth. Those who follow the ones that associate others with God shall find that they follow nothing but imagination and fancy. They are only fabricating. (66)

He made the night for your rest and the day for your vision, and in that there are signs for those who listen. (67)

They said: "God has begotten a son. God is self-sufficient, the owner of all that is in heaven and on earth. Do you have any authority for what you are saying? Or are you saying about God that of which you know nothing?" (68)

Say: "Those who fabricate lies about God shall never succeed. "(69)

They shall have some free rein on this earth, and then to us they shall return and they shall taste severe torture for their disbelief. (70)

Tell them the story of Noah when he said to his people: "My people if it has become intolerable to you for me to be living among you and continue to remind you of God's verses (*on whom alone I rely*) then why do you not get together with those that you associate with God (*idols*) and without secrecy make your judgement on me and then inform me of it without any other considerations? (71)

If you turn away from me, remember that I have never asked to be rewarded, for my reward only comes from God, Who ordered me to surrender myself to Him." (72)

They denied him and We saved him and those who followed him in the Ark and they replaced those who denied Our verses and were drowned, and thus contemplate how was the ending of those who were warned. (73)

After him We sent other apostles to their people bringing them veritable signs. They did not believe them and they denied Him like those before them. That is how We seal the hearts of the transgressors. (74)

After them We sent Moses and Aaron to the Pharaoh and his people with Our verses. They became arrogant and they were truly criminal. (75)

When the truth from God was presented to them, they said that is nothing but an obvious magic. (76)

Moses said: "Do you call the truth brought to you magic? Magicians never prevail." (77)

They said: "You came to entice us away from what we learned from our fathers, so that you become the center of glory on earth. We shall not make that possible by following you." (78)

The Pharaoh asked that the most knowledgeable magicians be brought in. (79)

When the magicians came, Moses said to them: "Go ahead and do whatever you can do." (80)

As they performed their magic Moses said: "Whatever you brought in here God will nullify. God does not permit the acts of the transgressors to succeed." (81)

God will reveal the truth in His words even if the criminals resisted. (82)

Only some of his own people believed Moses. They were afraid of the Pharaoh and his followers attempting to convert them as the Pharaoh had a lot of influence, and followed his fancy to extremes. (83)

Moses said: "People, if you believe in God you shall have to rely on Him if you have surrendered yourselves to Him." (84)

They said: "On God our Lord we shall rely, do not let us suffer at the hands of the transgressors. (85)

Save us with your mercy from the unbelieving people." (86)

We revealed to Moses and his brother the need to build for his people in Egypt homes and devote those homes to prayers and bring good tidings to the believers. (87)

Moses said: "Our Lord, you gave the Pharaoh and his people an abundance of cloth and money in this world and they only deviated from Your path. Lord, put to waste their riches and harden their hearts so they will not believe until they see the excruciating torture." (88)

He said: "I shall grant you the wish of your prayers. Be righteous, and do not ever follow the path of those who do not know." (89)

We helped the people of Israel cross the sea, and the Pharaoh and his soldiers followed them in out of arrogance and animosity. As he was about to drawn, the Pharaoh said: "I believe that there is only one God, the God of the people of Israel and we will surrender to Him." (90)

Now you believe when you disobeyed before and you were one of the corrupted? (91)

Today We shall let you survive with nothing but your own body to make you an example and a sign for those who succeed you, as many people remain oblivious to Our signs. (92)

We elevated the people of Israel to a position of truth and we blessed them with our bounty of the best of foods. They never disagreed among each other until knowledge was extended to them. Your Lord shall be the final arbitrator for them on the Day of Judgement, in whatever their disagreement is all about. (93)

If you have doubt in what We have revealed to you, ask those who have been reading the Book before you. The truth was given to you by your Lord; do not join the ranks of those afflicted with doubt. (94)

Do not be one of those who denied the signs given by God, or you will become a loser. (95)

Those who deserved the curse of your Lord do not believe. (96)

Even if they were presented with every sign and verse until they face the excruciating torture. (97)

Very few people believed early enough to benefit from their belief, except the people of Jonah. When they believed, We relieved the torture of their own shame in this life, and We permitted them to live comfortably for a while. (98)

If it was the wish of your Lord, all the people on earth shall become believers, and you are trying to pressure people into becoming believers. (99)

No soul can believe without God's permission, and He afflicts those who have no sense with the impurity of thought. (100)

Say look at what is in the heavens and on earth. Signs and warnings are of no value to people who do not believe. (101)

What is it they are waiting for other than the fate of those who came before them? Say to them: "Go ahead and wait and I shall be waiting with you." (102)

We always save Our apostles and those who believe with them, as We always save the believers. (103)

Say: "People, if you doubt my religion, you have to realize that I do not worship what you worship in place of God, but I worship God who is capable of taking you away, and was ordered to be a believer." (104)

Devote yourself to the true faith and do not join the ranks of the associaters. (105)

Do not ever direct your prayers to anyone other than God, and you shall find that no one other than God is capable of benefiting or hurting you.

If you do, you shall certainly be a transgressor. (106)

If it is God's wish that you be touched by harm, no relief can come from anyone but Him. And if God blessed you with His bounty no one can take away His favor. He targets whomever He wishes among His subjects and He is the Forgiving and the Merciful. (107)

Say: "People, the truth has come to you from your Lord. He who finds guidance finds it for himself and one who chooses to remain misguided does it against himself. I am not your keeper." (108)

Follow what is being revealed to you and remain patient until God's judgement arrives. He is the best of all judges. (109)

HOUD (11)

In the Name of God, Most Merciful, and Most Beneficent.

Alef Lam Raah (*A, L, & R*). A Book whose verses have been composed and detailed by the One who is Wise and Experienced. (1)

Do not worship any but God. On His behalf, I give you warning and good tidings. (2)

Ask your Lord for forgiveness and then direct your repentance to Him. He shall let you live comfortably for a while, and He will reward your good deeds, one for one. If you do not I shall be fearing for you the torture of the Big Day. (3)

To God you shall return, and He is Capable of all things. (4)

They cover their chests to conceal their thoughts from God, except when they are fully clothed, God knows everything they hide or declare. He has full knowledge of all that people try to hide. (5)

There is no creature on earth that God does not set up its sustenance, its residence and and where it will be stored after death. All recorded in a veritable book. (6)

He is the One who created the heavens and the earth in six days while His throne was above water. He did that to test you and find out who among you do better works than others. If you tell them that they will be resurrected after death, the unbelievers will say this is nothing but verifiable magic. (7)

If We delay their torture to a day that We determine, they ask: "How come their day of reckoning has not arrived?" It shall arrive and take them for all of the mocking they did. (8)

If We blessed a man with Our mercy and then We took it away from him, he becomes desperate and blasphemous. (9)

And if We gave him our blessing and bounty after adversity touched him, he starts saying that adversity has left him and becomes happy and boastful. (10)

It is only those who remain patient and do good works who will receive forgiveness and big reward. (11)

You may be tempted to ignore some of what is being revealed to you, or you may become irritated and feel tightness in your chest when you hear them saying: "Why did God not give him a treasure or sent an angel with him?" Remember that you are only to give warning. To God belongs everything. (12)

Or they may say he made it up (*the Book*). Say: "Try to imitate ten of its chapters. Solicit help from anyone other than God if you are truthful." (13)

When they fail they should know that it is revealed only with God's full knowledge, and then ask them if they surrender to God. (14)

Whoever wants this life, with of its decorations, We shall reward them for their works in it and shall not be cheated. (15)

They are the ones who the hellfire awaits. What they did will fail, and fruitlessness shall be the outcome of their efforts. (16)

This is to be contrasted from one who was confident in his Lord and in what He revealed to a witness sent by Him and before him the Book of Moses sent for guidance and mercy. They are the true believers. Whoever denies Him among the tribes is hereby promised the fire of hell. Do not be in doubt, it is the truth from your Lord, but most people are unbelievers. (17)

Those who transgress by creating lies about God; they shall be paraded in front of God, and witnesses shall say those are the ones who lied about their Lord. God's curse shall afflict the transgressors. (18)

Those who attempt to direct people away from the straight path of God into a crooked path, on the Day of Judgement they are the nonbelievers. (19)

Those are people who were not handicapped on earth and have not adopted other Gods. They shall receive twice the torture for they refused to hear or see. (20)

Those are the ones who lost themselves and became entrapped by their own lies. (21)

It is thus not a surprise that on the Last Day they shall be the losers. (22)

Those who believed and did good works and acted with humility before God; they are the owners of Paradise and in it they shall be immortalized. (23)

The difference between the two groups is like the difference between the blind and deaf, and one who sees and hears. Could you consider them equal? Make sure you contemplate that. (24)

We sent Noah to his people, and he said: "I bring you a veritable warning." (25)

Worship only God, otherwise I fear for you the day of an excruciating torture. (26)

His unbelieving people said to him: "We see you as only a human like us. Your followers are some of the lowest in our tribe who are imprudent in their judgement; we owe nothing to you and we believe you are lying." (27)

He said: "My people, if I was guided by God and the receiver of His mercy, you are oblivious, how can I force you to accept it? (28)

I am not asking you for a reward or compensation, as my compensation is from God, and neither will I reject those who believe, as they shall meet their Lord, and I find you to be ignorant people. (29)

Who will protect me from God if I sent them away. Do you have no sense? (30)

I never claimed that I have the treasures of God nor did I claim the ability to tell the future. I never pretended to be an angel, nor would I ever say to those who you look down with contempt to that they shall not get the blessing of God. God is more Knowledgeable with what they have in their hearts, and if I did I would classify myself among the transgressors." (31)

They said: "Noah, you argued and argued with us. Bring upon us what you warned us about if you are telling the truth." (32)

He said: "God will bring upon you anything He wishes, at the time He wishes, and you will have nothing to say about it. (33)

Even my advice will do you no good if God wanted to misguide you. He is your Lord and to Him you shall return." (34)

They also said that he made the revelations up, say: "If I did then the sin is mine and I am innocent of all your sins." (35)

He revealed to Noah that those who believed of his people are all of those who will. Do not be sorrowful over what they do. (36)

Build the Ark with my inspiration and blessing, and do not try to intercede on behalf of the transgressors for they shall be drowned. (37)

And as he was building the Ark, groups of his people passing by will mock him and make fun of him. He said: "If you mock us, we have good reason to mock you and we shall. (38)

You shall find out who will be the receiver of a shameful torture, which will stay with him forever." (39)

And as Our command was given and Hell boiled over with water, We said: Carry male and female pairs with you, in the Ark, of every species, your family, except for those already doomed, and all the believers; and those who believed in him were very few. (40)

He said: "Board it in the name of God who will be its sponsor as it sails and as it anchors. My Lord is Forgiving and Merciful." (41)

It sailed with them passing between waves that were as high as mountains. When leaving, Noah called upon his son who had isolated himself: "My son, come on board with us, do not stay with the unbelievers." (42)

He said: "I shall take refuge in a mountain which will protect me from the rising water." Noah said: "Today there is no refuge from God's command except for those He takes mercy upon." Then the waves separated them and he was among those who drowned. (43)

Then the earth was ordered to swallow its water and for the sky to cease raining. The water ebbed and the ark rested on the mount (*AL Judi*). And a voice from afar said: "The transgressors are gone." (44)

Noah called upon his Lord: "My Lord, my son is a member of my family, Your promise is the truth and You are the wisest of all judges."(45)

God said: Noah, he does not belong to your family, he committed bad sins, and do not inquire about things you have no knowledge of, and I warn you against being among the ignorant. (46)

He said: "My Lord, you forbid that I ever ask about things that I have no knowledge of, and if you do not forgive me and show mercy with me I will certainly end up with the losers. (47)

He said: Noah, disembark in peace with Our blessing on you and on those who are with you, and those who come after them who shall prosper for a while until they are touched by our excruciating torture. (48)

These pieces of the unknown past we reveal to you which you and your people were unaware of before now. Be patient and the final salvation is for the righteous. (49)

And as to Aad, when their brother Houd said: "My people, worship God for you have no other God but him, or otherwise you will be guilty of fabrication." (50)

I am asking for no reward from you as my reward comes from Him who created me; do you have no sense? (51)

My people, ask your Lord for forgiveness and repent and he will sends you the good rains and add more power to your strength. Do not recoil like guilty criminals. (52)

They said: "You, Houd, have never brought us a sign and we shall not be abandoning our gods on your word. We shall not believe in you." (53)

They said: "Some of our gods must have aflicted you mentally," and he said: "God is my witness that I am innocent of your association (54)

of others with Him. You go ahead and conspire against me and do not look back to me again. (55)

I have relied on God, my Lord and your Lord. No creature on earth can escape His absolute control. With Him is the straight path. (56)

If you choose to refuse, I will have delivered the warning that I was sent to deliver to you. My Lord shall replace you with others and you shall mean nothing to Him. My Lord is the guardian of all things." (57)

When our final verdict came, We saved Houd and those who followed him by Our mercy. We saved them from a heavy torture. (58)

This was Aad who denied the signs of their Lord and disobeyed His apostles and followed the path of intransigent tyrants. (59)

They earned a curse in this life and a curse in the Day of Judgement, and as Aad denied their Lord the curse shall always follow Aad, the people of Houd are gone. (60)

To Thamoud We sent their brother Saleh. He said: "My people, worship God for you have no other God but Him. He created you on earth and permitted you to thrive on it. Ask for His forgiveness and repent to Him. My Lord is always Near and Responsive." (61)

They said: "Saleh, prior to this we have put a lot of hope in you, and now you try to dissuade us from worshiping what our fathers worshipped. We have a grave doubt about what you ask us to do." (62)

He said: "My people, you see that I am well aware of my Lord, and have received mercy from Him. Who will protect me from God if I disobeyed Him? You can contribute no gain to me, but only loss." (63)

He said to them: "This female camel is God's sign to you. Let her feed on God's earth and do not touch her with harm or you shall be afflicted with an imminent torture." (64)

They killed her and He said: "You have three days left to enjoy your homes, and this is a promise that shall never fail to be realized." (65)

And as Our verdict arrived We saved Saleh and those who followed him by Our mercy and spared them the shame of that day. Your Lord is Powerful and Exalted. (66)

The transgressors were taken by the loud cry and they were left prostrate and frozen in their own homes. (67)

As if they never thrived there, but Thamoud denied their Lord and Thamoud are gone. (68)

Our emissaries brought Abraham good tidings. They greeted him saying: "Peace" and he responded with a similar greeting of wish for peace. Then He brought them food and served them a roasted veal. (69)

Then when he saw that they never touched the food he became suspicious and fearful of them. They said: "Do not be afraid, our mission mainly involves the people of Lot." (70)

And as his wife was standing cheerfully in their service, they gave her the good tidings of the coming of Isaac, and after him Jacob. (71)

She said: "Oh, my goodness, how can I bear a child? I am an old woman and my husband is an old man. This is definitely strange." (72)

They said: "Does the will of God surprise you? God's mercy and His blessings have been granted to the people of this house. He is the One to be thankful to and He is the Glorious One." (73)

As Abraham's fearfulness abated he started pleading with Us about the people of Lot. (74)

Abraham was a prudent, soft-hearted gracious man. (75)

Abraham, stop this intercession. Your Lord's verdict is in. Their coming torture is inevitable. (76)

Then Our emissaries came to Lot he became concerned about them (*as the angels appeared in the form of very good looking young men*), and said: "This is going to be a very hard day." (77)

His people came to him, interrupting their acts of depravity (*seeking his guests*), and he said: "My people, here are my daughters, they would be a cleaner target for your desires. Have fear of God, and do not shame me with my guests, is not there among you one prudent man." (78)

They said: "You know we have no interest in your daughters; you know what we want." (79)

He cried: "I wish I had some strength over you or I had a strong defensive corner where I could seek refuge." (80)

The emissaries said: "We are messengers from your Lord, they will never touch you. Flee with your people out at night, and never turn your head back, except for your wife who shall share their fate, and their appointment is the morning. Is not the morning coming soon?" (81)

As the time came for Our verdict, We turned everything upside down and rained upon them pieces of stone, one following the other. (82)

The stones were targeted by your Lord. Such a punishment shall not be far from those who are like them. (83)

To the people of Midian, We sent their brother Shoaib. He said: "My people, worship God, for you have no god but Him, and do not defraud and cheat people by rigging the weighing scales and the utensils for volume measurements. I see that you are living well and I am afraid for you from the torture of a day that none will escape. (84)

Use accurate weights and measurements with fairness, and do not cheat people out of their possessions, and do not spread corruption on earth. (85)

What truly remains from God's bounty is far better for you, if you are believers. I am not a guardian over you." (86)

They responded: "Tell us Shoaib; are you claiming that your prayers ordering us through you that we shall abandon what our fathers have worshipped, and tell us what we can do and not do with our own possessions, and yet you consider yourself prudent and wise?" (87)

He said: "My people, you can see that God has provided me with a sign from Him, and granted me ample amounts of His bounty. Why would I want to have a disagreement with you and tell you what you should not do? I only seek reform as much as I can, and my success only depends on God. On Him I shall rely, and to Him I shall always resort. (88)

My people, do not let your developing antagonism to me blind you from seeing what happened to the people of Noah, the people of Houd or the people of Saleh. The people of Lot are not so far from you either. (89)

Beseech God for His forgiveness, and then repent to Him. My Lord is Merciful and Approachable." (90)

They said: "Shoaib, we do not understand most of what you say to us. You are a single person and we do not have that much regard for you. If it was not for your relatives we would have had you stoned." (91)

He said: "My relatives are more importent to you than God, who you are trying to keep behind your backs. My Lord has full knowledge of what you do. (92)

My people, go ahead and do what seems fit to you, and I shall do what seems fit to me. You shall find out who will receive the torture which shall shame him and who is the liar. You wait and I shall be waiting with you." (93)

When it was time for Our verdict, We saved Shoaib and those who believed with him with Our mercy, then a shout took the transgressors, and the morning found them prostrated and frozen in their own homes. (94)

As if they never thrived in Madian and they were gone just like Thamoud was gone. (95)

We sent Moses with Our signs, and We granted him veritable powers. (96)

He was sent to the Pharaoh and his followers who followed the Pharaoh's directives and his directives were never well guided. (97)

He shall present his people on the Day of Upheaval, and they shall all be led to Hell; an ill-fated leadership indeed. (98)

They earned a curse in this life and a curse on the Day of Upheaval. What a gift to have on that day. (99)

These are the stories of many nations, some of them remain and others are gone. (100)

We did not persecute them, they persecuted themselves. Their gods did not do them any good. Those gods they claim instead of God. When it was time for God's verdict, those gods of theirs made their situation worse. (101)

Your Lord took away those people while engaged in their transgression. His taking is severely painful. (102)

In this there are signs for those who are afraid of the torture of the Last Day. It is a day for which people will be assembled, and it shall be a day to witness. (103)

That day shall be delayed only until a predetermined date. (104)

When that day comes, no soul can speak without His permission. Some are miserable and others are happy. (105)

Those who lived in misery, in Hell they shall inhale and exhale. (106)

Immortalised in it for as long as the earth and the heavens remain and for as long as your Lord wishes. Your Lord always acts on what He wants. (107)

The happy ones shall be immortalized in paradise for as long as the heavens and the earth remain and for as long as your Lord wishes. Their gift shall have no end. (108)

Do not have any doubt about what those people worship. They only imitate what their fathers did. We shall give them what they deserve with none missing. (109)

We gave Moses the Book, and they disagreed on it, and if it was not for a prior promise from your Lord, their disagreement would have ended long ago, for they retained a lot of doubt about it. (110)

All people shall be given what is deserved by their actions. He always has knowledge of what they do. (111)

Follow the straight path as you were ordered, you and those who repented with you and do not engage in tyranny, He sees what you do. (112)

Do not trust the transgressors for that can get you touched by the Fire. Without God you shall have no sponsors or support. (113)

Pray at the begining and the end of the day and during the night. Good deeds cancel bad ones. Something to be remembered by those who care to remember. (114)

Endure, for God shall never forget the deserved reward by those who do good. (115)

How would it have been if in all nations before you there were not a few who resisted corruption on earth? Those We saved, and all followed the example of the transgressors and their criminal behavior. (116)

Your Lord would not have annihilated nations while their people were reformers. (117)

If your Lord wished He would have made all the people one nation. They are not. They differ from each other. (118)

With the exception of those who earned God's mercy, it is the fulfillment of God's prediction: I shall fill hell with those belonging to man and jinn. (119)

All that We tell you of the stories of the apostles who preceded you We intend to strengthen your heart to carry what was revealed to you in righteousness, intended as an admonishment and a reminder to the believers. (120)

Say to those who are not believers: "Go ahead and work your way and we shall work our way." (121)

You wait, and we shall be waiting. (122)

God is the owner of all the secrets of the heavens and the earth. All matters shall return to Him. Worship Him and rely on Him. Your Lord is not oblivious to what you do. (123)

JOSEPH (12)

In the Name of God, Most Merciful, and Most Beneficent.

A, L, R, Those are the verses of the veritable Book. (1)

We revealed it as an Arabic Koran so you may understand. (2)

We tell you the best stories through revealing this Koran to you, and before it you were oblivious. (3)

As Joseph said to his father: "Father, I saw eleven stars, the sun and the moon bowing closer to the ground in front of me." (4)

His father said: "My son, do not inform your brothers of what you saw lest they become jealous and conspire against you. The Devil is clearly an enemy of man. (5)

Your Lord shall make you His choice, and He shall teach you the interpretation of predictions, and shall complete His blessings on you and on the house of Jacob as He did for your forefathers Abraham and Isaac. Your Lord is Knowledgeable and Wise." (6)

In Joseph and his brothers were signs for the inquisitive. (7)

They said: "Joseph and his brother (*Benjamin*) are favored by our father over us, although we are a bigger group. Our father has definitely lost the way. (8)

Kill Joseph or throw him somewhere on earth, and you shall have your father's undivided attention; then you can become righteous people after that." (9)

And one of them suggested: "Do not kill Joseph but rather throw him in the darkness of a distant well, and some travelers may pick him up, if you are going to do anything." (10)

They said: "Father, why do you not trust us with Joseph, when we desire nothing for him but his own good? (11)

Let him go with us tomorrow to run and play, and we shall watch out for him." (12)

He said: "I am concerned that you would take him, and then he will be eaten by the wolf. " (13)

They said: "It will be shameful for all of us to be there and then let the wolf eat him." (14)

And as they went with him and proceeded to place him in the darkness of a well. We revealed to him: You shall face them with what they did to you even if they are oblivious to that now. (15)

In the evening they returned to their father, crying. (16)

They said to their father: "We went racing and left Joseph with our belongings, and the wolf ate him. We know it will be hard for you to believe us, even if we were truthful." (17)

They brought back on his shirt false blood that they claimed to be his. Their father said: "There is something you are hiding, may God grant me patience and aid on tolerating what you describe." (18)

A caravan of travelers passed, and as their water supplier put down his bucket to fill it, he shouted: "I give you the good tidings of a boy." They took possession of him as property, and God was cognizant of what they were doing. (19)

They sold him for worthless pennies and never appreciated his true value. (20)

The man who bought him, from Egypt, asked his wife to treat him well as he may benefit them or they may adopt him, and through him We provided for Joseph on this earth. We taught him the interpretation of language. God can force what He wants to happen, but most people are not aware of that. (21)

And as he grew up to his prime We bestowed upon him wisdom and knowledge. This is the way we reward the righteous. (22)

The lady of the house where he lived then tried to seduce him. She closed all doors and then said: "come on." He said: "The Lord forbids that I do. He blessed me with his bounty. The transgressors will never succeed." (23)

She wanted him, and he wanted her, if it was not for the sign from his Lord. This is how We spared him the sin and the indecency. He was one of our faithful worshipers. (24)

They both raced to the door, and as they did she took hold of his shirt from the back and tore it. And at the door they came face to face with her husband. She said: "What penalty is suitable for one who does harm to your family except imprisonment and excruciating torture?" (25)

He said: "She was the one who was seducing me," and a member of her own family suggested: "Examine the shirt and if it is torn from the front she would be telling the truth and he would be a liar. (26)

But if his shirt is torn from the back then she is the liar and he is truthful." (27)

And as they found it torn from the back, he said: "These actions are treacherous on your part. Your treachery is great indeed. (28)

Joseph, you forget about this incident, and you, woman, repent for your sin, as you are a wrongdoer." (29)

Women of the town were now saying that the wife of Ezra tried to seduce her boy, and she is in love with him and obviously misguided. (30)

When she heard of their treachery she sent for them, prepared comfortable seating for them with food and provided each with a knife, then she had Joseph come out suddenly before them, and they all made cuts in their fingers of astonishment. They said: "By God, this is not human, he is none but a blessed angel." (31)

She said: "This is the one you blame me for. I tried to seduce him, and he refused, and if he did not he would have ended in prison and lost his status." (32)

He said: "My Lord, prison is far preferable to me over what I am being asked to do. I beseech You to help me thwart their plans for without Your help I would fail and become one of those who are ignorant." (33)

His Lord responded and protected him from their plotting. He hears and He is Knowledgeable. (34)

After all of the signs that were made clear to them, they still imprisoned him for a while. (35)

With him in prison were two young men. One of them said to him: "I see myself squeezing grapes to make wine" and the other said: "I see myself carrying bread over my head and the birds are eating from it. Interpret those visions for us, for we see you as a charitable person." (36)

He said: "The only reason I can give you as an interpretation, and I can even predict the food you will eat before you eat, is because of what my Lord has taught me as I abandoned the creed of people who do not believe in God and they shall be found to be unbelievers on the Last Day. (37)

Instead I followed the creed of my forefathers, Abraham, Isaac and Jacob, we associated none with God, and God has bestowed His favor upon us and upon all people yet most people do not say thanks. (38)

My prison mates, which is better, many useless gods or the One dominant God? (39)

Instead of God you worship nothing but names you and your fathers made up, which God never sanctioned. The final judgement belongs to God, worship none but Him. This is the valuable religion, but most people do not know. (40)

My prison mates, one of you shall serve his lord (*the king*) wine while the other shall be crucified and the birds shall be picking at his head, and this matter of your inquisition is done and over with." (41)

Joseph then said to the one who he thought would make it: "Please mention my case to your lord," but the Devil made him forget so that Joseph stayed in prison for several years. (42)

The king said: "I had a vision of seven fat cows being eaten by seven scrawny ones, and I also saw seven green ears of corn and seven dry ones. Can any of you people interpret this vision to me?" (43)

They said: "These are nothing but nightmares, and we are not knowledgeable in interpreting nightmares." (44)

In the presence of the king was the man who was in prison with Joseph and left it but forgot for a while to mention Joseph to the king as Joseph asked. He said: "I know someone who can interpret that if you will let me go and see him." (45)

He said: "My friend Joseph, interpret for us the meaning of a vision of seven fat cows being eaten by seven scrawny ones and seven green ears of corn and seven dry ones, so that I may go back with an answer to people who do not know." (46)

He said: "You shall plant corn for seven years and leave most of it in its ears except a small amount that you will need to use. (47)

Then you shall have seven very hard years, in which you will need to use most of what you have stored from the previous seven years of abundance. (48)

Then there will come a year in which abundance returns, and you can go back to producing other by-products from your corn." (49)

The king said: "Bring him to me," and as the king's messenger arrived, Joseph said: "Go back to your lord and ask him what happened with the women who cut their hands, for my Lord is quite knowledgeable with their intrigue." (50)

The king said to the women: "Did you try to seduce Joseph?" They said: "God forbids that we have known any evil of him," and the wife of Ezra said: "Now is the time for the truth, I am the one who tried to seduce him and he was nothing but truthful. (51)

I am confessing so that my husband is assured that I did not betray him behind his back, and that God does not help the cause of those who betray. (52)

I am not trying to absolve myself from seducing him, for one's self does tend to entice toward sin, except for my Lord's mercy and my Lord is Forgiving and Merciful." (53)

The king said: "Bring him to me, I can use him myself." And when he talked to him he told him that he was now held in a position of strength and trust. (54)

Joseph said: "Make me your treasurer and I shall knowledgeably preserve the earthly possessions." (55)

This is how We found for Joseph his niche on this earth in which he prospered and became prominent, and that is how our mercy envelops those We choose, and We never forget the rewards that belong to those who do good. (56)

The rewards of the next life are far better for those who are believers and those who are righteous. (57)

Joseph's brothers entered his presence, and he recognized them but they did not recognize him. (58)

After he gave them their share of rations he said to them that on their next trip to obtain rations they have to bring with them their youngest brother (*Benjamin*). He said: "As you see, I am very fair and I give each person his fair share." (59)

He said: "If you do not bring him you shall obtain no new rations from me." (60)

They said: "We shall do everything we can to convince his father to let him come back with us. We shall certainly try." (61)

Joseph then said to his workers privately to reload the merchandise that the brothers exchanged for the rations back on their rides, to ensure that they will have something to exchange for the rations on their next trip and thus ensure their return. (62)

As they went back to their father they said: "The next time we go back for rations we shall not get any unless our brother is with us, we promise you we shall take care of him." (63)

Their father said: "Should I entrust you with him the way I entrusted you with his brother before? God is the best protector, and He is the most Merciful of all." (64)

And as they unloaded their loads they found that their own merchandise had come back with them, and they said to their father: "You see, we will even bring more rations if our brother travels with us, and we will easily win an extra camel's load." (65)

He said: "I shall not let you take him until you swear and take oath on everything sacred that you will bring him back unless you are all left totally powerless; and when they did give him their solemn promise he said: "And God shall be a witness to what we say." (66)

Then Jacob said: "My children, when you enter the city enter it through several different doors. Although nothing will protect you from the will of God. The final judgement is God's, on Him I shall rely and on Him all shall rely. (67)

And as they entered the city like he told them nothing would have changed the will of God but that satisfied a need in Jacob's mind. He learned well what We have taught him, but most people do not know. (68)

And as they entered Joseph's presence, he took his brother aside and introduced himself and asked his brother (*Benjamin*) not to be too perturbed by his brothers' past actions. (69)

After he got their rations and merchandise ready and loaded, he planted a valuable water-pitcher into his brother's load, then someone shouted: "Those camel drivers are thieves." (70)

The brothers questioned them as they approached: "What are you missing?" (71)

"We are missing the king's drinking cup," said Joseph, "and he who comes up with it shall have a camel's load of rations as a reward." (72)

The brothers said: "You should know us enough to know that we did not come here to spread corruption in the earth, and we are no thieves." (73)

Joseph asked: "What should the penalty be for the responsible person if you are not telling the truth?" (74)

The brothers said: "He who the cup is found in his load shall become yours to own. This is how we punish the transgressors." (75)

Joseph started searching their loads before he inspected his brother's. When he produced it from his brother's load, the plot worked as Joseph planned. Joseph would not have taken possession of his brother under the laws of the local Egyptian rule, but he did only because it was the will of God. We elevate in stature those whom We favor and above all who have knowledge there is One Who is most Knowledgeable. (76)

They said: "If he stole, he had a brother who did the same before him." Joseph thought, without actually declaring it, your evil-doing was far worse and God is far more knowledgeable with what you describe. (77)

They said to Joseph: King's Minister, he has an old father, take one of us instead of him as we see in you an obvious benevolence. (78)

Joseph said: "God forbids that we take one other than the one in whose possession the stolen property was found, for otherwise we would by transgressors." (79)

As they gave up they got together for consultation and their oldest said: "Do you not know that your father has taken your solemn oath, and keeping in mind what you did with Joseph? I shall not leave this land until my father gives me permission or God makes a judgement on me, He is the best of all judges. (80)

Go back to your father and tell him: "Your son has stolen and we can only relay what we were told, and we have no way of discovering the unknown." (81)

Say: "You can ask in the town we came from and talk to the traders who accompanied us. We are being truthful." (82)

Their father said: "I know you are up to something, may God grant me patience and may God bring them all to me, He is Knowledgeable and Wise." (83)

He stayed away from them and said: "Alas for Joseph, and his eyes became white (blind) from sorrow and repressed anger." (84)

They asked him: "By God, are you going to continue thinking of Joseph until you become weak or among the dead?" (85)

He said: "I am simply relaying to God my burdens and my sorrows, for I know of God what you do not know. (86)

My children, go and seek information about Joseph and his brother and do not give up hope in God's help; only the unbelievers will do that." (87)

As they entered Joseph's presence they said: "King's Minister, we have been hurt by the famine and so were our people. We brought in some merchandise of small value, give us some rations and be charitable to us for God shall reward those who are charitable. (88)

He said: "Do you realize what you have done to Joseph and his brother if you continue to claim ignorance?" (89)

They asked: "Could it be that you are Joseph?" Joseph said: "Yes, and this is my brother. God has been benevolent with us. He who is righteous and patient shall see that God does not waste the compensation for those who do good." (90)

They said: "By God, He has certainly favored you over us. We have done wrong." (91)

Joseph said: "Nothing is lost today. God shall entertain forgiveness for you, He is the most Merciful of all Forgivers." (92)

He said: "Take this shirt of mine and throw it over my father's face and he shall see again and then bring all of your families to me." (93)

As the caravan left Egypt, Jacob said to his children who were with him: "At the risk of you accusing me of senility and illness, I tell you I feel the wind of Joseph." (94)

They said: "By God, you are but returning to your old afflictions." (95)

And as the bearers of good tidings arrived and the shirt was thrown over Jacob's face, his sight returned and he said: "Did I not tell you that I know of God what you do not know?" (96)

They said: "Father, plead for the forgiveness of our sins for we certainly were wrong." (97)

He said: "I will ask my Lord for your forgiveness for He is the Forgiving and Merciful." (98)

As they arrived to Egypt, Joseph received his parents and said: "Enter Egypt, with God's will you shall be safe here." (99)

He invited his parents to climb up and sit on the throne and they fell to the floor kneeling before him. He said: "Father, this is but the realization of my old vision (*of which you are aware*) made true by my Lord. He blessed me as He delivered me out of prison and then He brought you to me from the desert after the Devil incited a falling out between me and my brothers. My Lord is Considerate in whatever He wishes. He is Knowledgeable and Wise. (100)

My Lord, you have given me power and taught me the interpretation of stories. You are the Creator of the heavens and the earth. All belongs to You in this life and the life to come. Let me die while completely surrendered to You and permit me to follow the righteous who preceded me. (101)

These are news from the past We reveal to you (*Mohammed*). You were not with them as they planned for and decided on their treachery. (102)

Even with your best efforts, most people will not be believers. (103)

You never asked them for a reward for your guidance. It is but a reminder for all of mankind. (104)

All around them, in the heavens and on earth, are signs which they pass without paying any attention to them. Most of them believe in God only when they can retain associating someone else with Him. (106)

Will they believe only when they are hit with the overwhelming impact of God's torture or when the Day of Judgement finds them unaware? (107)

Say: "This is my chosen path. Seek God knowingly as I and those who follow me do. Glorified shall be God, and I will not be among the associaters." (108)

All those we sent before you were men who received our revelations in their different villages. Did they not walk about and see what were the outcomes met by those who came before them? The next life is far better for the righteous. Do you not have sense? (109)

When the apostles became discouraged, and believed they had been denied, our support reached them and we saved whomever we wished. There is no escape from our might for the transgressors. (110)

There stories represent a warning for those who have knowledge. These do not come in the form of stories that can be fabricated, for they are confirmation for what is already recorded and as elucidation, details, guidance and an act of mercy for those who believe. (111)

THE THUNDER (13)

In the Name of God, Most Merciful, and Most Beneficent.

A, L, M, R. Those are the verses of the Book and what was revealed to you, rightfully by your Lord, but most people do not believe. (1)

God Who raised the heavens with no visible support, then He occupied His throne. He dedicated the Sun and the Moon, each with its own orbit for a predetermined and limited time. He manages all things and recorded the details in verses so you may acquire faith in your Lord. (2)

He extended the earth and anchored on it high mountains and created rivers. For all fruits he created male and female components, and with the darkness of the night He covered the light of the day. In all there are signs for those who are thinkers. (3)

And on earth there are adjoining lots of gardens, vineyards, fields of wheat, and palm trees, some clustered and some not clustered, all watered the same yet do not taste the same. These are signs for those with reason. (4)

If you are to be amazed, be amazed at those who say: "Shall we be raised and brought back to life after we are dust?" These are the ones who disbelieved in their Lord; chains shall bind their necks. They are the owners of Hell and in it they shall be immortalized. (5)

They are faster to challenge you with evildoing than to test you with doing good, yet how many before them disappeared in punishment, and your Lord, though forgiving to people for their transgressions, He is quite stern in punishment. (6)

The unbelievers say: "Why did his Lord not supply him with a sign?" You are only to give warning and every nation has its own guidance. (7)

God has full knowledge of what a female carries in her womb, and which will be miscarried and which will be carried to term. He has everything predefined. (8)

He has full knowledge of what is hidden and what is witnessed. He is the Great and the Exalted. (9)

Whether one of you speaks in secret or openly, and whether he crawls in darkness or moves in daylight (10)

he is being watched from his front and behind his back and protected by God's command, and God shall not change the circumstances of people until they change what is inside their heart, and if God wished evil upon a nation they will have no protection from Him and without Him they shall have no sponsor. (11)

It is He who shows you the lightning which elicits in you fear and hopeful anticipation, and creates the heavy clouds. (12)

The thunder shouts praise for Him, and so do the angels in fear of Him. He sends the thunderbolts which may hit whomever He chooses, as they argue about God. His retaliation is quite stern. (13)

His call is the true call and those who respond to the call of others they shall find them unresponsive. They shall find that what they are responding to can be exemplified by one who extends his palms to collect water from the rain and then expects the water to reach his mouth on its own and without help from him; it shall not. The prayers of the unbelievers are all in vain. (14)

Those who dwell in the heavens and on earth, shall all prostrate themselves in front of God whether willingly or by compulsion. Even their shadows shall also kneel in front of Him, morning and evening. (15)

Ask them: Who is the Lord of the heavens and the earth? Tell them: It is God. Then ask them: Did you adopt as sponsors those who cannot even help themselves, or bring to themselves benefit or harm? Ask them if blindness equals eyesight, or if the darkness equals the light. Did the partners they invented for God ever create anything similar to what He created, and thus the similarity in creation caused their confusion!? Say: God has created everything, and He is the One, and the Dominant. (16)

He brings down water from the sky which fills the valleys with flooding waters covered by foam that is reminiscent of the scum that covers boiling water that is used to clean ornaments or metals. It is the scum that is washed and flows away while things of value remain in place. That is how God uses examples as reminders. (17)

To those who responded to their Lord shall come the reward, but those who did not respond shall not hesitate to use anything they have even if it all that is on earth and more to ransom themselves. Awaiting them is the worst form of reckoning, and their dwelling shall be Hell, a horrible resting place indeed. (18)

Is one who knows that what was revealed to you by God was the truth, equal to a blind person? It is those who have intellect who are the ones who take heed. (19)

They are the ones who remain faithful to their covenant with God and do not break it. (20)

They connect what God decreed to be connected, they fear God, and fear the ruthless reckoning. (21)

Those who persevered in anticipation of facing their Lord, held on to their prayers and spent from what God has blessed them with, covertly and overtly and prevent evil by doing good; they shall be rewarded with the ultimate dwelling. (22)

They shall enter the Gardens of Eden and with them they shall have those who are good among their parents, their spouses and their descendents. The angels shall welcome them as they pass through every door. (23)

We salute you for your perseverance. Blessed indeed is your final ultimate dwelling. (24)

Those who breach their covenant with God after having ratified it, and disconnect what God has ordered connected and propagate corruption on earth. Those shall be cursed and awaiting them is the worst of all dwellings. (25)

God extends His bounty to some and restrict it to others. Those who are happy with what they get in this life need to remember that all they have in this life they shall find in the next to be a burden. (26)

The unbelievers say: "Why did his Lord not support him with a miracle?" Say: God misguides whomever He wants and guides those who resort to Him. (27)

Those who believe and their hearts are comfortable when God is mentioned. Is not the mention of God enough to comfort the hearts? (28)

Those who believed and did good works, good for them. Their work shall give them an excellent final reward as they return. (29)

Thus We have sent you to a nation before which many nations have disappeared, so that you can recite to them what We revealed to you while they disbelieved in the Merciful. Say: "He is my Lord. No other God but Him, On Him I shall rely and to Him I will return." (30)

If the Koran were to move mountains, split the earth, or talk to the dead, for it is all up to God, would the believers then be satisfied that if God wished He would have guided all the people? The unbelievers shall continue to be afflicted with calamities earned by their deeds or those close to them may be afflicted until God's promise is realized. God's promise is never missed. (31)

Apostles before you were mocked, and I gave the unbelievers time then I took them and what a punishment it was. (32)

It is He who watches over every soul and over what it earns and yet they made partners for God; say: "Name them and tell us their origin." Do you think you can tell God of what He does not know on this earth? Or is it that you think words can deceive? God made them fall victims of their own cunning and miss the straight path. One who is misguided by God shall never find a guide. (33)

They shall be punished in life on this earth, but the torture on the Last Day shall be more severe, and from God they shall have no protector. (34)

This in contrast to Paradise, promised to the righteous, watered by rivers, with ample foods and vast areas of shade, a fitting ending for the righteous, while the unbelievers shall end in hell. (35)

Those to whom the Scriptures were revealed are pleased by what God revealed to you, although some factions shall deny some of it. Say I was ordered to worship God and associate none with Him. To Him I pray and to Him I shall return. (36)

We revealed it as a Book of judgement in Arabic, and if you ever follow their desires, after knowledge was revealed to you, you shall find that without God you have no sponsor, and from Him you have no protector. (37)

We sent apostles before you, and gave them spouses and descendents, and no apostle ever would have brought forward a verse without permission from God, and for each book we specified a period of validity. (38)

God may erase what He wants and confirm what He wants. In His possession he has the original Book of all. (39)

Whether We permit you to witness the realization of what we threatened them with or whether We let you die, your responsibility is only in the warning. Reckoning is Ours alone. (40)

Did they not see that the entire earth, with all its sides, is within our reach to destroy? God is the judge. His judgement is final and his reckoning is prompt. (41)

Those before them also conspired, but all conspiring is known to God. He knows what each soul commits and the unbelievers shall find out to whom does the final victory belong. (42)

The unbelievers will claim: "You are not an apostle." Say: "I need none but God as my witness. He shall be the arbiter between you and me, and who else has the knowledge of the Book?" (43)

ABRAHAM (14)

In the Name of God, Most Merciful, and Most Beneficent.

A, L, R. A Book We revealed to you so you may take people out from darkness into the light, and guide them with their Lord's permission to the straight path that belongs to Him, the exalted to whom thanks are due. (1)

God to whom belongs all that is in the heavens and on the earth. The unbelievers shall be afflicted with severe torture. (2)

Those who find this life preferable to the Last Day, and reject the way of God while going after this life abnormally, those are deep in their misguidedness. (3)

We never sent an apostle who did not approach his people using their native tongue to explain things to them. God may misguide whomever He wishes while He may guide whomever He wants; He is the Exalted and Wise. (4)

In our verses that We sent to Moses: "Take your people out of the darkness into the light and remind them of the days when God specially selected them for His bounty" and in that there are signs for those who are patient and grateful. (5)

When Moses said to his people: "Remember God's blessing which He bestowed upon you as He saved you from the Pharaoh and his people who were dealing to you the worst in persecution and torture, slaughtering your children and violating your women, in which there was great misfortune from your Lord," (6)

Your Lord has decreed that He will increase His bounty to you if you are thankful and if you disbelieve, His torture shall be severe. (7)

Moses said: "If you all disbelieve, and with you every one on earth, God shall remain unaffected and indifferent to lack of gratefulness. (8)

Did you not get the news of those people before you, the people of Noah and those of Aad and Thamud, and those who came after them, some of whom only God knows about? They had their messengers who brought them veritable signs, yet with their hands on their mouths, they indicated to those messengers that they should remain silent, and they disbelieved all that was sent to them, and indicated that they have strong doubts in regard to what they are being asked to believe. (9)

Their messengers said to them: 'How could you ever doubt God, the Creator of the heaven and the earth who is inviting you to be forgiven for your sins, and prolong your life for a while?'" They responded: "You are nothing but humans like us, wanting to drive us away from what our fathers worshiped; you will need to show us a powerful demonstration." (10)

The messengers said: "We are none but humans like you. We cannot provide anything more powerful than what God provides us with, although God sometimes does provide for His worshipers, and the believers always rely on God. (11)

We have no choice but to rely on God after He showed us the way, and we shall be patient with any harm that may come to us from you, and on God all shall rely." (12)

The unbelievers said to their messengers: "We shall drive you out unless you return to our religion," and their Lord told them: We shall annihilate the transgressors. (13)

You shall inhabit the earth after they are gone, for this is the reward of those who fear my position and fear my warning. (14)

They succeeded, while all stubborn despots failed. (15)

Hell is awaiting him ahead, and he shall be drinking water from his own body juices, (16)

drinking while he is hating it, while death is all around him and he will not die, and heavy torture awaits him. (17)

The earnings of those who disbelieved are like the ashes in the middle of a strong wind, on a stormy day; they shall get nothing from them, for that is how one can be far misguided. (18)

Do you not see that God who truly created the heavens and the earth can get rid of you and bring a new creation, (19)

and this is not that hard for God. (20)

And as they all become exposed before God, the weak followers ask the arrogant who they followed, are you going to help us and protect us from God's torture, and they will say, we would have guided you if God guided us, but whether we are afraid or patient, we will have no escape. (21)

On the day of reckoning, the Devil will say God's promise to you was true, while I have violated my promise to you. I had no authority over you except asking you and you responded; do not blame me but blame yourselves. I cannot save you and you cannot save me. I disbelieved like you did, and an excruciating torture awaits the transgressors. (22)

Those who believed and did good deeds were entered gardens under which flows rivers. There they shall be immortalized by the will of their Lord, and shall receive salutations of peace. (23)

Did you see how God brought the example of a nice word being the same as a good tree whose roots are stable in the ground and it branches point up to the sky. (24)

It brings out its fruits periodically by the will of God, and God brings examples for people as a reminder. (25)

The other example is that of a malicious word which is like a malicious tree which has its roots creeping above the ground, with no depth or stability. (26)

God lets the believers prove their worth with straight and stable talk in this life and in the next, while He misleads the transgressors, and God does whatever He wants. (27)

Did you not see those who replaced God's blessings with disbelieving and brought destruction on themselves and their people? (28)

They shall be the fuel of the hellfire, and it is a deserved ending indeed. (29)

They made partners for God, to misguide away from Him. Say enjoy yourselves, for your destiny is in hell. (30)

Tell my worshipers who believe, to attend to their prayers and spend in charity from what we blessed them with, overtly and in covert, before a day will come when there is no trade or ransom. (31)

God who created the heavens and the earth, and brought down water which makes crops grow a bounty for you, and gave you the ships with which to ride the oceans, and gave you the use of rivers. (32)

He also provided the sun and the moon alternating, and gave you the day and night. (33)

He brought you everything you may ask for, and if you try to count the blessings of God you shall find the count to exceed your ability to complete. Man is an ungrateful transgressor. (34)

And Abraham said: "My Lord, make this town safe and protect me and my children from worshiping idols. (35)

Idols have misguided many people. Those who follow me belong to me and those who do not will find You Forgiving and Merciful. (36)

My Lord, I have placed members of my family in an arid valley, next to your sacred house, so that they can attend to their prayers my Lord. I beseech you to warm the hearts of people towards them, and bless them with fruits so they may be hopefully grateful. (37)

Our Lord, you are aware of all we hide and declare. Nothing is hidden from God, on earth or in heavens. (38)

Thanks to God who granted me at an old age, Ishmael and Isaac. My Lord listens to prayers. (39)

My Lord, help me be attentive to my prayers, and help my descendents to do the same, and answer our prayers. (40)

My Lord, forgive me, forgive my parents, and the believers on the Day of Reckoning. (41)

Do not ever think that God is unaware of the deeds of the transgressors. God delays their reckoning until the day when the eyes widen with horror. (42)

They will be hurrying with their heads turned upward, cannot blink their eyelids, and with their hearts fluttering." (43)

Warn the people, that as the torture comes near, the transgressors will say: "Give us a short reprieve and we shall respond to your call and follow the messengers," and they are asked: Did you not say that you will always be as you were? (44)

You even resided where other transgressors against themselves resided, even as We were telling you what We did to them, and gave you examples. (45)

They deceived and God had their deception in hand, even as their deception was enough to make the mountains bend. (46)

Do not ever think that God will ever forget what He promised His messengers. God is Exalted and Revengeful. (47)

The day the earth is replaced with another and the heavens, and all are brought up before God, the One, the Defeater. (48)

You shall see the transgressors that day huddled together in their chains, (49)

their clothes made of tar and their faces on fire. (50)

God will punish those who earned such. God is fast in His reckoning. (51)

This is a declaration for the people to be warned, and to know it is he the One God, and those who have knowledge better remember. (52)

THE ROCK DWELLINGS (15)

In the Name of God, Most Merciful, and Most Beneficent.

Alef, Lam, Raah; these were verses of the Book, and a veritable Koran. (1)

It is probable that someday the unbelievers may wish they were Moslems. (2)

Let them eat and enjoy and delude themselves with false hopes, for they shall find out. (3)

We have never annhilated a village unless their predetermined day had come. (4)

No nation will have a reprieve beyond their fixed date or earlier. (5)

They accused him, he *(the apostle)* who received the "Mention" *(the read words of the Book)*: "You are crazy." (6)

They said: "Why do you not bring down the angels to testify for you, if you are truthful?" (7)

We would not bring the angels down, unless Our Judgement has already been made, and then they will have no chance of getting our attention. (8)

We have revealed the Mention *(the read word of the Koran)* and We shall preserve it *(for accuracy)*. (9)

Before you, We sent warnings to older generations. (10)

And they continue to mock every messenger they are sent. (11)

This is how We instill doubt in the heart of the criminals. (12)

They do not believe even after they saw what happened to the generations that disappeared before them. (13)

Even if We opened for them a door in heaven that they start climbing through (14)

they will nevertheless be saying: Our vision is blocked, we are under the effect of magic. (15)

We made towers in the sky and we decorated them for those who enjoy the view (16)

and preserved them from the cursed devils who want to destroy them (17)

and those who listen carefully shall also witness the spectacular falling star. (18)

The Earth, We spread it and put on it the mountain peaks. We brought on it all kinds of balanced vegetation. (19)

We have provided you with the means to make a living; who can make a living without us? (20)

We have the keys for all riches, which we dispense in certain amounts. (21)

We send the wind as a vehicle for fertilization, while we bring water down from the sky for you to drink while the originating stores for it cannot be under your control. (22)

We are the ones who bring life and death, and we are the eventual inheritors. (23)

We are familiar with those who came before you and those who followed you. (24)

Your Lord shall assemble all of them to His presence, He is Knowledgeable and Wise. (25)

We made man from solid dust, derived from smoothed and dried out mud. (26)

The jinn we created from the flames of poisonous substances. (27)

As your Lord told the angels: I am creating humans from solid dust derived from smoothed out and dried mud (28)

And as I create him and instill My spirit in him, I want all of you to prostrate yourselves in front of him. (29)

All of the angels fell down in front of Him. (30)

Except for the Devil who refused to prostrate himself. (31)

He (*God*) said: What about you? Why do you not prostrate yourself? (32)

He (*the Devil*) said: "I will never prostrate myself to a human you created from solid dust, derived from smoothed out and dried mud." (33)

He (*God*) said: Leave heaven, you are cursed. (34)

My curse will be on you until the Day of Judgement. (35)

He (*the Devil*) said: "My Lord give me a reprieve till the day of resurrection." (36)

He (*God*) said: You have the reprieve (37)

until the fixed day. (38)

He (*the Devil*) said: "Just like you misguided me, I will entice and misguide all of them (39)

except those who are faithful to you." (40)

He (*God*) said: This is the straight path. (41)

You have no control on my worshipers, except for those who may follow you among the misguided. (42)

And hell is a date for all of them. (43)

It (*hell*) will have seven doors, and an entrance for each is predefined. (44)

The pious will be in gardens with fountains. (45)

Enter it with peace and safety. (46)

We shall remove any proclivity for animosity in their hearts, and make them brothers, reclining on beds, opposite each other. (47)

They will not be touched by harm, nor can they be forced out. (48)

Tell my worshipers that I am the Forgiving and the Merciful. (49)

And my torture is an excruciating torture. (50)

Tell them about the guests of Abraham. (51)

They entered on him (*Abraham*) and said: "Peace be upon you," and he (*Abraham*) said: "I am actually afraid of you." (52)

They said: "Do not be afraid, for we are here to bring you good tidings of an intelligent boy." (53)

He (*Abraham*) said: "Are you bringing me tidings of what I am too old to have?" (54)

They told him: "We are bringing you the truth, do not lose hope. (55)

Only the misguided lose hope in their Lord's mercy." (56)

He then said: "What other messages did you come with?" (57)

They said: "We have been sent to people who are criminal (58)

except for the family of Lot, who will all be saved (59)

except for his wife who shall be gone." (60)

The messengers reached the family of Lot. (61)

And Lot (*seeing they are all handsome young boys*) said: "You are wicked people." (62)

They said: "No, we came to make you aware of what all the others were doing." (63)

They said: "We are relaying to you God's judgement and telling you the truth. (64)

Inform your family secretly late at night. Get them out and follow them, and none of you should look back, but rather go where you are ordered." (65)

They also told him that the rest of his tribe shall not go past the morning. (66)

People of the town came to him, happy upon seeing his guests. (67)

He said: "Those are my guests, do not disgrace me. (68)

Fear God and do not dishonor me." (69)

They said: "Did we not tell you not to have guests, and that you need to stay away from the rest of the world?" (70)

He said: "Here are my daughters, take them instead if you have to." (71)

He (*God*) said: I assure you, they are totally immersed in their being misguided. (72)

By sunrise they were taken by a loud cry. (73)

Everything was turned upside down, and We rained upon them stones from hell. (74)

These are examples for the believers who care. (75)

It is the straight path. (76)

And in that there is an example for the believers. (77)

People of the forest (*with the winding trees*) were also transgressors. (78)

And Our revenge was also a clear example. (79)

The rock dwellers also denied Our messengers. (80)

We brought them Our verses which they also shunned. (81)

They dug in mountain rock their homes for safety. (82)

They were also taken with a cry at sunrise. (83)

All their efforts did nothing for them. (84)

We created the heavens and the earth, and what is in between them; a symbol of the truth. The Last Day is coming. Resort to cheerful forgiveness. (85)

Your Lord is the Knowledgeable Creator. (86)

We brought you the seven riddles and the great Koran. (87)

Do not desire what We gave them for their enjoyment and the enjoyment of their spouses, do not be sad for them, and expose your soft side to them. (88)

Say: "I am the clear carrier of warnings" (89)

as We revealed the message to some who were dividers. (90)

Those are the ones who divided the Koran (*believing in some of it and not the rest*). (91)

By your Lord We shall ask all of them. (92)

About what they have been doing. (93)

So do what you are ordered, and stay away from those associaters. (94)

We have protected you from those who mocked you. (95)

Those who claim an additional God with God, shall find out. (96)

We know that what they say is upsetting to you. (97)

So praise and glorify your Lord, and be among those who prostrate themselves. (98)

And worship your Lord, so that you will be granted certainty. (99)

THE BEES (16)

In the Name of God, Most Merciful, and Most Beneficent.

God's will is already expressed, and there is no reason to hurry it on. The Glorious and Exalted God is far above their associating others with Him. (1)

He sends the angels with His spirit, by his command, to whomever He wants, so that they are warned that there is no God but Myself, so be righteous. (2)

He created the heavens and the earth as the supreme truth, and He is exalted over those who associate others with Him. (3)

God created man from a sperm, yet he is suddenly combative and audacious. (4)

He created cattle for you, and from them you derive warmth, make a living and from it you eat. (5)

Is it not wonderful when you bring your cattle in, and then take them out to pasture, the next day? (6)

They even carry your loads and make it possible for you to travel to places where you would have made it, otherwise, only with extreme difficulty. (7)

Horses, mules, and donkeys were provided for you to ride and to show off, and God creates what you do not know. (8)

God defines the right path, which some do not follow, and if God wanted He would have guided all of you. (9)

He is the One who brings water down for you to drink, and vegetation for feeding your cattle. (10)

The water brings up vegetation, olives, palm trees, and grapes and all other fruits. It is in this that there are examples for those with intellect. (11)

He provided you with the night and day, the sun, the moon and the stars. All move by His order, and in it also there is an example for those who have sense. (12)

All that He got together for you on earth of different colors and uses are things that serve as examples for those who can remember. (13)

He is the One who provided you with the sea, from where you get fresh meat, and get ornaments and jewelry that you wear. Ships also go through it, providing for you so you may be grateful. (14)

Mountains were set and anchored firmly on the earth so that they do not move under you, in addition to paths and rivers so that you may be guided. (15)

They use landmarks and the stars to find their way. (16)

Is He who creates the same as he who cannot create? It is a question of which you need to be reminded. (17)

If you try to enumerate the blessings of God, you shall find that hard to do. God is Forgiving and Merciful. (18)

God knows what you hide and you declare. (19)

What they worship other than God cannot create a thing, while they, themselves have been created. (20)

They (*the idols*) are dead with no life, and have no feelings, nor will they ever be resurrected. (21)

Your God is the One God, and those who do not believe in the Last Day. Their hearts are full with denial and they are arrogant. (22)

They are indifferent to the fact that God knows what they hide and declare and that He hates those who are arrogant. (23)

If they are asked: "What did your Lord reveal?" they answer: "He brought us the legends of the past." (24)

They shall be responsible for their own offenses and the offenses of those who follow them unknowingly. It is evil what they do. (25)

Those before them who resorted to deception, God discovered their intentions and the roots of those intentions, and the ceiling collapsed over them and directed the torture at them from where they would not expect. (26)

Then on the Day of Judgement He shall bring them shame and ask: Where are those you used to depend on, and associate with me? Then those who were given knowledge shall declare: "Today is the day for shame and real harm shall touch the unbelievers." (27)

Those who the angels will retrieve upon their death, after they have sinned against themselves, will try to say: "We have done nothing wrong;" yet God is knowledgeable with what they do. (28)

Enter the doors of hell, where you will be immortalized; a suitable ending for the arrogant. (29)

If the righteous were asked: "What did your Lord reveal?" They will answer: "Only good to those who did good things for this life and for the life to come, and blessed is the home of the righteous." (30)

They shall enter gardens of Eden, below which rivers run and where they will get what they desire. This is how God rewards the righteous. (31)

Those are the ones who will be retrieved by the angels upon death in a clean condition and will be told: "Welcome, enter the paradise as a reward for what you have been doing." (32)

Some pay no attention until the angels arrive, with the order of your Lord. Many before them did the same thing. God was never unfair to them, they were unfair to themselves. (33)

They received the results of their sins, and what they were mocking has just caught up with them. (34)

Those who associated others with God say: "If God wanted otherwise neither we nor our fathers would have associated anyone with Him nor would we have forbidden anything without His will." People who came before them did the same things. Did they think that apostles are expected to do anything but relay a clear warning? (35)

To all nations We sent apostles. They were told to worship God and avoid the Devil. Some of them God guided and some of them earned misguidance. Go around this earth and see how those who denied ended. (36)

Regardless of how much you like to see them guided, God will not guide those who He has already misguided. (37)

They swear heavily using the name of God claiming that God will never resurrect anyone after death. He will, it is a solemn promise, but many do not know. (38)

He shall show them what they have been arguing about and the unbelievers shall be shown to be liars. (39)

If We wished something to happen, all We need to say is: Be and it shall. (40)

Those who had to emigrate to avoid persecution can be predicted to do well in this life, and even better in the life to come, if they only knew. (41)

Those who are patient rely on their Lord. (42)

We sent before men to whom We made revelations, you can check with those who are familiar with the Mention (*the reading of the Koran*) if you want to know. (43)

With clear signs and books and the Mention which we revealed to you, people have clear signs of what was revealed to them if they want to ponder over them. (44)

Do those who engage in deception feel safe from God collapsing the earth under them, and sending them His torture from where they will not expect? (45)

He can take them while they are traveling, for they cannot make it difficult for Him. (46)

Or He can take them while they are terrorized, but God is Considerate and Merciful. (47)

Did they not see that everything God created casts a shadow, right and left (*morning and evening*) that they seek when they prostrate themselves for Him in obedience? (48)

All that is in heaven and on earth, of beasts or angels, kneel before God without arrogance. (49)

They are afraid of their Lord above them (*their master*), and do what they are told. (50)

God said: Do not adopt two gods, God is One and it is Me who you should be afraid of. (51)

To God belongs what is in the heavens and on earth, and religion belongs to Him always. Can righteousness be directed to anyone but God? (52)

Any blessings you have comes from God, and then if you are touched by harm, you resort to Him. (53)

Then if He protected you from harm, a group of you associate others with Him. (54)

They disbelieve what We gave them. Enjoy it for you shall find out. (55)

They assign to what they know nothing about (*such as their idols*) a portion of what God gave them. You shall answer to God on what you have fabricated. (56)

They give their daughter to God while they keep what they like. (57)

And if one of them was given the tidings of the birth of a female, the unhappiness becomes evident in his face, with his anger. (58)

Such a person would disappear from his people as his unhappiness takes hold of him, and starts wondering whether he should hold on to her or bury her in the earth. Evil are their choices. (59)

As to the unbelievers, these men are the perfect example for evil. Those who will meet God are those who provide the highest of examples. He is Exalted and Wise. (60)

If God was to punish people adequately for their transgressions, He would have left nothing living on earth, but He does grant reprieve for a limited time, but when that time is there nothing can change it to an hour earlier or later. (61)

They ascribe to God that which they do not like, while their tongues falsely ascribe that which is good to themselves, not bothered by the fact that the fire of hell is what belongs to them, and that they will be gone. (62)

In God's name We sent to many nations before you revelations, but they got seduced by the Devil who inspired their actions. He is their sponsor and they shall face an excruciating torture. (63)

We revealed the Book to you only to help them understand what they do not; guidance from God and an act of mercy to those who believe. (64)

God brings down from the sky water with which land is brought back alive after it was dead, and in this there is an example for those who hear. (65)

In livestock there is another learning example. From their bellies where there is blood and urine We give you clean and clear milk for the drinkers. (66)

And from the fruits of palm and vine you make sugar and earn a living, and in this also there is a lesson for those who use their head. (67)

Your Lord also inspired the bees to live in houses, in mountains and trees. Houses they built themselves. (68)

Then He told them to eat of all fruits, and follow the path of their God, so that from their bellies comes out a drink of different colors that is beneficial for people, and in this there is an example for those who think. (69)

God created you and He shall make you die, and some of you may revert to the worst of lives when he may lose what he had learned. God is Knowledgeable and Able. (70)

God has favored some with His bounty, yet why do they not also favor the slaves that belong to them, for the bounty is supposed to benefit them equally? Do they not fail to appreciate God's favor? (71)

God made you spouses who came from among you, then He gave you children and grandchildren and bestowed upon you further from His bounty. Yet they believe in falsehoods and disbelieve in the blessings of God. (72)

As an alternative to God, they worship what can provide them no bounty from the heavens or the earth, for they have none. (73)

So do not try to bring examples to God, for He knows and you do not. (74)

God brings the example of an owned slave who is capable of very few things on his own and of a person who received a lot of Our bounty and from which he spends overtly and covertly. Can they be considered equal? Thanks to God it is clear they are not. But most of them do not know. (75)

God will also bring the example of two men; one is dumb, helpless, unable to produce results wherever he is directed. Can he be compared to another who effectively spreads justice and always walks the straight path? (76)

To God belong the secrets of the heavens and earth. The Final Hour is as close as a twinkle of the eye or, even closer. God is Capable of all things. (77)

God extracted you from the bellies of your mothers knowing nothing, and gave you hearing, sight and hearts, so you may be grateful. (78)

Do they not see the birds flying in the sky, rising by God's will only? Is there not in this lessons for those who believe? (79)

God made for you houses in which to dwell, and from the skins of cattle He made for you temporary dwellings that you can carry with you, and from its wool, fur and hair, clothes that will cover you for a while. (80)

God gave you a shade from what He created for you, and He gave you in the mountains places you can seek protection, clothes that protect from heat and some that protect you from cold, and even some that give you protection from attack, so that you may submit. (81)

If they refuse all you can do is explain and warn. (82)

They know the blessing of God then they deny it. Most of them are unbelievers. (83)

The day is coming when on every nation We call a witness and then they have no excuse, nor could they complain. (84)

When the transgressors see the torture, it will not be ameliorated for them nor should they ever receive another consideration. (85)

The unbelievers shall meet their associates who they associated with or worshiped instead of God and they will say: "God these are the ones who induced us and their associates (*idols*) themselves will call them liars." (86)

And as they declare submission, their own associates shall turn away from them. (87)

The unbelievers who pushed others away from the path of God, We shall increase their torture over and above that of others because of the corruption they spread. (88)

The day We have a witness on every nation from among them, you shall be a witness on those unbelievers. We have sent you the Book to clarify everything, and also guidance, mercy and good tidings to the Moslems. (89)

God orders justice and charity to the relatives, and warns against indecency, evil and the spreading of oppression. He warns you in case you may heed His warning. (90)

Fulfill what you took an oath on, and do not violate a sworn promise after you take it, for you have made God your Guarantor and God knows what you do. (91)

Do not be like she who will unravel the threads that she has spun and violate treaties you make, and swear to, among nations upon one feeling stronger than the other. God will test you and then show you on the Day of Judgement the right on what you were having differences on. (92)

If God desired, He would have made you into one nation. But He misguides whomever He wishes and He guides whomever He wishes. You shall be interrogated in regard to what you did. (93)

Do not ever use swearing an oath in deception and let your foot slip after it was steadied, which will let you taste the hurt as much as you managed to deceive and thus deviate away from the path of God, and then become deserving of a stern punishment. (94)

Do not sell a pact with God for a cheap reward. God's reward is better for you if you know. (95)

What you have shall be exhausted, but what God has is inexhaustible, and We shall reward those who adhere to patience with much more than they thought they may get. (96)

He or she who does good, and is a believer, shall have a good life and shall be rewarded with what is appropriate for the best of their deeds. (97)

When you read the Koran seek God's help against the cursed Devil. (98)

For he has no power over those who believe and who rely on God. (99)

His power is over those who take him as a sponsor and those who associate him with God. (100)

When We replaced one verse with another, and God is the most knowledgeable with what He reveals, they claimed that you are not truthful. It is they who have no knowledge. (101)

Say: "It was a change that came through the holy spirit (*Gabriel*) in support of the believers and guidance and good tidings to Moslems." (102)

We knew that they said a human is teaching him (*the Apostle*). The human they are referring to is not even an Arab, while this book is in a clear and distinguished Arabic tongue. (103)

Those who do not believe in God's verses, God shall not guide them and awaits them an excruciating torture. (104)

The unbelievers are the ones fabricating the lies, and they are the liars. (105)

There are those who disbelieve after belief, when forced while their heart is comfortable with belief, and there are those who are open to and comfortable with renouncing their belief. The second group are those who earned the wrath of God, and awaiting them is a great torture. (106)

They have chose this life over that of the thereafter, and God does not guide the unbelievers. (107)

They are the ones whose hearts were stamped by God, and so was their hearing and sight, and they are the ones who do not heed. (108)

No wonder that on the Last Day they are the losers. (109)

Your Lord is Forgiving and Merciful with those who were forced to leave their homes and then struggled and persevered. (110)

This will occur on the day when each soul will have to fend for itself, and shall pay for what is owed on its actions, and none shall be unjustly treated. (111)

God's example is the village that was safe contented, receiving and blessed with bounty from everywhere, until its people disbelieved and failed to appreciate the blessings of God, and God made them taste hunger and fear for what they did. (112)

They were sent an apostle from among them, they denied him, they were afflicted with torture, and they were the transgressors. (113)

Eat from God's bounty, which is lawful, and be thankful for God's blessing upon you, if you are worshiping him. (114)

You are forbidden from eating carcasses, blood and the flesh of the pig and any flesh consecrated to a name other than the name of God, unless you become constrained with no intention of disobeying, for God is Forgiving and Merciful. (115)

Do not say this is lawful and this is forbidden falsely, falsifying the word of God. Those who falsify God's word shall not succeed. (116)

They may succeed for a short while then comes an excruciating torture. (117)

To the Jews, We have forbade what We did to you. We never treated them unjustly, but unjustly they treated themselves. (118)

With you Lord, those who transgressed with ignorance, then repented and corrected afterwards, your Lord is Forgiving and Merciful. (119)

Abraham was a leader, and faithful, and was never an idolater. (120)

He was thankful for His blessings and God chose him and guided him to the straight path. (121)

We rewarded him in this life, and in the next he is one of the righteous. (122)

Then We revealed to you to follow the creed of Abraham, for he never associated anyone with God. (123)

The Sabbath was ordered only for those who were in a dispute about it. Your Lord shall end their dispute on the Day of Judgement. (124)

Call to the pass of your Lord with wisdom and gentle persuasion. Your Lord is more Knowledgeable with those who lost the way and those who are guided. (125)

If you punish, do it in proportion to the affront, and if you hold off, it is better for those who do. (126)

Be patient for your patience is directed only towards God. Do not feel sorry for them, and do not let their deception bother you. (127)

God always supports those who are righteous and those who are charitable. (128)

THE JOURNEY (17)

In the Name of God, Most Merciful, and Most Beneficent.

Glory is His, He who sent His servant, at night, from the Sacred Mosque, to the far mosque, whose proximity We have blessed, to show Him some of our signs. He listens to all and sees everything. (1)

We revealed the Book to Moses, as guidance to the people of Israel, warning them to not take some one else to rely on. (2)

You are the descendents of those who were carried with Noah in the Ark. He was a thankful servant. (3)

We relayed our judgement to the people of Israel in the Book, that twice you have spread corruption in the land with achieving great heights. (4)

As the realization of the first became evident, We sent on you servants of Ours who were ruthless and who destroyed the land and fulfilled the promise of the threat that was made to you. (5)

Then We went again and granted you victory over them and blessed you with riches and children, and made you increase numerically. (6)

You were told that if you do good, you do it to yourself and if you do evil it shall afflict you. And as the threat of the second transgression comes due, your enemies shall again enter your temple and destroy anything they lay their hands on. (7)

Yet, you may hope that God be merciful, but if you return to your old ways, God shall be back also. We made hell a concentration for the unbelievers. (8)

This Koran is intended to guide to what is more just, and to bring good tidings to the believers who do good works, of the great compensation that awaits them. (9)

And for those who do not believe in the Last Day, we prepared an excruciating torture. (10)

Man is likely to pray asking for evil, as much as he prays asking for good. Man has always lacked patience. (11)

We made the night and day the two wonders, and while We made the night covered by darkness We made the day full of light, a gift from your Lord to make a living, learn how to count the years and other forms of calculation, and We revealed the details of many things elaborately. (12)

And for each man We made a record that he carries around his neck, which We shall bring out for him on the Day of Judgement plainly published for him to confront. (13)

Read your record yourself, for you shall answer to what it contains. (14)

He who was properly guided shall benefit himself, and he who went astray shall answer for himself. No one will ever answer for the actions of another and no people will be punished until a messenger was sent to warn them. (15)

If We decided to bring a community to an end, We rely on the rich among them to spread corruption, and then they earn the devastation We send upon them. (16)

Look at how many people We caused to perish since Noah. It suffices to say your Lord is well aware and mindful of the sins of His servants. (17)

He who is anxious to receive everything fast We may provide for him what We will, but then awaits him the fire of hell which shall consume him while defeated and disgraced. (18)

And he who wants the life next and made the effort it requires in good faith is among those whose efforts will be appreciated. (19)

Both shall be given, from your God, what they were working toward, and what your Lord gives cannot be denied. (20)

Look how We favored some over others, and favors of the life next are higher and more distinctive. (21)

Do not associate God with other gods, for you shall be left in disgrace and frustration. (22)

Your Lord has decreed that you worship none but Him, and that you be kind to your parents, and if one or both of them become old that you do not ever show them exasperation or disrespect or address them impolitely. (23)

Always show them your humble side, out of compassion, and say: "Lord, be compassionate with them as they were with me when I was small." (24)

Your Lord is quite Knowledgeable as to what is in your hearts if you are good intentioned for He always forgives those who return to the right path. (25)

Be charitable with your near of kin as they deserve and also to the destitute and the transient and avoid waste. (26)

For the wasteful is next of kin to the Devil and the Devil is always ungrateful to God. (27)

If unable to assist while waiting for help from God, be kind to them. (28)

Let your hand not be tightly held to your neck, nor let it be extended all the way until you are left in need and desperate. (29)

Your Lord extends his bounty freely to whom He wishes while sparingly to others for on His servants He is an expert and a keen observer, (30)

Do not ever kill your offspring in fear of poverty and want. We provide for you and them. Killing them is a huge sin. (31)

Do not be drawn to adultery for it is indecent and misguided. (32)

Do not ever kill a soul except in justice, and in an unjust killing, the guardian of the killed shall have satisfaction and control on the life of the killer. Let that satisfaction not be excessively on the side of killing, for the injustice was already avenged. (33)

Keep away from the property of the orphans, except in what is fair and permissible, until they are old enough to take care of it themselves. Fulfill your promises for promises are binding. (34)

Be exact in measuring and weighing, for that is better for your own sake. (35)

Do not take positions on what you have no full knowlege, for hearing, seeing and feeling are all parts of what you shall be held responsible for. (36)

Do not work on earth, so proud of yourself, for your feet will not make holes in the earth nor will your height give competion to the mountain peaks. (37)

Such behavior has always been a hated sin in the eyes of God. (38)

This is a part of what your Lord has revealed to you in wisdom. Do not make another god with Him, unless you want to be thrown in hell, guilty and defeated. (39)

Are you claiming that your Lord gave you sons while He took daughters for Himself from among the angels? This is none but a great blasphemy. (40)

We included so many details in this Koran to remind them, yet they appear to move more and more away. (41)

Say: "If there were other gods, as they claim, those would have tried to compete with Him and get to Him." (42)

So Glorified and Exalted He is that He is far above their claims. (43)

The seven heavens and the earth and what is on them, all glorify Him and sing His praise but they do not understand their singing. He is Beneficent and Forgiving. (44)

When you read the Koran, we place between you, the unbelievers, an unseen partition. (45)

We surrounded their hearts with a membrane that will inhibit their ability to understand it, while obstructing their ears from hearing it, and even the mention of God in the Koran by itself is enough to make them turn their back and run away. (46)

We know better what really happens when they listen to you. For after they are by themselves, the transgressors say: "You are only listening to a man who is possessed." (47)

Look at them when they tried to create for you their own examples, and it became apparent that they were lost, and that they knew not what they were talking about. (48)

They said: "Are you saying that after we become bones and dust we shall come back like a new creation?" (49)

Say: "Yes, even if you became rocks and iron." (50)

Or starting from any portion of you that may exist inside you, they will ask: "Who will bring us back?" Say: "He who made you to start with." They will shake their heads and say: "When?" And you say: "It may be very soon." (51)

The day He will call you and you will respond by His power, and you will think you were out but for a short time. (52)

Tell my worshipers to talk kindly, for the Devil creates divisiveness among them. The Devil has always been man's greatest enemy. (53)

Your Lord knows you the best. He will forgive you if He so desires and He shall punish you if He wishes, and We did not send you as a guardian over them. (54)

Your Lord is more Knowledgeable in what is in the heavens and on earth. We have favored some of the prophets over others, and to David we gave the Psalms. (55)

Say: "Call those who you claim to be gods other than Him, and you shall find that they are incapable of protecting you from harm or producing any change." (56)

In fact, those to whom they pray themselves would want to be closer to God and compete in trying to be closer to God, and seek His mercy and are afraid of His torture. Your Lord's torture is certainly to be avoided. (57)

At one point or another, before the Day of Judgement, all towns shall be visited by destruction or punished with severe torture. It is all decreed in the Book. (58)

Nothing prevented us from sending signs that will verify the warnings but the ancient people did not believe them anyway, just as We did with Thamoud when We brought them the she-camel as a clear visible sign and they transgressed by laying their hands upon her. We tend to provide signs only as a way of warning. (59)

We told you that your Lord has control over all people. We made the vision that we showed you (*the night of your journey*) and the tree that was cursed in the Koran (*the Zakkoum tree*), all as warnings, and all did nothing to decrease their transgressions. (60)

As We told the angels to prostrate themselves in front of Adam, they all did except for Satan, who said: "You want me to prostrate myself to one you created from mud." (61)

He said: "This one who you favored over me, if you give me time until the Day of Judgement, I shall show you that I will take control of and misguide most of his decendents." (62)

God said: Go, whoever follows you, and you will have hell as your reward. A suitable reward indeed. (63)

Try to instigate who you can among them, and control them with your voice, your power and the power of your followers, and share with them their riches and their descendents, and promise them whatever, for the promises of Satan are only deception. (64)

On my worshipers you shall have no power, as God will be all the guardian they need. (65)

Your Lord who made possible for you the use of navigation for sea travel in order to make a living, He was Merciful upon you. (66)

If you become in danger while sea traveling, you forget about all those you pray for, except Him, and then when He saves you, you return to your old habits. Man has always been ungrateful. (67)

Do you not think that as you start feeling safe on land, the rocks you are hanging on can fall in the ocean, or the land you are on can be hit with a storm and find you missing a guardian again. (68)

Or did you feel so safe that you did not consider that on another occasion a storm may hit you and get you to drown and die an unbelievers, and lose the opportunity to ever become His follower again. (69)

We certainly favored the descendents of Adam and enabled them to move on land and at sea, and bestowed upon them the best of Our bounty, and gave them preference over others of Our creations. (70)

The day when We call all people with their records with them and those who are handed their records in their right hands shall be able to read them and shall not be wronged a hair. (71)

While those who are unable to read their records are blind then, just as they were in the previous life and lost their way. (72)

They just about misled you away from what We revealed to you, so that you may lie and replace what We gave you with something else, and then you may have become their closest friend. (73)

And if We did not strengthen you, you were about to become somewhat comfortable with them. (74)

If that were to happen you would have received double the punishment in this life and double the punishment in the next life and you would have found no protector from Our wrath. (75)

They nearly succeeded in enticing you to leave your land and if they had succeeded they would have not survived much time past your departure. (76)

Our interference was according to precedents we established with other apostles before you, and Our precedents do not change. (77)

Recite your prayer at sunset and again as the night supervenes, and then again at sunrise. Reading the Koran at sunrise is a witnessed event. (78)

During the night you may also pray if you want your Lord to exalt you to an even higher status. (79)

Say: "My lord, let my exit be for the truth and my entrance be for the truth and grant me from Your power an ally." (80)

Also say: "The truth has come and falsehoods are defeated, for a falsehood is destined to defeat." (81)

Some of what We revealed in the Koran is healing and compassionate for the believers, and provides nothing to the transgressors except defeat. (82)

If We bestowed our bounty upon humans, they seem to draw away, and if they are touched by evil, they seem to become despondent. (83)

Say: "Each will react the way he is, for your God knows whose reaction is more appropriate." (84)

They ask you about the Spirit, say: It is in the realm of God's knowledge, and of all knowledge you were given but a small tiny portion. (85)

If We wished We can make all that We revealed to you disappear and you will find no one that can vouch for you with us (86)

except for your Lord's compassion, and His favors upon you have been enormous. (87)

Say: "If all the people and Jinn got together to produce something akin to the Koran they will fail even if they all helped each other." (88)

We revealed in this Koran examples representing all walks of life, but most people remain unbelievers. (89)

They said: "We shall not believe in you until you produce for us a spring of water from the ground (90)

or until you have a paradise of pine trees and vines and with water springs starting to burst from the ground among them (91)

or until you make the sky fall upon us in pieces as you threatened or until you bring God and the angels to meet us (92) or until you own a house in the sky made of gold and jewels or until you ascend to heaven, and we will not believe you ascended until you bring us back a book that we can read." Say: "Glorified be my Lord, am I anything but a human messenger." (93)

The only thing that seems to prevent humans from accepting guidance as it is sent to them, is their questioning of how could God send them a human as a messenger. (94)

Say: "If the earth was full with angels walking on it, we would have sent them an angel as an apostle." (95)

Say: "All I need is God as my witness between me and you. He has always had the full knowledge and the experience with His servants." (96)

He who God guides shall be guided and who is not guided by God shall find no sponsors. We shall bring them together on the Day of Judgement: dragged on their faces, blind deaf and dumb, their dwelling is hell, and as the flames die down We induce them to get stronger and hotter. (97)

Their punishment was earned by having disbelieved our verses and they did not believe that they can be resurrected after they are nothing but bones and remains, into a new creation. (98)

Did they not see that God who created the heavens and the earth is capable of creating them again and gave them a predetermined age, but the transgressors always are unbelievers. (99)

Say: "If you owned all the stores of God's mercy, you would have hoarded it and became afraid of dispensing it. Humans have always been stingy." (100)

We provided Moses with nine signs clearly demonstrated, yet ask the Israelites what happened when he appeared in front of them when the Pharaoh said to Moses: "I think you are a magician." (101)

Moses said: "You Pharaoh, no one more than you fully knows that these signs could have come from none but the Lord of the universe. I think you are doomed." (102)

The Pharaoh tried to intimidate them out of their land and We drowned him along with every one with him. (103)

We said to the Israelites: "Dwell in this land, and on the Day of Judgement I shall bring you together." (104)

We revealed it as the truth and it came down as the truth. We sent you only as a messenger and to give warning. (105)

The Koran is arranged so that you can read it to them in a logical sequence, and We revealed it gradually. (106)

Say: "Believe in it or do not believe in it." Those who are truly knowledgeable in what came before it, when it is recited in their presence fall to the floor on their faces. (107)

They say: "Glorified is our Lord, for His promise is always realized." (108)

They fall on their chins crying, and the more they hear, the respectfully emotional they become. Say: "Call on God, using God or the Merciful, for He has many good names." (109)

When you pray do not be loud or barely heard but somewhere in between. (110)

Say: "Glory to God who has no son nor did He share His kingdom with anyone and who answers to no one, and proclaim His greatness." (111)

THE CAVE (18)

In the Name of God, Most Merciful, and Most Beneficent.

Glory is to Him, He who revealed to His servant the Book containing no falsehoods, (1)

to warn of dire consequences coming from Him, and bringing good tidings to the believers who do good works, that good rewards are awaiting them (2)

that will stay with them forever. (3)

He warns those who said that God has begotten a son. (4)

It is obvious that neither they nor their fathers have any direct knowledge of that. It is but a blasphemous uttering and nothing but a falsehood on their part. (5)

You may hurt yourself while feeling sorry for them for not believing in this revelation. (6)

We made on earth beautifying ornaments to test mankind as to who is better in doing good works. (7)

We can certainly make it all into a useless desert. (8)

You may have thought that the cave dwellers, and the mountain where that cave was located were only one of Our miracles. (9)

They were young individuals who took refuge in the cave and said: "Lord bless us with your mercy and provide us with guidance in our situation." (10)

We caused them to lose consciousness and then left them as such for many years. (11)

Then We resurrected them and threw the challenge to the two parties who are after them to guess how long they have been in the cave. (12)

We tell you their true story for they were young individuals who truly believed and We blessed them with more guidance. (13)

We strengthened their hearts when they rose among their people and said: "Our Lord is Lord of the Heaven and earth and we shall not recognize any one but Him, for if we did we will be propagating a falsehood. (14)

Our people adopted gods other than Him, who never provided them with any signs of their existence, and who is a bigger transgressor than those who invents falsehoods against God."(15)

They abandoned their people and sought refuge in the cave. Their Lord extended His mercy to them with a salvation from their difficult situation. (16)

One in the cave would have seen the sun rising from the right and setting from the left (*facing north*) while they were in the deep part of it (*being hard to see from the outside*), and that was a sign from

God. A person who is guided by God is truly guided, and one who is misguided by God will never find a sponsor or a guide. (17)

If you looked at them, you would have thought they were awake while they were not. We caused them to move to the right and then to the left, and between them and the door sat their dog with his front legs extended. You would have run away from them with fear, and full of terror. (18)

We resurrected them to start questioning each other, One would say: "How long have we been here?" and the other said: "Probably a day or more." And one said: "Our Lord knows how long we stayed; one of us should go to town and find find us the best food we can eat, while he remains careful so that no one will recognize him, and know about us." (19)

They were afraid that if they became discovered, they would be stoned, or forced to rejoin their people's religion, and they would have been lost forever. (20)

We revealed their affair to the people so they may realize that the promise of God is true and that the Day of Judgement is beyond doubt while they go on arguing among themselves, some suggesting that they be returned to the cave and closed in, and others suggesting that a temple should be built over their bodies. (21)

Some say they were three and the dog was the fourth, and some said they were five and their dog was the sixth, and even others said they were seven and the dog was the eighth. Say: "My Lord is more Knowledgeable in what their true number was. He taught them but very little. Do not argue with them beyond the very obvious and do not put them in judgement on anything." (22)

Do not ever say: "I am doing this tomorrow." (23)

Unless God wills, and mention your Lord if you forget and say: "I hope my Lord will help me so I will be better guided." (24)

They stayed in the cave nine years over three hundred. (25)

Say: "God is much more Knowledgeable with how long they stayed. He has knowledge of all the unknowns in the heavens and on the earth go by what He shows you and tells you, who without Him they would have had no sponsor, and no one can ever share in His judgement." (26)

Recite what is revealed to you in your Lord's Book. No one can change His words or find a refuge from Him. (27)

Keep yourself with those who pray to their Lord morning and evening, wishing for His approval, and do not let those who are after the pleasures of this life out of your sight, and do not follow those who we have permitted their hearts to sway away from remembering us and followed their fancy, and thus ended their life in waste. (28)

Give them the truth from their Lord, and whoever wishes to believe can believe and those who wish can disbelieve, for We have prepared for the transgressors walls of fire surrounding them and when they seek help they will be helped with water that roasts the faces; the worst that one can drink, and the last that one needs in help. (29)

When one believes and does good works, We shall never forget to reward those who do good works. (30)

To those belong the Gardens of Eden, below which runs rivers, at the bottom of which they can find bracelets of gold. They shall be dressed with fine green silk and sparkling brocade, sitting on comfortable recliners; the best of rewards and the most equal distribution of ranks. (31)

Give them the example of two men. We gave one two gardens; one is full of growing vine and surrounded with palm trees and among which other crops were growing. (32)

Through it flows a river and both gardens produced generously. (33)

And as he benefitted from the crops he said, boasting to his friend: "I have more than you have in riches and family size." (34)

He entered his own paradise while transgressing against himself by saying: "I do not believe anything can wipe this out ever. (35)

I do not believe the Day of Judgement is coming, and if it does, it is obvious that God does favor me." (36)

His friend retorted: "Did you forget that God has created you from dust, then from a germinating particle, then formed you in the shape of a man?" (37)

He said to him: "It is God, He is my Lord, and I will never associate any one with Him." (38)

If I were you and entered heaven I would have said, "Glorified be God. Nothing occurs without him, even if you find me having les children and riches than you." (39)

Do you not know that God may one day give me more than He gave you and send on your gardens a storm leaving only a flat ground? (40)

Or its water can dry out and become unavailable to you?" (41)

Suddenly his fruits dried up. The vine was plants without grapes and he was wringing his hands and lamenting: "I wish I associated no one with my Lord." (42)

He had no support from any one in the absence God's support. (43)

In fact it is true loyalty to God that is rewarded by Him and is the favored ending. (44)

Give them as an example the life on this earth, the rain We bring down from the sky, vegetation uses it, and then they dry up and everything becomes dust blown by the wind and God is Capable of all things. (45)

Riches and children are the source of pleasure in this life, but the good works that remain earn better rewards with your Lord and represent a greater hope for you. (46)

The day when we make the mountains move and the valleys disappear until all earth becomes equally prominent, and We assemble all of them without missing one. (47)

They will be paraded in front of your Lord and will be told how they were brought back the way they were created, while they believed they will never meet that date. (48)

As they review their book of reckoning, the transgressors become astonished and blame on themselves all the details in it that leave nothing big and small not included, and start seeing the images of what they had done in front of them. Your Lord does not deal unfairly with anyone. (49)

When We asked the angels to kneel in front of Adam, they did prostrate themselves except Satan, who was a member of the Jinn, and deviated from his Lord's order. Are you going to follow him and his descendents instead of following me, and they are your enemies. It is the kind of cursed exchange that the transgressors deserve. (50)

I neither invited them to witness the creation of the heavens and the earth, nor did I invite them to witness their own creation, For I never intended for those who are misguided to have that type of importance. (51)

The day when We will ask them: Call those gods that you used to associate with Me. They did and they had and none answered, and antagonism started among them. (52)

And as the transgressors see the fire, they will know that they are its target and they shall find no salvation. (53)

We filled this Koran with varied examples for all people, yet humans have always been inclined to argue. (54)

Nothing ever will prevent people from becoming believers and asking their Lord for forgiveness, unless they become misguided by the stories of their previous generations, or the torture hits them before they do that. (55)

We send messengers only to warn and relay good tidings. The unbelievers argue, using falsehoods, trying to defeat the truth, and mock My examples and My warnings. (56)

Who is more of a transgressor than one who was reminded by the the signs of His Lord that he turned away from them and then forgot what have his hands committed? For We put covers over their hearts and plugs in their ears, and then even when invited to guidance They will never be guided. (57)

And your Lord the Merciful and Forgiving, if He was to deal to them what they deserve for their deeds? They will have a date with Him for torture and they will have no savior. (58)

There were the many towns that we annihilated for their transgressions, while We have different dates for many others. (59)

Moses said to His young companion: "I will continue to travel until I reach the point where the two seas meet. Even if I have to walk for hundreds of years." (60)

As they reached the place, they forgot their whale, which found its way into the water to the sea. (61)

And after they put some additional distance behind them, he said to his young companion: "With all the exhaustion of our travel we have yet failed. (62)

As we spent the night under that rock, I have forgotten the whale which only Satan could have made me do, and strangely it has found its way back to the sea." (63)

As they said that, they turned around and followed their own footsteps. (64)

They met with one of our servants who We blessed with Our mercy and increased tremendously with knowledge. (65)

And Moses said: "Can I follow you so I could learn from your knowledge and wisdom?" (66)

He said: "You will not tolerate travel with me." (67)

He said: "How can you do that, while I am given knowledge of certain information behind certain incidents that you have no knowledge of?" (68)

He said: "You shall find me patient and fully obedient to you." (69)

He said: "If you follow me, you are not to ask me any questions about anything unless I decide to talk to you." (70)

They went together until they boarded a ship and he made a hole in it, and Moses said: "You made a hole in it to drown its passengers; this is certainly a grave action." (71)

His companion said: "Did I not tell you that you will have no patience to travel with me?" (72)

Moses said: "Please excuse me in what I have forgotten, and do not be too hard on me." (73)

They continued together, and they met a young man, and his companion killed him. Moses said: "You just killed an innocent soul, and you committed a great crime." (74)

He said: "I told you, you will not be able to stand being with me." (75)

Moses said: "If I ask you anything more from here on, you can drop me from your company, because you will certainly receive the maximum of your tolerance." (76)

They went on until they reached a village, where they asked for food and were refused. His companion saw a wall about to fall down, and he repaired it and strengthened it. Moses said: "You could have easily asked for payment for that work." (77)

The companion said: "Here we part company, but I will explain to you what you found difficult to understand. (78)

About the ship, it belonged to a family making a living out of it, and a tyrant King has been confiscating ships for his own use, so I made a defect in it so that it will not be desirable to him. (79)

The boy was an unbelieving evildoer giving his believing righteous parents a bad time. (80)

I gave them an opportunity to have a nice believing son they can be proud of. (81)

The wall belonged to two young orphans in the village. Under it was buried a treasure left for them by their righteous father, and God did not want anyone else to discover the treasure before they had the opportunity to dig it up themselves. I did not do any of those things on my own, and this is the explanation for what you could not tolerate." (82)

They may ask you about the one with the two horns; say: "I will tell you something about him." (83)

We gave him strength in the land and the ability to achieve all things. (84)

He went after his assignments. (85)

He traveled west and found the sun going down behind a big dark black lake. And there he found people, and we said to the one with the two horns: "You either have to punish them or improve their lot." (86)

He said: "Those who have done wrong, we shall torture them and then God will torture them more later.

Whereas for those who did good, we will make their lives easier." (88)

Then he continued on his assignment. (89)

In the far east, He found people exposed to the hot rays of the sun without any protection. (90)

We became aware of it, and he took care of it. (91)

He traveled further, (92)

until he found an area between two levies and people near them who could barely understand what was going on. (93)

They said: "O' one with the two horns, Gog and Magog are corrupting and destroying the land. Can you build us an obstruction between us and them?" (94)

He said: "God certainly gave me the power to do that. If you supply me with workers I shall make between you and them an obstructive structure." (95)

He asked for iron which he held together with hot molten brass. (96)

He blocked the valley, and no one could penetrate or dig through it. (97)

He said: "This is mercy from my Lord, and He is capable at any time to destroy it totally." (98)

We left them after that doing their thing until the trumpet was sounded, and We brought them together. (99)

And hell was our offering to the unbelievers. (100)

Whose eyes were covered and their ears were impaired. (101)

Did the unbelievers think that they could use My worshipers as sponsors instead of Me? We have prepared hell as a residence for the unbelievers. (102)

Shall we tell you about those whose works were all at a loss? (103)

Those who remained misguided in this life thinking they were doing very well. (104)

They denied their Lord's verses, and all their works failed and became of no value. (105)

Their punishment is hell, for they denied my verses and mocked my apostles. (106)

Those who believed and did good works, paradise is their residence. (107)

Immortalizes in it with no way of leaving it. (108)

Say: "If the ocean was ink for the words of my God, the ocean will empty before my God's words end." (109)

Say: "I am only a human like you who receives revelations. Your God is one God, and those who want to meet Him should do good works and associate no one with him." (110)

MARY (19)

In the Name of God, Most Merciful, and Most Beneficent.

Kaf, Hah, Yah, Ain, Sad. (1)

Remember your Lord's mercy to His servant Zacharias (2)

when he called on his Lord in private. (3)

He said: "My Lord, my bones have become weak and my head white and with your blessings I have never been unhappy. (4)

I am afraid of what may happen among my folks with whoever is going to replace me, after I am gone and my wife is barren. Grant me from your mercy an heir. (5)

Who will inherit me and inherit the family of Jacob, and make him one who seeks your service?" (6)

God said: O' Zacharias, We give you the good tidings of a boy called John, a name that no one has carried before him. (7)

He said: "How would I have a boy and my wife is barren while I am at such an advanced age?" (8)

This is what your Lord has said: This is easy for me, for I have created you before after you were nothing. (9)

Zacharias said: "My Lord how can I demonstrate my everlasting gratefulness for this event?" He said: What I would ask you is not to say a word to any one for three consecutive nights. (10)

He went out to his people from the shrine and indicated to them that they should glorify God morning and evening. (11)

O' John, take the Book with strength, and We gave him wisdom when he was yet a boy. (12)

H e received tender care from us and he was righteous. (13)

He was loving and caring for his parents and was never arrogant or disobedient. (14)

He was blessed the day he was born, the day he died and the day when he will be brought to life again. (15)

In the Book, we shall recount the story of Mary, as she isolated herself from her family in a place in the east. (16)

She stayed away from them until We sent her our spirit in the form of a well formed man. (17)

She said: "I would seek the protection of God from you if you are a righteous man." (18)

He said: "I am a messenger from your Lord to grant you an intelligent son." (19)

She asked: "How can I have a child? No human has ever touched me nor have I ever sinned." (20)

He said: "That is what your Lord has said and it is: It is easy for me. We shall make him an example for mankind and a merciful gesture from us, and it is a pre-ordained event, an act of mercy from us. It is done and over with. (21)

She conceived and moved to a far away place. (22)

And as childbirth came upon her, she went and sat under a palm tree and said: "I wish I had died long before this and became one of those who became forgotten." (23)

A voice from below her said to her: Do not despair, for your Lord has provided a brook flowing below. (24)

Shake the bottom of the tree, and you will have fresh dates fall on you. (25)

Eat, drink and be happy, and any humans you see tell them: "I have promised God to fast, and today I will talk to no one." (26)

Then she went to her people carrying him, and they said: "O' Mary, you have committed something shameful. (27)

Sister of Aaron, neither your father was a man of sin nor was your mother a harlot." (28)

She pointed to him, and they said: "How can we talk to an infant in a crib?" (29)

He said: "I am the servant of God, he gave me the Book and made me a prophet. (30)

He blessed me wherever I am, and exhorted me to pray to Him and pay alms so long as I am alive. (31)

He ordered me to take care of my mother, and not become arrogant and wicked. (32)

I am blessed the day I was born, the day I will die and the day I will come to life again." (33)

This is the story of Jesus, son of Mary, the one about whom there is a lot that is not true. (34)

God, the Glorified, would not have a son, for whatever He wishes, all he needs to say is "Be," and it is. (35)

God is my Lord and yours, so worship Him and that is the straight path. (36)

They split on that among themselves. Awesome harm shall come to the unbelievers as they face the Great Day. (37)

You shall see them and hear about them the day they are brought to us, but today the transgressors are totally misguided. (38)

Tell them about the Day of Regrets, when they are caught unbelieving, when it is too late. (39)

We are the inheritors of the earth and what is on it, and they will be returned back to us. (40)

Also mentioned in the Book was Abraham who was a prophet and a friend. (41)

When he said to his father: "How do you worship something that neither hears nor sees, and cannot be of any use to you?" (42)

He said: "My father, I have been given knowledge that was never made available to you. Follow me and I will show you the straight path." (43)

He said: "O' father do not worship Satan, for Satan was disobedient to God. (44)

Father, I am afraid for you to be touched with torture from God, and then you become among the followers of Satan." (45)

His father said: "Are you denouncing my gods? If you do not stop, I shall stone you and you will have to leave my house soon." (46)

He said: "Goodbye to you, and I shall try to ask God to be merciful on you, because I am close to Him. (47)

I shall be away from you and what you pray for instead of God, and I shall pray to God so that my prayers will protect me from being an evildoer." (48)

And as he stayed away from them and from what they worshiped other than God, We gave Him Isaac and Jacob, and We made each one of them a prophet. (49)

We gave them our blessings, and We gave them the ability to favor the truth in what they say. (50)

And in the Book, there is the mention of Moses, who was faithful, a prophet and an apostle. (51)

We called him from the right side of the mountain, and had a friendly conversation with him. (52)

And We made his brother Aaron a prophet also included in Our mercy. (53)

Also mentioned in the Book is Ishmael. He was truthful, an apostle and a prophet. (54)

He exhorted his people to do their prayers and pay alms, and fully earned God's favor. (55)

Also mentioned in the Book Idris (*Enoch*), who was a friend and a prophet. (56)

We have put him in a high place. (57)

Those are the ones who earned God's favor among the prophets and the decendents of Adam. And among those that sailed with Noah and among the decendents of Abraham and the people of Israel and those We guided and blessed and who when they hear God's verses, they drop down on their knees, prostrating themselves and crying. (58)

After them came descendents who forgot their prayers and followed their whims, and they shall lose. (59)

Except those who repent and believe and do good works. Those shall not be losing anything. (60)

The gardens of Eden which were promised by God to His worshipers in the future is certain. (61)

In it they shall have no problems, and their supplies shall be provided to them morning and evening. (62)

This is the paradise that shall be inherited by the righteous of our worshipers. (63)

Every revelation you get reaches you by order of your Lord, who is the true owner of everything we have and everything we leave behind, and anything in between. Your God never forgets anything. (64)

Lord of the heavens and earth and what lies in between. So worship Him and be patient in your worship. Do you know of anyone higher than him? (65)

Some people say: "Are we going to die and be brought back to life again?" (66)

Do people not remember that We created them before when they were nothing. (67)

We shall assemble them together with devils and then bring them around hell kneeling. (68)

Then we shall isolate out of every group those that have history of being the most likely to challenge God. (69)

We are most knowledgeable of who are those who need to be fed to the fire first. (70)

Every one of you is passing through the fire, this is ordained by your Lord. (71)

Then We shall provide an exit for the righteous, while the transgressors remain the longest. (72)

As our clear verses are recited to them, the unbelievers will say to the believers: "Do these put you in a better and higher position in the future?" (73)

Do they not know how many nations before them we have destroyed who were better and stronger than they are? (74)

Say: "Those who have misguided, God may give them time so that when they finally come face to face with the torture that awaits them or the Day of Judgement, they will easily recognize who was in the weakest position and had the least means. (75)

God also increases the guidance of those who are guided. Good works always remain with your Lord, deserving a better reward and higher ending. (76)

Those who disbelieve our verses and say: "We are going to acquire more children and riches." (77)

Could they see into the future or did God give them a promise? (78)

Everything they say shall be recorded, and they shall be given enough time to deserve the torture awaiting them. (79)

We shall remind him with what he said on an individual basis. (80)

They have adopted gods other than God to bring the glory. (81)

Their gods will not accept their worship and be their adversaries. (82)

Did you not see us send the devils to help the unbelievers, when they become wary? (83)

Do not be in a hurry after them. We are counting every thing they do. (84)

The day the righteous will be assembled together and brought to God (85)

while the transgressors will be driven to hell. (86)

They will have no sponsorship from those who have a promise from God. (87)

They said: "God has begotten a son." (88)

You have committed a great wrong. (89)

It is so wrong that the heavens will cry, and the earth will split and the mountains will sink (90)

if they claim that God has a son. (91)

Why will God have son? (92)

Everyone in the heaven and earth is a servant of God. (93)

He has count of all of them. (94)

They will all face Him the Day of Judgement, one by one. (95)

Those who believed and did good works shall be close to God. (96)

We sent it to you in your tongue, to bring good tidings to the righteous, and warning to people who were deep in their transgression. (97)

Many people before them We annihilated. Do they ever see them or hear from them? (98)

TAHA (20)

In the Name of God, Most Merciful, and Most Beneficent.

Taah, Alef, Haah. (1)

We did not reveal the Koran to you to make you miserable (2)

but rather a reminder to those who fear God. (3)

It is being revealed by the One who created the earth and the upper heavens. (4)

God is the ruler on the throne of the universe. (5)

He is the Owner of what is in the heavens and the earth, and what is between them and what is under the earth. (6)

As you reveal the revelation loudly, God knows all that is secret and hidden. (7)

God who there is no other God but Him. And to Him alone belong all the good names. (8)

Did you hear the story about Moses? (9)

When he saw a fire and said to his people: "Stay awhile here, I see a fire. Let me see if I can bring you from it a lighted twig or get some light to guide our way." (10)

When he approached the fire, he was called: O' Moses, (11)

It is I, your Lord. Take off your shoes for you are in the sacred valley, Towa. (12)

I chose you, so listen to what is revealed to you. (13)

I am God and there is no other God but Me. Worship Me and institute prayers to mention My name. (14)

The Day of Judgement is coming. I have nearly kept it a secret to truly test and reward all souls for what they do. (15)

And do not let anyone who does not believe in the Last Day and followed his fancy to succeed in swaying you away from it. (16)

What is that in your hand, Moses? (17)

"That is my staff, I lean on it, and use it to get my sheep going in the right direction, and I use it for other purposes also." (18)

He (*God*) said: Moses, throw it. (19)

He (*Moses*) did, and it was transformed into a snake twisting. (20)

He (*God*) said: Take it and do not be afraid, it shall return to its original form. (21)

Put your hand under your arm then pull it back and it shall come shining white with no discoloration whatsoever, which is another sign. (22)

We shall show you even bigger signs. (23)

Go to the Pharaoh for he has transgressed excessively. (24)

He (*Moses*) said: "My Lord, help me feel better about myself. (25)

Help ease difficulties ahead of me. (26)

Help my speech to become more fluent (27)

so they may understand what I say. (28)

And give me a back-up from a member of my family. (29)

My brother Aaron, (30)

who will help to strengthen me, (31)

and share my hardship and travail. (32)

We will both glorify You always, (33)

and never tire of Your mention. (34)

You will always be watching what we do."(35)

He (*God*) said: We are going to grant you what you asked. (36)

And again you shall owe Us another big favor. (37)

We have revealed to your mother what she needed to do. (38)

Put him in a coffin, and throw him in the sea. And the tide will bring him to the shore, and he will be taken by an enemy of mine and yours, then I granted you love and a watchful eye. (39)

Then your sister went to them and told them that she can bring them one who will nurse him, and thus you are back in the arms of your mother, so as to remove her sadness and anxiety. Then you killed a soul and We saved you from your ordeal, and got you through difficulties. Then you stayed years with the people of Madian, until you came here by my ordinance. (40)

Now I have you for myself. (41)

Go, you and your brother, with my signs. And do not hesitate to mention Me. (42)

Go to the Pharaoh, for he has transgressed. (43)

Talk to him gently for he may still remember or fear. (44)

They said: "Our Lord, we are afraid that he may punish or torture us in excess and become more tyrannical." (45)

He (*God*) said: Do not be afraid, I will be with you, hearing and seeing everything. (46)

Go to him and say: We are the messengers of your Lord, send the children of Israel with us and do not torture them anymore. We brought you signs from your Lord, and peace shall fall on those who choose to follow the guidance. (47)

It has been revealed to us that torture shall fall upon those who lie and evade. (48)

He (*the Pharaoh*) said to Moses: "And who is your Lord?" (49)

He said: "Our Lord is the One who created all things and then provided guidance." (50)

He said: "What about the very ancient ages of mankind?" (51)

He said: "The real knowledge about them resides with my Lord in an all-encompassing and accurate Book. God is never mistaken or forgetful. (52)

He made the earth a place for you to live in, and provided you with guidance to survive on it. He brought down from the sky water we used to cultivate and grow plants and crops of different kinds." (53)

Eat, and feed your cattle (*God said*), and in these things are signs for those who understand. (54)

In it (*earth*) We have created you, and to it We shall return you, and from it We shall resurrect you again. (55)

We showed him all Our signs, and yet He lied and refused. (56)

He said (*the Pharaoh*): "Did you, Moses, come here attempting to get us out of power in this Land, with your magic (*sorcery*)? (57)

We shall bring you an equally impressive, if not better magic, of my own and there shall be a date between us. Do not miss it, and neither shall we, and it shall be a fair competition. "(58)

He (*Moses*) said: "Our date shall be the day of the festival when the crowds get together in the mid-morning." (59)

The Pharaoh left, got his people (*his best sorcerers*) together, and returned on the date set. (60)

Moses said to them: "You shall be cursed if you lie about God or He shall waste you with torture, for liars will never succeed." (61)

Then they quarreled among each other, and huddled together. (62)

They said: "These two are sorcerers who are trying to subvert your way of life, and push out with their sorcery." (63)

They coordinated their plot and came in front of him (*the Pharaoh*) in line, and agreed that it was a day when success will belong to those who are better. (64)

They said: "Moses, we either start, or we will let you start." (65)

He said: "You go ahead and start." And as they threw their sticks and their ropes, they seemed like snakes moving and twisting. (66)

And initially, Moses felt fearful. (67)

We said: Do not be afraid, you shall overcome. (68)

Throw what is in your right hand (*his staff*) and it shall swallow all that they produced with their sorcery. A sorcerer shall never succeed. (69)

All of the sorcerers fell on their knees, and declared: "We are believers in the Lord of Aaron and Moses." (70)

"You declared (*said the Pharaoh*) your belief in him without my permission. He must be your grand sorcerer who taught you sorcery. I shall cut off a hand and a leg for each of you on opposite sides and I shall crucify you on the trunks of palm trees, And I shall show you who among us has the most severe and lasting power to deliver torture." (71)

They said: "You are not going to influence what we have seen after the signs were revealed to us by our Creator. So go ahead and give your orders as you wish, for whatever you want to do you can do only in this life. (72)

We have believed in God so that He may forgive our sins in practicing sorcery which you have imposed upon us. God is better and truly lasting." (73)

It is He who arrived finally to his God. A transgressor shall have hell where he will neither die nor live, (74)

while those who come to their God believers and having done good works will enjoy endings at the highest levels. (75)

Gardens of Eden, below which flow rivers, immortalized in them; A reward for those who purified themselves. (76)

Our revelation to Moses was to take my people and strike for them a road through the sea, and do not be afraid or intimidated by anything. (77)

The Pharaoh and his soldiers followed them, and the sea closed over them. (78)

The Pharaoh misguided his people and failed. (79)

O' people of Israel, We saved you from your enemy and We promised you the right side of the Toor mountain, and We brought down to you Manna and quails for your eating pleasure. (80)

Eat and enjoy what We provided for you and do not transgress for those who do earn My wrath, and those who manage to earn My wrath shall be lost. (81)

But I am forgiving for those who repent, believe and do good works, and then become guided. (82)

Moses, What is the hurry for? Why did you come here and leave your people behind? (83)

"They are coming just behind me, I came fast to you to earn your approval. (84)

After you left, in your absence, your people failed our test and started quarrelling among themselves, and the Samiri has misguided them. (85)

Moses went back to his people angry and disappointed, and said: "My people, did your Lord not make you a good promise? Has it been a long time since I left you, or are you trying to earn the wrath of your Lord and violate your promise to me?" (86)

But we threw jewelry into the fire and so did the Samiri. (87)

He (*the Samiri*) made from it a statue of a calf, which when knocked on produces a resonance indicative of being empty inside. He then said to them: "This is your God and the God of Moses." (88)

Did they not see that it was not capable of answering them, nor could it do them bad or good? (89)

Aaron said to them: "You caused an uprising and disorder with this calf, and your Lord is the Great Forgiver, follow me and obey me." (90)

They said: "We will not give it up until Moses returns to us." (91)

He (*Moses*) said to Aaron: "Why did you just stand by while they became misguided? (92)

Did you not follow, or did you disobey my orders?" (93)

He (*Aaron*) said: "You, the son of my mother, do not take hold of my beard or my head, I was afraid of leaving them to catch up with you and they end up separating, and then you would find me guilty of causing the people of Israel to separate." (94)

He (*Moses*) said to the Samiri: "What happened to you? (95)

Why did you do that? I thought of something they did not think of. I took a handful of sand from the footprint of the apostle, and threw it out in the wind, and thus I thought I could get away with it." (96)

He (*Moses*) said (*to the Samiri*): "Go and you shall be an outcast. Then you shall have an appointment you shall not miss. Look at your god that you misguided people with it. We shall burn it then blow it into pieces and throw it in the sea." (97)

Your God is the God who there is no other god but Him, and in whom resides the knowledge that no other possesses. (98)

This is how we tell you the stories of those who came before you and We sent you from us a readable Book (*the Koran*). (99)

Those who turn away from it shall carry a big load with them to the Last Day. (100)

They shall carry it with them forever, and it is such a bad load to have on the Last Day. (101)

The day the trumpet sounds, and we bring all the criminals together, blue in color *(due to what they are passing through)*. (102)

They will be arguing with each other on how long have they been there, and they will say: "Ten days." (103)

We are more knowledgeable about what they are saying, for it is not more than a day. (104)

They ask you about the mountains, say: "My Lord will blow them up (105)

and make them like the straight bottom of an ocean, (106)

with no highs or lows." (107)

That day they will follow what they are told, and the different voices turn into whispers showing total obedience to God. (108)

On that day, no intercession is accepted on behalf of anyone unless God permits it or requests it. (109)

He knows what they are doing now and what they did in the past, while they know nothing about Him. (110)

All eye are turned to the Glorified Immortal, and failures are those who carry the burden of their transgressions. (111)

He who does good works and is a believer, will never have to fear unfairness, or his good works be overlooked. (112)

We revealed it: A Koran in the Arabic language, providing warnings in all forms and ways, so they may become righteous and be reminded. (113)

Glorified be God the true King, and take the Koran unhurriedly until the revelation makes its way to you, and say: "My Lord increase my knowledge." (114)

We made a covenant with Adam, but he forgot and proved to be not very studious. (115)

When We said to all the angels: Kneel in front of Adam, and they did, except for Satan who refused. (116)

We said to Adam: This is an enemy to you and your spouse. Do not let him cause you to leave paradise and become miserable. (117)

In it you shall never have to worry about being bare or hungry. (118)

In it you will never feel thirst or feel the effect of the scorching heat. (119)

Nevertheless, Satan got to him and said: "O' Adam, do you want me to tell you about the tree of immortality and the key to a non-ending kingdom?" (120)

They both ate from its fruit and they suddenly felt naked and ashamed of their genitals and started trying to cover them with the leaves of heaven. Adam disobeyed his Lord and was lost. (121)

And then God responded to his pleadings and repentance and forgave him. (122)

He said: Go down to earth, and some of you shall become enemies to each other. I shall provide you with guidance, and he who follows shall always be guided and shall not suffer. (123)

Those who do not heed my reminders, shall have a rough life, and shall be assembled blind on the Day of Judgement. (124)

One of them will say: "My Lord, You assembled me blind when I was a seeing person." (125)

He (God) said: Our signs came to you the same way and you forgot about them, and today We shall forget about your eyesight. (126)

This is the way We repay those who cross the line and did not believe in the signs of their Lord, for the torture of the Last Day is more severe and lasting. (127)

Did We not try to guide them? How many generations We have annihilated before them, as they walked inside their houses. There are signs in that for those who understand. (128)

And if it was not that your Lord has predetermined the life cycle of many and postponed their punishment, they would have been gone also. (129)

Be patient with what they say, and glorify your Lord before sunrise and before sunset, and during the night, and also during the day, until you are satisfied. (130)

Do not pay attention to what we let many couples enjoy in this life to reinforce their misguidedness, because the bounty of God is better and more lasting. (131)

Encourage your family to pray and be patient in doing that. You will not be asked to provide for anyone; it is rather God who will provide for you, and the good ending is for the righteous. (132)

When they say they wish you brought them a sign from your Lord, did they not get the signs in the previous books? (133)

If We had destroyed them with a torture before the Koran, they would have said: "Our Lord, we wish you had sent us a messenger to follow your signs before we were disgraced and insulted." (134)

Say: Keep on watching, because if you do you shall find out who are those who followed the right path, and who are those who were truly guided. (135)

THE PROPHETS (21)

In the Name of God, Most Merciful, and Most Beneficent.

The Day of reckoning is coming closer for people, and they do not seem to realize it. (1)

They continue to listen to reminders from their Lord while they are playing. (2)

While they are preoccupied somewhere else, the transgressors say secretly to each other: "He is only a human like you; could you not tell magic (*sorcery*) when you see it?" (3)

He (*Mohammed*) said: "My Lord knows the words in heaven or on earth, and He is always Hearing and Knowledgeable." (4)

They even said: "It is nothing but dreams made up by a poet. Let him bring us signs that were sent to the earlier generations." (5)

Many unbelieving towns We have annihilated in the past, are they going to believe? (6)

We sent before you only men, to whom We sent our revelations Tell them to ask people who are more knowledgeable if they do not know. (7)

They were not a body that did not need food, nor were they immortal. (8)

Then We gave them what We promised them, and wasted the transgressors. (9)

We sent you a Book that mentions you; do you not have any sense? (10)

Many a town that was inhabited by transgressors, We have annihilated and replaced with towns inhabited by others. (11)

And as they felt our power they left running. (12)

Do not run, return to what you are used to, and back to your residences where you may be asked for something. (13)

They said: "O' we have certainly been transgressors." (14)

And these continued to be their pleadings, until they were taken by Us unmoving. (15)

We did not create the heaven and the earth for Our entertainment. (16)

If We were to entertain ourself, We would have created something more to Our liking. (17)

We would have played a game throwing the right on the wrong and watch it demolish the wrong, but they will pay dearly for what they utter. (18)

He is the Owner of the heavens and the earth and those on His side are not ever too arrogant to worship Him nor do they ever get tired from or bored doing that. (19)

They glorify Him day and night, and never say falsehoods about Him. (20)

They do not adopt gods from earth who they know to be capable of nothing. (21)

If they (*the heavens and the earth*) contained a god other than the One God, they would have dysfunctioned. Glorified be He, the Lord of the Throne, over what they describe. (22)

No one can question Him about what He does, but they will be questioned about what they do. (23)

They took gods other than God. Say to them: "Give me your proof." This is my Book. It mentions those who are with me and those who were before Me. Most of them do not know what is right, and they are still in opposition. (24)

All of the messengers We sent before you We made revelations to them, I am the God and there is no other God but Me, so worship Me. (25)

They said: "God has begotten a son. He the Glorified has only honored worshipers." (26)

They do not rush to speak before He does, and they only obey His orders. (27)

He knows what is in their present and in their past. They will not intercede except for those He favors, and they are all afraid of Him. (28)

And whoever of them ever says that he is a god, other than God, shall be rewarded with Hell, for that is the way We reward the transgressors. (29)

Did not those who disbelieve know that the heaven and the earth were one melted mass and We separated them, and that from water We created everything living? Are they not going to believe? (30)

We made the mountains on earth to function as anchors, and we left passes between them so people can find their way. (31)

We kept the sky over them like a ceiling, and they still turn away from Our signs. (32)

He has created the night and day, and the sun and the moon, and they all travel in their own orbits. (33)

We never granted any one before you immortality, and if you die, do they think they are going to stay alive? (34)

Every soul shall face death, and We let you suffer through what is good and what is bad as a test, and to Us you shall all return. (35)

When the unbelievers see you, they start mocking you for what you say about their gods, while they themselves are unbelievers in the Merciful. (36)

He created humans who are always in haste. I shall show you My signs, so do not be hasty. (37)

They will say: "When is that going to happen if you are truthful?" (38)

The unbelievers shall not know when they shall be trying to protect their faces from the fire and protect their backs and they will have no help or support. (39)

It shall hit them suddenly, and they shall have no way of predicting it or seeing it. (40)

Messengers before you were mocked and made fun of, until what they were mocking got hold of them. (41)

Ask them who will give them the day and night other than the Merciful, while they are turning away from the mention of their Lord. (42)

Or do they have gods of their own, that keep them away from Us? Their companions cannot even help themselves. (43)

We have let those people and their fathers enjoy this life for a long time. Can they not see that frequently We make life harder by crimping away at the periphery of their landscape? Do they think they are going to win? (44)

Say: "I will warn you with what was revealed to me, but the deaf will not hear what they are being threatened with." (45)

If they were even touched with a little blow of your Lord's torture, they would have readily declared how much of transgressors they are. (46)

The scales We use on the Day of Judgement are very accurate, so that no one will be disadvantaged even the weight of a single mustard seed. We shall make absolutely sure of that. (47)

We revealed to Moses and Aaron the distinguisher (*the ten commandments*), a light and a reminder to the righteous. (48)

Those who are afraid of their God although they never saw Him, are always in an expectant state for the Day of Judgement. (49)

This is a new mention of God (*the Koran*) that I am revealing. Are you going to deny it? (50)

We brought Abraham to his youth and We were watchful for him. (51)

He said to his father and people: "What are those statues with which you keep company?"(52)

They said: "Our fathers used to worship them." (53)

He said: "You and your fathers have been totally misguided." (54)

They said: "Did you bring us the truth, or are you a joker?" (55)

He said: "Your Lord is the Lord of the heavens and the earth and the One who created you, and I am on that a witness." (56)

He said to himself: "Watch what I will do to your statues as soon as you turn your backs." (57)

He destroyed all of them to pieces except the largest one so that he may refer them to him. (58)

They said: "Who did this to our gods? He certainly is a transgressor." (59)

They said: "We heard a young lad say something about them who goes by the name of Abraham." (60)

They said: "Bring him in front of all the people as witnesses." (61)

They said: "Did you, Abraham, do that to our gods?" (62)

He said: "Actually their biggest one is the one who did that. Ask him if he can talk." (63)

They went back to each other and said: "We are really the transgressors." (64)

Then they reversed themselves and said: "We have always known that these things do not talk." (65)

He (*Abraham*) said: "Instead of God, you worship things that can do you no good or bad. (66)

I am tired of you worshiping objects instead of God. Do you have no sense?" (67)

They said: "Let us burn him and take revenge for our gods." (68)

We said (*God*): Fire, be cool and peaceful on Abraham. (69)

They wanted to destroy him, and We made them losers. (70)

We saved him and Lot and sent them both to the land which We blessed for the whole world. (71)

We gave him Isaac and then Jacob (*his grandson*), and We made both among the righteous. (72)

We made them leaders, providing guidance at our command. They engaged in prayers and paid alms, and they were Our worshipers. (73)

And to Lot We gave wisdom and knowledge, and saved him from a town whose inhabitants were engaged in wickedness and obscenity. They were evildoers. (74)

We entered him in the protection of our mercy. He was among the righteous. (75)

And Noah called Us and We responded to him. We saved him, he and his family from the great disaster. (76)

We gave him victory over the people who denied our signs and they were evildoers, so We drowned all of them. (77)

David and Solomon sat in judgement on the case when sheep encroached on a cultivated land, and on their judgement We were witnesses. (78)

We praised Solomon for his insight, and gave both of them wisdom and knowledge. We even made the birds and the mountains sing My praise with David. (79)

We even taught him how to make body armor so you can be provided with protection in your wars. Do you give thanks? (80)

To Solomon we gave the power to control the wind in the direction of the blessed land, and We had knowledge of all things. (81)

Devils were made to dive the ocean for him and perform for him other tasks, while We kept them under a very watchful eye. (82)

And Job who called upon his Lord: "I am not well, and you are the Most Merciful of all." (83)

We responded to him, and helped him with what ails him, and we brought him back his family, and many others, a mercy from Us and remembrance for the worshipers. (84)

Ishmael, Idris and Tha Al-Kifel, were all persevering worshipers. (85)

We entered them under Our mercy. They were among the righteous. (86)

And Tha Al-Noon, who left angry and thought: "We will have difficulty getting to him." And as soon as he found himself in the dark, he said: "There is none but you. God be glorified, I was a transgressor." (87)

We responded to Him and forgave him, and helped him out of his depression, and thus We save the believers. (88)

Zechariah who called his Lord: "I am one, by myself and have no heir. Your help on this matter is the best." (89)

We responded to him and gave him John, by removing his wife's infertility. They have always been at the front in giving, and pray to Us out of love and fear, and were always worshipers. (90)

And she who protected her chastity, we sent Our spirit to her, and made her and her son a sign for the world. (91)

Your nation is only one among many. I am your Lord. Worship Me. (92)

When they may disagree among themselves, they shall all return to Us at the end. (93)

He who does good works, and is a believer, shall have no way to lose the reward on his work. It is all written down. (94)

God decreed that any town that is annihilated, its people shall not come back to life. (95)

Until the time when Gog and Magog rush down the hills from everywhere. (96)

And as the true promise (*the Day of Judgement*) grows near, the unbelievers' eyes will be wide open, and they will say: "We are doomed, we sure were transgressors." (97)

You and whoever you worship other than God, are the fuel for hell, and you shall enter it. (98)

If those were true gods they would not have entered hell, and in it they shall be immortalized. (99)

In it they cannot even hear the sound of their own heavy breathing. (100)

Only those who have previously done enough good works to satisfy us will be spared. (101)

They will not hear the sound of the fire of hell, while they will be provided with everything their hearts desire, while immortalized. (102)

They will not be scared of the Great Scare (*Day of Judgement*), the angels will receive them. This is your day which you have been promised. (103)

The day We fold the sky like you fold a page of a book. Just like We started the first creation, We will restart again from the beginning. It is a promise from Us to do. (104)

We wrote in the Psalms, after the Mention (*the Torah*) that the righteous shall inherit the earth. (105)

In this there is a warning to those who worship. (106)

We sent you as a sign to the world. (107)

Say you: "God is the One God." Are you going to surrender to Him (*become Moslem*)? (108)

If they turn you down, say to them: "I am letting you go with that right now for I have no way to tell you whether what I am warning you about is near or far." (109)

He (*God*) knows what you declare and what you hide. (110)

I cannot even tell you for certain whether all you have is only a test that you shall for a while enjoy. (111)

Say: "My Lord is wiser as to what is right. Our Lord the Merciful who we rely upon to help us counter what you come up with." (112).

THE PILGRIMAGE (22)

In the Name of God, Most Merciful, and Most Beneficent.

People, worship and fear your Lord. The Quake of the Hour (*the Last Day*) is a big thing. (1)

That day you will see a nursing mother forget who she has been nursing, and those who are pregnant will deliver, and people walking like they are drunk and they are not. But the torture of God is severe. (2)

Some people argue about God with no knowledge and follow every rebellious devil. (3)

It is ordained that whoever follows the Devil, the Devil shall lead him to the torture of hell. (4)

People, if you are in doubt about resurrection, you need to know that We created you from dust, then from a germ, then from a clot, then from a mass of tissue, that may or may not produce a living fetus. Then there is a period of stay inside the uterus that We have predetermined. We bring you out a child, that grows until reaching maturity, and then some will die and some will reach the worst part of life, when he may not know anything after he knew a lot. You look at the earth and you find it barren until We bring down water from the sky, and vegetation grows in thriving colorful pairs. (5)

This is because God is the truth, and He does resurrect the dead, and He is Capable of all things. (6)

The Hour is coming, no doubt about it. God will resurrect people from their graves. (7)

Among people also are those who may argue about God with no knowledge, guidance or an enlightening book. (8)

They turn their back on guidance and participate in convincing others to do so. They shall be disgraced in this life, and shall taste the torture of fire on the Day of Judgement. (9)

This is for what they committed of sins and God is never unjust with his servants. (10)

There are those who worship God on the edge, and if they did well in life, they become settled, but if they face difficulties they take an about face. They will lose this life and the one next, and this is the true loss. (11)

They seek for help, others instead of God, and what can neither hurt them nor benefit them, and that is a severe deviation from the straight path. (12)

They seek what is more likely to hurt them than help them, it is the worst of sponsorships that they seek, and it is a doomed destiny indeed. (13)

God shall enter the believers' gardens, under which rivers flow. God does what He wants. (14)

Those who are angry and have enough hatred in their hearts, if they believe that God may neglect supporting him (*the prophet*) in this life and the life to come, should reason why should that happen and then to stop and see if that is enough to mollify their anger and hatred. (15)

We revealed It (*the Book*) with veritable signs, and God shall guide whomever He chooses. (16)

Those who believe, the Jews, the Sabaeans, the Christians, the Magians (*fire worshipers*), and those who associate others with God; God shall deal with the differences among them on the Day of Judgement. God is a witness on all things. (17)

All that is in the heavens and on the earth, on the sun, the moon, or other planets, and the mountains, the animals and many humans kneel before God, and many are due for torture. Those who are humiliated by God have no one that will honor them. God does what He wills. (18)

The two contenders argue about their Lord. The unbelievers shall have clothes made of fire, and scalding liquids will be poured over their heads. (19)

It will liquidate what is in their bellies and the skin. (20)

They will have restraints made of solid iron. (21)

And whenever they try to pull away, it pulls them back. Have a taste of the torture of fire. (22)

God shall enter the believers' gardens, below which rivers flow. In it they shall find bracelets made of gold and pearls, and shall be wearing pure silk. (23)

They have guided others to the best in speech and to the blessed path. (24)

The unbelievers who sway others from God's path and the sacred mosque, which We made with equal access for all, those that live near it and those who come from far, and those who commit transgressions inside it shall face an excruciating torture. (25)

We pointed to Abraham the site upon which the house needs to be. Do not associate any one with Me, and get My house ready to receive the pilgrims, to go around it and those who are praying on their knees or those who prostrate themselves. (26)

Announce the pilgrimage and they shall come from all directions, using all kinds of rides, from every gorge (27)

to remember and bear witness to the benefits God provided for them, like the animals that they use for food and to feed the poor. (28)

Thus they satisfy themselves spiritually, make true their yearnings and promises to themselves, and circle the sacred house. (29)

Those who glorify the Lord's sacred places help themselves with Him. It is lawful for you avail yourselves of what God has provided for you, except for when He stated otherwise. Avoid the paganism of idols, and avoid being the carriers of false witness. (30)

Be loyal to God and associate none with Him. One who associates others with God is likened to one who falls from the sky with the birds snatching at him and the wind blowing him to a faraway place. (31)

One who glorifies the symbols that refer to God, feels better about himself. (32)

This will be of help to you for a while and the place for it is the Old House. (33)

For every religion we made a symbolic place where they seclude themselves and repeat the name of God, and give thanks for what God gave them, such as animals to feed on, for your God is one God. Surrender to Him and bring good tidings to the fearing worshipers. (34)

Those whose hearts beat faster by the mention of God, and those who gallantly suffer whatever befalls them, and those who resort to prayers, and spend in charity from what We have bestowed upon them. (35)

We make the flesh of animals that you eat originate from the hay these animals eat. When it is butchered, mention the name of God over it, as each animal is done, and eat from it and feed the needy, especially those who are contented and proud enough to never ask. We gave it to you so you will be grateful. (36)

God will never benefit from its meat or its blood, but what reaches him is righteousness from you. God made it available to you, so you may glorify God for His bounty, and good tidings to the givers. (37)

God defends those who believe, and God dislikes the the disloyal and the unbelievers. (38)

Those who are persecuted are permitted to fight, and God is Capable of granting them victory. (39)

Especially those who will be driven out of their homes only because they said: "Our Lord is God." If it was not for the fact that God uses some to stop and defeat others, many places of worship, churches, monasteries and mosques, where the name of God is frequently mentioned, will be destroyed. God shall grant victory to those who struggle for Him. He is the Strong and the Exalted. (40)

Those We permit to take good hold and flourish on earth, are those who hold prayers, pay alms, exhort good works, and discourage evildoing, and to God belong all final results. (41)

If they deny you, many nations before them denied messengers send to them, such as peoples of Noah, Aad and Thamoud, (42)

the people of Abraham and Lot, (43)

and the people of Madian. Moses was denied, and We gave the unbelievers some time then We took them unaware, and God's revenge is so exercised. (44)

Many towns inhabited by transgressors We have annihilated and were left empty, with it buildings, wells and palaces left unused. (45)

Did they not walk in the land with souls that have senses of hearing and seeing? It is not blindness of the eyes but that of the soul. (46)

They seem to be asking for the torture earlier. Your Lord shall not miss His date with them, and a day to your Lord is like a thousand years of what you count. (47)

Towns that were warned about their transgression, We will take and they shall see the end destined for them. (48)

Say: "O' people, I am delivering a veritable warning to you." (49)

Those who believed and did good works, they shall have mercy and generous bounty. (50)

Those who did what they can to deny our signs, they are the owners of hell. (51)

All apostles and prophets before you, Satan attempted to interfere with their thought processes and their wishes. God erases what Satan installed, and then God applies His signs, and God is Knowledgeable and Wise. (52)

He lets the Devil influence only those who have sickness in their heart or those whose hearts are hardened. The transgressors are frequently in great dispute among each other. (53)

Those who are knowledgeable shall recognize it is the truth from you Lord, and their hearts shall open for it, and God shall guide those who believe to the straight path. (54)

The unbelievers shall remain in doubt about it until the Hour (*the Day of Judgement*) hits them suddenly or a great torture is delivered to them. (55)

On that Day judgement belongs to God, who is sitting on the throne, and He shall make the decision between them, and those who believed and did good works, are in the gardens of our bounty. (56)

Those who disbelieved, and denied our verses, they shall face humiliating torture. (57)

Those who immigrated, fought, or died in the cause of God, shall receive God's ample bounty, and God is the Best of all givers. (58)

He shall bring them to the entrance that satisfies them the most. God is knowledgeable and does not act in anger. (59)

Those who punish others in a way similar to the way they were punished, yet they are faced with excesses, they shall receive assistance from God. God is Forgiving and Merciful. (60)

God is the one who follows the day with the night and the night with the day. God hears and sees everything. (61)

For God is the truth, and what they claim are falsehoods, and God is Exalted and Capable of all things. (62)

Did you not see that God brings down water from the sky to fill the earth with greenery and vegetation? God is Considerate and Knowledgeable. (63)

He has all that is in heavens and on earth, every one owes thanks to Him and He owes no thanks to anyone. (64)

Did you not see that He made every thing on earth available for your convenience? Ships travel through the sea with His permission. He holds the earth safe from colliding with other planets in the sky unless He wished otherwise. God is Merciful and Beneficent to people. (65)

He is the One who gave Life and will take it again, then will give it back to you once more. Humans are very ungrateful. (66)

For every religion We made a sacred place of worship that they travel to for worship. Pray to your Lord that you remain on the straight path. (67)

If they argue with you, say: "God is more Knowledgeable with what you are up to." (68)

God shall be the judge on what you disagree on, among you, on the Day of Judgement. (69)

Did you not know that God knows what is in the heavens and on earth? It is all written in a Book, and that is all easy for God. (70)

They worship, other than God, what has never been revealed to have authority or power, and what they have no knowledge of, and the transgressors have no ally. (71)

As our veritable verses are read to them, you see in the faces of the unbelievers, the wickedness of their denial. They appear to want to hurt the ones who are reciting our verses on them, say to them: "I am predicting the pain of fire for you which God has promised for the unbelievers. A very miserable ending indeed." (72)

People, an example is given and listen to it. Those that you are worshiping will not be able to create a fly, even if all of them collaborated together. And if the fly takes something away from them, they will never be able to recover it. For one is weaker than the other. (73)

They did not appreciate God's real power. God is Powerful and Exalted. (74)

God selects messengers from among the angels and from among people. God hears and sees all things. (75)

He knows their present and what they left behind. All things eventually return to God. (76)

O' people who believe, kneel, prostrate yourselves, worship your Lord and do good works so you may succeed. (77)

Struggle in the way of God truly, for He chose you and never put in the religion any burdens upon you. You are following the religion of your great father, Abraham, who made the name Moslems. The apostle shall be a witness on you, and you shall witness others. Engage in prayers and pay alms, and hold on to the tenets of God, for He is Our sponsor, the best of all sponsors, and allies. (78)

THE BELIEVERS (23)

In the Name of God, Most Merciful, and Most Beneficent.

The believers succeeded. (1)

Those who in their prayers demonstrate fear of, and trust in, God. (2)

And those who do not engage in gossip and belittling others. (3)

And those who pay their alms obligations. (4)

And those who stay away from fornication. (5)

Except with their spouses, or those that belong to them, where they earn no blame. (6)

Those who cross beyond these limits are transgressors. (7)

Among the succeeding believers are also those who have solid respect for what they are entrusted with and for fulfilling their promises. (8)

And those who keep performing their prayers. (9)

These are heirs (10)

who will inherit paradise, and in it they shall be immortalized. (11)

We created humans from a creation sequence that started in mud. (12)

Then We made a germ into the deep part of it. (13)

Then from the germ We created a clot, then a mass of tissue, then from the tissue came bone, and then the bone was covered with flesh and from the flesh We made different creations. Glorified be God the best Creator. (14)

Then, later, you shall all die. (15)

Then, on the Day of Judgement you shall be resurrected again. (16)

We created above you seven layers of heaven, and We are fully aware of everything We did. (17)

We brought down water from the sky in moderate amounts and We established its presence on earth, and getting rid of it (*the water*) is always within our ability. (18)

With the water, We produced for you gardens of palm and vine and other fruits, from which you eat. (19)

A tree that grows in the Sinai (*olive tree*) produces oil and dyes for the use of humans. (20)

In cattle and sheep you have a lesson; you drink from its breasts and you eat its flesh. (21)

You also use it to ride on, just like you use ships to float on water. (22)

We sent Noah to his people to say: "My people, worship God, for you have no other God but Him. Is it not time for righteousness?" (23)

The unbelievers among his people said: "This is but a human like you, wanting to put himself in a position above you, and if God wanted, He would have sent angels, and we have never heard of such a thing from our predecessors." (24)

He is only a man who has some kind of mental illness. Just watch him for a while. (25)

He said: "God, give me support on what they are denying." (26)

We revealed to him to build the ship and helped him with our sight and revelations, and as the determined hour grew near, We ordered him to load on it male and female pairs of all animals. All shall die except those who I have already exempted. Do not try to intercede for the transgressors (*his son and his father*). They shall drown. (27)

As you are on your way on your ship say: "Thanks be to God who saved us from the transgressors." (28)

And say: "My Lord bring us safely to a place blessed by You. Your blessings are the best of all." (29)

In this there are signs. We do afflict those we wish with mishaps. (30)

We produced after them a new generation. (31)

And We sent to them an apostle from among them to tell them: "Worship God, for you have no other God but Him, for it is time for piousness." (32)

A lot of his people who are unbelievers denied that they will face the Last Day, because We permitted them to enjoy the luxuries of this life. They said he is only human like us; eats from what we eat and drinks from what we drink. (33).

They said: "If we obey a human like us, we shall be the losers. (34)

He is telling you that after you die and become dust and bones, you shall be resurrected again. (35)

These are empty claims that you are being promised. (36)

What counts only is our life in this life, we live it and die and then we shall never live again. (37)

He is a man who made up things in God's name; we shall not believe in him." (38)

He said: "God, support me against their denials." (39)

God said: In a short time they will be regretting what they said. (40)

We took them with a scream like thunder, that left them without motion. The transgressors shall be kept away. (41)

Then We created after them other generations. (42)

No people are ever gone a day before or a day after they are destined to go. (43)

Then We sent many messengers, one after the other, and as each people get their messenger they deny him, and again one people followed the other, until they all became subjects of conversation and example for those who came after them and those who do not believe. (44)

Then We sent Moses and his brother Aaron with Our signs and a veritable source of power. (45)

To the Pharaoh and his people and they became arrogant and disdainful. (46)

They said: "Are we going to follow two humans like us? Their people are our slaves." (47)

They denied them and they were annihilated. (48)

Then We gave Moses the Book so they may be guided. (49)

We made the son of Mary and his mother a sign, for all, and we sent her to a hill with vegetation and a flowing spring. (50)

O' messengers, eat from the best food and do good works, I have knowledge of all you do. (51)

Your people are all one people. I am your Lord. Show your piety to me. (52)

But their peoples divided into groups and parties and each one feels happy with what they had. (53)

Let them overwhelm themselves with their happiness for a while. (54)

Do they believe that We provide for them what We do because they have a special value for us? (55)

We actually, for a while, increase the rate of providing Our bounty to them, before they feel what will follow. (56)

Those who are watchful of what they do because of their fear of God. (57)

And those who believe in the signs God sent them. (58)

And those who do not associate others with their Lord. (59)

Those who appreciate what they are given with grateful hearts and with the knowledge that to their Lord they shall return. (60)

Those increase the rate of their giving as the rate of giving bounty to them is increased. (61)

God never requires a soul to provide anything above its ability to provide, and none will be treated unjustly. (62)

The others are not even concerned about it, because they are busy doing their own things. (63)

Those among them who are enjoying the highest luxury in living, make the loudest screaming and crying when faced with the consequences of what they did. (64)

Do not cry and scream today for you shall receive from Us no help. (65)

When My verses were recited to you, you used to turn your faces away. (66)

You were so proud of yourselves that you kept it up without relenting. (67)

Did they not understand the words, or did we bring them anything that was not brought to their predecessors? (68)

Or did they not know their messenger or did they suddenly decided to deny him? (69)

Or did they say he is crazy? He has rather brought them the truth, and to the truth they have none but hate. (70)

If the truth was to follow their whims, this would have corrupted all of the heavens and earth and everything in them. Instead, We brought them the Book and to the Book they are still in denial. (71)

Are you supposed to ask them for a fee for providing guidance to them (*and would they then have believed you*)? Your reward is from God and His rewards are the best of all rewards. (72)

You are simply inviting them to the straight path. (73)

Those who do not believe in the Last Day shall continue to deviate from the straight path. (74)

If We became merciful with them and took the pressure off of them, they shall go back to their transgressions as if nothing has happened. (75)

Even if we sent them what will hurt them, they will not return to their Lord or plead. (76)

Not even if they find themselves immersed in the severe torture of the Day of Judgement. (77)

He is the One who made for you the hearing the sights and the brains, yet you are rarely thankful. (78)

He is the one who spread you all over the earth, and back to Him you shall be assembled. (79)

He is the one who creates and destroys, and He is the reason behind the changing of the night and day. Do you not have sense?(80)

They even said like their predecessors: (81)

"Are we going to be resurrected after we are dead and become dust and bones?" (82)

Our predecessors have heard things like that in the past. These are nothing but ancient stories. (83)

Ask them: "To whom does the earth and everything on it belong, if you know?" (84)

They will say: "To God," and then say: "You'd better remember that." (85)

Say: "Who is the Lord of the seven heavens and and the Lord of the great throne?" (86)

They will say: "God." Say: 'Why do you not become pious?' (87)

Say: "Who has in his hand the total control of everything, and who can persecute any one, but no one can persecute Him, if you know." (88)

They will say: "God." Say: "So what is the mockery about?" (89)

We brought them the truth yet they continue to lie. (90)

God has never begotten a son nor does He have another God with Him, otherwise each God would have put a separate claim to what he has created, with one against the other. Glorified be God for He is far above what they describe. (91)

He is the One who has knowledge of the future and what all see and do, and He is far above their misguided associations. (92)

Say: "God, with what you show me of your promise to them (93)

please help me not ever be among the transgressors." (94)

We are capable of letting you see what will happen to them. (95)

It is better to repay the intention of harm with what is better. We are familiar with what they do. (96)

Say: "I seek your help my Lord from the Whispers of the devils." (97)

I also seek your help from even their presence. (98)

When one of them (*the unbelievers*) is facing death, they will say: "My Lord, let me go back (99)

so I may do some good works. It is just words they say, They shall remain trapped in an isthmus between now and the time they are resurrected." (100)

Once the trumpet is blown, they have no relatives or relations, and have no one to ask. (101)

Those who have a heavy load of good works shall be the winners. (102)

Those who have light loads of such are the ones who lost themselves, and in hell they shall be immortalized. (103)

Their faces shall be touched with fire and in it they shall suffer. (104)

Were you not denying My verses as they were being recited to you? (105)

They will say: "Our evildoing has caught up with us, we certainly were misguided people." (106)

They will say: "Please get us out of here, and if we went back again to what we were doing then we are definitely transgressors." (107)

The answer to them will be: "Stay shamefully where you are, no one will listen to you." (108)

My worshipers were saying: "Our Lord, we believed, forgive us and be merciful with us, and grant us Your mercy for You are the most Merciful of all." (109)

You mocked them and used them for your fun as you laughed. (110)

Today I will reward them for their patience, and they are the winners. (111)

He said (*God*): How many years did you stay on earth. (112)

They said: "We stayed a day or several days, ask those who are counting." (113)

He (*God*) said: You stayed a very short time, which you know. (114)

Did you think We created you for no reason and that to us you shall not return? (115)

Glorified be Him, God, the true King, No God other than Him, and He is the Lord of the High Throne. (116)

Those who claim other gods have no proof for such. Their reckoning is with their Lord, and the unbelievers shall not succeed. (117)

Say: "My Lord, forgive and have mercy. You are the most Merciful." (118)

THE LIGHT (24)

In the Name of God, Most Merciful, and Most Beneficent.

A chapter that We revealed and authenticated, and revealed in it clear verses to make sure you remember. (1)

The adulterers, men and woman, shall receive one hundred lashes each, and do not be reluctant to do that within the frames of the religion, if you believed in God and the Last Day, and the punishment shall be witnessed by a group of believers. (2)

An adulterer marries only an adulteress, or an associater (*a person who associate others with God*), and an adulteress marries only an adulterer or an associater. This is forbidden for the believers. (3)

Those who falsely accuse innocent women then fail to produce four witness to support their accusation, shall receive eighty lashes, and no testimony shall be accepted from them ever, and those are the real evildoers. (4)

Except for those who truly repent, and establish themselves in good works, for God is Forgiving and Merciful. (5)

Those who accuse their spouses, and have no witnesses but themselves, can take an oath four times, one for each witness, and then that spouse will be considered truthful (6)

unless the other spouse takes the same oath accusing the other of lying. (7)

That will protect the accused spouse from punishment. (8)

Both sides will earn the wrath of God when lying. (9)

This is an example of God's favor upon you, and mercifulness to you. God is Forgiving and Wise. (10)

If accusations come from a group of you that appear to be conspiring, do not consider it bad but rather good, because each one of them separately shall be considered responsible to God for this grave sin, and the organizer of the group shall have a great torture. (11)

Why did you not say to yourselves: "What you would have said if you were the accused, that the accusation represents clear evildoing?" (12)

For why did the accusers not produce four witnesses, and when they do not, they are the ones that are liars in the Eye of God. (13)

If it was not for God's favor to you and mercifulness upon you, you would have been touched with great torture for what you had helped spreading. (14)

You participated with your tongues and with what came out of your mouths in things you have no knowledge of. You may think it is trivial, but to God it is a very big thing. (15)

When you heard it, you should have said, we shall not repeat such a thing, and that in the eyes of God the glorified, it is none but a falsehood. (16)

God admonishes you never to do that again if you are believers. (17)

God clarifies the signs for you, He is Knowledgeable and Wise. (18)

Those who like to spread news of indecency among the believers, shall have great torture in this life and the life next; for God knows, but you do not. (19)

What saved you is God's favor and mercifulness on you. God is Caring and Merciful. (20)

People who believe, do not follow the steps of the Devil, for one who does is promoting indecency and evildoing. If it were not for God's favor and mercy towards you, He would not have passed one among you as a believer, but God will pass whomever He wishes, and God Hears and Knows. (21)

Those of you who have considerable resources and means, do not, out of anger or other reasons, deny the relatives and the destitute or those who immigrated serving God. It is better to forgive; do they not want God to forgive them? God is Forgiving and Merciful. (22)

Those who throw accusations on innocent, unaware and believing women shall be cursed by God in this life and the life next, and great torture shall await them. (23)

The Day when their tongues, their hands and their feet shall testify to what they were doing, (24)

on that Day God shall give them back their due, and they shall learn that God is the veritable truth. (25)

Wicked men are for wicked women, and wicked women are for wicked men. Good men are for good women, and good women are for good men, and the latter are innocent of what they are accused of, and to them goes God's forgiveness and His generous bounty. (26)

People who believe, do not ever enter homes that are not yours, without permission, and without saluting its owners, for that is better for you, so you may remember. (27)

If there is no one in the house do not go in unless you have permission. If you were told to stay out, stay out, for it is better for you, and God is Knowledgeable of what you do. (28)

You may enter houses that are uninhabited, only if it contains property that belongs to you, and God knows what you admit to and what you do not. (29)

Say to believing men to stay away from staring to where their gaze does not belong, and to avoid indecency, for that is purer for them. God is Knowledgeable of what they do. (30)

Say to believing women to also avoid staring, and to preserve their purity, and not to expose items of clothing intended to increase their attractiveness, except when it is on areas of their bodies that are normally exposed, and they should use a cover for their body skin folds, with the exception of their spouses, their fathers or the fathers of their fathers, or the fathers of their spouses, or their children, or the children of their spouses, or their siblings, or the children of their siblings, or other women, or those who belong to them or work for them, or to children who are at an age that would not be compatible with being attracted to women, and should avoid, while walking, to produce noises that will attract attention to them. All of you should submit your repentance to God, so you may succeed. (31)

Marry, the unmarried among you, and those women who are good among the population or your slaves, and if they are poor God will enrich them from His own bounty, and God is Generous and Knowledgeable. (32)

Those who cannot afford to marry, let them remain celibate, until God enrich them from his bounty, and those among your slaves who wishes to buy his liberty from you, do that and give him some of what God has given you. Do not ever force any of your female slaves into prostitution for your benefit, and these women who find themselves into such a situation against their will, God shall forgive them, and He is Forgiving and Merciful. (33)

We revealed to you clear verses, and examples from those before you, as an admonishment to the righteous. (34)

God is the light of the heavens and the earth. His light can be exemplified by a lighthouse and in it is a light. The flame of light is in a glass container, shining like a little star, and the flame is fed by oil from a sacred olive tree that grew neither in the east nor in the west. Its oil is practically shining without a fire touching it. Light upon light, and God guides to His light whomever He wants. God brings examples to people, and God is Knowledgeable of all things. (35)

In houses that God authorized that it be raised, where His name is mentioned and He is glorified in the coming and going. (36)

Men who are not diverted by a trade or sale from the mention of God, and the holding of prayers, or the giving of alms, who fear the Day when the eyes and the brains are turned upside down. (37)

God shall reward them in a way that is appropriate for the best they did, and even more from His bounty. God shall give to whomever He wishes, with no accounting. (38)

The deeds of the unbelievers are like a mirage, which is thought by the thirsty to be water, and as they come closer they find nothing, and God rewards them with what is equal. He is fast to bring forth His reckoning. (39)

Or like the darkness of a deep ocean and waves at the top, and above the waves are thick clouds. Layers of darkness one over the other, one in the middle of it will not be able to see one's hand if it is up. Those who are not provided with light from God, shall have no light. (40)

Do you not see that God is glorified by all that is in heaven and earth, and the birds in all their varieties, each learned their own methods of praying and glorification, and God has knowledge of what they do. (41)

To God belongs ownership of the heavens and earth, and to God belongs the destiny of all. (42)

Do you not know that God moves the clouds together until they appear like thick masses, and you see the rain come through it from the sky and even hail comes down, and it may hit some injuriously while it will miss others as He wishes, and God's lightning can nearly take away the eyesight. (43)

God turns the night into day, and in it there should be a sign to those who have insight. (44)

God created from water all kinds of animals. Some crawl on their bellies, and some walk on two legs and some walk on four. God creates what He wishes and God is Capable of all things. (45)

We have revealed veritable signs, and God guides whomever He wishes to the straight path. (46)

They say we are believers in God and the Apostle, and then a group of them denies, and those are not believers. (47)

And they ask for God and the Apostle to mediate between them, some of them refuse. (48)

Had the system of justice been in their hands, they would have come to it with obedience. (49)

They either had poor intentions, or they suspected that God and the Apostle may not be fair with them. Those are the transgressors. (50)

When the believers request that God and his Apostle mediate between them, they will say: "We shall listen and obey, and they shall be the ones who succeed." (51)

Those who obey God and His apostle, fear God, and worship Him, are the winners. (52)

They swear, using the name of God, that they will obey. Say: "Do not swear, it is the actual obedience that counts and not using God's name, for God is Knowledgeable with what you are doing." (53)

Obey God and obey the Apostle, and if they disobeyed, he carries the responsibility for his actions and they carry the responsibility for theirs. If you obey, you shall be guided; the apostle's obligation is only to warn clearly. (54)

God has promised those who believed and did good works to let them supervene on earth like He did people before them, and to strengthen the religion that He chose for them and to replace their fear with a feeling of security. So long as they worship Me and associate none with Me, and those who disbelieve after that are the real evildoers. (55)

Engage in prayer, and pay the alms, and obey the apostle so you may receive mercy. (56)

Do not ever think that the unbelievers are safe on earth. Hell shall be their residence, a miserable place to live indeed. (57)

People who believe, three times during the day, while in your home, your young children or those who belong to you or work for you, should ask your permission to enter, before they surprise you, early in the morning before the morning prayer, and before noon when you could be putting your clothes on, and after the evening prayer. Otherwise you can always get together. Thus God reveals his verses to you. God is Knowledgeable and Wise. (58)

As your children become adults, their permission should be sought for entry as they did to others when they were younger, and so God reveals His verses to you, and God is Knowledgeable and Wise. (59)

Older women who are not seeking marriage, can put their clothes on without some of the restrictions on younger women; also without using what may enhance their attractiveness, and if they dress conservatively it is better for them. God Hears and Knows. (60)

There should be nothing wrong with eating with a blind, lame or sick person, nor should you find a problem in eating at the homes of your fathers, mothers, brothers or sisters, uncles or aunts, on your father's or mother's side, or at any home whose keys were entrusted to you, or the home of your friend, together or separately. And if you enter a home, salute with words that mention God and ask for His blessing, and thus God reveals His verses to you so you may understand. (61)

Believers are those who believe in God and his Apostle, and when they are with him on a collective matter, they seek his permission before leaving. Those who ask your permission upon entry and for leaving are the believers in God and his apostle, and when they ask permission grant it to those you wish and ask for God's forgiveness for them. God is Forgiving and Merciful. (62)

Do not ever address the Apostle in the same way you address each other. God knows those who try to sneak out without His permission, let those who do things like that be careful about being hit with an affliction or excruciating torture. (63)

To God belongs all that is in heavens and on earth. He knows what you are up to, and when they are returned to Him, He shall tell them what they did, and God has knowledge with all they do. (64)

THE DISTINGUISHER (25)

In the Name of God, Most Merciful, and Most Beneficent.

Glorified be He Who revealed the Distinguisher to His servant, so he can deliver a warning to the world. (1)

The One to Whom belong the heavens and the earth, Who has never begotten a son nor did He ever have a partner. And Who created everything, after giving it careful evaluation. (2)

They took instead of Him gods that never created a thing, but were created by someone themselves, and they cannot do good or harm for themselves, not to mention others. They are unable to produce life, death or resurrection. (3)

The unbelievers said: "This is nothing but fabrication, in which he got help from other people. What they claimed was transgression and forgery." (4)

They said: "This is old fables and mythology of old times, being dictated to him night and day." (5)

Say: "It was revealed by God who knows the secrets of the heavens and the earth, and God is Forgiving and Merciful." (6)

They said: "Here is this apostle who eats food, and walks in the market, did he have an angel sent to him to guard him? (7)

Or was a treasure was thrown on him from above, or does he have gardens from where he eats?" The transgressors said: "You are only following a man who appears a victim of sorcery." (8)

Look at how they are blindly guessing, and they have become so misguided that they could never find their way again. (9)

Glorified be He who when He wants can provide for you much more than what they are imagining, such as gardens under which rivers flow, and can raise for you palaces. (10)

They have denied the Hour (*the Last Day*) and for those who have We have prepared a raging fire. (11)

If the fire even saw them from a far place, they shall hear its roaring and blowing of anger. (12)

And when they are thrown in it in a narrow place, near to each other, they shall start asking for death. (13)

They shall be told: "Here you have to ask for more than one death, but rather many deaths." (14)

Is this better or the eternal paradise, promised to the righteous, and it is to them a reward and destiny. (15)

In it they shall have what they want, and in it they will be immortalized, and it is a certain promise from your Lord. (16)

They will be assembled along with whatever they were worshiping, other than God, and they will be asked: "Did you misguide my servants or did they stray on their own?" (17)

They (*the Idols*) will say: "You be glorified. We should have never taken as sponsors anyone but You. You have provided for them and their fathers so much that they forgot your mention and became losers. (18)

They have denied you (*the idols*) and what you (*the idol worshipers*) say. You have no one to vouch for you. And the aggressors like you shall receive a great torture. (19)

All those We sent before you, did also eat and walk in the market. We have always used some of you to test the others. Be patient; God has all things in sight. (20)

Those who are not anxious to meet us say: "If we had angels sent to us, or we were able to see our Lord it would have been different." They have really given themselves too much importance, and were arrogant, and engaged in great deception. (21)

They will see the angels on a day when doing that is no good tidings to the transgressors, when their pass to hell will be written in stone. (22)

Whatever they may have thought their good deeds were, we shall reduce them to blowing dust. (23)

Those in heaven then shall have the best of all places, and the most comfortable of all residences. (24)

The day blinding light shall show through cracks in the thick clouds, and the angels will be coming down. (25)

The true monarchy that day belongs to the Merciful. It is a day that shall be very hated by the unbelievers. (26)

The day the transgressors shall be biting their hands, and saying: "We wish we had found our way to follow the apostle." (27)

Many will say: "How did we manage to adopt a sponsor other than God?" (28)

The Devil misguided me away from the Mention (*the Book, the Koran*). The Devil has always been the one who leads to failure. (29)

The Apostle said: "My Lord, my people are taking this Koran as something to be ignored. (30)

This is why God has had enemies among the transgressors." All you need as a supporter and guide is your Lord. (31)

Some unbelievers said: "Why did God not reveal the entire Koran all at once?" We did it gradually so that you understand carefully as it is being revealed to you and to give you support as events unfold, and to be able to recite it, as it is revealed. (32)

Thus every time they come up with something, We revealed to you the truthful answer, and the correct interpretation in light of the events. (33)

Those unbelievers are the ones who shall be dragged and assembled to hell so hard that their faces shall arrive first, which is the worst place for the most unguided. (34)

We brought Moses the Book, and We made his brother Aaron his lieutenant. (35)

We asked them to go to the people who denied our signs, until We ended up annihilating and destroying them. (36)

People of Noah, when they denied the apostles We drowned them, and made them an example for other people, and prepared for the transgressors an excruciating torture. (37)

Aad and Thamoud and the inhabitants of Rass and many generations between them were also annihilated. (38)

Each were given signs and examples and then destroyed and annihilated. (39)

Did people not see what happen to the town (*of Lot*) and the bad rain (*rain of stones*)? Probably they did not because they never believed they would be assembled on the Day of Judgement. (40)

Whenever they see you, they treat you sarcastically. Is this why God sent you an apostle? (41)

The unbelievers said: "He just about guided us away from our gods, if it were not for our holding on to them." They shall see the torture that will afflict those who depart from the right path. (42)

Do you not see those who worship, as gods, whatever they feel like? You cannot be responsible of every one. (43)

Do you think that most of them hear and are sensible? They are like animals, and even more misguided. (44)

Did you not see how your Lord produced the change in the length and direction of shadows? If He wanted He could have made it stationary, but He made it change following the change in the position of the sun. (45)

It shortens slowly as the day progresses, then it becomes longer again. (46)

He made the night for you as a cover for all to sleep for rest and the day to spread for work and activity. (47)

He sent the wind as good tidings for the arrival of the rain, and from His mercy. Water comes purified from the sky. (48)

To revive barn locations, and quench the thirst of many animals and people that We created. (49)

We distributed the reviving water among many locations, so they may remember God, but most insisted on being unbelievers. (50)

If We wanted to, We could have sent carriers of warning to every town. (51)

Do not obey the unbelievers, and you may have to struggle a lot to resist their influence. (52)

He is the Creator of both kinds of water, fresh water (*in rivers and wells*) and salty water in the seas and separated between them with isthmuses of solid stones and rocks. (53)

He is the One who created humans from water, and made them into relatives and spouses. Your Lord is extremely able. (54)

They worship as an alternative to God what cannot help them or hurt them. What unbelievers do is always evident to God. (55)

We sent you only to bring good tidings and warnings. (56)

Say to them: "I have never asked you for payment or reward for anything I brought you, all you need to do is find God's straight path." (57)

Rely on the Immortal who does not die. Glorify Him, and leave to Him the sins of His worshipers because He has the greatest expertise in that. (58)

He is the One who created the heavens and the earth, and what is in between in six days, then He sat on the throne. The Merciful keep on expecting the best for He is the Expert. (59)

As they were asked to prostrate themselves to the Merciful, they said: "Why should We do that by your order?" And they went deeper in the intransigence. (60)

Glorified be Him who created the different planets and constellations and among them the moon as a lamp emitting light. (61)

He is the One who brought the night and the day after it, for those who want to keep it in mind and be grateful. (62)

Worshipers of the Merciful walk on earth lightly and when they meet those who are ignorant they still give greetings. (63)

Those are the ones who glorify their Lord while standing or as they prostrate themselves. (64)

They say: "Our Lord, steer us away from the torture of hell for its torture is a huge punishment." (65)

It is the worst place to stay and the lowest rank to be. (66)

Those are the ones who spend neither too much nor too little and stay reasonably in between. (67)

Those are the Ones who do not worship, along with God, other gods. And do not ever kill a soul unless justifiably, and they do not commit adultery, and those who do shall pay the price in punishment. (68)

On the Day of Judgement torture will be doubled for them and they shall be disgraced forever (69)

unless they truly repent and do good works, then God may forgive their sins and God is Merciful and Beneficent. (70)

Those who repent shall have to do it in intention and practice. (71)

Also good are those who are never the bearers of false witness, and if they pass by gossip they do not pick it up. (72)

And good are those who when reminded of the verses of their Lord do not act like they are deaf and blind. (73)

They are the ones who say: "Our Lord, grant us descendents from our spouses who we shall be proud of and help us become leaders in righteousness." (74)

Those shall be rewarded with paradise for their patience, and they shall be greeted and welcomed as they enter it. (75)

Immortalized in it; the best place to reside. (76)

Say: "My Lord would not have paid any attention to you if it was not for your prayers, and if you denied Him you would have had to live with the consequences." (77)

THE POETS (26)

In the Name of God, Most Merciful, and Most Beneficent.

Taah, Saah, Meem. (1)

These are the verses of the veritable Book. (2)

You seem to be ready to exhaust yourself to death, unless they become believers. (3)

If We choose to We can reveal to them one sign in the sky that will make them raise their eyes upward, and bend their necks in submission. (4)

Every time they receive Mention (*verses*) from the Merciful in explanation to them, they seem to turn away. (5)

They are in denial, and they shall receive the appropriate corrections on what they have been sarcastic about. (6)

Did they not see how on earth We have caused pairs of all kinds of plants to grow? (7)

There is a sign in that, but most of them are not believers. (8)

And your Lord is Exalted and Merciful. (9)

When Your Lord called on Moses to go to the transgressing people, (10)

People of the Pharaoh who need to start fearing and obey God, (11)

He said: "My Lord, I am fearful that they may deny me. (12)

And I will have tightness in my chest and a knot in my tongue. Send my brother Aaron with me. (13)

The people of the Pharaoh already have a cause against me and they may choose to kill me." (14)

He said: Go, both of you, and I will be listening. (15)

They came to Pharaoh and said: "We are messengers from the Lord of the universe. (16)

He wants you to release and send the people of Israel with us." (17)

He said: "Did you not see how we brought you up from the time you were small, and you lived with us a major portion of your years? (18)

Then you committed the crime you did, and now you also became an unbeliever." (19)

He said: "Yes, I did the crime and it was a mistake. (20)

And I ran away because I was afraid of you. But God chose for me a different way and now I am one of His apostles. (21)

Are you telling me that it is a fair exchange in your eye to let me go while you are enslaving the entire people of Israel?" (22)

The Pharaoh said: "Who is the Lord of the universe?" (23)

"He is the Lord of the heavens and earth if you know anything." (24)

He (*the Pharaoh*) said to his people around him: "Do not listen to him. (25)

Your Lord is the one who inherited everything from your forefathers. (26)

This Apostle that was sent to you is crazy." (27)

He (*Moses*) said: "He is the Lord of the east and the west and what is between them if you have sense." (28)

Then he (*the Pharoah*) said: "If you take a god other than me, I shall put you in prison." (29)

He (*Moses*) said: "What I brought is a veritable sign." (30)

"Then bring it if you are telling the truth." (31)

He (*Moses*) threw his staff and it changed into a clear and deadly snake. (32)

Then he pulled his hand out and it became shining white in color. (33)

He (*the Pharaoh*) said: "This is nothing but an elaborate performance of a sorcerer. (34)

He wants to get you out of your land with his sorcery, so what do you think I should do?" (35)

They said: "Just give him time, him and his brother, and send out a call in your cities to assemble (36)

the best sorcerers our country has." (37)

He got them all together on a predetermined day (38)

and a public meeting was set up. (39)

People came to find out if the sorcerers would be able to defeat Moses. (40)

When the sorcerers came, they asked the Pharaoh: "Are we going to be rewarded if we are triumphant?" (41)

And he said: "Yes, and you shall be among the people who are closest to me." (42)

Moses said: "Go ahead and throw what you want to throw." (43)

They threw their ropes and staffs, and said to the Pharaoh: "We shall be the winners." (44)

Then Moses threw his staff, and it swallowed everything they produced. (45)

The sorcerers all fell down prostrated. (46)

They said: "We believe in the Lord of the universe, (47)

the Lord of Moses and Aaron." (48)

He (*the Pharaoh*) said: "You believed him without my permission, He must be your chief sorcerer, who taught you sorcery. I shall cut your arms and legs on opposite sides, and I shall crucify all of you." (49)

They said: "Do whatever you want, we are back to our Lord. (50)

We hope that the Lord will forgive our sins if we are among the first to become believers." (51)

We revealed to Moses to leave and that My followers will follow. (52)

The Pharaoh sent people to the cities assembling an army. (53)

He was telling them that these are nothing but a few rebels (54)

who managed to earn Our wrath. (55)

We are all watching for them. (56)

So as it turned out, We have gotten them (*the Egyptians*) out of their gardens, with the flowing springs. (57)

Leaving behind their treasures and plush homes (58)

while We rewarded the children of Israel elsewhere. (59)

The Egyptian army started behind them very early in the day. (60)

And as both sides were able to see each other, the people of Moses said: "We shall be caught." (61)

He said: "No, God will guide us." (62)

We revealed to Moses to hit the water of the sea with his staff, and the sea water split into two great mountains of water. (63)

While We permitted the others only to get close to the sea. (64)

We saved Moses and his people. (65)

Then We drowned the others. (66)

This is an example, for most of them were not believers. (67)

Your Lord is the Exalted and Merciful. (68)

Tell them of the news of Abraham. (69)

As he said to his father and people: "What are you worshiping?" (70)

They said: "We worship idols to which we are devoted." (71)

He said: "Do they hear you when you pray? (72)

Or do they help you or hurt you?" (73)

They said: "But we found our fathers doing the same." (74)

So, you see what you have been worshiping! (75)

You and your old fathers. (76)

These that you worship are enemies to me. Mine is the Lord of the universe. (77)

He is the One who created me, and He is the One who guides me. (78)

He is the One who feeds me and quenches my thirst. (79)

And if I became ill He heals me. (80)

He is the One who will cause me to die then resurrect me again. (81)

He is the One who I yearn to have Him forgive my sins, on the Last Day. (82)

Lord, grant me good judgement and let me follow in the footsteps of the righteous. (83)

And also grant me a tongue that is dedicated to truth, in regard to others. (84)

And count me among those who will inherit the Gardens of your blessings. (85)

Forgive my father, for he is among the misguided. (86)

Protect me from being sad on the Day of Resurrection. (87)

The day when no help can be expected from riches or children. (88)

Except for those who come to God with a clean heart. (89)

Paradise stands ready for the righteous (90)

while hell stands prominent in the future of the misguided. (91)

They will be asked where are what you have been worshiping. (92)

Without God, can they help you, or help themselves. (93)

They shall stay in it (*hell*) and they are the misguided. (94)

They and all of the soldiers of Satan. (95)

They will say as they fight among each other. (96)

It is a fact in front of God, that we have wronged ourselves (97)

when we considered you (*the idols*) equal to the Lord of the universe. (98)

It was the transgressors who misguided us (99)

and we have no one to intercede for us. (100)

Neither do we have close friends. (101)

They would say: "If we had another chance, we certainly would be among the believers." (102)

They are an example. They were not believers. (103)

Your Lord is the Exalted and the Merciful. (104)

The people of Noah denied the messengers sent to them. (105)

Their brother Noah said to them: "Are you not going to fear God and worship Him? (106)

I was sent to you with a veritable message. (107)

Worship and fear God and obey my message. (108)

I will not ask you for any reward, for my reward is only from the Lord of the universe. (109)

Fear God and follow my message." (110)

You want us to believe in what you ask us to, when your followers are the worst among us? (111)

He said: "How can I have anything to do with what they were doing? (112)

It should be obvious to you that their time of reckoning belongs to my Lord. (113)

I will not chase the believers away. (114)

I am only intended to deliver warning." (115)

They said to Noah: "If you do not desist, you will force us to become criminals." (116)

He (*Noah*) said: "My Lord, my people are denying the message." (117)

Noah said: "Separate between me and them, and save me and the believers with me." (118)

We saved him and those with him in the floating ship (119)

and caused the rest to drown. (120)

In this there is an example, and most of them were not believers. (121)

Your Lord is the Exalted and the Merciful. (122)

The people of Aad denied the messengers sent to them. (123)

When their brother Houd said: "Why do you not worship and fear God? (124)

I am a faithful apostle sent to you. (125)

Worship, fear, and obey God. (126)

I have never asked you to reward me for my reward is on the Lord of the Universe. (127)

You build on every hill a huge mansion for your own satisfaction. (128)

You build manufacturing plants like you are going to live forever. (129)

You tend to show your power always by forceful terror. (130)

Fear and worship God and obey Him. (131)

Worship God and fear Him for He is the One who gave you the knowledge that you have. (132)

He gave you luxuries and families. (133)

Gardens and flowing springs. (134)

I fear for you the torture of a Great Day." (135)

They said: "It shall make no difference whether you gave us advice or not. (136)

What we are doing is only what our predecessors were doing. (137)

And no one is going to torture us." (138)

They still denied, and We annihilated them, and in that was an example to all, for most of them were not believers. (139)

Your Lord is the Exalted and Merciful. (140)

Thamoud also denied apostles We sent to them. (141)

And their brother Saleh also said to them: "Worship and fear God. (142)

I am a faithful apostle to you. (143)

Worship, fear and obey God. (144)

I will never ask you for a reward because my reward is on God. (145)

Do you want to leave the safety that you have here? (146)

Gardens and flowing springs. (147)

Vegetation, palms and other plants. (148)

You dig your homes as caves inside the mountains. (149)

Worship and fear God and obey Him. (150)

And do not obey those who indulge themselves in excesses. (151)

They are the ones who corrupt the earth and not reform it." (152)

They said: "You are nothing but a sorcerer. (153)

You are nothing but a human like us; bring us a sign if you are truthful." (154)

He said: "Here is a female camel. She needs to drink just like you do, until a predetermined day. (155)

Do not do any harm to her or you shall receive the torture of a great day." (156)

They slaughtered her and they woke up regretful. (157)

They were taken and slated for the torture, because most of them were not believers. (158)

Your Lord is the Exalted and the Merciful. (159)

The people of Lot also denied their apostles. (160)

As their brother Lot told them: "Are you not going to worship God and fear Him? (161)

I am your faithful apostle. (162)

Worship, fear, and obey God (163)

I shall not ask you for a reward for my reward is on the Lord alone. (164)

You choose males to have sex with. (165)

And you turn away from your wives that God created for you, you sure are transgressors." (166)

They said: "If you (*Lot*) do not desist, we shall throw you out." (167)

He said: "To what you do, I shall always be objecting." (168)

He said: "Lord, save me and my family from what these people are doing." (169)

We saved him and his entire family (170)

except for an old lady. (171)

We destroyed them all. (172)

We sent a rain on them, and a rain sent to people who were warned is a damning rain. (173)

In that there was a sign, and most of them were unbelievers. (174)

Your Lord is the Exalted and the Merciful. (175)

The jungle dwellers (*city of Midian*) also denied apostles We sent to them. (176)

Shoaib said to his people: "Are you not going to worship and fear God? (177)

I am your faithful apostle. (178)

Worship, fear and obey God. (179)

I do not expect a reward from you, for my true reward is from the Lord of the universe. (180)

Be accurate in what you weigh and sell, and do not be among the cheaters who are losers. (181)

Use accurate scales for weighing. (182)

Do not cheat people out of their property, and do not spread corruption on earth. (183)

Fear the One who created you, and created those who came before you." (184)

They said: "You are possessed. (185)

We think you are only a human like us, and we believe you are lying. (186)

Bring down on us a part of the sky, if you are truthful." (187)

He said: "My God is more Knowledgeable with what you do." (188)

They still denied Him, and they were taken by the torture of the Dark Day, and it is the torture of a great day. (189)

In that was a sign, and most of them were not believers. (190)

Your Lord is Exalted, and Merciful. (191)

It (*the Koran*) is revealed by the Lord of the universe. (192)

It was transmitted by the faithful spirit (*Gabriel*) (193)

to your heart to engage you in warning (194)

in a clear Arabic language. (195)

This revelation was predicted in the old scriptures. (196)

Is it not enough for them that the prediction of its arrival was known to the knowledgeable of the children of Israel? (197)

Even if We had revealed it to a non-Arab, (198)

they still would not have believed in it. (199)

This is the way it affects the hearts of the transgressors. (200)

They will not believe in it until they face excruciating pain. (201)

It shall hit them suddenly while unaware. (202)

They will say: "Are we truly seeing what we are seeing?" (203)

Are they trying to speed up what is certain to come to them? (204)

Did you see how we let them enjoy themselves for years? (205)

Then they get what they are promised. (206)

What they were enjoying shall be no help to them now. (207)

We never destroy a town unless they were warned first. (208)

We do remind and We are never unjust. (209)

We do not use the devils as messengers. (210)

They will never be able even to play that role. (211)

But their hearing is insulated. (212)

Do not worship any one other than God, if you do not want to end among those who will be tortured. (213)

Warn the people who are nearest to you. (214)

Be kind to those who follow you. (215)

If they refuse, say: "I am innocent of what you do." (216)

And depend on the Exalted and the Merciful (217)

who sees you when you rise (218)

and when you lead those who prostrate themselves. (219)

He is the One who hears and knows. (220)

Do you want to know to whom the devils are revealed? (221)

They are revealed to every determined transgressor. (222)

Those who pretend like they are listening, but they are liars. (223)

The poets are many times followed by the misguided. (224)

Did you not see how they keep on going from one place to another. (225)

They also tend to say what they will not do. (226)

Except for those who believe and do good works. and mention God often and achieve victory after they are treated unjustly. And those who are transgressors and treat others unjustly, shall find what kind of an ending they will get. (227)

THE ANTS (27)

In the Name of God, Most Merciful, and Most Beneficent.

Taah, Seen. These are the verses of the Koran, a veritable Book. (1)

Guidance and good tidings to the believers (2)

who engage in prayers, pay the alms, and are certain of the Day of Judgement. (3)

Those who do not believe in the Last Day, their actions are being recorded and they shall remain in their deep state of misguidedness. (4)

Those are the ones who will receive the worst torture, and on the Day of Judgement they are the losers. (5)

You are getting the Koran, from the Knowing and the Knowledgeable. (6)

Moses said to his people: "I see evidence of a fire. I will go to it, find out what is going on, and bring you a torch from which you can light up a fire for warmth." (7)

As he got close to it, he was called by a voice that said: This fire and those around it are blessed. Glorified is God, the Lord of the universe. (8)

Moses, it is I, God, your Lord, the Exalted and the Wise. (9)

He said: Throw your staff. And when he did it began to move and shake. He was scared and he ran away. The voice said: Do not be afraid. My apostles are never afraid of me. (10)

Except for those who transgressed and then changed to good work from bad. For I am Forgiving and Merciful. (11)

Put your hand in your pocket, then pull it out and it shall come out glowing white, which will be one among nine signs you shall present to the Pharaoh and his people, because they are transgressors. (12)

When he brought Our veritable signs to them, they said: "This is obviously sorcery." (13)

They denied the signs, even after they felt it was true due to arrogance. So you can see what was the ending for the corrupted. (14)

We brought David and Solomon wisdom, and they said: "Thanks to God who gave us preference over many other people." (15)

Solomon inherited David and he said to his people: "We were taught the language of birds, and we were given all kinds of things. This is a big veritable favor." (16)

Solomon assembled his soldiers from humans, the jinn and from among birds. (17)

As they reached the valley of ants, one ant said to the others: "Enter your homes, so that Solomon and his soldiers do not crush you unknowingly." (18)

Solomon smiled as he heard her statement and said smiling: "God, help me to remember always to thank You for Your blessings on me and my son, and to be always among Your servants who do good works." (19)

He inspected his birds and said: "Where is the lapwing, for I do not see him anywhere. (20)

If he is absent I shall torture him or slay him, unless he brings me a clear important excuse." (21)

He was not far and he said: "I know something you do not know. I brought you true news about Sheba. (22)

I found out they are led by a queen who has everything and a very big throne." (23)

We found her and her people prostrate themselves to the sun, and not to God. The Devil is behind what they do, and he led them astray, and they became misguided. (24)

They do not prostrate themselves in front of God who knows all the secrets of the heaven and the earth, and knows what is hidden or revealed by anyone. (25)

God, who there is none but Him, Lord of the great throne. (26)

He (*Solomon*) said: "We shall find out if you are telling the truth or you are among the liars." (27)

He (*Solomon*) said to the bird: "Take this letter from me and throw it to them, then leave, but stay at a distance where you can see what will they do." (28)

She said: "My people, I had a letter thrown on to me from a high level source. (29)

It is from Solomon, in the name of God, the Merciful and the Beneficent. (30)

He is asking that we humble ourselves and surrender ourselves to God." (31)

She said: "I want you to tell me what you want, for I am not making a decision on that until I hear from you." (32)

They said: "We are people who have a lot of power and courage, so contemplate it yourself, and then give us you orders." (33)

She said: "When kings enter a town, they make its proud people, less than proud and actually insult them. This is their mode of operation. (34)

I am sending them a present and I shall see how they respond." (35)

Solomon's answer was: "Are you so proud of yourselves that you send me money? God has given me far more than anything you can give me. (36)

Go back to them and tell them to expect soldiers they cannot handle, and we shall get them out subjugated and with total loss of pride." (37)

Solomon said to his followers: "Who among you will bring me her throne before they even had a chance to decide on surrendering?" (38)

A demon from among the jinn said: "I will bring it before you had a chance to stand up from your chair. I have the power and the trustworthiness." (39)

The one who had knowledge of the Scriptures said: "I will bring it to you before your eyelid can blink." And when he noted that Solomon will most likely trust him with the job, he said: "This is a favor from God to test me, whether I will be thankful or engage in denial, and one who thanks, does for himself, and one who denies does against himself. My Lord is Rich and Generous." (40)

Then Solomon said: "Make some changes in her throne and let us see if she will recognize it or if she going to be clueless." (41)

When she appeared, she was asked: "Is this your throne?" and she said: "It does resemble it." Solomon said: "We were given knowledge before her, and then surrendered ourselves to God. (42)

Her problem is what she has been worshiping instead of God. She comes from an unbelieving nation." (43)

She was asked to enter the palace and as she entered she thought that the floor was a big pool of water, so she pulled her dress up higher over her legs, and he told her that the floor of the palace was made of glass derived from glass bottles. She said: "Lord, I have transgressed against myself. I have, like Solomon, surrendered to the Lord of the universe." (44)

As We sent to Thamoud their brother Saleh, who said to his people: "Worship God," and they divided into two parties fighting each other. (45)

He said: "My people, why are you quicker in doing bad, rather than good? Instead, ask God for forgiveness so you may receive mercy." (46)

They said: "We shall protect ourselves from any harm that may come to us from you or your followers." He said: "Harm will not come to you from us if it comes, but it will come from God, for you are a corrupt people." (47)

In town there was a band of nine transgressors, who spread corruption in the land. (48)

They conspired to kill him (*Saleh*) and his family then say to their relatives that they never saw who did the crime. (49)

They conspired and so did We while they were unaware. (50)

See what were the consequences of their conspiracy. We annihilated them, and their people together. (51)

There are their houses empty, as a consequence to their transgressions, as a sign to those who understand. (52)

We saved those who were believers, and those who worshiped and feared God. (53)

And Lot who said to his people: "You are committing an indecency and you know it. (54)

You have sex with men in preference to women. You are ignorant people." (55)

The answer of his people was: "Get Lot and his people out of your town for they are puritanical." (56)

We saved him and his family, except for his wife who We considered to be among the transgressors. (57)

We brought on them a rain, and the rain We send on people who have been warned is not a good rain. (58)

Say: "Thanks to God and a salutation to His worshipers that God chose for they will never associate one with God." (59)

He Who created the heavens and the earth, and brought down water from the sky with which He raised gardens that are pleasant to see. They would not have been able to bring up the trees; they with their gods could not do it, yet they are putting them on an equal standing with God. (60)

The One Who made the earth as a base and ran through it rivers, and raised on it mountains, and We created isthmuses as a wall between two seas. Then they put other gods with God. Most of them do not know. (61)

The One Who responds to those in dire straits when they call on Him and has the ability to relieve what weighs hard on humans and He made them inherit the earth. Yet you associate others with God. How little are you aware of. (62)

He (*God*) is the One who guides you through the darkness of the seas and land, and the One who sends the wind as good tidings from His mercy. There is no God but Him. And His glory is far above what they associate Him with. (63)

Who can start the creation and repeat that again, and then He facilitates for you making a living from what He sends you from the sky and on earth. Say: "Give us your proof if you are truthful." (64)

Say: "No one knows the secrets of what is in the heavens and on earth other than God. And no one will know when they will be resurrected again. (65)

They know nothing about the Last Day; they even doubt it will ever happen, for they are blind." (66)

The unbelievers say: "If we become dust like our fathers, are we going to be brought back again. If that is true, where are our fathers? (67)

We and our fathers have been promised that before. This is nothing but the mythology of the old ages." (68)

Tell them they shall see on earth what is the ending for the transgressors. (69)

Do not be sorry for them and do not let it bother you, how they conspire. (70)

They say: "When is this threat going to come true, if you are truthful?" (71)

Say: "Some of what you seem to be doubting? Could be closer than you think?" (72)

Your Lord is owed a lot of favors by people, but most of them are not grateful. (73)

Your Lord knows what their chest holds, things that they declare and things that they hide. (74)

There is nothing in the heavens or on earth that is not predetermined in a clear Book. (75)

This Koran explains to the children of Israel most of what they are in doubt about. (76)

It is guidance and mercy to the believers. (77)

Your Lord shall resolve all of the disagreements among them. He is Exalted and Knowledgeable. (78)

Rely on God for you have on your side the veritable truth. (79)

You cannot make the dead or the deaf hear your call, especially after having run away. (80)

You are not going to guide the blind away from being misguided. You will only reach those who already believe in Our verses, and have surrendered themselves to the faith (became Moslems). (81)

When it is time (the Day of Judgement) if We brought out a creature from the earth it may be able better to communicate with them, if Our verses cannot make them understand. (82)

That day We shall assemble from every nation a group of those who denied Our signs and distribute them as they belong. (83)

As they come they will be asked: "When you denied My verses without even knowing what they are or what they mean, what were you trying to do?" (84)

On that day they shall be facing the consequences of their transgressions, without being able to say a word. (85)

Did they not see that We made the night for them to rest and the day for them to see their surroundings well and go to work? In that there are signs for people who believe. (86)

The Day the trumpet will sound, and all that is in the heavens and on earth will be terrorized except for those who God wishes not to be afraid, but all shall be there. (87)

You look at the mountains, thinking that it is still due to their size, yet it keeps on passing like clouds, the work of God who mastered everything and He is Knowledgeable with what you do. (88)

One who does a good deed, shall be rewarded with a better one, and those are the ones who will not need to be afraid as the trumpet sounds. (89)

One who does a bad deed shall go face first into hell. You will be punished only for what you did. (90)

Say: "I am simply ordered to worship the Lord of this town, which He made sacred. He owns everything and He ordered me to surrender myself to Him." (91)

Recite the Koran, and to those who become guided shall do that for themselves, and those who remain unguided, simply say: "My job is only to deliver warning." (92)

Say: "Thanks to God who will show you His signs," and you shall recognize it, and God is not unaware of what you do. (93)

THE STORIES (28)

In the Name of God, Most Merciful, and Most Beneficent.

Taah, Seen, Meem. (1)

These are the verses of the veritable Book. (2)

We relay to you the true news of Moses and the Pharaoh for the benefit of people who believe. (3)

The Pharaoh has gotten strong and arrogant in the land, and created divisions among the people, as he persecuted some of them, by killing their children, and taking liberties with their women. He was truly corrupted. (4)

We intended to do a favor to those who were persecuted and make them leaders and have them inherit the land. (5)

To strengthen their position on earth, and show the Pharaoh, Haman, and their army what they were doing to others. (6)

We revealed to the mother of Moses: Nurse him, and if you become concerned about him throw him in the sea, and do not be afraid or sad, because We shall return him to you, and We shall make him an apostle. (7)

He was picked up by the family of the Pharaoh, so that he eventually became their enemy and caused them a lot of sadness. The Pharaoh, Haman, and their army paid a heavy price for that. (8)

The Pharaoh's wife said to her husband: "Do not kill him, he may become very dear to me, and we may adopt him." They did know what they were doing. (9)

In her heart, Moses' mother was conflicted, with a sense of emptiness without him, and was about to give him up if We did not strengthen her heart, and paved the way for her to become a believer. (10)

His mother had his sister follow him and find out to where he was taken. (11)

Then We caused him to refuse nursing at the breast of all nursing women they tried to have for him, so that his sister had an opportunity to suggest to them a nursing mother that they will be happy with. (12)

Thus We returned him to his mother, to relieve her anxiety, and for her to know that the promise of God is always true, but most people do not know. (13)

When he grew up straight, and correct, We taught him and gave him wisdom, and that is how We reward those who do good works. (14)

Then Moses entered the city, unknown to its people, and found two men fighting, one of his own people and the other from among their enemies. The one from his own people asked for his help. Moses hit him and killed him. He then said: "This is what the Devil has made me do; he is an obvious misguiding enemy." (15)

He (Moses) said: "I have transgressed against myself; forgive me," and God forgave him, for He is the Forgiving and Merciful. (16)

He (Moses) said: "My Lord, with Your favor and forgiveness, I shall never become a supporter of criminals." (17)

The following morning, he (Moses) was back in the city walking with fear in his heart, and the person from his people who asked for his help against the Egyptian the previous day called upon him for help again against another Egyptian, and Moses said to him: "You are obviously a trouble maker." (18)

As he was about to get in a fight with another Egyptian again, the Egyptian said: "Moses, do you want to kill me like you killed the other poor soul yesterday? Do you just want to be a tyrant in the land? Do you not want to be among the peacemakers?"(19)

A man came from the other side of the city, and said to Moses: "The people here are getting together to kill you, and I strongly advise you to leave." (20)

He left afraid, and said: "Lord save me from the transgressors." (21)

He headed towards Madian and said: "I hope my Lord will lead me to the straight path." (22)

As he got to the main water hole at Madian, he found it surrounded by a group of men, watering their animals and two women, (*Arab women*) standing aside with their sheep. He asked about what they were waiting for, and they said that they are unable to water their sheep until the men are done, and that their father is very old and home by himself. (23)

He helped them water their sheep, and then went and sat in the shade and said: "Lord, I am in great need for the kindness with which you have always blessed me." (24)

One of those two women came back walking towards him, appearing to be embarrassed and bashful, and informed him that her father extends an invitation to him to reward him for his assistance to them in watering their sheep, and as he (*Moses*) met him and told him his story, he (*the Arab Bedouin father*) said: "Do not be afraid, you are safe from those tyrants." (25)

One of the old man's daughters said to her father: "Why do you not hire him, for he would be the best you can hire, being strong and faithful." (26)

He (*the old man*) said: "I would like to offer you to marry one of my two daughters, and in return you will work for me eight years, or ten if you wish. I will not be hard on you or take advantage of you, and you shall find me a good man." (27)

He (*Moses*) said: "That shall remain between you and me, in regard to which of the two alternative dates. It shall be your choice, and God shall be the witness on what we agreed upon." (28)

When Moses finished his agreed upon time, he left with his family, and as he came to the side of a mountain, he said to his family: "I just saw a fire far away, stay here and let me find out, and I may be able to get you a torch so that we can have a fire of our own for warmth." (29)

As he got closer, he was called from the right side of the valley at the blessed spot at a tree: O' Moses, It is I, Lord of the universe. (30)

Throw your staff, and as he saw it shaking and twisting he ran away back with fear. O' Moses return, and do not be afraid, for you are safe. (31)

Put your hand in your pocket, and upon pulling it out you shall find it shining white in color, without being hurt. Whenever you become afraid hold your arm close to your chest and you shall feel better. We want you to take these signs as proofs to the Pharaoh, and his people, for they have become true evildoers. (32)

He (Moses) said: "My Lord, I have killed a soul from among them and I am afraid they will kill me. (33)

And my brother Aaron, he is better spoken than I am, send him with me so he can support me if they did not believe me." (34)

He (God) said: We shall strengthen you by your brother, and endow both of you with a great power, and they will never lay a hand on you, and with our signs, you and those who follow you shall prevail. (35)

When Moses brought them our veritable signs, they said: "This is nothing but manufactured sorcery, and we have never heard of anything like it from our predecessors." (36)

Moses said: "My Lord is far more knowledgeable with who shall be guided and end up receiving the ultimate reward. The transgressors shall never succeed." (37)

The Pharaoh said: "O' people, I am not aware of any god for you, other than me," and he said to Haman: "Build a memorial for me that would get me to the level of the God of Moses, and I believe he is a liar." (38)

He and his soldiers behaved arrogantly in the land with no reason, and thought that they will never answer to Us. (39)

We destroyed him and his soldiers, and threw them in the sea. Remember always how the transgressors ended. (40)

We made them in a position of leadership, and towards hell they led. The Day of Judgement they shall find no supporters. (41)

They earned themselves a curse from us in this life, and on the Day of Judgement they shall look uglier. (42)

We revealed the Book to Moses, after We destroyed many generations, as warning for people and guidance and mercy to them so they may remember. (43)

You were never a witness to what happened in the lands west of you, when We assigned the job to Moses. (44)

We brought up generations that lived for many years, but you were not the messenger to the people of Madian, reciting Our verses to them, but others were. (45)

You were not the one in the sacred valley, near the mountain when We called, but We did send you as an act of mercy to warn people who have not been warned before you, so they may be reminded. (46)

And as they are afflicted with a catastrophe, caused by what their own actions brought upon them, they would say: "Our Lord if you sent us an apostle, to help us follow what You reveal to us, we would have been a believing people." (47)

As the truth was revealed to them, they said: "If what was revealed to us was similar to what was revealed to Moses our attitude would have been different. Did not people deny what was revealed to Moses? And did they not call it sorcery? They refused everything." (48)

Say: "If that is the case, why do you not bring a book which is a guide to the truth, better than these two men are, and follow it if you are truthful." (49)

If they do not respond to you that will tell you they follow nothing but their whims, and who is more misguided than those who follow their whims instead of following the guidance of God? God will not provide guidance to the transgressors. (50)

We have delivered the calling to them in case they may remember. (51)

There are those who were given the Scriptures before this Book, and believed in them. (52)

And then when this Book is recited to them, they believe in it as they see the similarity in the truth, and say: "It is from our Lord, to whom we have surrendered even before hearing this one." (53)

Those will be rewarded twice, first for their patience, in responding to evil with good, and for spending from what We gave them to pay alms. (54)

And second for when they hear others remonstrating and arguing, they turn away from it, and say: "We shall answer for what we do and you shall answer for what you do; we salute you, but we shall not seek ignorance." (55)

You do not bring guidance to whomever you want; it is God who guides whomever He wishes. He is far more knowledgeable on those who are truly guided. (56)

Some of the unbelievers say: "We are afraid to follow your guidance lest the other unbelievers threaten our existence on this land." Did We not make their city safer, by making it a sacred place? Did We not fill their land with places where vegetation of all kinds grows? It is a bounty from Us, yet most of them do not appreciate it. (57)

How many a city did We annihilate as they became abusive of what We granted to them? Their dwellings remained mostly empty, and We were the only heirs. (58)

Your Lord has never annihilated a town before He sent to its inhabitants an apostle reciting to them our verses, and no town will be annihilated unless its people are transgressors. (59)

What God has is better, and more lasting, than anything you may acquire in this life in pleasure and property. Do you not understand? (60)

Those who are made a good promise shall find it, and those who are granted the pleasures and properties of this life shall be answering for them. (61)

The day when He shall call: "Where are those associates of Mine that you claimed?" (62)

Those associates said: "Lord, those who we misguided have misguided us like we misguided them. We resort to you for forgiveness for the actions of those who worshiped us." (63)

The associaters were asked to call their partners, and when they did not respond, they faced the torture, from which they refused to be guided away. (64)

As they (*the unbelievers*) are called and asked: "What was your answer to the apostles?" (65)

And on that day they shall have no answers regardless of the questions. (66)

But those who repented, believed and did good works may manage to end up succeeding. (67)

Your Lord creates what He wills, and chooses, but a choice they do not have. God is Glorified and Exalted over what they associate Him with. (68)

Your Lord knows what they hide in their bosoms and what they declare. (69)

He is God and there is no God but Him, in this life and the life to follow. He rules superior and to Him you shall return. (70)

Do you not see that God imposed night on you until the day of judgement, and only He can follow it with light.? Do you not hear? (71)

Do you not see that God imposed the day on you until the Day of Judgement, and only He can bring the night for your tranquility. Do you not see? (72)

It is out of His mercy that He gave you the night and day, to rest and to make a living, as a favor from Him, so you may be thankful. (73)

The Day (*Day of Judgement*) He (*God*) calls and asks: Where are those associates of Mine that you claimed? (74)

We shall pick a witness from each nation and say: Provide us with your proof. They shall know that the truth is with God, and they shall find no support for their lies. (75)

Korah was one of the people of Moses. He treated them with arrogance, for We gave him such treasures that the keys to those treasures would have been hard for a group of strong men to carry. The people said to him: "Do not be boastful, for God does not like those who are." (76)

They said: "Use what God gave you to approach the Last Day, never forgetting the share you were given of this life, and be generous to others as God has been generous to you. Do not seek corruption for God does not like those who are corrupted." (77)

He (*Korah*) said: "Do you not realize that God gave me what I have because He felt I deserved it?" Did he not know that God annihilated generations before him, who were stronger than he was and more numerous? It makes no difference how sinful the transgressors are. (78)

He came out to his people with all his rich garments and jewelry. Those who are mostly interested in this life said: "We wish we have what Korah has, he is a tremendously lucky man." (79)

Those who have knowledge said: "Be careful; God's rewards are far better for those who believe, and do good works and shall be obtained only by those who are obviously righteous." (80)

We sunk him and his house into the earth, and without God he found no support, and he never was a winner. (81)

Those who wanted to have what he had woke up saying: "God bestows His bounty on those He wishes, which is not necessarily a measure of God's favor, for if we had what we had, God may have sunk the earth with us also." The unbelievers do not end up successful. (82)

The final dwelling We made for those who do not seek prominence on earth, nor do they seek corruption, and the lofty end belongs to the righteous. (83)

Those who do good shall be rewarded with better. Those who choose to do evil shall be afflicted only with what they did. (84)

He who imposed on you the burden of delivering the Koran shall be calling you on the Day of Judgement. Say: "My Lord is more knowledgeable with who received the guidance and who is totally misguided." (85)

You did not expect God to have you shoulder the burden of delivering the Koran to others. It was an act of mercy upon you, so do not help the unbelievers by being discouraged due to their opposition. (86)

Let nothing discourage you away from spreading God's verses as they are revealed to you. Seek help from God and do not join the ranks of the associaters. (87)

Do not pray to any other god with God. Everything shall be gone but His face. He is the Ruler and to Him you shall return. (88)

THE SPIDER (29)

In the Name of God, Most Merciful, and Most Beneficent.

Alef, Lamm, Meem. (1)

Do people think that they are going to be able to claim being believers, without their claim being put to the test? (2)

We put to the test the claims of people before them. God shall distinguish between those who are truthful and those who are liars. (3)

Or do evildoers think that they can outrun Our judgement? Evil is their judgement. (4)

Those who look forward to meeting God, their appointment with Him is coming. He listens and He is Knowledgeable. (5)

Those who have to struggle, struggle for their own benefit. God has no need for the world. (6)

Those who believed and did good works, We shall forgive their sins, and We shall reward them for what they did. (7)

We exhorted humans to respect their parents and care for them. If they try to get you to associate others with Me, about which you know nothing, do not obey them. To Me you shall all return, and I shall tell you what you have been doing. (8)

Those who have believed and did good works We shall include them with the righteous. (9)

Among the people are those who say: "We believe," and then when they get hurt because of it, they equate the harm they receive with the torture of God, then when the believers prevail they say: "We were with you all along." Do they not realize that God is far more knowledgeable in what people keep hidden in their chests? (10)

God knows who are the true believers and God knows who are the righteous. (11)

The unbelievers said to the believers: "Follow our way and we shall carry your sins." They shall not be carrying anyone's sins but their own. They are only liars. (12)

They shall carry the weight of their sins many times over, and on the Day of Judgement they shall answer for their lies. (13)

We sent Noah to his people and he lived among them for nine hundred and fifty years, and then they were taken by the flood for they were transgressors. (14)

We`saved him and his companions on the ark, and made out of it an example for the whole world. (15)

And Abraham who said to his people: "Worship God and fear Him, for it is better for you, in case you did not know. (16)

Instead of God you worship idols and create forgeries. Those that you worship instead of God cannot grant you what you need to make a living. Seek God's bounty, worship Him and be thankful to Him, for to Him you shall return." (17)

If you decide to deny this revelation, many nations before you denied revelations revealed to them also. The apostle is obligated to deliver warning only. (18)

Did they not see that God starts all creation, and then He ends it and He starts it back again? It is all so easy for God. (19)

Say: "Why do you not walk the earth and see how creation started? Then God shall create the last generation." God is Capable of all things. (20)

He tortures whomever He wishes and grants mercy to whomever He wants, and to Him you shall all return. (21)

You are incapable of escaping God's reach, in heavens and on the earth, and without Him you have no sponsors or supporters. (22)

Those who deny God's verses or the certainty of meeting Him are the ones who should not expect mercy, and shall have excruciating torture. (23)

The answer of his people was: "Kill him, or burn him," and God saved him from the fire and in that there were signs for those who are believers. (24)

He said to them: "You worship idols instead of God to maintain a social way of life among you. But in the life next, you shall fight with each other and curse each other, and your dwelling shall be hell, and you shall have no supporters." (25)

Lot believed in him and said: "I am immigrating to my Lord, He is the Exalted and the Wise." (26)

We gave him Isaac and Jacob, and We established prophethood and the Book among his descendents, and We rewarded him in this life and the life next, and he shall be among the righteous. (27)

Lot said to his people: "The indecency of your behavior has reached an extent never reached by any other people on earth. (28)

You go after men, you obstruct peoples' path, and indecency prevails socially in your meetings with each other." His people's answer was: "Bring upon us the torture of God if you are truthful." (29)

He said: "My Lord, support me against these corrupted people." (30)

When Our messengers brought Abraham the news of the imminent annihilation of the town of Lot for its people's transgressions (31)

he said: "But Lot is in there, and he was assured that We are more knowledgeable of who is in there, and that Lot and his family shall be saved except for his wife, for she was one of them." (32)

And as Our messengers reached Lot, he was very concerned about their presence. They said to him: "Do not be afraid or sad. We shall save you and your family, except for your wife who proved to be one of them. (33)

We shall bring down on them a rain of stones from the sky for their corruption." (34)

We left them as a sign from Us to people who think. (35)

In the city of Madian, their brother Shoaib said to his people: "Worship God and anticipate the Last Day, and do not spread corruption in the Land." (36)

They denied him, and they were taken by the shaking of an earthquake, and their lives ended with them flat faced in their own homes dead under the rubble. (37)

Aad and Thamoud who you knew by their unusual dwellings very well; their actions were planned for them by the Devil, who caused them to deviate from the straight path, while they knew well what they were doing. (38)

Korah, the Pharaoh and Haman were brought Our veritable signs by Moses, yet they became arrogant and followed those who did the same before them. (39)

They all perished with what they sinned, those who died with a rain of stones, those who were buried in the ruins of a quake, those who died by being sunk into the ground, and those who We drowned. God would never have been unfair to them. They have been unfair to themselves. (40)

The example of those who took sponsors for themselves other than God, is similar to the spider making its own home. No house is flimsier than the house of a spider. (41)

God knows to whom they look to, besides Him, and He is Exalted and Wise. (42)

These are examples We bring to people, but only those of intellect understand it. (43)

God is responsible for the truth of the creation of the heavens and the earth, and in that creation there are signs for the believers. (44)

Recite what God has revealed to you in the Book, and do your prayers, for prayers have an inhibiting effect on indecency and evildoing. The mention of God by itself is even stronger. God knows what you do. (45)

Do not have arguments with people of the Book, unless it is friendly, and to those of them who are aggressive say: "We believed in God and what He revealed to us, and what He revealed to you. Our God and your God are one, and we surrendered ourselves to Him." (46)

We also revealed the Book to you, and those to whom We revealed the Book believe in it. Some of the people of the Book believe in it, and only the unbelievers totally reject it. (47)

You have never recited another Book before, nor have you ever writtten another book with your own hand, which if it occurred may have provided a pretext for the doubters. (48)

It is rather veritable verses in the bosoms of those who have knowledge, and only the transgressors deny Our verses. (49)

They said: "It would have been different if his Lord has given him some signs." Say: "The signs come from God, I am only to deliver warning." (50)

Has it not been enough that We revealed to you the Book, recited to them? In that there is mercy and a reminder to a believing people. (51)

Say: "Let God be the witness between you, and me, He knows what is in the heavens and on earth, and who are the ones who have claimed being believers insincerely, and did not truly believe in God." They are the losers. (52)

They seem to invite God's torture early, and if it was not for a predetermined timing, they would have been hit with it as they stand. (53)

They ask of earlier infliction of God's torture, and hell shall be all around the unbelievers. (54)

The day when torture shall come to them from above them and from beneath their feet, and they shall have a taste of what they have been working for. (55)

My worshipers who believe, My Land is large (*to immigrate through*), so worship Me. (56)

Every soul shall taste death, and then you are all coming back to Me. (57)

Those who believe and do good works shall reside in paradise, in chambers below which rivers flow, and they shall be immortalized in it; a suitable reward for their works (58)

for those who waited and depended on their Lord. (59)

How many creatures that cannot provide for themselves? God provides for them and you. He is Knowledgeable and hears all things. (60)

If you asked them who has created the heavens and the earth, and established the rhythm of the sun and the moon, and when they answer God, say: "Where do you get the other fabrications from?" (61)

God provides from His bounty what He wishes, and to whom He wishes from among His worshipers, and God is Knowledgeable of all things. (62)

And if you ask them: "Who brought down water from the sky, and revitalized the earth after it was dead?" And when they say: "God," say: "Glorified be God;" but most of them do not understand (63)

This present life is nothing but fun and games. The Last Dwelling is the true life, if they can understand. (64)

If they ride in a ship they pray to God with all the enthusiasm of true believers, and when they arrive to solid land they are back associating others with God. (65)

Let them deny what We gave them, and enjoy it, for they shall find out. (66)

Did they not see that We created for them a sacred place which provides them security? Yet they believe in fraudulence and deny the bounty of God. (67)

Who is worse than one who is untruthful in regard to God or denies the truth when it comes to him? Is not there in hell a special place prepared for the unbelievers? (68)

Those who struggle for Us, We shall lead them Our way, and God is with those who are charitable. (69)

THE BYZANTINES (30)

In the Name of God, Most Merciful, and Most Beneficent.

Alef, Laam, Meem. (1)

The Byzantines were defeated (2)

on your side of the earth, but after defeat, they shall have a victory of their own. (3)

It shall occur in a few years, and God is the One who controlled what happened before and will control what happens in the future; and then the believers can rejoice. (4)

It is God's victory, and He will grant victory to whomever He chooses. He is the Exalted and the Merciful. (5)

It is God's promise, and God always fulfills His promises, but most people do not know. (6)

They may know a little about this life, but are totally oblivious of the life next. (7)

Did they not contemplate what God has created in the heavens and on earth, and in between; all in truth, and to a predefined time, yet a lot of people deny that they will meet their Lord and are thus unbelievers. (8)

Do they not walk on earth, and see how did those who were before them end? They were stronger than them and they dug in the earth and built it, much more than they are doing, and their apostles also brought them veritable signs. God would have never been unfair to them, yet they have been unfair to themselves. (9)

This was the ending of those who got used to evildoing, and were denying God's verses and making fun of them. (10)

God starts the creation, then ends it, then to Him you shall return. (11)

On the Final Hour, the transgressors shall be astonished. (12)

They shall not find character witnesses among their partners, and they shall be denying them. (13)

On the Final Hour they shall be separated from each other. (14)

Those who believed and did good works are then in a garden enjoying themselves. (15)

But those who did not believe Our verses and denied they will ever meet God on the Last Day, they shall meet torture. (16)

Glorified be your God every morning and every evening. (17)

To Him belongs all thankfulness, in the heavens and on earth, when you go to bed and when you rise. (18)

He extracts life from death and death from life, and this is why you even exist. (19)

One of his signs is that He created you from dust, and from there you multiplied. (20)

One of His signs also is that He created for you from yourselves spouses that you can feel comfortable with, and He created between you a loving and caring relationship, and in that there are signs for those who think. (21)

Among His signs also is the creation of the heavens and the earth, and your different languages and skin colors. In that there are signs for those who are knowledgeable. (22)

Among His signs also is your sleeping at night and your working during the day; all favors from Him, and these are signs to people who listen. (23)

Among His signs also is that He shows you the lightning, which induces fear but also anticipation of rain, which comes down from the sky and revitalizes the soil after it was dead, and in that there are signs for those who understand. (24)

Among His signs also is His total control, and if He made one call to you, from the earth you shall emerge. (25)

To Him belongs all that is in heaven and on earth, and everything is under His command. (26)

He is the one who started the creation and can repeat it, and it is easy for Him. He makes the best of all examples, in the heavens and on earth, and He is the Exalted and Wise. (27)

God shall bring you an example of yourselves. Do your slaves share equally in the bounty that God has given you, and are they afraid of you and obedient to you as you are afraid of them? These are the verses that We clarify for people who can think. (28)

The transgressors follow their own whims, ignorantly, and who can guide those who God has misguided, for they have no supporters. (29)

Devote yourself to the new face which God has designed for you, and there is no change to what God has designed. It is a valuable religion, but many people do not realize that. (30)

You will return to Him. Worship and fear Him and pray to Him, and do not be one of those who associate others with God (31)

or one of those who divide their religion into different sections and parties where each party is so happy with what they have. (32)

If a catastrophe touched people, you see them praying to their Lord, then as they are touched with the taste of safety, some of them go back to associating others with their Lord. (33)

As they again stop believing in what We revealed to them, We tell them: Enjoy it for you shall find out. (34)

They behave as if We gave them permission to go back to their old ways. (35)

If We let people have a taste of our favor or mercy they become happy and then of they become hit with a misfortune caused by what they did themselves, they become desperate. (36)

Did they not see that God provides His bounty to whomever He wishes and decides? In that there are signs to people who believe. (37)

So give your relatives what is their due, in addition to the wretched souls or the homeless. This is better for those who want to see the face of God, and those are the ones who shall succeed. (38)

We did not provide them the money so that they can put their hand in the pockets of others through usury. But those who pay alms seeking only the face of God are the ones who will be rewarded with twice of what they gave. (39)

God who created you, then He provided for you from His bounty, then He shall cause you to die and then to live again. Do any of those you associate with God do that? Glorified be Him and Exalted over associations that they try to make. (40)

Corruption occurred over the seas and lands with what people have been doing. God shall give them a taste of what they did themselves in case they may back off. (41)

Say walk on this earth and see for yourself what was the final ending of those who were mostly unbelievers. (42)

Concentrate your effort on the great religion, before a day comes when there will be no recourse from the will of God, which will hurt them. (43)

Those who do not believe shall face the consequences of what they earned, and those who do good works pave the road for themselves. (44)

God shall reward the believers, and those who did good works from His bounty, for He does not like the unbelievers. (45)

Among His signs is sending you the winds as good tidings and to give you a sample taste of His mercy, and for the ships to sail on His order, and for men to earn a living from His favor. So you may be thankful. (46)

We sent many apostles before you to their people, and they brought them veritable signs, and We had to retaliate against those who transgressed, for We had the obligation to protect the believers. (47)

God sends the wind which brings the clouds which God stratifies in any pattern He wishes. You see the rain coming down from the clouds, and He provides the rain to whomever He wants of His worshipers, who look upon it as good tidings (48)

after they have been in despair before it came down to them. (49)

Look at the effect of God's mercy, who revitalizes the earth, after it is dead, and He is also the one who can resurrect the dead, and He is Capable of all things. (50)

If We sent them dry wind that leaves everything yellow in color, they will remain unbelieving in its wake. (51)

You cannot make the dead or the deaf hear the call, especially if they turn their back and run. (52)

There is nothing you can do about the blind remaining misguided, You will be able only to reach those who hear Our verses and surrender to them. (53)

God who created you from weakness, then following the weakness comes strength, and the weakness again as the white hair comes; He is the Capable and the Knowledgeable. (54)

On the day of the Hour, the transgressors shall swear that they have not been out for no more than an hour. It is similar to what used to come out of their mouths all the time. (55)

Those who have knowledge and believe shall say: "You have stayed out in God's Book until the Day of Resurrection." This is the Day of Resurrection about which you knew nothing. (56)

On that day the transgressors shall not be excused from their ignorance nor will anyone even question them on it. (57)

We have brought in this Koran all kinds of examples, and if they are brought a sign, the unbelievers will say that it is invalid. (58)

That is how God seals over the hearts of those who are lacking in knowledge. (59)

Be patient, for God's promise is true, and do not let the unbelievers drive you to despair. (60)

LUKMAN (31)

In the Name of God, Most Merciful, and Most Beneficent.

Alef, Lam, Meem. (1)

These are the verses of the wise Book. (2)

Guidance and mercy for those who do good works. (3)

Those who do their prayers, give alms and believe in the Last Day. (4)

These are the ones who are following the guidance from their Lord, and these are the ones who will succeed. (5)

There are some who use clever conversation to mislead people away from the path of God using mocking and sarcasm. Those shall face a humiliating torture. (6)

If Our verses are recited to them, they will turn away arrogantly as if they never heard them or as if they had plugs in their ears. Relay to them the certainty of an excruciating pain. (7)

Those who believed and did good works shall have blissful gardens awaiting them. (8)

Immortalized in them; a true promise from God, and He is the Exalted and Wise. (9)

He created the heavens without supporting columns that you can see, and through over the earth anchors, so it will not veer away from under you. And filled the earth with all kinds of animals and brought down from the sky water which brought up vegetations in pairs. (10)

This is the creation of God; show Me what those below Him created. The transgressors are so clearly misguided. (11)

We gave Lukman wisdom, and said: Thank God, and those who do thank God, do it for themselves, and for those who do not believe, God is in no need of anyone, but many need Him. (12)

Lukman said to his son, advising him: "Do not associate anyone with God for doing that is a great transgression." (13)

We exhorted humans to care for and respect their parents. Their mother has carried them, and then nursed them, one burden after another for nearly two years. Be thankful to me and to your parents to the Last Day. (14)

If they make an effort to make you associate someone else with me, of which you know nothing, do not obey them, but keep their company in this life gracefully, and follow the path of those who are returning to me and to me you shall all return, and then I shall tell you what you have been doing. (15)

He said: "My son if there is something as small as a mustard seed, on a rock, or in the heavens or on earth, God will find it. God is Expert and Merciful. (16)

My son, do your prayers, exhort good works, and discourage evildoing, and be patient with what befalls you, and that is how you remain in control of yourself. (17)

Do not turn your face away from people scornfully, nor should you walk on earth so proud of yourself, for God does not like those who are arrogant or boastful. (18)

Be modest in the way you walk, and do not be loud, and remember that in voices there is none that is uglier than that of the donkey. (19)

Do you not see that God granted you the benefit of many things in the heavens and on the earth, and gave you of His bounty things that are evident and other things that remain hidden?" Still there are some people who ignorantly and misguidedly argue about God, even without the benefit of an enlightening Book. (20)

If they are asked to follow what God has revealed, they say: "We will follow what we found our fathers following." These are the ones who have been following the invitation of the Devil to the torture of hell. (21)

One who turns his face early in the direction of God reserves for himself a front row place, and to God, everything shall return. (22)

If one does not believe, do not be disturbed about his lack of belief. He shall come back to us and We shall tell him what He did; for God knows what is inside his bosom. (23)

We let them enjoy themselves for a while, then they are driven to a great torture. (24)

If you ask them who created the heavens and the earth, and when they say: "God," you say: "Glorified be God," but most of them do not know. (25)

To God belongs everything that is in the heavens and on earth. God is in need of no one and to Him belongs all the thanks. (26)

If every tree was a pen and all the oceans, and seven more behind them were full of ink, they would become empty before writing all the words of God. God is Exalted and Wise. (27)

As you were created and as you will be resurrected, you will feel as if all was happening to you alone. God hears all, and sees all. (28)

Did you not see that God ends the night with a day and the day with a night, and rotates the sun and the moon each in its own orbit for a while? God is Knowledgeable with what you do. (29)

For God is the truth, and those they pray for other than Him are forged, and God is Exalted and Great. (30)

Do you not see that the ships travel at sea with his favor, so as to show you His signs, and these are signs to all who are patient and thankful? (31)

If the waves at sea threatened them, they call upon God, declaring the truthfulness in their belief, and as He saves them, some of them reject our verses, and each one of them is an unbelieving liar. (32)

O' people, worship and fear God, and be mindful of the day when no parent will be rewarded for a child nor a child for a parent. The promise of God is true and do not be seduced by what is in this life, or let God's bounty in this life seduce you away from God Himself. (33)

God has exclusive knowledge about the Hour. He brings down the rain and knows what is in the womb, while no soul knows what it will face the next day nor will it know where on earth will it depart. God is an Expert and Knowledgeable. (34)

THE PROSTRATION (32)

In the Name of God, Most Merciful, and Most Beneficent.

Alef, Lam, Meem. (1)

The revelation of this Book is undoubtedly from the Lord of the universe. (2)

Alternatively, they say: "He made it up," but it is the truth from your Lord intended to warn people who were never warned before you, so they may be led to the right path. (3)

God who created the heavens and the earth, and what is in between them, then sat on the throne. Without Him you have no sponsor, nor any one who can intercede for you. (4)

He observes all affairs between the heavens and the earth, and the information that reaches Him in one day is equivalent in time to a thousand years of what you count. (5)

He is the One who has knowledge of the future, and the accuracy of testimony (*whether false or true*). He is the Exalted and the Merciful. (6)

He created all to perfection, and started the creation of humans from dust. (7)

Then He continued the creation of human descendents from mere drops of liquid. (8)

Then He perfected the creation of humans by instilling in His creation some of His own spirit, and included inside you is hearing, eyesight, and a heart, yet you are rarely thankful. (9)

They said: "If after we are created on earth we are lost, shall we be recreated again?" In effect they are denying whether they will ever meet their Lord. (10)

Say: "The angel of death shall take their life away, which is an assignment of his," and then you shall be taken back to your Lord. (11)

You will see the criminals with their heads lowered, stating in the presence of their Lord: "Our Lord, we have seen and we have heard; turn us back and we shall do good works; we are now absolutely convinced." (12)

If We wished, We could have granted guidance to every soul, but it is I Who made the decision that I will fill hell with willful sinners from jinn and humans. (13)

Taste the result of your forgetting the meeting of this day. We shall also forget you as you taste the permanent torture for what you have done. (14)

Those who believe in our verses are the ones who whenever these are recited to them they fall prostrated glorifying and praising their Lord, and remain free of arrogance. (15)

Their sides are aching from lying down and getting up, and they pray for their Lord in fear of Him and in seeking His approval, and they spend of what We granted to them of our bounty. (16)

No soul shall know what I have in reserve for it in reward for what it did. (17)

Those who were believers, and those who were blasphemous cannot in any way be equal. (18)

Those who believed and did good works shall have gardens as their residence and shelter, in recognition of what they did. (19)

Those who committed blasphemy shall have hell as their residence. Every time they shall try to get out, they shall be thrown back, and told: taste the torture which you have been denying. (20)

Some may receive the lesser torture of this world, rather than the greater torture of the world to come, so they may correct themselves. (21)

None is a bigger transgressor than the one who was reminded of God's verses, and still manages to steer away. We shall be revengeful with the transgressors. (22)

We gave Moses the Book. Meeting God you should never doubt the Book. We made it guidance for the people of Israel. (23)

We made from among them leaders who guided based on our will, and who persevered, and were absolutely certain of our verses. (24)

If they had differences among them, it is up to your Lord to settle these on the Day of Judgement. (25)

Did God not tell them how many generations before them We have annihilated? They now walk in their previous houses, and in that are signs to those who hear. (26)

Do they not see that We drive water into the earth to water roots from which vegetation grows that feeds them and from which their animals are fed? (27)

They say: "When will that Day of Judgement that you are talking about come? If you are truthful (28) say: "The Day of Judgement is of no use to the unbelievers, for then they will most likely believe, but no one will even look at them." (29)

So ignore them and wait, for they shall be waiting. (30)

THE PARTIES (33)

In the Name of God, Most Merciful, and Most Beneficent.

O' Prophet, worship and fear God and do not yield to the unbelievers or to the hypocrites. God has always been Knowledgeable and Wise. (1)

Follow what is revealed to you by your Lord, and God is an expert on what you do. (2)

Rely on God, and He is all you need to rely upon. (3)

God has not given anyone two hearts inside him, nor is it enough to divorce your wife to make her your mother (*referring to a pagan habit of considering a woman divorced by saying: "she is now to me like my mother's back"*), nor do those you adopt become actually your own children. Those are simply words you say with your mouth, but God says the truth, and He leads to the straight path. (4)

Call the adopted by the name of their fathers, for that is better in the eyes of God, and if you do not know their fathers call them your adopted or your brothers in religion. You will not earn penalty for making a mistake with good intention, and God is Forgiving and Merciful. (5)

The prophet has a special status among the believers, which makes him closer to them than to each other, and his wives are their mothers, and those who are blood relatives are closer to each other in the Book of God than they are to other believers or to those who immigrated. When you are favoring others by adopting them or doing good to them it is nevertheless a charitable act that shall be in the Book forever. (6)

We made a covenant with the prophets. We did with you, with Noah, Abraham, Moses, and Jesus, the son of Mary. It was a heavy covenant indeed. (7)

The truthful shall be examined on their truthfulness, and an excruciating torture shall be readied for the unbelievers. (8)

People who believe, remember God's favor to you, as you were attacked by an army, and God assisted you with a strong wind and another army that you could not see, and God was very Knowledgeable with what you were doing. (9)

As they attacked you from above and from below, and the eyeballs rolled, and the hearts seemed to have ascended to become a lump in the throat, and you started doubting your faith in God. (10)

Then the believers were put to the test, and were shaken very severely. (11)

The hypocrites and the deceitful said: "What God and his apostle have promised us was only wishful thinking." (12)

A group of them said to the people of Madina: "What are you doing here? You had better leave," and some of them asked the prophet's permission to leave, saying: "Our houses are exposed," and they were not. They just wanted to run away. (13)

If the city was penetrated from its periphery and they were asked to rebel, they would have done that, but nothing of the kind would have lasted long. (14)

They have made a covenant with God that they will stand their ground and not run, and a covenant with God shall always be expected to be abided with. (15)

Say: "A flight from dying or being killed shall produce benefits that are short lived." (16)

Say: "Who will insulate you from God if He wished you harm or mercy?" They shall not find for themselves, apart from God, a sponsor or a supporter. (17)

Say: "God knows the obstructionists among you who say to the others: 'Stay on our side, and do very little fighting.'" (18)

They are dependent on you, and when they are hit with fear, they look at you with their eyes rolling as if they are facing death, and then when fear eases they hit you with the lashes of their tongues that are short on praise. These are not true believers, and God shall make their designs fail, which is a matter easy for God. (19)

They think that the warring parties were not going to abandon the siege, and if they ever return they would rather be out among the other Arabs. They will follow the news about you, but if they are among you, they will do very little fighting. (20)

In God's Apostle you have a good example to follow, if you yearn to get to the Last Day, and mention God frequently. (21)

As the believers met the warring parties, they said: "This is what God and His apostle promised us," and the confrontation did nothing but strengthen their faith and increase their surrender to God. (22)

Among the believers are those who adhered to what they promised God. Some of them die and some are waiting for their pre-assigned day, and never waver. (23)

God shall reward the truthful for their truthfulness, while the hypocrites He may torture or forgive. God is Forgiving and Merciful. (24)

God left the unbelievers with their anger to live with, having achieved nothing else. The believers were spared from having to fight a cruel battle. God is Exalted and Mighty. (25)

God brought down from their towers people of the Book who provided assistance to the warring parties with terror in their hearts. A group of them you killed, and another group you took prisoners. (26)

You inherited their lands, their homes and their properties, lands that you never set a foot on before. God is Capable of all things. (27)

O' Prophet, tell your wives: If you prefer this life and its luxuries, so state that and I shall make sure you enjoy yourselves and you will be let go in a pleasant way. (28)

But if it is God, His Apostle and the Last Residence is what you prefer, God has prepared for your good works a tremendous reward. (29)

Wives of the prophet, if one of you commits a clear and obvious indecent act, she shall receive twice the appropriate punishment, and this is easy for God. (30)

Those among you who remain faithful to God and His apostle, and do good works, shall receive twice the appropriate reward, and they have awaiting them a generous bounty. (31)

Wives of the Prophet, you are not like other women, when you speak do not be overly submissive in words and attitude, so as to avoid having those with bad intentions take an unintended wrong message, while maintaining being graceful and appropriate. (32)

Resort to your homes and do not engage in exhibiting your beauty and jewelry like the pagan women used to do. Engage in your prayers and pay alms, and obey God and His apostle, for God would like to help you. Family of the prophet keep an impeccable reputation and social acceptability. (33)

Try to remember all that is recited in your homes of God's verses and wisdom. God has always been considerate and well informed. (34)

Moslem men and women, believing men and women, men and women who dedicate themselves to God, faithful men and women, enduring men and women, men and women who give in charity, fasting men and women, men and women who keep their purity, and men and women who mention God frequently; to all God prepared forgiveness and huge reward. (35)

No believing man or women ever has a choice after God and His apostle relay to them that a matter has been decided. Those who disobey God and His apostle have clearly taken the wrong path. (36)

You say to one who received God's bounty and your blessing to hold on to his wife, and fear God, while you hide inside you what God does not wish to be hidden. Thus you became afraid of others when your fear should have been directed to God alone. When Zaid did not want her any longer, We married her to you. Believers should have no problem marrying the divorced wives of their adopted children, and this is God's ruling. (37)

The prophet committed no sin by following the decree of God, and God's precedent that was created with prophets before him, and a decree from God is final. (38)

Those who relay the message from God and fear Him, and fear no other than God, need to worry about no one else. (39)

Mohammed is a father to no one among you, but he is rather the Apostle of God and the last of the prophets, and God is Knowledgeable of all things. (40)

People who believe, mention God frequently. (41)

And glorify His name morning and evening. (42)

He is the One who, with His angels, took care of taking you out from the darkness into the light, and has always been Merciful with the believers. (43)

They shall be greeted the day they see Him, and He has prepared for them a great reward. (44)

O' Prophet, We sent you as a witness, a bearer of good tidings, and to deliver warning. (45)

And also to call people to God by His permission, and to be a beacon of light. (46)

Bring good tidings to the believers, and tell them that they have earned a big favor from God. (47)

Do not obey the unbelievers, or the hypocrites, and ignore their attempts to harm you, and rely on God, and He is all you need to rely upon. (48)

People who believe, if you marry and then divorce a believing woman without the marriage having ever been consummated, you do not owe them anything and they do not have to go through a waiting period for that, but deal with them fairly and let go of them amicably. (49)

O' Prophet, it is lawful for you to marry those women you pay a dowry to, and slave girls you may own, by whatever circumstances that may occur. You can also marry your female cousins, on your father, or your mother's side who immigrated with you, and a believing woman if she gives herself to you and you wish to marry her, so long as no other believer has a claim on her of any kind. We are aware of what has been imposed on the believers in regard to their spouses, and their slave girls, but these rules also have been extended to you so that you will never feel embarrassed or uncertain, and God is Forgiving and Merciful. (50)

It is your choice which one of them (*your wives*) you recline with, or you may want to recline with one you have stayed away from for a while, it is actually better if you did the latter, so that you keep them all contented and satisfied. God knows what is inside your heart, and God has always been Knowledgeable and Forgiving. (51)

It shall not be permissible for you to take more wives, or to exchange any of your wives for new ones even if you are attracted to them, except for slave girls that you may own, and God shall give consideration to all things. (52)

People who believe, do not enter the houses of the prophet until you receive permission, not expecting to be fed, unless you are invited to eat, and after you are fed, do not stay too long, but rather leave even if the conversation was inviting, for this may make the prophet uncomfortable, and yet he may be shy to tell you. God does not shy away from the truth. If you ask questions of the prophet's wives, do it from behind a partition, for this is purer for your hearts and theirs. You are not to ever hurt the prophet, or marry his wives after him, for that would be a grave thing to do in the eye of God. (53)

Whether you reveal things or hide them, God is Knowledgeable of all things. (54)

Wives of the prophet do not need to be as restricted in regard to their interactions with their fathers or their children, nor in regard to their brothers or their sisters, nor in regard to the children of their brothers or sisters, nor in regard to their slaves. Worship and fear God, for He is a witness to all things. (55)

God and His angels pray and seek blessings for the prophet. People who believe also pray and seek blessings for him, and greet and salute him. (56)

Those who do harm to God and His apostle shall be cursed by God in this life and the next, and humiliating torture awaits them. (57)

Those who cause harm to believing men or women, which they did not instigate themselves have committed a wrong and a grave sin. (58)

O' Prophet, tell your wives, your daughters and the believing women (*similarly situated*) to pull their robes over their heads, so they can be easily recognized and not interfered with, and God is Forgiving and Merciful. (59)

If the hypocrites, those who carry hate in their hearts, and the rumor mongers do not seize and desist, I shall order you to get rid of them, and they shall never be your neighbors again. (60)

They shall be cursed wherever they live, and they may be killed or eradicated. (61)

This was God's sentence against those who behaved similarly in the past, and you shall find that God's rulings change very little. (62)

They ask you about the Hour (*Day of Judgement*), say: "Knowledge about it is with God. For all you know it may be very soon." (63)

God has cursed the unbelievers and prepared a fire for them. (64)

They shall be immortalized in it, and they shall find no sponsor or supporter. (65)

As their faces are turned in the heat, they will say: "We wish we had obeyed God and obeyed the apostle." (66)

They say: "Our Lord, we obeyed our masters and our elders and they misled us. (67)

Our Lord, give them (*the masters and the elders*) twice the torture and curse them severely." (68)

People who believe, do not be like those who caused Moses harm, and God exonerated him and He was noble in the eyes of God. (69)

People who believe, worship and fear God, and be certain of the accuracy of your utterances. (70)

He (*God*) will straighten your path and forgive your sins, and those who obey God and His apostle will achieve a great victory. (71)

We offered the responsibility for Our trust to the heavens, to the earth, and to the mountains and they were all afraid to accept the undertaking, except for the human, who took it. He has erred and was ignorant. (72)

God shall subject the hypocrites, men and women, and the unbelievers, men and women, to torture, and He shall forgive the believing men and women, and God is Forgiving and Merciful. (73)

SHEBA (34)

In the Name of God, Most Merciful, and Most Beneficent.

Glorified be God, to whom the heavens and the earth belong, and He shall be glorified on the Last Day. He is the Expert and the Wise. (1)

He knows what enters the earth and what comes out from it, and what comes down from the sky, and what ascends to it, and He is the Forgiving and the Merciful. (2)

The unbelievers said: "We shall never see the Hour (*Day of Judgement*)." Say: "O' yes, you shall see it by my Lord. He knows the future and not a speck of dust is missed by Him in the heavens or on earth, neither does He miss anything smaller or bigger. It is all recorded in a veritable Book." (3)

So He will reward those who believed and did good works, and awaiting them is total forgiveness, and generous bounty. (4)

And those who spent a lot of effort trying to falsify our verses, awaiting them is a severe torture. (5)

Those who have knowledge realize that what was revealed to you is the truth, and is guidance to the straight path of He who is Exalted and is deserving of thanks. (6)

The unbelievers said: "Shall we point out to you a man who claims that after you are torn up to pieces in the dust, you shall be brought back into a new creation?" (7)

Is he a liar or is he crazy? It is the unbelievers who shall find themselves totally misguided, and face torture on the Last Day. (8)

Do they not pay attention to what is behind them and what is ahead of them in the heaven and on earth? If We want We can sink the earth with them, or send on them, or bring to them lethal rain from the sky, and in that there are signs for repentant worshipers. (9)

We granted David favors from Us. We called upon the mountains and the birds to be responsive to him, and made iron more resilient to him. (10)

We showed him how to make body armor out of mail (*iron links*). We exhorted him to do good works, and informed him that We are watching all that they do. (11)

To Solomon We gave power over the wind, to blow one month at a time in different directions. He was also provided with a fountain of melted brass, and authorized some jinn to work with him under strict control, and knowledge that if one deviated a hair from Our instructions, they shall taste hell. (12)

They helped him in whatever he wanted to build, in shrines, statues or large troughs that can hold water, and the family of David were thankful, and very few of My servants usually are. (13)

When We decided it is time for his death, the only thing that indicated to the jinn working for him that he died was an earth creature starting to eat at the end of his staff which caused him to fall down. It was then that they realized that had they been given knowledge of the future they would not have had to be obeying slaves that long. (14)

The people of Sheba had where they lived an example of God's favor. Two stretches of paradise-like gardens on each side. Eat from God's bounty and be thankful to Him for a good place to live and a forgiving Lord. (15)

Nevertheless they became misguided, and We sent upon them a flood that replaced their gardens with stretches of a desert that contains bitter thorny shrubs and cactus plants. (16)

They were punished for their refusal to believe, and We only punish the unbelievers. (17)

Then We made between them and the towns We have blessed, small stopping villages that permit travel with ease and without too many supplies, and said: Travel safely in the day or in the night. (18)

They said: "Our Lord, make our travel more challenging and the stop distances longer." They transgressed against themselves, and We made them stories on the tongues of many, and tore them far apart from each other, and in that was an example for the benefit of those who are enduring and thankful. (19)

They proved the Devil's thoughts about them to be correct, and they followed him, except a group of believers. (20)

The Devil would have had no power over them, except for Us wanting to see who believes in the Last Day, and who is in doubt. God is the Keeper of all things. (21)

Say: "Call those that you have been praying for, instead of God, and you will find out that they do not own not a speck of dust in the heavens and on the earth, and that they share in nothing anywhere, and that God has no need for them." (22)

No one can intercede with Him, except by His permission, and as fear starts relenting and eases off their hearts, they start asking each other: "What did your Lord say?" The others will answer: "The truth, He is the Exalted and the Great." (23)

Say: "Who will provide your sustenance from the heaven and the earth?" Say: "God, we and You both are either right or strongly misguided." (24)

Say: "You will not answer for our sins, and we shall not be questioned about what you did." (25)

Say: "Our Lord shall have us together one day, and He shall make the final judgement between us correctly. He is the problem solver and the Knowledgeable." (26)

Say: "Show me the partners you annexed to God. He is rather God, the Exalted and Wise." (27)

We sent you only to bring good tidings and warnings to all people, but most people do not know. (28)

They ask: "When is that promise going to materialize if you are truthful?" (29)

Say: "For that you have a pre-ordained date which you cannot bring forward or delay one hour." (30)

The unbelievers said: "We will not believe in this Koran nor shall we believe in what is said to occur later," and you shall see the transgressors later, as they are brought to God, quarrelling among themselves. The weaker will say to the stronger and more arrogant: "If it was not for you, we would have been all believers." (31)

And the arrogant will say: "Are you now claiming that it was we who stood in your way and diverted you away from being guided?" It is the opposite, you were transgressors on your own. (32)

The weaker will answer back to the stronger: "Are you going to deny all the conspiracies, day and night, to pressure us to not believe in God and to associate others with Him?" They all start conveying regret after they face the torture; We made the chains and iron collars for the necks of the unbelievers, so as to punish them for what they knew very well. (33)

Every time We sent one to carry the warning to a town, those among its residents who live well denied the warning. (34)

They say: "We have bigger families and more property and we shall not be tortured." (35)

Say: "My Lord provides his bounty to whomever He wishes. It is His choice, but most people do not understand." (36)

It is not your property nor is it your children that bring you closer to Us, but rather being believers and doing good works. These are the things that bring even double the reward for what they do, and make them safe in their homes. (37)

Those who make an effort to frustrate Our verses, shall have torture catch up with them fast. (38)

Say: "My Lord grants His bounty to whomever He wishes from among His worshipers and decides how much." Everything you spend in the way of God, God shall replace it, and He is the best of all givers. (39)

All that they associate with God shall be assembled to Him, and the angels shall tell them: "You are the ones they have been worshipping." (40)

They will say: "Glorified be You our true sponsor," they were rather worshiping jinn, and most of them used to believe in them. (41)

Today, not one of you can help or hurt another one, and We shall say to the transgressors, taste the tortures of fire that you have always been denying. (42)

As Our verses are recited to them, clear and veritable, the unbelievers say: "This is a man who wishes to turn you away from what your fathers have worshipped, and this is just evil fabrication." The unbelievers described the truth as it was sent to them to be veritable sorcery. (43)

We never gave them books to read, nor have We sent them anyone to deliver warning before you. (44)

Many denied the message We sent before them, and those were given by us many times the bounty We gave them, yet they also denied the same way. (45)

Say: "I am giving you a clear single warning, and try as singles and couples to contemplate whether your man is crazy or is he delivering a warning to you." Ahead awaits you severe torture. (46)

Say: "I have asked you for no compensation, for my compensation is on God. He is a witness to all things." (47)

Say: "My Lord throws only the truth, He has full knowledge of what is ahead." (48)

Say: "The truth has come, and fallacies have ended and shall not return." (49)

Say: "If I have become misguided, I have done that to myself, and if I am guided that is a favor from God through what He reveals to me." God hears and He is always Near. (50)

As they get close and they become fearful, (51)

They will say: "We believe," which is contrary to what they said when they were far away. (52)

Before, they did not believe when they were looking at the unknown from a far-away place. (53)

They were prevented from getting what they wanted, just like those before them. They were in great doubt. (54)

THE CREATOR (35)

In the Name of God, Most Merciful, and Most Beneficent.

Thanks to God, the Creator of the heavens and the earth, and the Maker of the angels, as messengers, who have wings in twos, threes and fours. He adds creations as He wishes; God is Capable of any and all things. (1)

When God opens the door for a blessing to people, no one can stop it and when His door is closed, no one can open it other than Him. He is the Exalted and the Wise. (2)

People, remember God's blessings upon you, for there is no Creator but Him who can bless you with His bounty, in the heavens or on earth, so how can you still manage to go wrong? (3)

If they deny you, people have denied apostles before you, and to God all things return. (4)

O' people, God's promise is true, do not be seduced by this life, and do not let your arrogance lead you to underestimate God. (5)

The Devil is your enemy; take him as an enemy and be aware that his party shall be those who are heading towards hell. (6)

Those who did not believe shall find severe torture awaiting them, and those who believed and did good works shall find forgiveness and great rewards. (7)

As to those who mistake their evildoing for good works, remember that God misleads whomever He wishes and guides to the right path whomever He wishes, so do not let yourself be very much concerned about them, God is far more knowledgeable with what they do. (8)

God Who sent the wind which causes clouds to collect, and then clouds are driven over to a dead land, and the earth is resurrected after it was dead. Resurrection is like that. (9)

One who seeks greatness, greatness belongs to God, all of it; and to Him goes the words of praise and the good works help elevate the words, while those who use deception to cover their evildoing shall meet severe torture, and they shall find that their deception was a failure. (10)

God created you from dust, then from a sperm, and made you in couples. No female shall conceive or deliver without His knowledge. No one reaches old age, or His age is decreased except as written in the Book, which is all so easy for God. (11)

The two bodies of water are not alike. One is fresh water that is good to drink and the other is salty and bitter. You get meat that you eat from both, and make cloth that you wear. Both are traveled by ships that you use to seek a living. All so you may be thankful. (12)

He ends the day with night and the night with day, and employs the sun and the moon, each in its own orbit, for a predetermined time. This is the work of your Lord who reigns supreme, and all of those you pray to besides Him own absolutely nothing. (13)

If you pray to them they shall not hear you, and even if they do, they shall not respond to you, and on the Day of Judgement they shall condemn your associating others with God. No one will tell you the truth about them but an Expert. (14)

O' people, all of you are poor and only God is rich, and to Him goes all thankfulness. (15)

If He chooses He can take you away and bring a new creation. (16)

That is not difficult for God. (17)

No one carries the burdens of others, not even a tiny portion of them, and not even the burdens of close relatives. Deliver the warning to those who fear God even without having all the answers, and pray and purify themselves, and those who do, do it for themselves, and all are destined to God. (18)

The seeing and the blind are not the same. (19)

Neither is darkness equal to light. (20)

Nor is shade equal to the heat of the sun. (21)

Nor are the living equal to the dead. God makes whoever He wishes hear. You will not be able to make those in their graves hear you. (22)

You are only to deliver warning. (23)

We sent with the truth a bearer of good tidings and warning, and every nation had a deliverer of warning. (24)

If they deny you, be reminded that many before them did so even after they were brought by their apostles veritable signs, Scriptures, and a Book with illuminating light. (25)

Yet in the end I had to take away the unbelievers, and that was severe indeed. (26)

Do you not see that God brought down from the sky water that caused all kinds of fruits to grow in different colors? He gave the mountains different colors also, white, red and many a strange black. (27)

Among people, animals, and cattle are differences in color also.It is those who have knowledge among God's worshipers are the ones who fear him the most. God is Exalted and Forgiving. (28)

Those who recite God's Book, do their prayers and spend from what God has given them covertly and overtly are engaged in a trade that will never lose. (29)

God shall pay them for their work, and more from His own bounty. He is Forgiving and Grateful. (30)

What We have revealed to you from the Book is the truth confirming what We have already sent (*in the Scriptures*) before. God is always Seeing and Knowledgeable in the affairs of His worshipers. (31)

We let the Book pass on to those of our worshipers whom we chose. Some of them transgressed against their own souls, some were more careful than that and others went beyond the call in their good works with God's blessing. This was what will favor them greatly. (32)

Gardens of Eden they shall enter, wearing bracelets of gold and pearls, and dressed with silk. (33)

They will say: "Thanks to God who took away our sorrow. He is our Lord, Forgiving and Grateful. (34)

He is the One who provided for us this dwelling from His bounty, and where we shall suffer no tiredness or exhaustion." (35)

The unbelievers shall have hell where they shall not die and be finished, nor will their torture ease. That is how We punish those who do not believe. (36)

They will scream, saying: "Our Lord, let us out and we shall do good works different from what we were doing before." Did We not let you live long enough to remember whatever you needed to remember, and were you not provided with an apostle who gave you warning? Taste the pain; the transgressors shall have no help. (37)

God is Knowledgeable with all the secrets of the heavens and the earth. He knows what is concealed in their bosoms. (38)

He is the one who permitted you to inherit the earth. Those who are unbelievers shall carry the burden of their lack of belief. Their lack of belief does nothing but increase their Lord's anger with them and increase their great loss. (39)

Say: "Have you seen those that you associate with God to have ever created what is on earth, or to have anything in the heavens to belong to them? Were they ever given a Book with veritable signs?" The transgressors support each other's arrogance. (40)

God is the One who holds the heavens and the earth and prevents their disintegration. And if that is to happen, no one else can prevent that from happening. He is always the Patient and the Forgiving. (41)

They (*Kouraish*) have taken an oath that if they were sent an apostle of their own, they will be more guided than any other nation to whom apostles were sent, yet an apostle of their own only increased their resistance. (42)

They only engaged in arrogance on earth and deceptive evildoing, and that only hurts those who engage in it. Do they not look at the pattern of behavior of the older generations? When you do, you shall find that God's pattern of behavior can neither be replaced or changed. (43)

Do they not travel around and see what was the destiny of people before them who were stronger? But nothing can stand in the way of God, in the heavens and on earth. He is Knowledgeable and Capable. (44)

If God was going to be strict in holding people to what they have done, He would have left no one on earth, but He tends to defer many destinies for a while, and when their final time comes, God always has full knowledge of what His servants did. (45)

YAAH SEEN (36)

In the Name of God, Most Merciful, and Most Beneficent.

Yaah, Seen. (1)

It is in the wise Koran (2)

that you are an apostle (3)

treading on the straight path (4)

revealed by the Exalted and Merciful (5)

to deliver warning to people whose fathers were not warned and remain oblivious. (6)

It is already apparent that most of them are not believers. (7)

They shall have rings of iron around their necks that are so thick that they will touch their chins, and keep their heads up. (8)

They have obstructions in front of them and behind them that overwhelm their senses, and render them effectively blind. (9)

To them, it makes no difference whether you warn them or not, for they shall not believe. (10)

The warning is for those who follow the Word and fear the Merciful without direct proof; relay to them the good tidings of forgiveness and a generous reward. (11)

We are capable of resurrecting the dead and We keep records of what they did, and the effects of their deeds, which is all kept in a clear book. (12)

Tell them the example of a town to whom apostles were sent. (13)

We sent them two apostles that they denied, and We followed them with a third. They all said: "We are sent to you." (14)

The answer they received was: "You are nothing but humans like us, and the Merciful has revealed nothing to you and you are only liars." (15)

The apostles said: "Our Lord knows that we have been sent to you (16)

our obligation is only to deliver warning." (17)

The townspeople said to them: "We are fed up with you, and if you do not desist, you shall be stoned, and you shall receive excruciating torture." (18)

"You should be fed up with yourselves," the apostles answered. "You have been warned, but you are excessive in your evildoing." (19)

A man came running from the far end of the town, and said: "My people, follow the apostles. (20)

Follow those who warn you and seek nothing from you, while they are guided themselves." (21)

Why would I not worship Him, He who created me, and to Him we shall all return? (22)

Why would I adopt gods other than Him, when I know that if the Merciful wished me harm, they will be useless to intercede for me, or save me? (23)

If I did such a thing, I will be badly misguided. (24)

He said to the apostles: "Please hear me, I believe in your Lord." (25)

He was told to enter heaven, and he said: "I wish my people knew (26)

how my Lord forgave me and made me among those whom He distinguished." (27)

We did not need to send an army against his people from heaven, nor do We ever need to do that. (28)

But all it took is a shout, and they were all lifeless. (29)

It is unfortunate that all of those people are wasted, and every time an apostle is sent to them, they make a mockery out of him. (30)

Did they not see how many a generation We have annihilated before them and they will never see them again? (31)

When it is time they shall all be brought back to us. (32)

They should take a sign from the dead earth that We revive, and all of a sudden it is producing the wheat that you eat. (33)

We also created gardens of palm and vine from it and caused springs of water to burst out from it (34)

thus making it possible for them to eat fruits grown from their own toil; should they not be thankful? (35)

Glorified be Him who created the pairs of plants that grow from the earth, and the pairs of humans themselves and other things that they do not know. (36)

Another sign for them is the night which We create by taking away daylight, and they are suddenly in the dark. (37)

The sun follows a predefined course, as set by the Exalted and Knowledgeable. (38)

The moon We made to rotate in its own orbit and always returns with an old and lasting regularity. (39)

The sun cannot catch up with the moon, nor can the night and day change sequence and all are floating in their orbits, in the same universe. (40)

A sign for them that We have at one point in history, carried their predecessors in a ship, (41)

and with them We also preserved the animals they ride. (42)

If We wished We could have drowned them and they would have found no rescuer (43)

if it was not for Our mercy, and for a while. (44)

They are told to take example from what happened before them and fear what is coming ahead of them, so they may receive mercy. (45)

Yet they turn away from all signs provided to them by their Lord. (46)

When they are asked to spend in charity from what God has given them, the unbelievers said to the believers: "Why should we feed someone who could have been fed by God if He wanted? You are clearly misguided." (47)

They also said: "When is that day that you are promising us, if you are truthful?" (48)

All they will hear is one shout and they shall be taken where they stand, and as they remonstrate with each other. (49)

They will have no time to make a will or to ever return to their families. (50)

As the trumpet sound, they shall be extracted from their graves, and on their way to their Lord. (51)

Then they will say: "Who has brought us out from our resting place? This must be what the Lord has promised, and the apostles must have been correct." (52)

It will take one shout and they shall be in front of Us. (53)

On that day no soul shall ever be wronged, and all shall answer to what they have done. (54)

Those in heaven shall be busy enjoying themselves that day. (55)

They and their spouses shall be sitting on couches and leaning on soft cushions. (56)

They shall be having fruits and anything else they may desire. (57)

A greeting and a fulfilled promise from a Merciful Lord. (58)

You, the transgressors, shall be tasting a different day. (59)

O' humans, did I not tell you not to worship the Devil, because he is your clear enemy, (60)

and worship Me for this is the straight path? (61)

Many generations before you have been misguided; can you not see that? (62)

This is the hell that you were promised. (63)

Be its fuel today for what you were doing. (64)

Today We shall seal their mouths, their hands shall talk and their legs shall testify to what they have been doing. (65)

If We wish, We can cover their eyes so they cannot see their way. (66)

And if We choose, we can change them so that they are cripples, unable to come and go. (67)

Those who We permit to live longer, usually live less well; do they not see that? (68)

We never taught him (*the apostle*) poetry nor should he have been. It is the word of God in a veritable Koran. (69)

To warn those who are alive, and to set the limits for those who do not believe. (70)

Did they not see that We created for them, with our own hands, cattle that they are able to own? (71)

We tamed some of those animals so they can ride them, and some of them they eat. (72)

In these animals they have benefits from which they derive food and drink, yet they are rarely thankful. (73)

They adopted gods instead of God and sought their support. (74)

They will not be able to support them even if they were true soldiers in an army. (75)

Do not let what they say affect you, for We know everything they hide and they declare. (76)

Is it not obvious that the human that We created from a sperm has become clearly contentious? (77)

He asks contentiously, while forgetting his own creation, who can resurrect bones after it is dust? (78)

Say: "It will be resurrected by Him who created it the first time, and He is Knowledgeable of all creation." (79)

He who made for you firewood from green trees, that you use to make fire. (80)

Is not the One who created the heavens and the earth able to create like them again? He is the Knowledgeable Creator. (81)

If He wishes to have something done, all He needs is to say, Be, and it will be. (82)

Glory be to Him; the One who holds the reigns of the kingdom and all things, and to Him you shall return. (83).

THE ROWS (37)

In the Name of God, Most Merciful, and Most Beneficent.

Swearing by those who stand in tight rows (*the angels*) (1)

and by those who keep their devils away by cursing them (*the jinn*) (2)

and those who recite the words of God (*humans*). (3)

Your God is One. (4)

Lord of the heavens and the earth and what is in between, and Lord of where all had started. (5)

We have made the stars ornaments of the sky, (6)

protectors from devilish demons. (7)

They are kept out of touch with the upper creations, by continuing to be hit from every side by meteors, (8)

to be defeated, and awaiting them is a certain torture. (9)

And those who manage to escape are followed by a piercing comet. (10)

Ask them (*the unbelievers*) and find out if they think they are the strongest of what We created. We created them from soft sticky mud. (11)

You were amazed at their mockery. (12)

When reminded they never remember. (13)

When given a sign they mock it (14)

and say: "This is obviously sorcery." (15)

Are we going to be resurrected after we die and become dust and bones? (16)

Are our forefathers going to be resurrected also? (17)

Say: "Yes, and you shall be humiliated. (18)

It will take only an indication from Him and they shall be watching what will happen." (19)

They will be saying: "We shall be damned if it is not the Day of Religion (*Day of Judgement*)." (20)

This is the Day of Judgement that you were denying. (21)

Assemble the transgressors and their spouses, and what they used to worship, (22)

instead of God and guide them to the path towards hell, (23)

to be held responsible. (24)

They will be asked about why they do not support each other that day. (25)

In effect, the opposite, on that day they shall surrender themselves. (26)

They will start questioning each other. (27)

Some will say to the others: "You used to to come at us from the right (*impose your will on us*)." (28)

Those will answer: "No, you were not believers anyway. (29)

We had no power over you, but you were transgressors. (30)

We are here because the true word of our Lord caught up with us both. (31)

We may have misguided you, but we were misguided ourselves." (32)

They shall both be sharing the torture. (33)

That is what awaits the transgressors (34)

who, when told that there is no god but the One God, they became arrogant. (35)

They even said: "We shall not leave our gods for a crazy poet." (36)

In effect the truth has become evident, and the apostles were proven to be right. (37)

You shall taste the excruciating pain. (38)

You will be punished only for what you did. (39)

Except for the faithful worshipers of God; (40)

they shall have God's known bounty. (41)

The best fruits to eat while being honored (42)

in the blissful gardens, (43)

reclining on luscious beds positioned opposite each other, (44)

served glasses filled with a special juice, (45)

white and delicious to drink. (46)

It does them no harm, nor will they become addicted to it. (47)

Sitting next to them will be young and bashful women. (48)

As innocent as covered and protected eggs. (49)

And as they engage each other in conversation. (50)

One will say to the other: "I used to know a person. (51)

He asked me if I was one of the believers. (52)

Are we going to return after we die, and become dust and bones?" (53)

He said: "Can I find out about him?" (54)

He does and he finds him in hell. (55)

He will say: "O' my God, he just about misguided me. (56)

If it was not for God's mercy upon me, I would have been among those brought for punishment." (57)

Some will ask themselves: "Are we going to ever die again, (58)

other than for the first time we died, or are we ever going to be tortured?" (59)

This is the great triumph. (60)

And this is what all should work for. (61)

Is this not a better reception than that provided by the Zakoum tree? (62)

We made it a special treatment for the transgressors. (63)

It is a tree that grows at the bottom of hell. (64)

Its pollen looks like the heads of devils. (65)

They shall eat from it until their bellies are full. (66)

It will make them feel like they have put on a gown of flame. (67)

They shall always return to hell. (68)

They found their fathers to be misguided. (69)

And they seem to be in a hurry to follow them. (70)

Before them, most of the earlier generations were misguided. (71)

We sent to them apostles to give warning. (72)

Look at how those who were warned ended. (73)

Except for those who are God's faithful worshipers. (74)

Noah called upon us, and who can respond better than Us? (75)

We saved him and his family from the great catastrophe. (76)

We made his descendents the only survivors. (77)

We got rid of the others, (78)

a special salute to him from the entire world. (79)

That is the way We reward those who do good works. (80)

He is one of Our believing worshipers. (81)

And then We drowned all the others. (82)

Among those who are like him is Abraham (83)

who came to his Lord with a receptive heart. (84)

As he said to his father and his people: "What are you worshiping? (85)

Is it these forgeries that you want, instead of God? (86)

How do you think this will be looked upon by the Lord of the universe?" (87)

He looked at the stars in the sky, (88)

and said: "I feel sick." (89)

They walked away from him. (90)

He went to their idol gods and said to them: "How come are you not eating while the food is offered to you? (91)

How come do you not say a word? (92)

He (*Abraham*) started smashing the idols with his right hand. (93)

People came back to him running. (94)

He (*Abraham*) said: "Are you are going to worship what you made with your own hands? (95)

when God is the One who created you and you do not even seem to know it?" (96)

They built for him a big oven and then threw him in the fire. (97)

They conspired and had designs against him, but they came out at the bottom. (98)

He said: "I am going to my Lord, who will guide me." (99)

He (*Abraham*) said: God grant me an offspring of God-worshiping and fearing people. (100)

We gave him good tidings of a nice boy. (101)

And as the boy grew up and he got used to his help and company, he said to him: "I saw in my dream that I am slaying you, so tell me what you think?" He answered: "My father, do what you are ordered, and you shall find me obedient." (102)

And as they surrendered themselves to the calamity at hand, (103)

We called upon Abraham. (104)

We declare what you saw fulfilled, and that is how we reward good works. (105)

That is the height of obedience to God. (106)

We ransomed his son with a great sacrifice. (107)

We also left for him with others, (108)

an everlasting salute, (109)

and that is how We reward good works. (110)

He was one of Our believing worshipers. (111)

We gave him good tidings of Isaac, a God-worshiping and fearing prophet. (112)

We blessed him and blessed Isaac, and among their descendents those who did good works and those who clearly transgressed against their own souls. (113)

We granted favors also to Moses and Aaron, (114)

and saved them with their people from a great calamity. (115)

We gave them support, so they became triumphant. (116)

And also We revealed the veritable Book to them, (117)

And We led them to the straight path. (118)

And We left for them with others, (119)

a salute to Moses and Aaron. (120)

This is the way We reward good works. (121)

They are among our true believing worshipers. (122)

Elias was also one of the apostles. (123)

He said to his people: "Fear and worship God. (124)

You worship an idol called Baal instead of the accomplished Creator. (125)

God is your Lord and the Lord of your ancestors." (126)

They denied Him and they shall be among the assembled. (127)

Except for those who are God's faithful worshipers. (128)

We also left for him among others, (129)

a salute to all the family of Yaahseen. (130)

That is the way We reward good works. (131)

He is among Our worshiping believers. (132)

Lot was also among the apostles. (133)

We saved him and his family. (134)

Except for an old woman. (135)

Then We destroyed all the others. (136)

You will pass them by in the morning, (137)

and at night. Do you not understand? (138)

Jonah also was an Apostle. (139)

He took a ride on a fully loaded ship. (140)

As the ship was about to sink for being overloaded, he cast a lot with other shipmates on who will jump off to keep the ship afloat and he lost. (141)

He jumped off and was swallowed whole by a whale unaware. (142)

If it was not for the fact that he was a praying believer, (143)

He would have stayed in his belly until the Day of Resurrection. (144)

He was then thrown out, with little clothes and sick, on a desolate beach. (145)

We caused a gourd shrub to grow next to him and cover him. (146)

Then We sent him as an Apostle to over one hundred thousand people. (147)

They believed and We let them enjoy themselves for a while. (148)

Try to ask the unbelievers (*as they talk about idols being the daughters of God*) does the Lord get the girls and you get the boys? (149)

Just as false when they say the angels are females. Did they witness their creation? (150)

In their blasphemy they attribute (151)

children to God, and they are liars. (152)

Or in claiming that God has chosen female children over male. (153)

How do you exercise such poor judgement? (154)

Do you not remember? (155)

Or do you have such veritable high level knowledge? (156)

If that is true, then why do you not reveal to us your book, if you are truly truthful. (157)

Some of them made a relationship between their gods and the jinn, but even the jinn themselves know that they shall be assembled in front of God. (158)

Glorified be Him who is Exalted above all that they describe (159)

except God's faithful worshipers. (160)

You and what you worship (161)

and appear to be devoted to (162)

shall all taste hell. (163)

Every one has a special predetermined position. (164)

We (*the angels*) are the ones who determine the order of the rows in which all are arranged. (165)

We (*angels*) who worship and glorify Him. (166)

The unbelievers say: (167)

"If we received admonishment from our elders, (168)

we would have been faithful worshipers." (169)

Yet they do not believe in the Koran and they shall find out about that. (170)

Our word has been given to Our worshiping apostles. (171)

They shall receive Our support. (172)

Our armies shall vanquish them, (173)

so leave them for the time being. (174)

Watch them and you will see when they see the truth. (175)

They must be in a hurry to see our torture. (176)

And when it hits them, the morning of the warned shall be spoiled. (177)

Leave them for a while. (178)

And you shall see when they see the truth. (179)

Glorified be Him, your Lord, who is Exalted far above what they describe. (180)

A special salute to the apostles. (181)

And thanks to God, Lord of the universe. (182)

SADD (38)

In the Name of God, Most Merciful, and Most Beneficent.

Sadd, and I swear with the Koran, that is so much worthy of mention. (1)

The unbelievers are merely arrogant, and are fighting with each other. (2)

How many generations We have annihilated before them, who kept on screaming for help with no answer. (3)

Yet when they had warning from amongst them, the unbelievers called it an untruthful sorcery. (4)

He is trying to make all the gods One God, is this not strange? (5)

Many of them were saying: "Go ahead and be patient and keep on relying on your gods." Driving you away from your gods is what the believers desire. (6)

We have never heard about any of this before, this is only confabulation. (7)

Would God choose to send His message to him from among all of us? They are expressing doubt in My Book. They shall change their tune when My torture touches them. (8)

Or do they have a key to cabinets full of your Lord's abundant mercy, (9)

or do they own the heavens and the earth and what is in between, and if they do, why do they not climb up to higher places? (10)

What will happen to them will be like what happened to allied armies before them. (11)

Apostles were denied before them by the people of Noah, Aad, and the Pharaoh with the sticks (*he used to impale his enemies on sticks*). (12)

Also Thamoud, the people of Lot, the people of Madian, and the other parties. (13)

They all denied the messengers sent to them and they earned their punishment. (14)

All they needed was one shout that cannot be silenced by anything, (15)

and they will start saying: "Our Lord bring our punishment on us now, rather than wait for the Day of Judgement." (16)

Be patient with their claims, and remember our servant David who was very strong and yet he sought God's mercy and forgiveness always. (17)

We have made the mountains glorify God with him morning and evening. (18)

We made the birds in all of their variety answer to him. (19)

We caused him to control a huge kingdom, and gave him wisdom, and an unerring judgement. (20)

Have you heard the story of the two disputing individuals who came over the wall into David's temple? (21)

And as they entered on him, he became apprehensive, and they said: "Do not be afraid; we have a dispute between us, and we want you to arbitrate our dispute, and be just and guide us to the straight path." (22)

One of them said: "This is my brother and he owns ninety nine ewes, and I own one. He has been arguing that I should give it to him, and has managed to embarrass me in his argument." (23)

David said: "He was not being just to you by wanting to add your ewe to his," and many times when people have common or mixed property, they try to take advantage of each other, unless they are believers who did good works, and those are not many. David then thought that to be a test for him and he fell down on his knees asking for forgiveness. (24)

We forgave him; Our door was always open to him, and he will always be close to Us. (25)

We said David: We made you in a position of leadership, in the land. So judge among people rightly, and do not follow your whims, for you could be led away from God's straight path, and those who drift away from God's path shall have excruciating torture awaiting them for what they may have forgotten, on the Day of Judgement. (26)

We did not create the heavens and the earth and what is in between them for nothing, as the unbelievers may think, but the unbelievers shall have no savior from hell. (27)

Does anyone think that We may treat the believers the way We treat the transgressors on earth, or could those who worship and fear God be ever treated like the loudmouths? (28)

A blessed Book We revealed to you, so they can contemplate its verses, and to serve as a reminder to those who have sense. (29)

Then We gave Solomon to David, a best worshiper, and seeker of God's approval. (30)

As he was being shown his fine horses in the evening, (31)

He said: I have permitted my love for fine things to make me forget my prayers until the sun went down. (32)

He ordered the horses to be brought back and ordered them killed. (33)

To test Solomon, We threw a body over his chair, and he repented. (34)

He said: "Lord forgive me, and grant me a kingdom that will not be given to anyone after me. You are the greatest of all grantors." (35)

We gave him control over the wind, which will run in the direction he commands. (36)

We had devils under his control, some were building for him and others were diving at his command, (37) and many others waiting in chains. (38)

This is what we can give or withhold at will, and with no count. (39)

He will always have with us a listening ear and a respectable place. (40)

Remember our servant Job, who called on his Lord saying: "I have been touched by a state of depression and suffering from the Devil." (41)

Hit the earth with your foot (*We said*), and the earth will burst with a fountain. Wash, drink and refresh yourself. (42)

We then blessed him with a family, and just as many others, a mercy from us, and a reminder to those of intellect. (43)

Take a bunch of a hundred thin twigs and use it to hit with lightly once, instead of a promise to hit with a whip a hundred times (*symbolic gestures can be used to avoid the appearance of having not fulfilled a solemn promise made in haste or anger to punish*). We found him to be among the best of My servants, and a trustworthy one. (44)

Also remember Abraham, Isaac and Jacob, who all had the strength and the sound judgement. (45)

We purified them and made them direct their attention to the Last Day, rather than this life. (46)

They are our select group of good people. (47)

Also remember Ishmael, Elisha (*Yasaah*) and Isaiah (*Thalkifl*) and other good people. (48)

This is a reminder; and to those who worship and fear God belongs the best of all destinies. (49)

To them the doors of the Gardens of Eden shall be open. (50)

There they shall be reclining while served with fruits and drinks. (51)

They and their spouses shall pay attention to no one but each other. (52)

This is what you are promised on the day of reckoning. (53)

This is from our bounty, which is inexhaustible. (54)

To the transgressors belongs the worst destiny. (55)

They shall be consumed by the fire of hell. A deserved ending indeed. (56)

They shall have their own drinks; alternating hot scalding water, and stinging venom of snakes and insects, (57)

and other drinks inflicting different kinds of torture, (58)

As a new group is ushered in, unwelcome, to feed the fire. (59)

They will say to their predecessors: "Unwelcome to you also for what you handed down to us, damned was your judgement. "(60)

They will say: "God give those who handed bad things over to us, twice the torture of hell." (61)

Some will say: "Where are those bad individuals among us?" (62)

We used to mock them (*the believers*). Did they slip out of sight? (63)

That is an example of how those in hell shall quarrel. (64)

Say: "I am only to deliver warning from the One and only God, the Vanquisher." (65)

Lord of the heavens and the earth and what is in between, the Exalted and Merciful. (66)

Say: "It is such a great call I am giving you, (67)

and you are turning away from it." (68)

Say: "How would I have known what is up there as you are fighting each other? (69)

If it was not for the revelation that I am to deliver a clear warning." (70)

When your Lord said to the angels: I am creating humans from mud. (71)

I have completed his creation, and installed in him some of My spirit, so prostrate yourselves in front of him. (72)

The angels, all of them, fell down. (73)

Except for Satan, who became arrogant and ended an unbeliever. (74)

He (*God*) said: You, Satan, what prevented you from prostrating yourself in front of what I created with My own hands. Did you simply become arrogant, or did you think you knew something? (75)

He (*Satan*) said: "I am better than him, You created me from fire and created him from mud." (76)

He (*God*) said: Then get out of it (*heaven*) for you have become deserving of stoning, (77)

and My curse is on you until the Day of Religion (*Last Day*). (78)

He (*Satan*) said: "Give me a reprieve until the day of their resurrection. "(79)

He (*God*) said: You are reprieved; (80)

only until then. (81)

He (*Satan*) said: "If you permit me I shall entice them all, (82)

except for the faithful among them." (83)

He (*God*) said: I hereby say, and it is the truth. (84)

I shall fill hell with you, your descendents, and those of them who follow you. (85)

Say (*God to the Prophet*): "I have asked you no reward for what I bring you, and I have no personal gain from it." (86)

It is a reminder for the whole world. (87)

The absolute proof to what I am telling you shall come to you after a while. (88)

THE GROUPS (39)

In the Name of God, Most Merciful, and Most Beneficent.

This revelation of the Book is from God, the Exalted and the Wise. (1)

We revealed the Book to you rightly, so worship God and be faithful to Him in your religion. (2)

The pure religion is that which is directed exclusively to God, and those who assume sponsors other than God, and then they say that we use them only to bring us closer to God, God shall adjudicate the differences among them. God does not guide those who are unbelieving liars. (3)

If God was desirous of having a child, He would have chosen whomever He wishes from among those he created. Glorified be Him, God the Vanquisher. (4)

He rightly created the heavens and the earth. He eases the night into the day and the day into the night. He deployed the sun and the moon each in its own orbit for a predetermined duration. He is the Exalted Merciful. (5)

He created you from one soul, then from you He created your spouses. He also created cattle for you in eight different pairs. He creates you inside the bellies of your mothers, one after the other, in three sacs of darkness. This is God, your Lord. To Him belongs the kingdom of heaven. How do you dare to look for alternatives? (6)

If you do not believe, God has no need for you, and He will never approve of lack of belief on the part of His worshipers, but no soul shall ever answer for another, and to your Lord you shall return, and He shall tell you what you have been truly doing. He knows what is inside your bosoms. (7)

When humans are touched with harm, they start praying to God for salvation, but when they are extended a blessing they forget what they were praying for before and associate others with God to mislead others away from Him. Say: Enjoy your lack of belief for a while, but you are among the owners of hell. (8)

The believer prostrates himself part of the night worshiping, and warns of the Last Day during the day. Say: Can you equate those who are knowledgeable with those who are ignorant? Those of intellect are those who remember. (9)

Say: O' worshipers who believe, worship and fear your Lord. Those who do good works in this life shall receive good. God's earth is big and wide (*you can move to other areas on earth where there is more tolerance of your way of life*). Those who endure shall be rewarded without measure. (10)

Say: I was ordered to worship God and be faithful to Him in my religion.(11)

Say: I was also ordered to be the first Moslem. (12)

Say: If I disobeyed my Lord, I will be afraid of the torture of a Great Day. (13)

Say: I worship God, and to Him I am faithful in my religion. (14)

Say: Worship whomever you want instead of Him. The losers are the ones who are going to lose themselves and their families on the Day of Judgement, and that is a most prominent loss. (15)

The heat of the fire shall attack them from above and from below, The horror of this is why God warns His servants. My servants, worship and fear Me. (16)

Those who avoided idol-worshipping, and instead surrendered themselves to God, shall receive good tidings, so deliver these good tidings to the worshipers. (17)

It is those who listen to what is said and follow the best of it, who are the ones who are guided by God and are the ones who have true intellect. (18)

Do they think that those who are deserving of torture can be saved by you from the fire? (19)

But those who worship and fear God, shall have chambers above chambers, under which rivers flow. God never fails to deliver on a promise. (20)

Do you not see that God brought water down from the sky, and channeled it into fountains and springs that bring up plants from the earth of varying colors, then it turns yellowish and dries out? In that there are signs for those with intellect. (21)

Those who God opens their hearts to Islam are guided by their Lord's light, and those whose hearts are hardened, away from the words of God; those are the ones who are clearly misguided. (22)

God revealed the best in discussions, many of which tend to reiterate the same message, and many may initially make the skin crawl, then the skins and the hearts soften to the words of God.

This is God's guidance which He provides to whomever He wishes. Those who God misguides can never find a guide. (23)

Those whose face shows their surrender, on the Day of Judgement shall save themselves from torture, while the transgressors shall be told to taste the result of their actions. (24)

Those who denied the message before them were hit by torture from places they never expected. (25)

God afflicted them with the taste of shame in this life, and the torture of the Day of Judgement is bigger if they knew. (26)

We brought examples to people in this Koran from all kinds so they can be reminded. (27)

A Koran in the Arabic language, that contains no errors or deviations, so they may worship and fear. (28)

Is a slave with multiple masters pulling on him from different directions the same as a free man who can choose the path he wants? Thanks to God, but most of them do not know. (29)

You are going to die, and they will die, too. (30)

Then, on the Day of Judgement, you shall return to God who shall provide the final judgement. (31)

Who is a bigger transgressor than the ones who lie about God, and deny the truth when it comes to them? Do they think that hell is not going to have enough room for the unbelievers? (32)

Those who bring the truth, and believe in the truth, these are the ones who worship and believe God. (33)

They shall get what they want from their Lord, for that is the reward for those who do good. (34)

God shall forgive some of the worst of what they have done, and reward them based on the best they have done. (35)

Is not God's confidence sufficient for his worshipers? Yet they try to scare you with those who are far beneath Him. Those who are misguided by God shall find no guide. (36)

While those guided by God cannot be misguided by anyone. God is Exalted and Vengeful. (37)

If you asked them: Who created the heavens and the earth? and they say: "God," say: Do you not see that those you pray for instead of God cannot prevent harm from reaching me if God wished it, and they cannot prevent a mercy from reaching me if God wished it? Say: I will leave my fate in the hands of God, and on God rely those who need some one to rely on. (38)

Say: My people, work on improving your status with God like I am doing, and you shall find out. (39)

Those who earn torture shall shamefully get a lasting torture. (40)

We have revealed the Book to you, to relay the truth to people. Those who become guided do it for themselves, and those who remain misguided err against themselves, and you are not the keeper. (41)

God retrieves the souls of those who die. Some die in their sleep, and their souls are retrieved, unless it was decided to let them live longer for a while, and in that there are signs for people who think. (42)

Are they going to adopt others to intercede for them? Others who cannot claim ownership of anything, nor could they even think straight. (43)

Say: Power to intercede belongs only to God. To Him belongs the kingdom of heavens and earth, and to Him you shall return. (44)

The hearts of those who do not believe in the Last Day shrink when the name of the One God is mentioned in front of them, while they take the mention of those they worship instead of God to bring them good tidings. (45)

Say: "God, the Creator of the heavens and the earth; He who has knowledge of the future and the truthfulness of testimony. You shall adjudicate what your servants were in disagreement about. (46)

If the transgressors owned all that is on earth, and even twice as much it will not be enough to ransom them from the torture awaiting them on the Day of Judgement, and they shall face from God what they have never expected. (47)

They shall face the willfulness of their mocking, and what they have mocked will catch up with them. (48)

If a human was touched with harm he prays for Our help, while if We gave him a blessing he acts like he deserved it while in reality it is a test, but most people do not know. (49)

Many before them said the same thing, and it was no help to them in changing what they earned. (50)

They will face the consequences of their action, and those among them who transgressed shall be harmed by the harm they caused, and they shall not escape. (51)

Did they not know that God extends His bounty to whomever He wishes and determines? In that there are signs for those who believe. (52)

My worshipers who may have crossed the line of righteousness; do not despair in seeking forgiveness, for God forgives all sins; He is the Forgiving and the Merciful. (53)

Repent and surrender to your Lord, before you get the torture and after which you have no way out. (54)

Follow the best of what your Lord has revealed to you, before you are surprised with the torture unaware. (55)

When a soul will say: "Alas, I have wasted time in not being on God's side, instead of joining the mockers." (56)

Or for one to say: "If God has guided me I would have been fearing and worshiping Him." (57)

Or to say when facing the torture: "If I get another chance I will be among those who do good works." (58)

My verses reached you and you denied it, and became arrogant, and thus joined the unbelievers. (59)

On the Day of Judgement you shall find those who denied God with black faces. Is there not always a place in hell for those afflicted with arrogance? (60)

God shall save those who worshiped and feared God as a prize and no harm shall touch them, nor shall they be sad. (61)

God created everything, and He is in control of all things. (62)

He owns the heavens and the earth, and those who denied God's verses are the losers. (63)

Say to them: "Are you expecting me to worship someone other than God, you ignorant people?" (64)

He revealed to you and to those who came before you that if you associate others with Him, you shall fail and become losers. (65)

It is God you should worship, and be grateful. (66)

They never appreciated God's true power, when the earth, on the Day of Judgement shall be in His hand, and the heavens stacked under His right arm; Glorified and Exalted, He is above the associations they make. (67)

When the trumpet will sound, all those in heaven and on earth shall fall to the ground unconscious, except for those spared by God. As the trumpet sounds again, they shall all rise and start looking around them. (68)

The earth shall light up with its Lord's light. The Book shall be brought, and so will the prophets and the witnesses, and they shall receive the appropriate adjudication of their cases rightly, and no one shall be wronged. (69)

Each soul shall receive the appropriate judgement for what it had earned. He is most Knowledgeable with what they did. (70)

The unbelievers shall be taken to hell in groups, and as they come to its doors and the doors open, the keepers shall ask them. Did you not get apostles from among you, reciting to you verses from your Lord, and warning you in regard to this day, and they will say: "Yes." The truth of the hour of torture is now evident to the unbelievers. (71)

They will be told: "Enter the doors of hell where you will be immortalized." What a suitable place for the arrogant. (72)

Those who have worshiped and feared God shall be driven in groups to heaven, and as they get to the doors and those are opened, and its keepers shall greet them and inform them that they earned it, and in it they shall be immortalized. (73)

They will say: "Thanks to God who truthfully extended the promise to us and permitted us to inherit the earth, and then elevated us to wherever we want in paradise. It is the best of all rewards." (74)

You shall also find the angels surrounding the throne, praying and glorifying their Lord, and He shall also give them His judgement rightly, and they shall thank the Lord of the universe. (75)

THE FORGIVING (40)

In the Name of God, Most Merciful, and Most Beneficent.

Haah Meem. (1)

The Book is revealed by God, the Exalted and the Knowledgeable. (2)

The Forgiver of sin, the Acceptor of repentance, the Bountiful, and the One who can deal severe punishment. There is no God but Him, and to Him is the destiny. (3)

Only the unbelievers dispute the verses of God. Do not be mislead by their apparent success in the land. (4)

Before them the people of Noah denied, and so did numerous tribes after them. Many tried to kill apostles sent to them, and they disputed the right with what they knew to be false. I took them away, and what a punishment was that. (5)

Thus the word of your God was realized on the unbelievers, for they are the owners of hell. (6)

Those (*angels*) who carry the weight of the Throne, and those who stand around it, and glorify with gratefulness their Lord and believe in Him, and ask for forgiveness to the believers, they say: "Our Lord Who has knowledge of all things, and the unlimited capacity to forgive, forgive those who repented and followed your path, and protect them from the torture of fire." (7)

Lord, enter them the Garden of Eden that you promised them and to the righteous from among their fathers, spouses and their descendents, for You are the Exalted and Wise. (8)

Protect them from harm, and those who You protect from harm on that day will have received Your mercy, and that is the greatest of all victories. (9)

On that day, the unbelievers shall be called and told that regardless of how much you despise yourselves, God despises you even more, as you were invited to believe and yet you denied. (10)

They say: "Lord, you have caused us to die twice and to live twice, and now we admit to all of our sins, is there not a way out?" (11)

The answer they will receive is: When you were asked to worship God alone, you denied, and when asked to associate others with Him you always responded affirmatively; now the judgement is in the hand of God, the Exalted and the Great. (12)

He is the One who shows you His signs, and brings you down sustenance from the sky, which only those who repent remember. (13)

So pray to God faithfully, and believe in your religion, whether the unbelievers like it or not. (14)

He is the superior and owner of the throne. He grants the gift of the spirit to whomever He wishes among His worshipers to warn about the day of the great meeting (*Day of Judgement*). (15)

The day when all are exposed, and nothing about them is hidden from God. To whom does sovereignty belong that day other than to the One God, the Dominant? (16)

On that day every soul shall reap what it has planted. On that day no one shall be shortchanged, and God's accounting is quite swift. (17)

Warn them of the day when their hearts will feel like they have jumped up and blocked their throats. On that day the transgressors shall have no one who will claim their friendship or intercede for them. (18)

He (*God*) knows what the eyes try to disclose and what the chests hide. (19)

God renders judgement fairly, and those that they worship, instead of God, shall be judging nothing. God listens and sees everything. (20)

Did they not walk the earth and see how did those that preceded them end up? They were stronger than them, and left a much bigger impact, yet God took them for their sins, and they had no protection from God. (21)

Their apostles brought them veritable signs, yet they denied, and God took them. He is the Powerful, and the One whose punishment is quite severe. (22)

We sent Moses with Our revelations, supported by Our power, (23)

to the Pharaoh, Haman and Korah, and they said: "He is nothing but a sorcerer and a liar." (24)

As he (*Moses*) brought them the truth from Us, they said: "Kill the believers' children, and take liberties with their women." The vindictiveness of the unbelievers will always fail. (25)

The Pharaoh said: "I shall kill Moses and let him ask his God for help. I am afraid of letting him change your religion and spread corruption in the Land." (26)

Moses said: "I shall resort to my Lord and yours to protect us from all those who are arrogant and do not believe in the day of reckoning." (27)

A truly believing man from the family of the Pharaoh, who kept his believing a secret, said: "Are you going to kill a man because he said God is my Lord, and brought veritable signs from your Lord? If he is lying then he bears the consequences of his lies, but if he is truthful, you may suffer from what he is warning you about. God provides no guidance to those who are transgressors and liars." (28)

He said: "My people, today you have the throne and you are prominent on earth, but who will protect us from the wrath of God when it comes?" And the Pharaoh said: "I am showing you what I see, and guiding you to the right path." (29)

The believing man said: "My people, I am afraid for you from a day like that which hit on the day of the groups, (30)

like the people of Noah, Aad, and Thamoud and those who came after them, and God will not wrong the worshipers." (31)

He said: "My people, I am afraid for you from the day of the calling when people start calling each other — the Day of Judgement." (32)

The day you shall be running away in terror, and you shall find no protection from God. Those who are misguided by God shall find no guidance. (33).

Joseph was sent to you with veritable signs, and you continued to remain in doubt about what he brought you until he died and then you claimed that God shall send no apostle after him, and this is how God misguides those who are excessive in their doubtfulness. (34)

Those who argue in God's verses with no knowledge, earn the indignation of God and the believers. That is how the hearts of those who are arrogant and domineering are stamped and sealed by God. (35)

The Pharaoh said to Haman: "Build for me a structure that will permit me to reach new heights, (36)

heights that permit me to look at the God of Moses, for I suspect him to be a liar," and so were the designs of the Pharaoh that led to his misdeeds, and his deviation away from the straight path, and the Pharaoh's designs were decidedly a failure. (37)

The believer said: "My people, follow me, and I shall show you the way to wisdom. (38)

In this life there are only vanishing treasures, and in the next life lies our stable dwelling. (39)

Those who commit sins shall be facing the consequences, and those who do good works and are believers, whether male or female, shall enter heaven and be rewarded with no accounting." (40)

He also said: "Tell me, my people, why do I invite you to salvation, and you invite me to hell? (41)

You ask me to disbelieve in God, and to associate others with him, of which I have no knowledge whatsoever, while I invite you to the Exalted and the Forgiving. (42)

That is not to mention that what you invite me to is something that has no support in this life or the next. We shall all be returned to

God, and those who are excessively misguided are the owners of hell. (43)

You shall see the truth of what I tell you, and I shall put my trust in God, and God has total knowledge of all that worshipers do." (44)

God protected him from the evil of their designs, and the people of the Pharaoh earned the worst of God's torture. (45)

They shall be shown hell morning and evening, and at the final hours, people of the Pharaoh shall enter it and taste the worst of it. (46)

They will start arguing about hell, and the weak among them shall say to the more arrogant: "We were following you, so now are you going to shoulder a larger share of this hell-torture?" (47)

To this the arrogant ones will respond, saying: "We are all in it, and God has already passed his judgement on the worshipers." (48)

Those who are already in hell shall say to the caretakers: "Pray to your Lord so that He may lessen our torture." (49)

The caretakers will say: "Did you not receive apostles who brought you veritable signs?" and they will answer: "Yes, and they (*the caretakers*) will say: "Then you pray for yourselves," but prayers of the unbelievers shall be in vain. (50)

We shall always support the believers, in this life and on the Day of Judgement when all shall rise. (51)

The day the transgressors shall have no use of any excuses, and they shall be cursed and given the worst of all dwellings. (52)

We gave Moses guidance and the people of Israel were made to inherit the Book. (53)

Guidance and a reminder to those who have knowledge. (54)

So be patient, and realize that God's promise is true. Ask for your Lord's forgiveness of your sins, and glorify Him in the evening and early in the day. (55)

Those who argue in God's verses with no strength of validity, in their hearts there is inside them a motivating feeling of superiority that they will never succeed in justifying. So rely on God, He is All Hearing and Seeing. (56)

The creation of the heavens and the earth is a far bigger task than the creation of humans, but most people do not even understand that. (57)

The blind is never the same as one who can see, just like the believers who do good are not the same as sinners, but most tend to remember very little. (58)

The Hour (*Day of Judgement*) is coming, with no doubt, but most people do not believe. (59)

Your Lord said: Pray to me and I shall respond to you, and those who are too arrogant to worship Me shall enter hell for certain. (60)

God made the night for you to rest and the day to look around. God has done a lot of favors to people, yet people rarely give thanks. (61)

This is God, your Lord, who created everything; there is no other god but Him, and yet you find reasons to be disloyal. (62)

This is the same disloyalty exhibited by those who denied God's verses. (63)

God who made you the earth as a place to dwell, and built the heavens above you, and created you in images that are the best of all images. He is God your Lord, glorified be Him, Lord of the universe. (64)

He is the Immortal, no god but Him, pray to Him and be faithful to Him in your religion. Thanks to Him; Lord of the universe. (65)

Say: I have been ordered to desist from worshiping those that you worship, other than God, upon receiving the signs from my Lord and was ordered to surrender myself to the Lord of the universe. (66)

He is the One who created you from dust, then from a sperm, then from a clot, and then He brought you out an infant to grow until you reach your peak, and then you become old, although some may die earlier, yet all live to a predefined time, so you may be prompted to think. (67)

He is the One who gives life and determines death, and if He decrees something, all He has to say is "Be," and it shall. (68)

Do not be puzzled by those who argue in denial of God's verses, as to how their brain works. (69)

Those who denied the Book and what We revealed in it shall find out. (70)

As they carry iron around their necks, and pull their chains behind them (71)

while moving from scolding liquids to excoriating fire. (72)

Then they will be asked where are they, (73)

Those that you were worshiping instead of God, and they will say: "We lost them," and then deny that they were worshiping others. That is how God misguides the unbelievers. (74)

This is because of all that used to make you happy and gleeful on earth. (75)

Enter the doors of hell where you shall be immortalized, a suitable final dwelling for the arrogant. (76)

Be patient and confident that God's promise is true, and you shall either see them get what we had promised for them or you shall die, and later you shall all be brought to Us. (77)

We sent apostles before you, and We told you about many of them, and We did not tell you about some, and no apostle could ever bring a verse without God's permission. When it is time for the ruling from God, God shall rule lightly, and those who are wrong shall find themselves on the losing side. (78)

God who made animals that you ride and cattle from which you eat. (79)

Your benefits from them, and your dependence on them and on the ships that move you across the world is obvious. (80)

He shows you His signs, yet the signs of God you continue to deny. (81)

Did they not walk the earth and see the ending of those who came before them, and who were more powerful than they are and left a much larger impact on earth, and yet their power and impact never saved them. (82)

When apostles were sent to them, they were so proud of the level of knowledge they had achieved that they resorted to mocking the messages they received, which ended up catching up with them. (83)

And as they witnessed Our crushing power, they said: "We believe in God alone and deny whatever we have been associating with Him." (84)

Their believing after they saw Our power did them no good. It is the rule of God for His worshipers (*belief is accepted upon revelation and call, but prior to absolute certainty*), and that is where the unbelievers lost. (85)

IN FULL DETAILS (41)

In the Name of God, Most Merciful, and Most Beneficent.

Haah, Meem. (1)

Revealed by the Merciful and the Beneficent. (2)

A Book whose verses were revealed in full details. A Koran in Arabic to those who have knowledge. (3)

It is a Book of good tidings and warning, yet most declined, for they cannot hear. (4)

They said: "Our hearts are sealed from what you are inviting us to. Our ears are plugged, and a curtain is drawn between you and us, so you keep working and we shall do the same." (5)

Say to them: I am a human like you, receiving a revelation. Your God is One God, so correct your course towards Him, and seek His forgiveness, and doomed indeed are those who associate others with Him. (6)

Also those who do not spend in alms, and who are not believers in the Last Day. (7)

Those who do good works are rewarded with no expectations. (8)

Say to them: You do not believe in Him, He who created the earth in two days, and you ascribe associates to Him and He is the Lord of the universe. (9)

He made on it high mountains extending upward, and blessed it and created in it sustenance for all who need it in four more days. (10)

Then He ascended to heaven which was all smoke and said to the heavens and the earth: Are you going to submit to my will by choice or by force? They all said: "By choice." (11)

So He stratified the heavens into seven layers, and specified for each layer its contents, in two days. In the lowest layer (*closest to the earth*) We installed ornaments of sparkling lights, and balancing forces for stability. These were the rules from the Exalted and the Knowledgeable. (12)

If they reject your invitation, tell them that you have already warned them of a thunderbolt similar to the one that hit Aad and Thamoud. (13)

As the apostles were sent to them and to those before them exhorting them to worship only God, they said: "If God wished He would have sent us angels, but we are not believers in your revelations." (14)

Aad have become arrogant on this earth, with no justification, and said: "Who is stronger than us?" Did they not see that God who created them is stronger than they are? But they disbelieved our verses. (15)

We sent on them a huge wind storm, on several consecutive days, so they tasted the torture of shame in this life, and shall face a different torture, just as shameful, on the Last Day, and shall find no supporters. (16)

As to Thamoud, We provided them with guidance, yet they chose being blind instead of being guided, and they were taken by the thunderbolt. A humiliating torture, appropriate to what they have earned. (17)

We spared the believers who worshiped and feared God. (18)

The day when the enemies of God will be assembled to hell, and distributed in it. (19)

As they arrive there (*hell*), their own senses of sight and hearing, and their skins shall testify against them, as to their deeds. (20)

They will ask their own skin, why did it testify against them? Their skins will say: "It is God that enabled us to speak, as He did every one. He created you to start with, and to Him you shall return." (21)

You thought that you could hide, and that your hearing, sight and skins will not betray you, and that God will be oblivious to what you do. (22)

This was what you thought of God; you were wrong, and you became losers. (23)

If they wait, hell is their final destiny, and if they try to blame someone, none will take them seriously. (24)

They all had others like them, who encouraged them on what they did before and what they are doing now or will in the future. They have earned what is coming to them like many nations before them of jinn and humans, and they shall be losers. (25)

The unbelievers said: "Do not pay attention or consideration to the Koran as it is being recited, so you may prevail." (26)

Those unbelievers shall taste the most severe torture, and they shall receive far worse than they have been delivering. (27)

That shall be the punishment for the enemies of God, for to them there is immortality in hell, for they were subverting Our verses. (28)

The unbelievers will say: "Our Lord, show us who are those who contributed to our misguidance among the jinn or among humans and we shall trample them with our feet until they have a resting place among the lowest among us." (29)

Those who say: "Our Lord is God" and adhere to the straight path, the angels shall descend upon them and assure them and tell them to not be sad or afraid, and bring them good tidings of paradise which they have been promised. (30)

We are your sponsors in this life and the one next, and you shall have what your hearts desire, or anything you ask for, (31)

a gift from the Forgiver and the Merciful. (32)

Who could talk better than one who prays to God, does good works, and declares: " I am surrendered to Him"? (33)

A good deed and a bad deed can never be equal. Give priority to the good deed, and suddenly one with whom you have animosity may become a close sponsor. (34)

This exhortation is rarely followed successfully but by those who are extremely patient. They are the ones who will be truly fortunate. (35)

As such, one needs to pull himself away from the Devil by praying for God's help. He is the One who is always Hearing and Knowledgeable. (36)

Among His signs are the night and the day, and the sun and the moon. Do not prostrate yourself for the sun or the moon, but rather to the One who created them, if you are among His worshipers. (37)

As to those who are too arrogant, they shall realize that those on God's side glorify Him at night and during the day, and never get tired of it. (38)

Among His signs is when the earth appears to be silent in respect, and as the rain comes down, it is shaken with a characteristic noise. The One who created it shall resurrect the dead, and He is Capable of all things. (39)

Those who disbelieve and subvert Our verses cannot hide themselves from Us. Is the one who is thrown in the fire the same as the one who reaches the Last Day safely? You do whatever you want. He sees everything you do. (40)

Yet there are those who disbelieve the Book (*the holy Mention*) as it is revealed to them, with all the superior things it contains. (41)

A Book that is protected from all that may affect it, from before, in the present, or in the future. A revelation from the Wise and the One to whom all should be grateful. (42)

What is being said to you was said to apostles before you. Your Lord is the One who has a huge capacity for forgiveness, and also for delivering an excruciating torture. (43)

If We had made it a Koran in a foreign language they would have said: "Unfortunately the verses are not clear enough." Yet whether it is foreign or Arabic, it is for the believer's guidance and healing. As to the unbelievers, their ears are plugged and to it they are blind and they simply make noises from a far place. (44)

We brought Moses the Book and it was also a subject for controversy, and if it was not for a prior decision by your Lord to postpone, for awhile, His final judgement, they would have seen His displeasure earlier, and doubts about it would not have continued. (45)

One who does good works helps himself, and one who sins does against himself, and your Lord does not wrong His worshipers. (46)

God has all the knowledge about the Last Day. No fruit grows out of its budding branches, and no female is impregnated without His knowledge. As He calls, where are those that you associated with me, all will answer, none can testify to ever seeing them. (47)

They are suddenly denying what they claimed before, after they thought no one will ever find out. (48)

Humans do not tire from praying for the good to happen, and if they are touched by evil they become hopeless and desperate. (49)

If We show mercy to a human after having been touched by misfortune, he will say: "This is my lot, and I do not think the Last Day is coming, but if I have to return to my Lord, it is obvious that He has good intentions for me." We shall inform the unbelievers of what they did, and they shall taste severe torture. (50)

If we grant humans generously from Our bounty, they turn away and become reluctant to follow directions, but when touched by harm, their prayers are ample. (51)

Say: "You knew it was from God and yet you disbelieved it." Who could be more misguided, and farther away from the straight path? (52)

They shall see Our signs in the horizons, and inside themselves, until they know it is the truth. Is it not enough that your Lord is Witness to all things. (53)

They are in doubt of ever meeting their Lord, but He is aware of all things. (54)

ADVICE AND CONSENT (42)

In the Name of God, Most Merciful, and Most Beneficent.

Haah, Meem. (1)

Ain, Seen, Kaaf. (2)

This is the way We revealed to you, and to those before you, by God, the Exalted and the Wise. (3)

Owner of what is in the heavens and on earth, and He is the Superior and the Great. (4)

The heavens nearly crack for fear of Him, and the angels glorify their Lord, and pray for forgiveness to those on earth, for God is the Forgiving and the Merciful. (5)

Those that assume for themselves sponsors other than God, He shall always remember them, and you are not their keeper. (6)

We revealed to you an Arabic Koran so that you may warn the residents of the mother of villages (*Mecca*) and all that is around it. Warn them of the day of assembly (*Day of Judgement*) of which there is no doubt, when a group will be in paradise and the other group in hell. (7)

If He wished He would have made them all one nation, but He enters those He wishes in His mercy, and the transgressors shall find no sponsors or allies. (8)

It is strange to assume sponsors other than Him while He is not just the only sponsor, but the One Who will resurrect the dead, and He is Capable of all things. (9)

Any thing you have a disagreement on, the final ruling on it shall belong to God, my Lord. I rely on Him, and to Him I shall return. (10)

The creator of the heavens and the earth, who made spouses for you from yourselves, and created pairs from all animals, that provides for continuation of the species, He knows and He sees. (11)

He has total control of the heavens and the earth, providing for whomever He wishes, and chooses. He is Knowledgeable of all things. (12)

God decreed for you the religion similar to the way He decreed to Noah, and to Abraham, Moses and Jesus. They were all ordered to establish the religion and not let it be used to split people apart. The unbelievers shall prove to be too arrogant to accept what you invite them to. God leads to Himself whomever He wishes, and guides whomever He prefers. (13)

Some split only after they receive the revelation, due to rivalry among them, and if it was not for a prior decision by your Lord to hold off for a predetermined time, He would have forcefully settled the differences among them. Usually those who inherit the Book from those before them are highly more suspicious than people before them. (14)

Because of that you need to pray and straighten out as you were ordered and do not follow their whims and say: "I have believed in what God has revealed in His Book, and I was ordered to deal fairly with you. God is our Lord and yours. We shall answer for our actions and you shall answer for yours. There is no argument between you and us. God shall bring us together, and our destinies are to Him." (15)

Those who continue to argue in God with those who already decided on their response to Him, their argument is in error with their Lord's wishes, they shall earn His displeasure, and will face severe torture. (16)

God is the One who revealed the Book in a balanced truth, and who knows how close the Hour (*Last Day*) shall be. (17)

Those who are not believers wish it to come faster, whereas the believers are weary of it, and know it is the truth, but those who argue about it are very misguided. (18)

God is merciful with His worshipers, and provides for whomever He wishes, and He is the Exalted and the Mighty. (19)

One who wants to reap what he cultivates on the Last Day, we add to what he cultivated, and one who wants to reap what he cultivated in this life, he shall get it, but he shall have no share in the harvest of the Last Day. (20)

Those who have partners who legislate for them what they desire in religion, and what God has never permitted, God would have settled things with them, if it was not for His prior decision to hold off till the time He has predetermined arrives. The transgressors shall earn excruciating torture. (21)

You shall see the transgressors terrified of what they have done (*on the Last Day*) while those who believed and did good works shall be in the gardens of heaven, and they shall get what they want from their God, and that is the greatest of all rewards. (22)

As to what God brought good tidings to his worshipers about: it is, to believe in God and do good works, and you can tell them, you are expecting no recompense from them, and all they need to do is show goodwill and neighborliness and every good deed shall be returned with a better one, and God is Forgiving and Grateful. (23)

Or they will say: "The prophet told lies about God," but they should realize that if that was true, God is Capable of responding to that by sealing over your heart, and erasing the wrong and establishing the truth with His own words. He is Knowledgeable with what is inside the chests of humans. (24)

He is the One who accepts repentance from His worshipers, forgives sin, and knows what you do. (25)

He responds to those who believed and did good works, and reward them from His bounty, and the unbelievers shall have severe torture. (26)

If God provided plentifully to all his worshipers they will misbehave on earth; thus, He trickles down in as much, and to whomever he wishes. God is an Expert, and knows well His worshipers. (27)

He is the One who brings down the rain after the need for it becomes desperate, and spreads His mercy, and He is our sponsor to whom thanks belong. (28)

One of His signs is the creation of the heavens and the earth, and the creatures We filled the earth with, and He is the One capable of bringing everything together. (29)

Misfortunes that befall you are your own doing, and God forgives a lot. (30)

On earth you are not without significant limitations, and without God you have no sponsor or ally. (31)

Among His signs also, the floating of ships sailing in the ocean like flags. (32)

If He wishes to hold the wind still, they will stay stationary on its (*the ocean's*) back, and in that there are signs for grateful anxious travelers. (33)

Some times people are held responsible for what they do, but many a transgression He forgives. (34)

And those who continue to argue about our verses, know that they do not have far to go. (35)

Everything you have is the property of this life, and what God has is better and more lasting, for the believers who rely on their Lord. (36)

Those who avoid the worst of sins and indecencies, and when angered they can forgive. (37)

Those who responded to their Lord, and attended to their prayers, ran their affairs by advice and consent among them, and who spend in charity some of what We give them. (38)

They are the ones who when afflicted with adversity, they overcome. (39)

The punishment for an evil act is a similarly evil act, and if you forgive it is rather preferable with God, for He does not like the transgressors. (40)

Those who retaliate after they have been hurt by transgression from others shall not be punished. (41)

But the punishment is for those who persecute others and spread tyranny in the land and deviate from what is right. They shall face excruciating torture. (42)

Those who forbear and forgive, shall deserve the best of rewards. (43)

Those who are misguided by God, shall find no sponsor besides Him, and the transgressors, as they face the torture shall say: "Is there any way out of that?" (44)

You see them suffering, humbled, and degraded, stealing glances through the corner of their eyes. The believers will say: "The losers are the ones who lost themselves and their families on the Day of Judgement." The transgressors shall live in a lasting torture. (45)

Without God, they shall have no sponsors or allies, and one who is misguided by God shall not find his way. (46)

Respond to your Lord, before a day with no return arrives. Then you shall have no shelter or protection from God. (47)

If they turn away remember that We have not sent you to them as their keeper, We sent you only to warn, and if We give a human mercy from Us, he becomes exulted, and if he is afflicted with a calamity he becomes inclined to disbelieving. (48)

To God belongs what is in the heavens and on earth. He gives female children to some, and male children to others. (49)

He may marry males to females and cause some of them to be sterile. He is Able and Knowledgeable. (50)

No human shall be communicated with by God except through closely held revelations, or from behind a screen, or through an apostle, who will convey revelations as He wishes being whispered in his ear. God is Superior and Wise. (51)

We also revealed to you a spirit (*the Koran*) from our will, before you knew what is the meaning of the Book and faith, and We made it a light with which We guide whomever We wish from among Our worshipers, and for you to use it to guide to the right path. (52)

It is the path established by God, to whom belongs what is in the heavens and on earth, Who is the final arbiter on all things. (53)

THE ORNAMENTS (43)

In the Name of God, Most Merciful, and Most Beneficent.

Haah, Meem. (1)

I swear with the veritable book. (2)

We made it an Arabic Koran so you may understand. (3)

In the mother of the Book We included superior logic and wisdom. (4)

Did you think that We are going to forgive you even if you engaged in excesses? (5)

How many apostles did We send to the old generations? (6)

They were mocking every prophet We sent them. (7)

We have annihilated people who were far more fierce and stronger than they are. Those generations disappeared. (8)

Those unbelievers, they will admit that God, the Knowledgeable and the Exalted, created what is in the heavens and on earth. (9)

He who made the earth a place you seek shelter in, and also sustenance, so you may be correctly guided. (10)

He brought down water from the sky in enough amounts to revive dead towns, which permits you to survive. (11)

He is the One who created all living creatures in pairs and provided ships and animals for travel. (12)

So that as you are riding the backs of animals or floating on the surface of the seas, you will remember what God's bounty to you has been, and you will say: "Glorified be Him who provided us with all of that, and which We could have never duplicated." (13)

To your Lord you shall always be indebted. (14)

Some people started dividing what God has created into portions they want and the rest they grant to God. Humans have always been clearly unbelievers. (15)

You even assign the girls to God, and the boys to yourselves. (16)

If one of them is informed of what God has chosen for him, his face becomes darkened, and he becomes angry. (17)

They claimed that females grow wearing jewelry, and are useless in confrontations or fighting. (18)

They even made the angels who are worshipers of God females, did they ever witness their creation, and they shall be interrogated about that. (19)

Then they said: "If God wished, we would have not worshiped the idols," (*who are females, and called the daughters of God*) but they really have no worthwhile knowledge about any of these things, they are only inventing stupid excuses. (20)

Did We even bring them a book before it, and now they are trying to hold on to it? (21)

They rather say: "We found our forefathers on the track we are in, and we shall continue to follow this track for guidance. (22)

Even before you, every time We sent a warning to a town, the people said: "They are simply following the tracks of their forefathers." (23)

Even when they are shown that they were brought a far superior guidance than what their fathers had, they say: "We still disbelieve what you brought." (24)

We retaliated against them, and look how those who denied the truth will end. (25)

Abraham told his father, and his people: "I declare my innocence from having anything to do with what you worship. (26)

The One who created me shall guide me. (27)

He let His word stand firm after that, hoping they may see the light." (28)

We have permitted those people to enjoy life, along with their fathers, until the truth was delivered to them through a veritable messenger. (29)

When the truth was sent to them they said: "This is nothing but sorcery," and they did not believe. (30)

They said that if the Koran was revealed to a great man, from one of the two cities (*Mecca, and the Taaeff*), it would have been different. (31)

Are they trying to second guess God's decisions and redistribute His mercy, when He was the One who distributed wealth and status to them in this life. He made some of them higher than others, yet some of them mock others and do not realize that the Lord's mercy is far more valuable than anything they collect for themselves. (32)

If it was not for Our reluctance to unify and strengthen the unbelievers into one power, We would have given those who disbelieve in the Merciful houses with silver roofs, and high towers from which they can be seen. (33)

Their homes will have many doors and be full of comfortable couches on which they can recline. (34)

And countless ornaments, for all of these are properties of this life that has little value, and your Lord saves the next life for those who worship and fear God. (35)

One who refuses to acknowledge the Merciful, We shall assign him a special Devil of his own to be his partner. (36)

He will lead him away from the straight path, while making him think that he is rightly guided. (37)

On the day he returns to us he shall say to his partner: "I wish the longest distance separated us from each other." (38)

On that day you shall not benefit, even if you recognized your transgressions, and you shall be all sharing the torture. (39)

Do you think you can make the deaf hear or the blind find his way after being clearly lost? (40)

We can actually take you away, and retaliate against them (41)

or let you witness them being hit with what We promised them, and that at any time We wish we can bring them under Our control. (42)

So hold on to the One who sent you the revelations, for you are on the straight path. (43)

It is a reminder for you and for your people, for you shall be asked. (44)

None need to doubt that the messengers We sent before you have never been sent to call for worshiping any but the Merciful Himself. (45)

We sent Moses to the Pharaoh and his people with Our signs, and he said: "I am a messenger from the Lord of the universe." (46)

As he started presenting Our signs to them, they broke out laughing. (47)

As they saw signs, one bigger than the other, they continued. We hit them with the torture so they might desist. (48)

They addressed Moses like he was a sorcerer, and said: "Please pray to your Lord to help us, and We shall be guided." (49)

As We gave them relief, they reneged. (50)

The Pharaoh called upon his people, and said: "Am I not the king of Egypt and do these rivers not pass below me? Do you not see that? (51)

Am I not better than he who brings you humiliation, who you can hardly see where he stands? (52)

How did he not get gold bracelets, nor were the angels sent down in his support?" (53)

He took advantage of his people's ignorance and they obeyed him, for they were corrupted people. (54)

When they denied Us We retaliated and drowned all of them. (55)

They became a precedent and an example for others. (56)

Jesus, son of Mary, was used by some of your disbelieving people as an example of a person, other than God, being worshiped as one (*and yet those who do are not considered unbelievers*). (57)

They said: "Are not our Gods better than him?" They did this only to be argumentative, and they are a very contentious people. (58)

He is our servant who We granted Our mercy, and made him a guiding light for the people of Israel. (59)

I could have replaced all of you with angels on earth (*who will do what they are told*). (60)

This is all relevant to the certainty of the Hour (*the Last Day*) about which you never have a doubt, and follow my straight path. (61)

Do not let the Devil misguide you for he is your unquestionable enemy. (62)

Jesus said: "I brought you veritable signs and wisdom, to try to throw light on some of what you have disagreements about, so worship and fear God and obey Him. (63)

God is my Lord and your Lord, worship Him, for it is the straight path." (64)

They still divided into opposing factions, and doomed are the transgressors, for awaiting them is an excruciating torture. (65)

Do they realize that the Hour (*Day of Judgement*) may hit them suddenly with no warning? (66)

On that day, friends become each other's enemy, except for those who worship and fear God. (67)

My worshipers, today there is nothing for you to fear or be concerned about. (68)

Those who believed our verses and surrendered to them (*became Moslems*). (69)

Enter heaven, you and your spouses to enjoy. (70)

They are served with trays and cups of gold. Everything that the soul may wish or the eyes may enjoy is available, and in it you shall be immortalized. (71)

This is the paradise that you inherited with your deeds. (72)

In it there shall be all kinds of fruits from which you will eat. (73)

The transgressors are immortalized in the torture of hell. (74)

Their torture never ceases, and they remain devoid of hope. (75)

We have not wronged them, but the transgressors wronged themselves. (76)

They call upon Malek (*the angel in charge of hell*) saying: "Ask your Lord to kill us and He will answer, you shall continue to be around." (77)

We brought you the truth, but most of you hated the truth. (78)

They have made an unalterable decision, and so did We. (79)

They think We are not aware of what they said in secret, but We did and We had some who record. (80)

Say: "If the Merciful has a child, I shall be among the first to worship." (81)

Glorified be Him, Lord of the heavens and the earth, and Lord of the throne, Exalted above what they describe. (82)

Let them play, stumble, and fall, until they get to the day they are promised. (83)

He is the One who is God in the heavens, and God on earth, and He is the Knowledgeable and the Wise. (84)

Glorified be Him the Owner of the kingdom of the heavens and the earth, and what is in between them, and has the full knowledge about the Hour (*the Last Day*), and to Him you shall return. (85)

Those who pray to someone other than Him do not have hope for any intercession, unlike those who recognized the truth and are aware of what they know. (86)

Many of those who disbelieve, when asked who created them, they will say "God," so is it not strange that they worship others. (87)

And as he (*Mohammed*) said: "My God these are disbelieving people. (88)

Forgive them and with your blessing they shall learn." (89)

THE SMOKE (44)

In the Name of God, Most Merciful, and Most Beneficent.

Haah, Meem. (1)

I swear with the veritable Book. (2)

We revealed it in a blessed night. We did provide warning. (3)

On that night, the distinctions between many appropriate things were provided. (4)

It was an act of mercy from your Lord. (5)

He Hears and He is Knowledgeable. (6)

He is the Lord of the heavens and the earth and what is in between, if you are believers. (7)

No other God but Him, and from Him comes life and death. Your Lord and the Lord of your fathers before you. (8)

They oscillate between variable degrees of doubt. (9)

Wait for the day when the sky may bring an easily seen smoke. (10)

It will surround people from everywhere, and it is an excruciating torture. (11)

They will say: "God, lift the torture away from us, and We shall believe." (12)

Why would they need this type of intimidation when a messenger was sent to them? (13)

They denied him and said he was mad. (14)

We shall ameliorate the torture somewhat, and see how much of worshipers you are. (15)

But the day We finally lower the boom, shall be the true day for retaliation. (16)

Before them We tested the people of the pharaoh, as We sent them a man of respect as an apostle. (17)

He invited them to join God's worshipers, and said: "I am a faithful messenger to you. (18)

Do not be arrogant with God, for I am bringing you news of a veritable immense power. (19)

I do not want to see you stoned by your Lord's immense power. (20)

If you do not want to believe in me, at least manage to stay away from me." (21)

Then he talked to his Lord, telling Him that those are transgressors. (22)

Take my worshipers out during the night, and you shall be followed. (23)

After you cross the sea, leave it split, for they are going to be drowned soldiers. (24)

How many gardens and springs they are going to be leaving behind. (25)

Also crops and a status of respect, (26)

in addition to God's bounty that they were enjoying. (27)

This way We let it be inherited by other people. (28)

The heavens and the earth did not weep for them, nor did anyone care. (29)

We saved the people of Israel from a humiliating torture. (30)

And from the Pharaoh, for he was one who is excessive in his transgressions. (31)

We chose them openly over the rest of the world. (32)

We also brought in signs that showed them a clear favor. (33)

Those who say: (34)

"If We die it shall be the first and the last, and We shall not be brought up again." (35)

So bring signs like ours, if you are truthful. (36)

Do they think they are better than those who came before them, who We annihilated for being transgressors? (37)

We did not create the heavens and the earth, and what is in between as a game. (38)

All We created was the truth, but most of them do not know. (39)

The Day of Judgement is the appointment day for them all. (40)

The day when no one can make a difference for another, and none have defenders. (41)

Except for those on whom God will have mercy, for He is the Exalted and the Merciful. (42)

The Zukkoum tree, (43)

shall be the fruit of sin, (44)

that feels like boiling in the belly, (45)

like boiling oil. (46)

Take him and elevate him to a prominent place in hell. (47)

Then pour over his head the boiling torture. (48)

Taste it, for you were supposedly the exalted and the noble. (49)

This is what you refused to accept that will happen. (50)

Those who worshiped and feared God are in a safe place, (51)

with gardens and springs. (52)

They shall be wearing silk and brocade, (53)

and they shall be paired with beautiful women, (54)

offered every fruit they wish in safety. (55)

They will be immortalized in it, and they shall be protected from the torture of hell. (56)

It is a favor from your Lord, and it is the greatest of all victories. (57)

We made it available to them through what We revealed using your tongue. (58)

So watch for it, and they shall be watching. (59)

SHE WHO IS KNEELING (45)

In the Name of God, Most Merciful, and Most Beneficent.

Haah, Meem. (1)

The Book was revealed by God who is the Exalted and the Wise. (2)

In the heavens and on earth are signs for the believers. (3)

In your own creation, and the creation of animals are signs for those who have a little doubt. (4)

The alternation of night and day, and what God brings down from the sky that produces life and sustenance on earth, many times after the earth is arid and dry, and also the movement of the winds, all signs for people who can think. (5)

These are the verses from God that We recite to you as the truth; so after the verses from God and His signs, what is yet needed for them to believe. (6)

Cursed by God are the deceiving scoundrels. (7)

They hear God's verses being recited, and they recoil arrogantly as if they did not hear them, so relay to them the tidings of an excruciating torture. (8)

Even when they understand something from our verses, they use it for mockery, and to those belong humiliating torture. (9)

Awaiting them is hell, and they shall have little benefit from their works, or those who they took as their sponsors instead of God. (10)

This is the guidance, and those who disbelieve in the signs from their Lord shall have torture from the painful kind. (11)

God made it possible for you to use the sea for the ships that sail in it by God's will, for your transportation, and to earn a living so you may be thankful. (12)

He provided you with the ability to make use of all that he provided for you, in the heavens and on earth; all of it from Him, and in that there are signs for those who contemplate. (13)

Tell the believers to be forgiving with those who have no hope of getting in, on God's days, because God shall reward people only with what is appropriate for what they have earned. (14)

One who does good works does them for oneself, and one who does evil, does it against oneself. Then to Him you shall all return. (15)

We gave the people of Israel the Book, wisdom, and prophethood, in addition to the other good things in life, and We gave them preference over the rest of the world. (16)

We brought them clarity on all subjects, yet they were having disputes after all that We brought them. Your Lord shall provide the final mediation among them on the Day of Judgement. (17)

Then We made sure that you are starting on the right path, so follow it and do not follow the whims of those who do not know. (18)

They will never make a difference between God and you. The transgressors are sponsors for each other, and God sponsors those who worship and fear God. (19)

This is enlightenment and guidance for people, and for those who are certain of their belief. (20)

Did those who commit sin think that We are going to treat them, like those who believed and did good works, whether they are alive or dead. If they think that , this is a huge miscalculation. (21)

The truth is in God's creation of the heavens and the earth, and each soul shall reap what it has earned, and none shall be wronged. (22)

Look at the example of the one who worshiped whatever his whims lead him to, and God intentionally misguided him, and closed over his hearing and his heart, and covered his eyes with a non-transparent membrane, so who can then guide him after God did not. (23)

They said, there is nothing but life on this earth for us, and whether we live or die, only our age will end our life, they know nothing about that and they are only guessing. (24)

As our veritable verses were read to them, all they could come up with is saying, bring back our forefathers if you are truthful. (25)

Say: "God created you, then He will cause you to die, then He will bring all of you together on the Day of Judgement, of which you should have no doubt, but most people do not know." (26)

To God belong the kingdom of the heavens and earth, and when the Hour comes, on that day, the deniers shall lose. (27)

You shall see women kneeling, and others called to their books. Today, all of you shall get the reward for what you did. (28)

This is Our Book, which pronounces the truth to you, and We have record of what you used to know. (29)

Those who believed and did good works, God shall enter them into His mercy, and that is the biggest of all winnings. (30)

Those of you who disbelieved, did you not have my verses recited to you? Yet you grew arrogant, and you became transgressing people. (31)

If it is said that the promise of God is the truth, and there is no doubt about the Hour, You would say: "We do not know what it is, and We have suspicions, but we are not absolutely certain." (32)

On that Day they shall see the bad things they have done, and they shall be caught up with what they have been mocking. (33)

On that Day they shall be told that We have forgotten about them, the same way they forgot about this day, and their residence shall be the fire, and they shall have no supporters. (34)

It is the payment they have earned for mocking the signs from God, and for being seduced by the life on earth. They shall not exit from it (*the fire*) without hearing any further admonishment. (35)

The thanks go to God, Lord of the heavens, the earth and the universe. (36)

To Him goes all the pride of the heavens and the earth, and He is the Exalted, and the Wise. (37)

THE CAVE DWELLINGS (46)

In the Name of God, Most Merciful, and Most Beneficent.

Haah, Meem. (1)

The Book was revealed by God who is the Exalted and Wise. (2)

We created the heavens and the earth and what is in between symbolizing the truth, and for a predefined stretch of time, and the unbelievers are turning away from the warning. (3)

Say to them: "Show me what did those that you worship instead of God create on earth or in the heavens, or did they even participate in formulating a Book like this one, before it or after it, if you are truly truthful?" (4)

Who is more misguided than one who worships something that cannot respond to him until the Last Day, and who cannot even acknowledge their worship. (5)

On the day when all are assembled, these that they worship shall be their worst enemies, and they shall disclaim their worship. (6)

As Our veritable verses are read to them, the unbelievers response to the truth shall be to call it a veritable sorcery. (7)

Or some will say: "You made it up." Say: "If I did, I certainly have nothing I want from you, and God is more knowledgeable with what you accuse me of. I need no one but Him as a witness against your accusations, and He is the Forgiving and the Merciful." (8)

Say: "I am certainly not the first apostle sent, and I have no idea what is my final destiny or yours. I only follow what is revealed to me, and I am only a clear deliverer of warnings." (9)

Say: "You saw that it was from God, and yet you disbelieved it, even after a witness from the people of Israel testified to the truth in it, having been revealed long before it. Then he believed it and you continued in your arrogance. God does not provide guidance for people who are transgressors." (10)

The unbelievers said to the believers: "If it was good for us those early believers would not have jumped on it ahead of us (*because a lot of them were slaves and from the lowest caste*)." As they refused the guidance, they were prepared to call it old lies. (11)

Before it there was the Book of Moses, providing guidance and mercy, and this Book that certifies what was in the older one in the Arabic tongue, to warn the transgressors, and bring good tidings to those who do good works. (12)

Those who said our Lord is God, and then accordingly straightened their path, shall face no danger, and shall not be sad. (13)

They shall be the immortalized owners of paradise, as a reward for their good works. (14)

We exhorted man to be good to his parents. A mother suffers by carrying a child, and suffers by delivering a child. Carrying a child, delivering a child, and then nursing a child takes thirty months. Then when a human reaches his full strength, followed by full maturity at forty, he should say: "My Lord, let me thank you for your blessings upon me, and upon my parents, and help me do good works that will please you, and bring up good descendants who will worship you. I am offering my repentance to you and I am one who surrendered to you as a Moslem." (15)

Those are the ones We shall have measured by the best they have done, and We shall forgive their sins, and make them the owners of paradise, a true promise made to them as their reward. (16)

To mention the one who said to his parents: "Why do you not leave me alone? You promise me that I shall be resurrected, yet many generations have come and gone before me, and none showed up." While his parents are screaming for God's help, they say to him: "Believe, for the promise of God is the truth," and he will respond saying: "These are the fables of the old." (17)

These are the people who will be soon be caught-up by the truth of the word of God, like many nations before them of humans and jinn, and they are the ultimate losers. (18)

For each there are ranks consistent with what they did. They shall be rewarded for their works, and they shall not be wronged. (19)

The day when the unbelievers shall face the fire, they shall be asked if they had used and enjoyed all the good things made available to them, for today is the day when you will face the humiliating torture for what you spent your pride and arrogance on earth on, ignoring the truth, while indulging yourselves. (20)

Also mention the brother of the people of Aad, who warned his people, the cave dwellers, as all the apostles before him who at his time were all gone: "Do not worship anyone but God, for I am afraid for you from the torture of a Great Day." (21)

They said: "Are you trying to get us to become disloyal to our gods? Bring on us what you are warning us from if you were truly truthful." (22)

All knowledge is from God, and I am simply relaying to you what I was sent with, but I can see that you are very ignorant people. (23)

As the first of the winds arrived to their valley bringing rain with it, they liked it and said: "But we do need rain." No, this is what you brought on yourselves earlier, which is only the front of a wind which shall bring in its wake an excruciating torture. (24)

A wind that shall destroy everything by order from its Lord, and in the morning you could see only their caves. This is how we punish the transgressors. (25)

We have given them a lot of what We have given you, and strengthened them just like We have strengthened you, and gave them hearing, eyesight and hearts, but their hearing, sight and hearts did little for them, as they were denying the signs of God, until they were caught by what they were mocking. (26)

We have annihilated many villages and towns all around you, after we revealed signs to them so they might self-correct. (27)

As they needed help, did those that they were worshiping in preference to God, give them help. They had to see firsthand the consequences of their lack of belief, and their false claims. (28)

We shall also relay to you the news of a group of jinn who heard the Koran being recited, and they listened to it, and then went back to their people with a warning. (29)

We just listened to a book, that was revealed after Moses, confirming what Moses had. It guides to the truth and to the straight path. (30)

They said to their people: "Respond to God's call, and believe in Him, and He shall forgive your sins, and save you from an excruciating torture. (31)

Those who do not respond to God's call shall have no escape on earth, and shall find no alternative sponsors, and those are clearly misguided. (32)

Could they not see that God who created the heavens and the earth without even getting tired is capable of resurrecting the dead? He is Capable of all things. (33)

The day the unbelievers shall be confronted with the fire, they shall be asked: "Is this not the truth?" And they shall say, swearing by the Lord: "It is." He shall say: "Taste the torture for your lack of belief." (34)

So be patient, like many among the apostles were, and give them time, for on the day they see what they have been promised, they shall think that their entire previous existence was an hour of one day (*compared to what they are facing*). It is a warning, but only the corrupted shall perish. (35)

MOHAMMED (47)

In the Name of God, Most Merciful, and Most Beneficent.

Those who do not believe, and misguide people away from God's path, God shall misguide all of their actions. (1)

Those who believed, did good works, and believed that what was revealed to Mohammed was the truth from their Lord, He shall forgive their sins, and make them more comfortable with themselves. (2)

This is because the unbelievers followed what is wrong, while the believers followed the truth from their Lord, and God brings such things as examples to people. (3)

As you face the unbelievers in war, there is going to be killing, but once you prevail over them, secure the prisoners by tying them down until the war ends, and then you can either let them go or demand a ransom for their freedom. If God wished, He would defeat them Himself, but God tests you against each other, and those who die defending the cause of God, their work shall never go unrewarded. (4)

God shall guide them, and make them feel better of themselves. (5)

They shall enter paradise, which was identified for them. (6)

People who believe, if you uphold the cause of God, He shall grant you victory and steady your feet. (7)

The unbelievers shall be unhappy, and their actions misguided. (8)

For as they hate what God has revealed, their efforts shall fail. (9)

Did they not walk on this earth, and observe the destinies of those before them whom God has destroyed? A similar destiny awaits the unbelievers. (10)

God is the sponsor for the believers, while the unbelievers have no sponsor. (11)

God shall enter those who believed and did good works, gardens below which rivers flow, while the unbelievers shall eat and enjoy themselves in this life, just like animals do, but fire is their final residence. (12)

Many towns, far bigger and stronger than your town that displaced you, We have annihilated, and they found no help or support. (13)

Can anyone equate one who is clear on what God expects from him with one aware of his misdeeds, yet continued to follow his whims? (14)

Can anyone equate one in paradise, which God promised to those who worship and fear Him, in which rivers of pure water flow, and rivers of milk which does not spoil, and rivers of wine that is delicious to taste, and other rivers of purified honey, to one who is immortalized in hell, drinking boiling water that burns his intestines? (15)

Some of them will listen to you until they are no longer in your presence, and after they leave you, they will say to other informed people: "What was he talking about?" These are the ones whom God stamped on their hearts, and they follow their whims. (16)

Those who become guided, God increases their guidance, and rewards them for their worship and fear of God. (17)

Do they ever consider that the Hour can hit them suddenly unaware, for they have already seen some of its signs? What kind of warning do they expect? (18)

Know that there is no god but God and seek forgiveness for yourself and for the believers, men and women. God knows well what is going to happen to you and how you will end up. (19)

The believers may say: "We wish a new chapter will be revealed to us," and as one is revealed, and if it contains the mention of a possible war, those with sick hearts (*the hypocrites*) shall look at you like they are about to faint from their fear of death. Yet it is better for them. (20)

They could obey and speak their mind, but once a decision is made, believing and trusting God is the best for them. (21)

Were you worried that if you left to fight, you would spread corruption on earth and lose contact with your relatives and your kin? (22)

It is people like that who are cursed by God, and are made by Him deaf and blind. (23)

Do they not contemplate the Koran, or have locks been installed on their hearts? (24)

Those who turn back after guidance has become clear to them, the Devil has reached them and dictated to them. (25)

They say to those who hated what God has revealed: "We shall be with you on certain matters, but God knows all their secrets." (26)

How are they going to feel when they die and the angels claim their souls, and hit them on their fronts and their backs? (27)

As they followed a track that angered God, and did not like His blessings, He made their efforts fail. (28)

Did those who have sickness in their hearts (*the hypocrites*) think that God would not expose their inner feelings? (29)

If We wished We would have pointed them out to you, but you shall recognize them by their facial expressions, and the tone of their voices. God knows what you do. (30)

We let you be tested, to identify those of you who are studious and steadfast, and spread the good news about them. (31)

Those who do not believe and try to dissuade people away from the path of God and give the Apostle a hard time, after guidance had become clear to them, shall not affect God in any way, and He shall make their effort fail. (32)

People who believe, obey God and obey the apostle, and do not permit your good deeds to be wasted. (33)

Those who do not believe, try to dissuade people from the path of God, and then die unbelievers, they shall not be forgiven by God. (34)

Do not become weary and accept peace after you paid the price and gained the upper hand. God is with you, and will not forget your deeds. (35)

This life is only play and games. If you believe in Him, worship Him and fear Him, you shall receive your rewards, and you shall need to provide no accounting for what you have, or be required to make any payments. (36)

If He were to ask you, you will surely become stingy and show a lot of what you hide inside you. (37)

You are invited to spend some of what God has given you, in the way of God. One who is stingy, he is being stingy only with himself. God is the One who is rich and you are the poor, and if you do not comply, he will replace you with those who will, and ones who are different from you. (38)

THE SUCCESS (48)

In the Name of God, Most Merciful, and Most Beneficent.

We have granted you great success. (1)

God shall forgive your sins, the ones that already occurred and those that are yet coming. He shall complete the bounty He blessed you with, and continues to guide you on a straight path. (2)

And God shall bless you with a great victory. (3)

God is the One who brought the feeling of tranquility to the hearts of the believers to make their believing even stronger. To God alone belongs all the worriers (*angels*) in the heavens and the earth, and God is Knowledgeable and Wise. (4)

He shall enter the believers' gardens below which rivers flow, and forgive their sins. With God that is a great prize. (5)

God shall torture the hypocrites, men and women, those who associate others with God, men and women, and those who permit themselves to think the worst of God, shall be surrounded by the worst, and they shall earn the wrath of God and His curse and awaiting them is hell which is the worst of all destinies. (6)

The warriers (*angels*) of the heavens and earth, all belong to God, thus God is Exalted and Wise. (7)

We sent you as a witness, and a carrier of good tidings and warning. (8)

To believe in God and His apostle, and to worship God, pray to Him and revere Him morning and evening. (9)

Those who put their hands in your hand, pledging to you loyalty and faithfulness, God's hand is over their hand, and those who violate that promise are violating themselves and their chances with God. Those who remain faithful to their pledge to God, He shall reward them handsomely. (10)

Those who among the Arab tribes stayed behind and did not take the walk in support of the Apostle, said: "We are busy with our trade, assets and family, so ask for forgiveness for us." But they say with their tongues what is not in their hearts. Ask them who can shield them from God, if He wished them harm, or prevent good from reaching them if God wished it for them. God knows very well what you do. (11)

Did you think the Apostle and the believers are not coming back to their families ever? You thought the worst would happen to them. You were rather failed people. (12)

Those who do not believe in God and his apostle need to remember that We have prepared for the unbelievers a flaming destiny. (13)

To God belongs the kingdom of the heavens and the earth. He forgives whomever He wishes and tortures whomever He wishes, and God is Forgiving and Merciful. (14)

Those who stayed behind said: Let us participate with you, and share in the spoils of the next march, trying to change the word of God. Say to them: You shall not follow us, and this is an order from God. They shall claim that you are envious of them. Little do they know about anything. (15)

Say to the Arabs that stayed behind: You shall be called upon to resist people who are far stronger, if you truly join the religion and obey God, He shall give you good rewards, but if you stay behind as you did before, you shall receive excruciating torture. (16)

Those who are blind or lame and those who are infirm are not required to participate in the effort. Those who obey God and his apostle shall enter gardens under which rivers flow. Those who refuse to participate shall receive an excruciating torture. (17)

God became happy with the believers who made pledges of loyalty to you under the tree, thus knowing what is in their hearts, He granted them tranquility, and rewarded them with a soon-to-occur resolution. (18)

Much spoils and winnings they shall earn, and God is Exalted and Wise. (19)

God promised you many winnings and spoils, and kept the hands of others away from you, so that it is a sign to the believers, and He shall guide you on the straight path. (20)

There were other conflicts in waiting, of which God was aware, and God is Capable of all things. (21)

If the unbelievers chose to fight you, they would have been forced to run, for they would have found no sponsor or supporter. (22)

It is the will of God, that showed itself many times before, and no one shall find an alternative to His will. (23)

He is the One who kept their hands away from you and your hands away from them in the valley of Mecca, and actually gave you victory over them (*in the confrontation at Houdaibiah, outside Mecca so that no war resulted, but rather a negotiated peace treaty*). God was seeing all that you did. (24)

It was the unbelievers who prevented you from reaching the sacred mosque to pray, and obstructed guidance from reaching its final target, and if it was not for the efforts of believing men or women, who were hiding being guided, while living among them (*the unbelievers*) to protect themselves, and who in case of war might have been trampled upon by both sides, unintentionally, I would have ordered you to fight them. But the right path was to let those who want to believe do so without interference. God shall enter in His guidance whomever He wishes, and those among them who remain unbelievers shall receive excruciating torture. (25)

He made the unbelievers have in their heart the anxiety of ignorance, while He granted tranquility to the hearts of His Apostle and the other believers. Which helped them stick to worshiping and fearing God, thus deserving God's watchfulness, and God is Knowledgeable of all things. (26)

God fulfilled His Apostle's vision of entering the sacred Mosque, safe by the will of God, with your hair shaved, or shortened, and with no fear. He knew what you did not know, and made out of that a soon-to-occur victory. (27)

He is the One who sent His Apostle with the guidance and the religion of truth, so that the truth become dominant over the entire religion. (28)

Mohammed is the Apostle of God, and those who are with him are strong on the unbelievers and kind with each other. You see them kneeling and prostrating themselves, seeking favor with God and asking for His approval. You see the effect of frequent prostration on their faces, and there are people like them in the Bible and the Gospel. They are like the growing plant: as it grows up, it becomes stronger with a thicker stalk, a wonder to the farmers and an irritant to the unbelievers. God has promised the believers who did good works forgiveness and great reward. (29)

THE CHAMBER WALLS (49)

In the Name of God, Most Merciful, and Most Beneficent.

People who believe, do not engage in impertinent behavior while you are in the attendance of God and His Apostle. Worship and fear God; He hears all and He is Knowledgeable. (1)

People who believe, do not raise your voices above that of the Prophet, and do not use explicit language with Him like you do with each other. This type of behavior can hurt you without realizing it. (2)

Those who lower their voices in the presence of God's Apostle are the ones who God has tested their hearts for worshiping Him and fearing Him, and they shall attain forgiveness and great rewards. (3)

Those who call upon you from behind the walls of the chambers of your residence have little sense. (4)

If they had waited until you came out to them, it would have been better for them. God is Forgiving and Merciful. (5)

People who believe, if one with a shady reputation brings you a piece of news, check on it. Otherwise you may afflict other people with an injustice and find yourselves regretting that deeply the following day. (6)

Living among you is the Apostle of God, and you have to realize that if he submits to your will too many times, you will find yourselves in trouble. God has made the faith dear to your heart, and turned your hearts away from disbelieving, evil-doing, and disobedience; and these are the wise ones. (7)

This is a favor and blessing from God, and God is Knowledgeable and Wise. (8)

If two groups of believers are in dispute, try to make peace between them, and if one of them committed aggression against the other one, fight the aggressor until the aggressor desists and returns to the shade casted by believing in God, and then mediate between them with fairness and justice. (9)

Believers are brothers; mediate to resolve disputes among them. Worship and fear God so that you are treated with mercy. (10)

People who believe, do not mock other people for they may be better than you, nor should women do that to other women because the other women may be better than them. Do not ever engage in backbiting and in calling each other names, for evil names are the worst that one can use after becoming guided, and those who do not repent are the transgressors. (11)

People who believe, do not engage in a lot of suspicions, for some suspicions are a sin. Do not spy on each other nor backbite each other. Would one of you like to eat the flesh of his dead brother? You will surely hate that. Worship and fear God, He is Forgiving and Merciful. (12)

O' people, We have created you as males and females and made you different tribes and people, so you may learn to recognize your differences and live with them. Those who are superior among you are those who are best in worshiping and fearing God; God is Knowing and Knowledgeable. (13)

Many Arabs said: "We believe." Say you did not believe, but you have rather become Moslems, even though faith may not yet be established in your hearts (*a statement that faith is more specific than Islam*), but if you obey God and his apostle you shall not waste any rewards on your good deeds; God is Forgiving and Merciful. (14)

The believers (*faithful*) are those who believed in God and His apostle, and then never doubted their belief, and struggled using their possessions and themselves in the way of God. These are the truthful. (15)

Say: Do you think you need to inform God of your religion and your faith? He knows all that is in the heavens and on the earth. God has knowledge of all things. (16)

They try make it as if they have done you a favor by becoming Moslems. Say: You do me no favor by becoming Moslems. It is God who did you the favor by guiding you towards the faith, if you are truthful. (17)

God knows the secrets of the heaven and the earth, and does see what you do. (18)

KAAF (50)

In the Name of God, Most Merciful, and Most Beneficent.

Kaaf; I swear in the name of the glorious Koran. (1)

They were surprised that they got a man warning them from among them, and the unbelievers said, that is a strange thing. (2)

After we die, and become dust, coming back is a farfetched thing. (3)

We know what the earth takes away from them (*when buried*) every day, and it is all kept in an ever-preserved book. (4)

They denied the truth when it was revealed to them; they are really in trouble. (5)

Did they not look at the sky above them, how We built it, and dressed it with ornaments and far distances in between? (6)

The earth We have spread, and made in it huge anchoring mountains, and made beautiful pairs grow in it of all colors. (7)

A scene and a reminder to every God-fearing worshiper. (8)

We brought down blessed water from the sky to grow gardens and grain-producing plants. (9)

And the high palm trees loaded with pollen that will flower into a fruit. (10)

Providing sustenance for people that will revive a dead town; such is His ability at transformation. (11)

Before them, the people of Noah, and those who lived in the Rass, and the people of Thamoud also denied. (12)

In addition to Aad, the Pharaoh, and the people of Lot. (13)

The forest people (*people of Midian*), and the people of Tobba (*the king of Hamyar*), all denied apostles sent to them and earned my displeasure and punishment. (14)

Did they master all the secrets of the first creation, and now they are knowledgeable enough to deny a new one? (15)

We created the human, and We know what occurs to his mind, and We are closer to him than the vein in his neck (*meaning the angels on a human's shoulders who keep abreast of his actions*). (16)

It is in him that the two (*the angels*) seated on the right and left meet. (17)

Whatever a human says, he has two careful listeners. (18)

When death truly comes, it is what you have been trying to avoid. (19)

As the trumpet sounds, it is the promised day. (20)

Every soul shall arrive with an escort and a witness. (21)

You (*humans*) have been oblivious to this, and now We removed the cover off your eyes, and your eyes have a steely eyesight. (22)

The watchful angel will say: "Here is a very arrogant man, (23)

throw in hell every unbelieving stubborn human." (24)

One who stood in the way of good works, and was always a suspicious aggressor. (25)

He made a god other than God, and was thrown in severe torture. (26)

His counterpart (*a devil chained to him*) will say: "Lord, we did not encourage him, but this one was deeply misguided." (27)

He (*God*) said: Do argue in front of me, for my promises were made clear to you. (28)

With Me utterances never change, and the worshipers are never wronged. (29)

The day hell is asked: are you full? And the response will be: "Is there more?" (30)

While paradise grows nearer to those who worshiped and feared their Lord. (31)

This is what you were promised to be the reward for every repentant who remembered all the right things. (32)

The one who feared the Merciful without direct knowledge and came (*to the Last Day*) with a clear undoubting heart. (33)

Enter it (*paradise*) with peace, for that will be your day of immortality. (34)

They shall have in it all they may want, and We have even more. (35)

Many generations did We annihilate before them who were far stronger than they are, and yet found no escape in the land. (36)

This is something to remember by those who have heart, or those who will heed what they hear. (37)

We created the heavens and the earth in six days, and We were not even touched by fatigue. (38)

So be patient with what they say, and pray to and glorify your Lord, before sunrise and sunset. (39)

At night glorify Him, especially after you prostrate yourself. (40)

Wait for the day when the call will come from a place that seems close. (41)

The day they will hear the shout resonating with the truth, and that is the day to go out. (42)

We are the One who resurrects the dead, causes them to die, and to Us belongs the final destiny. (43)

The day the earth shall be splitting, and such an assembly is easy for Us to achieve. (44)

We are far more knowledgeable with what they say. You are not a tyrant over them, but remind of the Koran those who pay attention to warning. (45)

THE SQUALLS (51)

In the Name of God, Most Merciful, and Most Beneficent.

I swear with the squalls that gust and elevate dust. (1)

I swear with those that are laden with rainwater. (2)

Then with the ships that sail easily on the surface of the water. (3)

Then the angels that help set things as they need to be. (4)

What you are being promised is the truth. (5)

And the religion is an established fact. (6)

The heavens are many layers, with multiple stars. (7)

What you are saying differs from the truth. (8)

Intended to misguide those who are already lost. (9)

Those who fabricate shall be killed. (10)

These are the ones who shall be engrossed in themselves, (11)

asking when is the Day of the Religion (*Last Day*)? (12)

On that day they shall meet the fire which they have been denying. (13)

Taste what you have been denying, and what you have actually asked that it be brought on you earlier. (14)

Those who worshiped and feared God are in gardens and springs, (15)

using what was provided for them by their Lord, for the good they have done before. (16)

When they slept little of the night. (17)

Early in the morning they were still repenting. (18)

In their money their was always a share for the poor and the beggars. (19)

On this earth there are always signs for the believers. (20)

Even in themselves; do they not see that? (21)

In the sky is your sustenance, and what you have been promised. (22)

And with the name of the Lord of the heavens and the earth, He is the truth and as true as the fact that you are able to talk. (23)

Did you get the story of the respectable guests of Abraham? (24)

They entered his presence and said: "Peace be upon you," and he welcomed people who were not truthfully showing themselves to him. (25)

He went to his family and brought back to them a cooked good-sized calf. (26)

He brought it closer to them and asked them why they were not eating. (27)

He became afraid of them, but they said: "Do not be afraid, for we are here to bring you the good tidings of an intelligent boy." (28)

His wife came out with a scream, and slapped her forehead with her hand, and said: "Could that occur to a sterile old woman?" (29)

That is what your Lord has willed, He is the Knowledgeable and the Wise. (30)

He (*Abraham*) said: "O' messengers, is there other reason for your being here?" (31)

They said: "We have been sent to a group of transgressors (*people of Lot*). (32)

We brought down over them stones of mud. (33)

Chosen by your Lord for those who engage in excesses. (34)

First, We got out from the town those who were believers. (35)

We actually found one single house that had in it Moslems (*those who surrendered themselves to God*). (36)

We left in that town a sign for those who fear the excruciating torture." (37)

And Moses who We sent to the Pharaoh with a strongly supported and veritable authority from Us. (38)

He denied it and turned away, and said: "He is practicing sorcery, or he is mad." (39)

We took him and his soldiers, and threw them in the sea, for which he is to blame. (40)

To Aad We sent the wind that leaves nothing behind. (41)

Anything it comes onto, it leaves in ruins. (42)

To Thamoud We said: Enjoy yourselves for a while. (43)

They ignored their Lord's order, and the thunderbolt took them as they were looking. (44)

They could not get up nor could they succeed. (45)

The people of Noah were all truly transgressors. (46)

The sky We built big and then made it bigger. (47)

The earth We straighten out, and in doing that We are the best. (48)

We created a pair from everything, so you may contemplate. (49)

He (*Noah*) said: "Make God your refuge, for I have been sent to deliver from Him a warning that is quite clear. (50)

Do not make with God another God, for I am unquestionably warning you especially against this." (51)

So were the people before them, every time they were sent an apostle, they said: "He is a sorcerer, or he is mad." (52)

They kept on relaying this from one to the other, and they were all transgressing people. (53)

If they do that leave them, you will not be blamed for them. (54)

Remind people, and reminders are helpful to those who believe. (55)

I created the humans and the jinn so they may worship. (56)

I do not expect otherwise anything from them, and I am the One who provides for them. (57)

God is the One who provides and to Him belongs the power, and He is the strong. (58)

The transgressors have sins similar to those who transgressed before them; let them not be in a hurry. (59)

It is ugly, that which the unbelievers will face, on the day they were promised. (60)

THE WOODED MIOUNTAIN (52)

In the Name of God, Most Merciful, and Most Beneficent.

By the wooded mountain (1)

and the Book that is written (2)

on open paper. (3)

And the built house, (4)

with the raised ceiling, (5)

and the sea whose water is not fit for drinking or cultivating. (6)

God's torture is certain. (7)

Nothing can keep it away. (8)

The day the sky shall collapse, (9)

and the mountains shall move, (10)

it shall be a bad day for those who denied. (11)

Those who are up to their ears in games. (12)

That day they shall receive invitations to hell. (13)

This will be the hell they said did not exist. (14)

Is this sorcery or can you not see? (15)

You shall be feeding this fire, and it matters not whether you are patient or not, you are simply being punished for what you did. (16)

Those who feared and worshiped God are in blissful gardens. (17)

They will be enjoying what their Lord granted them, and their Lord insulated them from torture of hell. (18)

Eat, drink and enjoy the result of your work. (19)

They shall be reclining on arranged recliners, and they shall be mated to whomever their choice of mate from the people in paradise, who are slender and beautiful. (20)

The people who believed and were followed by their own family shall have their families join them. They shall not be wronged in any of the good they did, and each person and his or her deeds cannot be separated. (21)

They shall be supplied with the fruits or meats that they desire. (22)

They shall enjoy together a drink of wine that is associated with no drunkenness or sin. (23)

They shall be served by young individuals who are so handsome and clean that they are glowing like pearls. (24)

They started approaching eath other and asking questions. (25)

We were initially worried about our families, (26)

but God did us a favor, and protected us from the torture of poisons. (27)

Because we have been praying to Him; He is the Grateful and the Merciful. (28)

Remind people, and you are, by the grace of God, neither a monk nor mad. (29)

Or, they say, a poet waiting for his death. (30)

Say to them: "Why do you not wait, and I shall wait with you?" (31)

Do they see these things in their dreams or are they simply transgressors? (32)

Do they think you made it up, or are they just unbelievers? (33)

Why do they not produce something like it, if they were truthful? (34)

Were they created by no one, or did they create themselves? (35)

Or did they even create the heavens and the earth, which they know with certainty? They have not! (36)

Maybe they think they are in possession of all the stores of the kingdom of heaven, and that they are in charge? (37)

Or do they have a high listening place, and the listener is capable of bringing a veritable great power? (38)

Or do they have the girls and the rest of you have the boys (*sarcasm in regard to the nasty custom of the pagan Arabs to sacrifice their daughters, while keeping the boys, thus returning the daughters of God to their father*)? (39)

Or are you asking them for a fee for the guidance, and they are running out of money to pay? (40)

Or maybe they have knowledge of the future, and they are busy writing? (41)

Or are they expecting a scheme? And only the unbelievers are good in scheming! (42)

Or they believe they have a god other than God. God is Glorified far above their blasphemies. (43)

If they see missiles from the sky falling on them, they will attribute that to heavy clouds. (44)

So leave them till they meet their day when they shall be thunderstruck. (45)

The day their schemes shall yield nothing for them, and they will receive help from no one. (46)

The transgressors shall receive yet another type of torture, but most of them do not even know. (47)

Be patient under your God's judgement, for Our eyes are on you, and Glorify your God every time you wake up. (48)

And glorify Him sometime during the night, and after the stars disappear (*the morning*). (49)

THE STAR (53)

With the star as it falls. (1)

Your man (*Mohammed*) is not misguided, nor is he relaying to you anything but the truth. (2)

Nor does he speak following whims. (3)

It is a revelation being revealed to him. (4)

It is taught to him by the one with the multiple powers (*the angel Gabriel*). (5)

Who combines powers with good looks. (6)

His place is in the upper horizons. (7)

And as he hangs down, he becomes much closer; (8)

as close as the length of two bows. (9)

Through him God revealed what he revealed to his servant. (10)

His heart did not deny what his vision was. (11)

Do you question him on what he saw? (12)

And he saw more than once. (13)

He saw him also at the 7th heaven (*during the night journey*). (14)

Where the paradise refuge stands. (15)

Veiled with all that it is veiled with. (16)

There was nothing wrong with his vision. (17)

He witnessed his Lord's greatest signs. (18)

Look at the Lat and the Azza. (19)

And the third one called al Manwa (*female names for the pagans' most important idols – they used to call them the daughters of God*). (20)

So you always want the males and to God belongs the females (*sarcasm*)? (21)

Then surely this is an unfair division. (22)

These are names you devised, you and your fathers. God has never authorized such a thing. They follow their own thinking and whims; but now guidance has arrived from their Lord. (23)

Humans do not get what they want. (24)

To God belongs this and the second life. (25)

How many other kingdoms exist in the heavens where no one's intercession is of any value except with God's permission, which is given to whomever He wishes. (26)

Those who attribute a gender (*female*) to the names of the angels are unbelievers. (27)

They only follow their suspicions, and suspicion is of no value next to the truth. (28)

So turn away from one who refuses to glorify Our Mention, and insists on wanting only this life. (29)

This is the extent of their knowledge, and your Lord is more knowledgeable with those who are misguided away from His path and those who are guided. (30)

To God belongs what is in the heavens and on earth. He punishes those who transgress, and rewards those who did good works. (31)

Rewarded will be those who avoid the biggest of all evildoing and indecency. As to the minor sins, God has a large capacity for forgiveness, and He knows you for He raised you from the earth, and then as fetuses in the wombs of your mothers. So do not try to praise yourselves, for He is far more knowledgeable with those who are worshipers and fear God. (32)

Did you not see the one who turned away? (33)

Who gives a little then he stops. (34)

Does he have knowledge of the future (*and thus he knows that he will continue to have what he has*)? (35)

Did he not know what came in the tablets of Moses? (36)

And all that Abraham relayed to all? (37)

No one's sins are passed to, or carried by, someone else. (38)

Humans have nothing but what they have worked for. (39)

And their toil shall be rewarded. (40)

Then finally one would get the best of all awards. (41)

And to your Lord all return. (42)

He shall cause you to laugh and to cry. (43)

He shall cause you to die and to live. (44)

He is the One who created the pairs, the male and the females. (45)

From a sperm when He so wished. (46)

And from Him shall come the next life. (47)

He is richer than all, and owns all. (48)

He is the Lord of the star Sirius (*a star that some Arab tribes used to worship*). (49)

He is the One who annihilated the people of Aad. (50)

And annihilated Thamoud and left none of them. (51)

He similarly treated the people of Noah who were even stronger aggressors and transgressors. (52)

He did even worse with the city of the people of Lot, (53)

which has become buried. (54)

So which one of your Lord's signs are you not believing? (55)

He is a messenger like the earlier ones. (56)

For the Hour is near. (57)

Nothing but God is changing that. (58)

You continue to seem perplexed with this subject. (59)

You seem to laugh instead of crying, (60)

while you are resisting. (61)

Prostrate yourselves in front of God and worship. (62)

THE MOON (54)

The hour grew nearer, and the moon split. (1)

Whenever they see a sign, they turn away and call it continuing sorcery. (2)

They denied, and followed their whims, and their inclination to keep things the way they were. (3)

They have received all kinds of news that should give them clear warning. (4)

When eloquent wisdom is not enough, what is the value of warning? (5)

Stay away from them on the day of the call, for what will be a very bad day. (6)

With their eyes looking down with fear they will be coming out of their graves like a spreading locust. (7)

Answering the caller, and the unbelievers shall be muttering: "This is going to be a difficult day." (8)

Before them the people of Noah denied Our servant, and said he was mad and mistreated him. (9)

He called his Lord, saying: "I was defeated," and he became victorious. (10)

And We open the doors of the sky with a steady stream of water. (11)

The earth also exploded with numerous fountains, and the two waters met on a predestined purpose. (12)

We carried him on what was built with boards of wood and nails. (13)

And watched it move away leaving those who disbelieved. (14)

We left it as a sign for those who are willing to be warned. (15)

This was how My torture came after warning. (16)

We have provided the Koran as a reminder. Will people remember? (17)

Aad also denied and with them also My torture followed the warning. (18)

We sent on them a devastating wind on a day that was a curse on them from beginning to end. (19)

A wind that carried people like they were the stalks of empty and dried up palm trees. (20)

And that was also my torture following warning. (21)

We made the Koran to easily remind people. Will any be reminded? (22)

Thamoud also denied the warning. (23)

They said: "Are we going to follow one human from among us? If we did we would be truly misguided. (24)

He is going to receive a revelation by himself. He is nothing but a pathological liar." (25)

The next day they shall find out who is the liar. (26)

We are sending to them a female camel (*created from the side of a rock as they requested*), so watch them and wait. (27)

Tell them that they will have to alternate using the water with the camel. (28)

They called upon one of them, and he killed the camel. (29)

And then My torture following the warning came. (30)

It was the sound of one cry and they were all like ashes in the wind. (31)

We made the Koran as an easy reminder. Are any people being reminded? (32)

The people of Lot also denied the warning. (33)

We sent upon them a rain of stones that wiped them out except for the family of Lot, who We miraculously saved (*except for his wife*). (34)

It was a blessing from Us and that is how We reward those who are thankful. (35)

We have warned them of Our crushing power yet they repudiated it. (36)

They tried to get their hands on his guests, and we first took away their eyesight, which was just an early taste of My torture that follows my warnings. (37)

The rest came to them in the morning, and that was My lasting torture. (38)

So taste My torture that follows My warning. (39)

We made the Koran an easy instrument to remind people. Are they being reminded? (40)

The people of the Pharaoh also received their warning. (41)

They denied all of Our signs, and We took them the way the highly Exalted and Capable does. (42)

Are your unbelievers better than all of those or do you somehow have an exemption? (43)

Or do they think that they will prevail if they all get together? (44)

They will all be defeated together and they shall be put to flight. (45)

Their hour is the Hour (*the Last Day*) and it is far more damaging and bitter. (46)

The transgressors are in a state of misguidance and confusion. (47)

They shall find themselves in the fire on their faces. Taste what God can deliver. (48)

Everything We have created is with a predefined destiny. (49)

Our wishes are carried out faster than the blink of an eye. (50)

We have annihilated many before them, are people going to ever remember. (51)

Everything they have done will be recorded. (52)

The recording shall include the big and the small. (53)

Those who fear and worship God shall be in gardens with rivers. (54)

In a truly promised seat, by a King who has the greatest of all capabilities. (55)

THE MERCIFUL (55)

In the Name of God, Most Merciful, and Most Beneficent..

The name of the Merciful (1)

marked the Koran. (2)

He created humans (3)

and created in them the ability to learn. (4)

The sun and the moon alternate in a predetermined rhythm. (5)

The stars and the trees kneel before Him. (6)

He raised the heavens, and established the criteria for honesty. (7)

Do not ever cheat on what you sell with a scale. (8)

Use accurate scales, and do not adjust them to your benefit. (9)

He made the earth hospitable for all kinds of life. (10)

On it grow fruits and palm trees, where the dates come out from the opening of sleeve-like structures. (11)

And grain that hides under covering leaves, and scent emitting flowers. (12)

So which of the blessings of your God do you deny? (13)

He created humans from wet dust, like the bricks. (14)

He created the jinn from pure and clean fire. (15)

So which of the blessings of your Lord do you deny? (16)

The Lord of the two easts and the two wests (*the two extremes of the sunsets and sunrises in the winter and the summer*). (17)

So which of the Lord's blessings do you deny? (18)

Two large oceans may come close, (19)

but an isthmus of land in between may never let them touch. (20)

So which of your Lord's blessings do you deny? (21)

Pearls and corals are found there (*in the oceans*). (22)

So which of your Lord's blessings do you deny. (23)

To Him belong the ships traveling on the sea with its sails like flags. (24)

So which of your Lord's blessings do you deny? (25)

All that are on it shall die. (26)

But the face of your Lord, the Exalted and the Majestic shall always be there. (27)

So which of your Lord's blessings do you deny? (28)

Those who are in the heavens and on the earth pray to Him daily with requests of all kinds. (29)

So which of your Lord's blessings do you deny? (30)

We shall yet certainly find the time to make a judgement on all that you bear in deeds. (31)

So which of your Lord's blessings do you deny? (32)

You people and jinn, if you can penetrate through the layers of heaven and the regions of the earth, go ahead, but you shall not succeed until you identify a source for a great power. (33)

So which of your Lord's blessings do you deny? (34)

God can send upon you a stream of flames and melted brass, and then you shall not succeed. (35)

So which of your Lord's blessings do you deny? (36)

As the sky splits, and opens like a rose with different colors. (37)

Which of your Lord's blessings do you deny? (38)

On that Day, no one among humans or jinn shall be asked about their sins. (39)

So which of your Lord's blessings do you deny? (40)

The transgressors shall be identified by the look on their faces, and shall be taken by their hair and their feet. (41)

So which of your Lord's blessings will you deny? (42)

This is hell that the transgressors deny. (43)

They shall be alternating between the fire on their skins and the drinking of fiery liquids. (44)

So which one of the blessings of your Lord do you deny? (45)

To the one who fears the status of his Lord belongs two gardens. (46)

So which of the blessings of your Lord do you deny? (47)

And in them there are branches loaded with fruits. (48)

So which of the blessings of your Lord do you deny? (49)

Inside them there are two flowing brooks. (50)

So which of your Lord's blessings do you deny? (51)

Inside them, also, there are pairs from each fruit. (52)

So which of your Lord's blessings do you deny? (53)

They shall be reclining on seats lined with brocade, and the fruits are as close to them as the reach of their arms. (54)

So which of your Lord's blessings do you deny? (55)

The spouses in these gardens have limited interest; only in their spouses, and have never been touched by humans or jinn. (56)

So which of your Lord's blessings do you deny? (57)

In their beauty, they are like corals and rubies. (58)

So which of your Lord's blessings do you deny? (59)

Is there a reward for charity but charity itself? (60)

So which of your Lord's blessings do you deny? (61)

In addition there are two other gardens. (62)

So which of your Lord's blessings do you deny? (63)

Stretched as a green carpet. (64)

So which of your Lord's blessings do you deny? (65)

Watered by two high flowing fountains. (66)

So which of your Lord's blessings do you deny? (67)

On it there are trees of different fruits, palm and pomegranate. (68)

So which of your Lord's blessings do you deny? (69)

In them also there are good and beautiful spouses. (70)

So which of your Lord's blessings do you deny? (71)

Beautiful shapely women, sitting under tents. (72)

So which of your Lord's blessings do you deny? (73)

They have not been touched by humans or jinn before. (74)

So which of your Lord's blessings do you deny? (75)

They shall be reclining on plush carpets, and soft pillows, over green meadows. (76)

So which of your Lord's blessing do you deny? (77)

Glorified be the name of your Lord, the Exalted and the Majestic. (78)

THE GREAT EVENT (56)

In the Name of God, Most Merciful, and Most Beneficent.

As the great event is occuring, (1)

there is no question that it will occur. (2)

It will bring down many (*who were high in this life*) and bring up others (*who were in low positions*). (3)

As the earth shakes, (4)

and the mountains become crushed, (5)

and turn into blowing dust, (6)

then you shall be divided into three groups. (7)

Those on the right are the winners. (8)

And those on the left are the losers. (9)

And those on the front are held closer. (10)

They are the closest to God, (11)

in the blissful gardens. (12)

They shall consist of some from the older generations, (13)

and some from the newer ones. (14)

They shall be reclining on comfortable beds, (15)

opposite each other. (16)

Served by young boy servants, who are immortalized in their service. (17)

With cups and pots, and glasses of wine, (18)

which do not give them a headache, nor do they impair their judgement. (19)

They will get fruits of their choice, (20)

and bird meat of the kind they desire, (21)

and beautiful and slender spouses, (22)

who are like well preserved pearls, (23)

as a reward for what they did. (24)

There they will not hear harsh words or condemnations. (25)

But only greetings and salutations. (26)

Those on the right shall be treated right. (27)

They shall recline on beds raised over green Sidrah trees, and tall bushes (28)

that have no thorns, but instead, clusters of fruits, (29)

in a long stretch of shade, (30)

and flowing water, (31)

and varied fruits. (32)

None of it is unavailable or forbidden. (33)

They shall sleep on high beds. (34)

Their spouses are recreated (35)

to be virgins. (36)

The spouses will entertain each other, and be interested in each other only. (37)

Among those on the right (38)

are also those from older (39)

and newer generations. (40)

Those on the left are truly cursed, (41)

drinking poisons and boiling liquids. (42)

In hell there is not a spot of shade (43)

that is cool or relieving. (44)

Prior to this, they used to be spoiled rich. (45)

They used to insist on the greatest of all blasphemies. (46)

They used to say: "We could not be resurrected, after we have died and become dust. (47)

Nor could our forefathers." (48)

Say to them: "The forefathers and the descendents (49)

shall all be brought together at a predefined time. (50)

Then, you, the misguided who denied, (51)

shall eat from the fruits of the Zakkoum tree, (52)

from which you shall fill your bellies. (53)

Then you shall drink the boiling liquids, (54)

and taste how it will all feel inside." (55)

This will be their stay on the Day of the Religion (*Last Day*). (56)

We created you, yet you do not believe. (57)

Can you not see the transgression you are committing. (58)

Do you create humans or do We? (59)

We destined you to die, and our decision is irrevocable. (60)

If We wish, We can change the way you look on the Last Day, and bring you back unable to recognize yourselves. (61)

You know how you looked the first time you were created; do you not remember? (62)

Do you not observe when you cultivate? (63)

Are you really the ones who are planting or are We? (64)

If We wished We can make it all dry up, and left you wondering what happened. (65)

You shall find yourselves penalized (66)

and wonder why are you being punished. (67)

Do you see the water you drink? (68)

Did you bring it down from the sky or do We? (69)

If We desired We can make it a useless poisoned liquid. Why do you not give thanks? (70)

Do you not see the fire that you light up? (71)

Did you create the tree from where the wood that you burn come from, or did We? (72)

We made it as a reminder and help for all the uses that humans have for fire. (73)

So glorify the name of your Lord, the Greatest. (74)

I swear by the location of the stars. (75)

And it is a sacred oath indeed, if you knew it. (76)

It is a great Koran (77)

included in a treasured Book, (78)

the true meaning of which is touched only by those who are receptive to it. (79)

Revealed by the Lord of the universe, (80)

it is this that you are denying. (81)

You lie instead of being thankful, (82)

and as the soul reaches the throat (*on its way out*), (83)

and as you are watching, (84)

We are nearer to him (*the dying person*) than you are, but you cannot see it. (85)

If you are not believers, (86)

why can you not push it (*the soul*) back inside him, if you are truthful. (87)

If the dying person was among those who are held close, (88)

his soul shall be waiting, in wonderfully smelling, blissful gardens. (89)

If the dying person happens to be from among the people on the right, (90)

greetings to him from all of those on the right. (91)

But if the person is from among the misguided who denied, (92)

then awaiting him is a very hot place of residence. (93)

With the fire surrounding him from all directions. (94)

This is the certain truth. (95)

Glorify the name of your great Lord. (96)

THE IRON (57)

In the Name of God, Most Merciful, and Most Beneficent.

All that is in Heavens and on earth glorify God. He is the Exalted and the Wise. (1)

To Him belongs the kingdom of the heavens and earth. He grants life and takes it away, and He is capable of all things. (2)

He is the First and the Last, He is the Evident and the Hidden, and He is Knowledgeable of all things. (3)

He is the One who created the heavens and the earth in six days then sat on the throne. He knows what enters the earth and what leaves it, and what comes down from the sky and what moved in the heavens. He is with you wherever you are, and has full knowledge of what you do. (4)

To Him belongs what is in the heavens and on the earth, and to God all things shall return. (5)

He causes the day to end with the night, and the night ends with the day. He also has knowledge of what is hidden inside every human's chest. (6)

So believe in God and His Apostle, and spend from what We made you trustees over in this life. The believers and givers among you shall have a great reward. (7)

How do you not believe in God and His Apostle, after you made an oath to Him to be believers? (8)

He is the One Who reveals to His servant veritable verses so that He may take you from the darkness out into the light. God is Compassionate and Merciful with you. (9)

How do you not spend in the way of God? To God belongs all that is in the heavens and on the earth. Those who spent their money and fought before the victory cannot be held equal to those who spent their money and fought after the victory, although both have earned the goodness that was promised to them by God, and God is quite Knowledgeable with what you do. (10)

All who make God a good loan by spending their money in His way, shall be rewarded with more than twice what they spent, and shall deserve a great recompense. (11)

A day will come when the believers, men and women who the light of their faith shall precede them, and in their right hands they shall carry the good tidings of gardens, below which rivers flows, and that is the great triumph. (12)

On that day, the hypocrites, men and women, shall say to the believers: "Watch us how we will use some of your light," and they were told to go back and seek the light of the faithful, and suddenly a fence appears between them and the believers, which has a door that has the appearance of being merciful, but in reality it is an instrument of torture. (13)

They will start calling on the believers: "Have we not been with you?" The believers will answer: "That is true, but you have deceived yourselves. You conspired and have been overtaken by your fantasies, until God set the record straight and your real intentions were brought up to light." (14)

Today, no ransom will be accepted from you, or from the unbelievers. Your permanent residence shall be hell, and you shall belong to it; a very bad ending indeed. (15)

Is it not time for the believers to fill their hearts with fear of God, upon the mention of God and what He has revealed of the truth? They should not be like those who got the Book before them, who as the time went on their hearts became harder, and many of them have become transgressors. (16)

Know that God is the One who revives the earth after it is dead. We have revealed the verses to you so you may contemplate. (17)

The believers, men and women, who in good faith make a loan to God (*contribute money in God's way*) shall be repaid double, and they shall have a generous reward. (18)

Those who believed in God, and His apostles, men and women, those are the true people of truth, along with the martyrs, their recompense and true light of faith is with their Lord. Those who did not believe, and denied our signs; they are the owners of hell. (19)

Know that this life is a life of play and entertainment, where you engage in boasting to each other, and acquire riches and children, like the rain which the unbelievers admire the vegetation it produces; after maximum growth, it becomes yellow and turns into dust. On the Day of Judgement their will be severe torture and forgiveness from God and blissful living. This life is only an instrument of seduction. (20)

Compete for forgiveness from your Lord and gardens as wide as the heavens and the earth, stand ready for those who believed in God and His apostles, and this is a favor from God which He gives to whomever He wishes. He is the great Grantor of all favors. (21)

No catastrophe shall afflict the earth or yourselves that We did not destine it long before the creation of anything, and that is easy for God. (22)

So that you do not need to grieve over what you lost, or be so enthralled with what God gives you, for God does not like the arrogant nor the boastful. (23)

Those are the stingy who recommend stinginess to others, and those who do need to remember that God is rich and to Him thankfulness belongs. (24)

We sent apostles with signs and with them Books and just scales, so that people deal with each other justly, and We created iron, with a lot of strength in it, and benefits for people, and for God to know who will stand up for Him and His apostles without prior knowledge; God is Strong and Exalted. (25)

We sent Noah and Abraham and created prophethood and books in their descendents; some of them became guided and many of them were transgressors. (26)

We followed them with other apostles, including Jesus, son of Mary, and revealed the Gospel to him, and filled the hearts of those who followed him with mercy which became associated with a life of priesthood, which they invented, but we never imposed it on them. We only required them to seek the bliss of God's approval and they did not follow that fully. Those who believed and did what We ordered among them shall be adequately rewarded, but many of them are transgressors. (27)

People who believe, fear and worship God and believe in His apostles, and He will reward you with a double portion of His mercy and provide you with the light of faith guiding your way. He will also forgive you, and God is Forgiving and Merciful. (28)

People of the book need to know that God's favor is not in their hands but rather in God's hands, and He grants it to whomever He wishes. He is the One who is the greatest of all givers. (29)

SHE WHO ARGUED (58)

In the Name of God, Most Merciful, and Most Beneficent.

God has heard the argument of the woman complaining to God and to you about her husband, and God heard your conversation with her. God hears and knows. (1)

Those of you who declare a separation from their wives by calling them by the name of their mothers need to know that the separation is invalid. Their mothers are only those that gave birth to them. Statements of that kind are acts of sin and forgery. God is Forgiving and Merciful. (2)

Those of you who say words intended to mean separation or divorce, cannot go back on what they said without paying a ransom, such as freeing a slave. You cannot go back to her and touch her without the satisfaction of the ransom requirement, and God is Knowledgeable with what you do. (3)

If such a prescribed ransom is not possible or available, then the fasting of two months in succession is required before they can touch each other again. Another alternative, available if the other two are impossible, is feeding sixty needy persons, if you believe in God and His Apostle. These are the limits imposed by God, and awaiting the unbelievers is an excruciating torture. (4)

Those who resist and complain about the limits imposed by God and His Apostle are just like many before them who did the same. After We revealed our verses clearly, they need to remember that for the unbelievers We prepared humiliating torture. (5)

The day when God has resurrected them, He will tell them of all that they have done, including many deeds they have forgotten, and God is the Witness to all things. (6)

Do you not see that God knows what is in the heavens and on earth, and no secret shall be among three, without God being their fourth, or among five without God being their sixth, or even less or more without being one of them, wherever they are? He shall tell them what they did on the Last Day; God is Knowledgeable of all things. (7)

Did you not see those who were told to stay away from a wicked practice of intimidation (*they speak to each other threatening some one else in a way intended for that person who is being intimidated to hear as he is passing by*). Although they were instructed to refrain from it, they plot indecency and aggression against others, and disobey the apostle. They salute you with words intended to be different (*though similar sounding*) from what God salutes you with, and then they sarcastically wonder why God does not torture them for what they do. We tell them they shall be fed to the fire of hell. A bad destiny indeed. (8)

People who believe, do not ever exchange with each other words of indecency, aggression, and disobedience to the Apostle, but rather, exchange words of charity, fear of God, and worship, and fear God and worship Him for to Him you shall all be assembled. (9)

Conversations of conspiracy originate from the Devil, intended to make the believers feel bad. The believers can never be hurt by anything without God's permission, and on God the believers shall rely. (10)

People who believe, if you are requested, in a meeting, to make room, do make room. When you make room, God will make room for you, and if you were asked to rise, also do so. God will elevate the believers among you, and those who were given knowledge higher. God is Expert, and Knowledgeable. (11)

People who believe, if you desire to confide in the Apostle, it is advisable that you perform before that an act of charity. This is better for you, and more appropriate, unless you do not have the financial means to do that, and God is Forgiving and Merciful. (12)

Did you become reluctant to talk to the Apostle in confidence to avoid the charities before hand? If you did obtain confidential advice and yet failed to make the charity, and God forgave you, then do your prayers, and pay the alms, and obey God and His apostle. God is Knowledgeable with what you do. (13)

Did you not see the people who betrayed you? They have earned God's wrath; they are not with you nor are they with them (*the enemy*). They take oaths and swear, while they know they are lying. (14)

They have severe torture awaiting them, and what they did was disgraceful indeed. (15)

They swore falsely, and deviated from God's path. Awaiting them is a humiliating torture. (16)

Their riches and their children shall be of no help to them. They are the owners of hell, and in it they shall be immortalized. (17)

When they are resurrected by God they shall swear to Him just like they swore to you, thinking that would work, then, but they are nothing but liars. (18)

The Devil has taken them over, and that made them forget the mention of God. They belong to the party of the Devil, but the party of the Devil are the real losers. (19)

Those who resist God and His Apostle, they are the ones who will be in the lowest of all ranks. (20)

God wrote: I shall always win with My apostles. God is Strong and Exalted. (21)

You will not find people who believe in God, and the Last Day, trying to be subservient to those who antagonize God and His Apostle, even if they were their fathers, their sons or members of their tribe. Those are the ones that God wrote the faith in their hearts, and aided them with a spirit from Him, and shall enter them gardens below which rivers flow, immortalized in them. He is happy with them and they are happy with Him. They are the party of God, and those who belong to the party of God shall be the ones who succeed. (22)

THE EXILE OF THE TRIBE OF NOODAIR (59)

In the Name of God, Most Merciful, and Most Beneficent.

Glorify God, for to Him belongs what is in the heavens and on earth, and He is the Exalted and the Wise. (1)

He (*God*) is the One who pushed out the unbelieving group of people of the Book out of their homes, and sent them into exile. They thought that their castles and high defensive positions would protect them from God, but God came at them from where they did not expect. Due to the fear in their hearts, they started destroying their own homes by themselves, and some were destroyed by the believers. So those of you who have eyes, take heed. (2)

If God did not decide on letting them go into exile, He would have tortured them in this life in addition to the torture awaiting them in hell on the Last Day. (3)

This was because they tried to oppose God and His Apostle, and those who oppose God shall find that God is severe in His punishment. (4)

Whatever of their palm trees you cut down or leave standing, it all occurred with God's permission, for God wanted to humiliate the transgressors. (5)

All of the spoils left by those exiled, which did not result from fighting, such as horses and camels is under the direction of the apostle. God gives His apostles authority over whomever He wishes, and God is Capable of all things. (6)

The spoils that God put under the authority of His Apostle belong to the Apostle, his relatives who are in need, the orphans, the destitute, and the homeless. God does not wish that you have among you a dynasty of the rich. What the Apostle gives you, take, and what he denies you, stay away from it. Fear and worship God, for His punishment is truly severe. (7)

The destitute and the immigrants who were expelled away from their homes and possessions, who are seeking God's favor and pleasure, and side with God and His apostle; those are the true believers. (8)

Those who were early in adopting the faith, and are welcoming of those who immigrated to them, and their hearts are clear of envy of those who may have adopted the faith before them, and even prefer them over themselves when they receive special attention, those who resist the lower trends in a human's soul, these are the ones who will succeed. (9)

Also those who came after them, who say: "Lord forgive us and forgive our brothers who came before us, of the faithful, and clear our hearts of any envy of other believers. Our Lord, you are Merciful and Beneficent." (10)

Did you see the hypocrites say to their brothers, the unbelievers, among people of the Book: "If you are expelled, we shall leave with you, and we shall not join anyone against you, and if you fight, we shall support you, and God is a witness to the fact that they were liars." (11)

If they are expelled they shall not leave with them, and if they fight they shall not support them, and if they did support them they shall be put to flight before them, and they shall find no real supporters. (12)

You scare them more than God does, because they are ignorant people. (13)

They shall not all fight you unless they are in fortified towns, or behind walls separating them from you. With each other they seem very strong, but their hearts are not together, for they are people who have no sense. (14)

Like people before them, soon they will taste the result of their own actions, and awaiting them is an excruciating torture. (15)

They are like the Devil who encourages humans to disbelieve, and when they do, he says: "I are apart from you. I am afraid of the Lord of the universe." (16)

Their punishment both is that they shall be immortalized in hell, and in that there is appropriate punishment for the transgressors. (17)

People who believe, fear God and worship Him, and every soul should look carefully at what it had done. Fear and worship God, for God is an Expert on what you do. (18)

Do not be like those who forgot God. He made them forget themselves, and these are the transgressors. (19)

Owners of heaven cannot be equated with owners of hell, because the owners of heaven are the winners. (20)

If We revealed this Koran to a mountain, you would have found it scared and will crack from the fear of God. These are the examples We bring to people so they may think. (21)

He is God; no other God exists but Him, and He has knowledge of the future and the truth. He is the Merciful and the Beneficent. (22)

He is God; there is no God but Him, and He is the Sacred King, Free of all weaknesses, the One in charge, the Dominant, the Exalted, the Mighty and the Arrogant. Glorified He is above their unbelieving associations (*associate others with God*). (23)

He is God, the Creator, the One who designs the way anything looks, and to Him belong the good sacred names. He is glorified by all that is in the heavens and on earth, and He is the Exalted and the Wise. (24)

WOMEN WILL BE TESTED (60)

In the Name of God, Most Merciful, and Most Beneficent.

People who believe, do not take those who are my enemies and yours as your sponsors and people you behold to (*in a position of advice and control over you*). You are showing them affection, and they have denied the truth that came to you. They repelled the apostle and you because you believed in your Lord. If you have immigrated as a part of your struggle to adhere to my path, and please me, do not be entrusting your secrets, and seeking advice and affection from them. I have full knowledge of what you declare and what you hide, and whoever among you who does that has missed his way. (1)

If they were able to, they will be your bitter enemies, and use their hands and tongues against you, and would love to be able to have you renounce your religion, and disbelieve. (2)

On the Last Day you shall derive no benefit from your children or your relatives, because you shall not be together. God always sees what you do. (3)

Abraham and those with him would be a good example for you. They said to their people, we are free from you, and from what you worship, instead of God, We have no longer any faith in you. We already have hate and animosity among us, and will most likely continue until you believe in the One God. Abraham said to his father: "I shall ask God for forgiveness on your behalf, otherwise I have nothing that I can do for you with God. God, we shall rely on You, and resort to you, and to you belongs our destiny. (4)

Our Lord, do not let us have the intransigence of the unbelievers, and forgive us, our Lord. You are the Exalted and the Wise." (5)

Those were the best example for you, and for those who have hopes concentrated on God and the Last Day. Those who deviate need to realize that God is in need of no one and to Him belong all thanks. (6)

It is possible that God may create affection between you and those who were your enemies. God is Able and God is Forgiving and Merciful. (7)

God does not forbid you from being fair and affectionate with those who have not fought you because of your religion, and did not force you out of your own homes, for God likes those who are fair. (8)

Those who God orders you away from seeking their sponsorship are those who fought you, because of your religion, forced you out of your homes, or helped others to do so. Those who seek them are transgressors. (9)

People who believe, if believing women immigrated and came to you, test them. These are women from the tribe of Kouraish who, due to the provisions of the Houdaibyah treaty are to be returned intended for their protection so they are not returned to their tribe and be subjected to retaliation. God is more knowledgeable with who is the truthful in faith. Once you are convinced they are faithful do not return them to a state of lack of belief. The unbelievers are not suitable for them to marry and they are not suitable for each other. Instead pay a ransom for them equal to what the unbelievers spent to have them. You are permitted to marry them if you pay them what they have spent or deserve, and do not marry the unbelievers. Each side shall be compensated for any cost. This is God's judgement for you, and God is Knowledgeable and Wise. (10)

If any of the wives of the believers defected to the unbelievers, the believers can be compensated for their loss from the spoils of war. Fear and worship God in whom you believe. (11)

If women who believed come to you, and swear their loyalty to the faith, and promise to associate none with God, and to not steal, commit adultery, kill their children, or attribute their children to a father other than their true father (*equally sinful for a man to refuse to recognize a child that is his*) or refuse to obey you in anything lawful, accept their oath, ask God's forgiveness for them, on their behalf. God is Forgiving and Merciful. (12)

People who believe do not seek the sponsorship of people who earned God's wrath. They have no more hope for the Last Day than the unbelievers who already died. (13)

THE ROW (61)

In the Name of God, Most Merciful, and Most Beneficent

God is glorified by all that is in heavens, and on earth, and He is the Exalted and the Wise. (1)

People who believe, why do you say what you do not do? (2)

It incurs the wrath of God to say what you do not do. (3)

God likes those who fight in His way, standing in rows just like a solid building. (4)

As Moses said to his people: "My people, why do you do harm to me, while you know I am God's Apostle sent to you? And as they continued to deviate from the truth, God made their hearts go astray, and God does not guide the transgressors." (5)

Jesus, the son of Mary said to the people of Israel: "I am God's Apostle to you, confirming what you already have in the Bible and bringing you the good tidings of a new Apostle, whose name is Ahmad." As he brought them veritable signs, they called it a clear sorcery. (6)

Who is more of a transgressor than those who spread lies about God as they are being invited to Islam? God will not provide guidance to the transgressors. (7)

They would like to put out the fire emitting the light of God by blowing air from their mouths, but God shall maintain His light, whether the unbelievers like it or not. (8)

He is the One who sent his Apostle with the guidance and the right facts so that He makes him prevail even if the associaters hated it. (9)

People who believe, let me draw to your attention a trade that shall save you from an excruciating torture. (10)

Believe in God and His apostle, and struggle in the way of God with your properties and yourselves, for that is better for you if you knew. (11)

He shall forgive your sins, and enter you gardens, below which rivers flow, and blessed residence in the gardens of Eden, and that is the great triumph. (12)

And you can expect from God even more, including good tidings to the believers of a victory from God, and the resolution of threats. (13)

People who believe, be supportive of God just like Jesus, son of Mary, asked His followers: Are you going to support me and God? And the followers said: "We are supporters of God. A group of the people of Israel believed and another group denied. We supported those who believed, and they prevailed over those who did not." (14)

THE FRIDAY (62)

In the Name of God, Most Merciful, and Most Beneficent

God is glorified by all that is in the heavens and on earth, the Sacred King, the Exalted and the Wise. (1)

He is the One who sent an apostle to the gentiles, reciting to them his verses, purifying them and providing them with the Book and wisdom, for they were clearly misguided prior to that. (2)

Including others that may follow, and He is the Exalted and the Wise. (3)

This is God's favor that he grants to whomever He wishes, and God is the greatest Grantor of favors. (4)

The example of those who carried the Torah and did not abide by it, is similar to the donkey simply carrying what belongs to someone else. It is an uncomplimentary example for people who denied God's verses, and God does not guide the transgressors. (5)

People, let them wish death, if what they claim is true. (6)

They will never wish that, knowing what they have done, and God is far more knowledgeable with the transgressors. (7)

Say to them: "The death that you are running away from shall certainly catch up with you, and then You shall be turned to a world that is unknown and where only reliable testimony is of help." (8)

People who believe, if the call to prayers is heard on Friday, discontinue trading to join in mentioning the name of God, for this is better for you if you knew. (9)

When prayers are completed, spread back again to resume making a living from God's favor, and remember God often, so you may succeed. (10)

When they find the opportunity for trading or entertainment they leave you standing and run. Say to them: "What God has is better than entertainment and trade, and God is the Best of all providers." (11)

THE HYPOCRITES (63)

In the Name of God, Most Merciful, and Most Beneficent.

If the hypocrites come to you and say: "We declare that you are God's Apostle," they know you are His Apostle. God also knows that the hypocrites are liars. (1)

They used their oaths as a method for deception. They deviated away from the way of God, and what they did is bad indeed. (2)

They believed and then disbelieved again, so their hearts were stamped shut by God, and they will never understand. (3)

You look at them, and you get attracted to their looks, and if they speak, you are tempted to listen to them. They behave always uneasy and unsure and hardly moving, like boards of wood. They think that any shouting is against them. They are the enemy. Be careful with them. God shall take care of them for their deception. (4)

If they are told: "Come and ask the Apostle to pray to God for your forgiveness," they turn their heads, and decline arrogantly. (5)

Whether you do ask for their forgiveness or you do not, God shall not forgive them, and God does not guide the transgressors. (6)

It is they who advise others not to spend in charity on anyone of the Apostle's followers until they leave him, while they know that to God belongs all the treasures of the heavens and the earth, but the hypocrites are ignorant of that. (7)

They say: "When We return to Medina, the high among the people shall repel the low." To God belongs the high position and to His apostle and the believers, but the unbelievers do not know. (8)

People who believe, do not let your riches or your children keep you away from the mention of God, and those who do are the losers. (9)

Spend from what we provided for you, before death catches up with you, and then you try to say: "My Lord, if you gave me a little more time, I would have spent more and I would be among the righteous." (10)

God shall never provide a reprieve to a soul after its time has come. God is quite Knowledgeable with all that you do. (11)

DAY OF THE LOSING DEAL (64)

In the Name of God, Most Merciful, and Most Beneficent.

God is glorified by all that is in the heavens and on earth. To Him belongs the kingdom, and the glory, and He is Capable of all things. (1)

He created you, and some of you are unbelievers and the others are believers, and He sees all that you do. (2)

His creation of the heavens and the earth is the truth. He created your features (*the way you look*) and perfected it, and to Him belongs the final destiny. (3)

He knows what is in the heavens and what is on earth, and He knows what you declare and what you hide, and God knows what you hide in your hearts. (4)

Did you not hear the news of those that disbelieved before you, and tasted the price of their actions? Awaiting them is an excruciating torture. (5)

Their apostles also brought them veritable signs, yet they said: "Are we going to have humans guide us?" and they disbelieved and denied, and God gave up on them. God is in need of no one, and He is the One to give thanks to. (6)

The unbelievers claimed that they shall not be resurrected, say: "O' yes, by my Lord, you shall be resurrected, and you shall be informed of all that you did, and that is so easy for God." (7)

So believe in God and His apostle, and in the light We revealed to him. God is an Expert on what you do. (8)

He will assemble you on the day of assembly, or the day of the losing deal. One who does good works and adheres to righteousness, He shall forgive his sins, and enter him gardens under which rivers flow, immortalized in them, and that is the great triumph. (9)

Those who disbelieved and denied our verses, they are the owners of hell, immortalized in it; a very bad destiny indeed. (10)

No catastrophe occurs without God's permission, and one who believes in God, God guides his heart, and God is Knowledgeable of all things. (11)

Obey God and obey the Apostle, and if you do not, Our apostle is only obligated to give clear warning. (12)

God who there is no god but Him, and on God rely the believers. (13)

People who believe, it is not uncommon for your children and your wives to be enemies to you, so watch out for them. If you pardon, forgive and forget, God can also be Forgiving and Merciful. (14)

Your riches and your family can be an element of temptation for you in this life, but God has the most valuable of all prizes. (15)

Worship and fear God as much as you can. Listen carefully and obey, and spend in charity for your own good. Those who resist their own selfish possessiveness are the ones who will succeed. (16)

If you make a good loan to God, He will double it for you, and He will forgive you. God is Grateful and Prudent. (17)

He is the One who has knowledge of the future, and the truthfulness of allegations. He is the Exalted and the Wise. (18)

DIVORCE (65)

In the Name of God, Most Merciful, and Most Beneficent.

O' prophet, if you (*in the plural*) divorced women, they will immediately start on their waiting (*limited contact*) period. Count the days of the waiting period (*90 days*), and worship and fear your Lord. Do not ever force them out of their homes unless they committed a grave act of obvious indecency. These are the limits imposed by God, and one who transgresses over God's limits has transgressed against himself. Before the end of the waiting period God may cause things to happen (*minds may change*). (1)

As the waiting period ends, you either hold on to them in good faith or let them go the same way, and have witnesses to such decisions by people among you who have impeccable reputations. The witnessing process ought to be done with an admonishment from God to those who believe in God, and the Last Day, and those who worship and fear God as to truthfulness. God shall always find an out for them from entanglement. (2)

One who abides by God's wishes, He shall provide for him from where he does not expect. One who relies on God, God is his resort, and God shall recognize his plight. God gives a value to everything. (3)

Those women who are having no menstruation, or cannot menstruate, their waiting period is three months. Women who are pregnant their waiting period is until they deliver, and those who worship and fear God, God shall make their way easier. (4)

These are the wishes of God that He reveals to you, and for one who worships and fears God, He shall forgive sins, and increase rewards. (5)

Let them live where you have lived, and do not show them animosity, or tighten things up on them, and if they are pregnant, pay all of their expenses until they deliver, and if they nurse their child for you pay them for doing that, and manage interactions between you nicely, If you cannot reach agreement, find someone else to do the nursing. (6)

He who is well to do should spend based on his ability, and from what his riches permits him to do, which was what God gave him to start with. God does not ask one to do beyond what he is able to, and God shall provide ease after hardships. (7)

Many towns deviated from the admonishments of the Lord and His apostles, and We extracted from them severe punishment and subjected them to severe torture. (8)

They suffered for their misdeeds, and their final destiny was a total loss. (9)

God prepared for them severe torture. So, believing people of intellect, worship and fear God. God Has revealed to you a reminder. (10)

An apostle reciting to you God's verses clearly to deliver the believers out from the darkness into the light, and one who believes in God, and does good works shall be entered into gardens below which rivers flow, immortalized in them forever, and God will provide for such people the best of His bounty. (11)

God who created the seven heavens, and an equal number of solid grounds, all under His control. You should know that God is Capable of all things, and has full knowledge of all things. (12)

THE FORBIDDANCE (66)

In the Name of God, Most Merciful, and Most Beneficent.

O' prophet, why do you forbid what God Has permitted for you? You are seeking approval of your wives, and God is Forgiving and Merciful. (1)

What God permitted for you cannot be made forbidden by your own oath. God is your Sponsor, He is the Knowledgeable and Wise. (2)

The prophet confided something to one of his wives and she informed others about it. The prophet recognized some of what she conveyed and did not recognize some other parts that she conveyed, and when he told her of the contradiction (*what he said and what he did not*) she asked: "Who told you?" and he said: "The Knowledgeable and the Knowing." (3)

If you repent to God, and cleanse your hearts, that is one thing, but if you conspire against him remember that God is his sponsor, in addition to Gabriel and the rest of the believers, with the angels backing them up. (4)

If he decides to divorce you, maybe God will help him replace you with wives more righteous than you, believing Moslems, worshiping and fearing God, and repent and glorify Him, whether maiden or previously married. (5)

O' people who believe, protect yourselves and your families from a fire whose fuel is people and rocks, attended to by angels who are rough and powerful, who will never disobey God in anything He orders them, and they do what they are told. (6)

O' unbelievers, do not commit transgressions today, for you shall be punished for everything you do. (7)

People who believe, repent to God fully and in good faith, for God may forgive you for your sins, and enter you gardens below which rivers flow, and the day when God's pride in his prophet and those who followed him will be justified, and their own light of faith shall illuminate the path before them, and on their right. They will say: "Our Lord, complete our enlightenment for us, and forgive us. You are Capable of all things." (8)

O' prophet, resist the unbelievers, and the hypocrites, and be hard on them if necessary, for their residence shall be hell. A bad place to reside indeed. (9)

God gave the unbelievers examples from the wives of Noah and Lot, who were close to two of the very righteous among our servants, and when they betrayed them, their relationship with them did not produce a difference with God, and they will enter hell with all the others who will enter. (10)

Another example by God to the believers is the wife of the Pharaoh who said: "My Lord, build for me a house in paradise and save me from the Pharaoh and his deeds, and from the transgressing people." (11)

And Mary the daughter of Imran, who preserved her chastity, and We blew in her womb from our spirit. She believed in the word of her Lord and His Books, and was one of those who worshiped and feared God. (12)

THE KINGDOM (67)

In the Name of God, Most Merciful, and Most Beneficent.

Glorified be He, who holds in His hands the reins of the kingdom, and He is capable of all things. (1)

He is the One who created death and life, in order to test you and find out who among you does better works. He is the Exalted and the Forgiving. (2)

He is the one who created the heavens in seven layers. You do not ever see in the creation of the Merciful contradictions or incompatibilities. Review the entire creation; do you see any deficiencies? (3)

Even with a second review, the result will come back a negative. No deficiencies will be found. (4)

We decorated the Lower heaven with lanterns, and provided astrological stoning to the devils (*the falling stars*) and prepared for them the torture of hell. (5)

The torture of hell awaits those who denied their Lord, a very bad appointment indeed. (6)

If they are thrown in it they will hear a suction sound as it boils over. (7)

Hell will appear like it is mad, and every time a new group are thrown in it, the attendants shall ask: "Did you not get a messenger with a warning?" (8)

They will say: "Yes, we did, but we denied everything revealed, and accused those who followed of being misguided." (9)

They said: "If we had listened, and done some thinking, we would not be among the owners of hell." (10)

So they admitted their sins, and thus they deserved to be in hell. (11)

Those who fear their Lord, covertly earn forgiveness and a great reward. (12)

Whether you talk covertly or openly, He knows what is in your hearts. (13)

Would He not know what he created? He is an Expert and Fair. (14)

He is the one who facilitated the use of this earth for you, so spread on it, and eat from what He gave you, and to Him you shall be assembled. (15)

Do you feel safe from Him who is in the heavens, if He decided to make the earth sink, and move with you on it? (16)

Or do you feel safe enough that you are sure that He in the heavens will not send on you a destroying wind, so you will have a taste of the value of My warning? (17)

People before them denied and they know how bad the results had been. (18)

Do they not see birds above them flying in lines, sometimes striking the air with their wings and other times simply extending them? Only the Merciful keeps them up there. He is aware of all things. (19)

Who is He who is going to have soldiers bringing victory to you, other than God? The unbelievers are in a state of arrogance. (20)

Who is going to provide for you if He withholds his bounty from you? Yet they persist in their denial and intransigence. (21)

Is one who walks with his face down on the ground better than one who walks straight on a straight line? (22)

Say: "He is the One who brought you up, and gave you hearing, eyesight, and hearts, yet you infrequently say thanks." (23)

Say: "He is the One who caused you to spread on earth, and to Him you shall be assembled." (24)

They ask: "When is that going to happen if you are truly truthful?" (25)

Say to them: "Only God knows that, and I only deliver a clear warning. "(26)

As they face the day, their faces shall show their fear, and they will be told: "This is what you were being promised." (27)

Say to them (*the unbelievers*): "If God annihilated me, and those with me, who is going to protect the unbelievers from an excruciating torture?" (28)

Say to them: "He is the Merciful. We believe in Him, and rely on Him, and you shall find out who is clearly misguided." (29)

Ask them: "If their water sank away in the earth, who is going to provide them with a new spring?" (30)

THE PEN (68)

In the Name of God, Most Merciful, and Most Beneficent.

Noun. I swear by the pen and what they write with it. (1)

By the grace of your Lord, you are not crazy (*as the unbelievers claim*). (2)

You shall be rewarded with no limitations. (3)

You are very superior in character. (4)

You shall find out and they shall, (5)

who is the misguided (*you or them*). (6)

Your Lord is far more knowledgeable with who lost his way, and He is far more knowledgeable with those who are rightly guided. (7)

Do not obey those who denied. (8)

They would love to see you ignore what they are doing, so that they can ignore what you do. (9)

Do not pay attention to those despicable individuals who swear using the name of God falsely. (10)

They are backbiting, two-faced liars. (11)

They stand in the way of others doing good works, transgressors and evildoers. (12)

They are obnoxious and vindictive. (13)

While they have riches and many children (*as a way of thanking God for His bounty*), (14)

they call them old fables, when our verses are recited to them. (15)

On the Last Day, they shall have the facial characteristic of a nose that looks like a trunk. (16)

We tested them like We tested those who owned a fruit garden, and as the trees became fully loaded, they promised themselves that they wouldharvest it all in the morning. (17)

They did not express the slightest uncertainty about their next day harvest. (18)

A visitor from your Lord landed on them as they slept. (19)

He left it dried up and black in color. (20)

They called each other in the morning: (21)

"Let us start collecting our harvest if we want it all." (22)

And they got on their way while whispering and conversing with each other: (23)

"We need to finish the work before it is raided by some wretched or hungry people." (24)

As they approached their property able and ready to work on it (25)

they saw what happened and said: "We certainly were misguided." (26)

We now denied everything. (27)

The one of them who is middle-aged said: "Did I not tell you to glorify God and be thankful?" (28)

They said: "Glorified be Our Lord, we were transgressors." (29)

And they started blaming each other. (30)

They said: "It was bad for us, we have really transgressed." (31)

They said: "May Our Lord find it possible to replace our misfortune with something better, and to the Lord we shall be praying." (32)

This was a form of torture in this life, But the torture of the life next is far more severe, if they knew it. (33)

Those who worship and fear their Lord, awaiting them are blissful gardens. (34)

Do you think We will ever equate Moslems with transgressors? (35)

How can you make a judgement like that.? (36)

Or did you study that in a book? (37)

Maybe it contains something that will support your claims! (38)

Or maybe you think you have solid promises from us, that you can rely on, on the Day of Judgement, that makes you talk the way you do! (39)

Ask them who among them will win this way. (40)

Or maybe they have associates who they associate with God. Let them bring them along if they are truthful. (41)

The day the magnitude of the true horror of the Last Day becomes evident. They try to prostrate themselves and they fail. (42)

They are looking down with absolute fear, exhausted with their humiliation, yet when they were invited to prostrate themselves, and they could, and they did not while they were perfectly safe. (43)

So leave the one who will deny this (*the Koran*) to Me. We shall give them the opportunity to do even worse, without them knowing it. (44)

I shall prolong things for them, for their deception by Me shall be complete. (45)

If you were asking them for compensation for what you are bringing them, it should have cost them a lot. (46)

Or do they have knowledge of the future and they are busy recording it? (47)

Be patient until you receive His final verdict, and do not be like the man of the whale (*Jonah*) who called (*on His God*) while distressed in the darkness (*inside the whale*). (48)

If it was not for the blessing of his Lord, He would not have ended in the arid land where he was eventually thrown. (49)

His Lord responded to him, and he became a righteous man. (50)

The unbelievers just about penetrated through you with their eyes, as they heard the Mention (*the Book – the Koran*) and said: "You were crazy." (51)

It is mentioned as a reminder for the whole world. (52)

THE CERTAIN DAY (69)

In the Name of God, Most Merciful, and Most Beneficent.

The certain day. (1)

What is the certain day? (2)

How do you know what is the certain day? (3)

Thamoud and Aad denied the Last Day. (4)

And Thamoud were annihilated following the great cry. (5)

While Aad were annihilated with a powerful, unrelenting wind (6)

which He (*God*) had directed at them for decisive seven nights and eight days, that left their dead bodies stretched like the empty trunks of dead palm trees. (7)

Do you see any of them left? (8)

The Pharaoh came before them, and others who engaged in the same blasphemous denial (9)

they disobeyed the Apostle from their Lord, and He took them in a wave of annihilation. (10)

The day the water rose, We carried you on a sailing ship. (11)

To make it a reminder for you, directed towards listening ears. (12)

As the trumpet is sounded once. (13)

And the ground and the mountains are pressed together into a single flat mass. (14)

That is then the certain day. (15)

The sky will split open into holes. (16)

The angels will be roaming around, and eight of them will be carrying the throne of your Lord. (17)

On that day you shall be exposed and not a thing in you will remain hidden. (18)

One who gets his record in his right hand, shall say: "This is my record, read it." (19)

I have thought I will be subjected to an unrelenting accounting. (20)

He will actually be living satisfied (21)

in a high above garden (22)

with low hanging fruits available. (23)

Eat, drink, and enjoy yourselves, as a result of what they have done in the old days. (24)

One who gets his record book in his left hand shall say: "I wish I have not gotten mine (25)

and I wish I never found out what would I be accounting for. (26)

I wish this was my final death. (27)

For all my money did not do me any good. (28)

All my power has been destroyed." (29)

Take him and put him in chains (30)

and then in hell he shall remain. (31)

Such is the torture of the Last Day, which is much worse. (32)

Such is the one who did not believe in the great God. (33)

He was not even inclined to feed the wretched poor. (34)

Today he has no one close. (35)

His food shall be garbage. (36)

food eaten only by sinners. (37)

I swear by all that you can see (38)

and all that you cannot see. (39)

That is all relayed by an honorable apostle. (40)

It is not the work of a poet; little do you believe. (41)

It is not the work of a priest either; little do you remember. (42)

It is rather a revelation from the Lord of the Universe. (43)

If one (*Mohammed*) were to say what We did not say. (44)

We would take it forcefully away from him by our right. (45)

And We would have cut his aorta. (46)

No one among you would have been able to protect him from Us. (47)

It is a reminder to those who worship and fear God. (48)

We know that among you some who deny. (49)

It is too bad for the unbelievers. (50)

For it is the absolute truth. (51)

Glorify the name of your great Lord. (52)

PATHS OF ASCENT (70)

In the Name of God, Most Merciful, and Most Beneficent.

A questioner asked for an earlier torture. (1)

For the unbelievers it is coming for certain. (2)

It is coming from God, the Owner of all the Paths of ascent. (3)

The angels and the spirit (*Gabriel*) ascend to Him in one day that is equal to fifty thousand years. (4)

So wait and be patient. (5)

They see it very far. (6)

We see it very close. (7)

The day the sky shall look like molten metal (8)

and the mountains like tufts of cotton. (9)

Close friends will not even talk to each other. (10)

The transgressors would wish they can sacrifice their children to save themselves. (11)

He will sacrifice his friend and his brother, (12)

and even his clan who protected him. (13)

He will sacrifice everyone on earth to save himself. (14)

No, he will feel the heat. (15)

A fire that takes away the skin. (16)

Receptive to all of those who denied and turned away. (17)

And those who accumulated riches assuming no one has a share in that. (18)

Humans are created easy to terrorize. (19)

And harder to satisfy. (20)

And if they are touched by a blessing they are stingy. (21)

Except for those who pray. (22)

And those who persist in their prayers. (23)

And those who have in their riches a known portion. (24)

For the beggar and the deprived. (25)

And those who believe in the Last Day. (26)

And those who are afraid of the torture of their Lord. (27)

For their Lord's torture is very unpleasant. (28)

And those who guard their chastity. (29)

Except with their spouses, and those they own, to which no sin attaches. (30)

Those who cross these limits are the transgressors. (31)

The ones who are honest in what they have custody of, and truthful in what they promise. (32)

And the ones who are straight in what they testify on. (33)

And those who are persistent in their prayers. (34)

Those are the ones who will be in gardens as honored guests. (35)

How is it that those who disbelieved before you are hurrying on their way away, (36)

spreading to the right and to the left? (37)

Do they all think that they are going to make paradise. (38)

No, We have created them from what they are familiar with (*sperm*). (39)

I swear by the Lord of the east and the west that We are able (40)

to replace them with others better than them, and that shall take no time at all. (41)

So let them play their games until they meet the day they are promised. (42)

They shall come out from their graves hurrying as if they are going to be awarded prizes. (43)

Their eyes are directed downwards exhausted by the humiliation of the Day they were promised. (44)

NOAH (71)

In the Name of God, Most Merciful, and Most Beneficent.

We sent Noah to his people, and told him: Warn your people before they receive an excruciating torture. (1)

He said: "My people, to you I am clearly ordered to deliver a clear warning. (2)

Worship God, fear Him and obey me. (3)

He will forgive your sins and give you a reprieve for a defined period of time." (4)

Then he said: "My Lord, I have been inviting my people to believe day and night. (5)

My call to them has only served to increase their turning away. (6)

Every time I invited them to have You forgive their sins, they put their fingers in their ears, and they even wear different clothes so that I do not recognize them, and they became as arrogant as arrogance can be. (7)

Then I started seeking their support publicly. (8)

I have actually used both approaches, the overt and the covert. (9)

I said: 'Ask your Lord's forgiveness, for He is Forgiving.' (10)

He sends rain to you from the sky. (11)

He provides for you riches and children, and bestows upon you gardens and rivers. (12)

Why do you not give God the glorification He deserves? (13)

He was the One who put you through the stages of creation. (14)

Did you not see how He created the heavens in seven layers? (15)

God caused plants to grow out from the ground. (17)

Then He will put you, yourselves, in the ground, and bring you up later. (18)

He made the earth flat enough for you to travel on. (19)

And hospitable enough to seek and dwell in its different regions.'" (20)

Noah said: "My Lord, they have shunned me, and followed those whose riches and children will give them only a great loss." (21)

They also engaged in a great deception. (22)

They said to each other: "Do not disavow your gods, neither Aad, nor Sowa, nor Yaghuth, nor Yauq, nor Nassr." (23)

They have misguided a lot of people, and We shall misguide the transgressors even further. (24)

Because of their sins, they were drowned. Then they shall entered the great fire and they shall find no support instead of God. (25)

Noah said: "My Lord, do not leave for the unbelievers a single place of residence. (26)

If you leave any of them, they shall misguide worshipers, and only bring children who will grow as equal transgressors and unbelievers. (27)

My Lord. forgive me and my parents, and all those who entered my house believers, and the other believing men and women, and grant the transgressors one loss after another." (28)

THE JINN (72)

In the Name of God, Most Merciful, and Most Beneficent.

Say: "It was revealed to me that a group of jinn (*unseen creatures, believed to be created of fire, unlike angels, some are believers and some are not, and like humans have a will of their own*) said they have heard the Koran being recited, and they called it a wonder." (1)

It guides and makes a lot of sense. We believed in it (*the Koran*) and we shall associate no one with our Lord. (2)

Our Lord is Glorified and Exalted and has never taken a spouse or a son. (3)

Many of us committed blasphemies, and one of us used especially (*the Devil is originally a member of the jinn*) to say horrible things about God. (4)

They said: "We have erroneously assumed that humans or jinn will not say falsehoods about God." (5)

But obviously, some humans have been collaborating with some jinn, and they misguided each other. (6)

They thought, just like you did, that God will not resurrect anyone. (7)

We (*jinn*) have touched the heavens, and found it full with powerful guards, and flying well-aimed comets (*believed to be used to hit and kill the devils*). (8)

There used to be places in the heavens where we could sit and listen to a lot of things, but now whoever tries to listen shall find a well aimed comet waiting. (9)

We have no idea if those measures were intended because some harm was intended by someone (*the Devil*) to people on the earth, or did God simply wanted to permit them to be guided, and drive away some misguiding influences away from them (*by driving the Devil away*)? (10)

Among us are the righteous, and many are far less than that. We were many groups and beliefs. (11)

We knew we could not escape God on earth or by running away from Him. (12)

When we heard the guidance, we believed in it, and one who believes in his Lord shall not have to fear loss, or stress. (13)

Among us are Moslems and devious unbelievers. Those who became Moslems chose the judicious way. (14)

The deviants are fuel for hell. (15)

If they had chosen the right path, we would have provided them with fresh water to drink. (16)

We have tested them with it, and one who shuns the mention of his Lord shall start on an ascending path of suffering. (17)

Mosques belong to God, and do not use them to glorify anyone but Him. (18)

As they heard the servant of God call on God, they just about descended all on him. (19)

Say: "I am simply calling on my Lord, and I shall never associate any one with Him." (20)

Say to them: "I cannot do you good or harm." (21)

Say: "Nothing will ever protect me from God, and I shall find none to resort to but Him. (22)

I can only relay the message from God and His warning, and one who disobeys God and His apostle shall be immortalized in the fire of hell." (23)

Until they see what they were promised, and find out who has less supporters, and lesser numbers. (24)

Say: "I do not know whether what God has promised is close, or we may still have some time. (25)

He (*God*) is the One who has knowledge of the unknown, and does not reveal that knowledge to anyone." (26)

He may impart selective portions of that knowledge to whomever He chooses of His apostles, and to make sure that they also fulfill their obligations. (27)

And to make sure that they have relayed the messages of their Lord, and acquired full knowledge of what they have, and have a record of everything by accurate numbers. (28)

UNDER THE COVER (73)

In the Name of God, Most Merciful, and Most Beneficent.

You who are under the cover, (1)

stay up the night, except for some of it. (2)

Half of it, or a little less. (3)

Do that even a little longer and recite the Koran. (4)

We shall throw on you even a heavier load. (5)

Using the hours of the night for that has a better impact and permits better enunciation. (6)

You spend a lot of time on other things during the day hours. (7)

Mention the name of your Lord, and spend as much time as you can, thinking of Him and worshiping to Him. (8)

Lord of the east and the west, no other God but Him, and make Him the one you rely on. (9)

Be patient with what they say, and abandon them gently. (10)

Leave to me those who are receivers of my bounty, and yet they deny. Give them a little time; (11)

then We shall have for them humiliation and hell. (12)

Also food that sticks in the throat, and an excruciating torture. (13)

The day the earth and the mountains shall shake, and the mountain rock becomes grounded like sand. (14)

We have sent you an apostle who will be a witness on you, the same way We sent an apostle to the Pharaoh. (15)

The Pharaoh disobeyed the Apostle, and We took him in a very catastrophic way. (16)

How would you have time to worship and fear God if you were unbelievers, on the day when young kids will have white hair? (17)

On the day the sky shall split open, and God's promise shall be fulfilled. (18)

This is a reminder, and whoever chooses can find his way to God. (19)

Your Lord knows that you are up close to two thirds of the night, if not sometimes a half and a third, along with a group of those around you, and God knows that the length of the night and day, relative to each other does vary, so He forgave your sins. Read what you can from the Koran. He knows that some of you may be sick, and others traveling on the earth seeking God's bounty, and even others may be fighting in the way of God. So read what you can from it, and attend to your prayers, and pay the alms, and make a good faith loan to God (*spend in charity*), and whatever you extend in good works you shall find it, or more, in reward from God. Seek God's forgiveness for God is Forgiving and Merciful. (20)

TIGHTLY COVERED (74)

In the Name of God, Most Merciful, and Most Beneficent.

You, the one who is tightly covered, (1)

get up and warn, (2)

and glorify your Lord. (3)

Cleanse your clothes (4)

and stay away from all that is indecent. (5)

Do not expect a lot for what you give. (6)

Let your relationship with God be characterized with patience. (7)

The day it is blown in the horn, (8)

that shall be a day that is hard, (9)

especially on the unbelievers, not easy. (10)

Leave to me those who I created myself, (11)

and I provided them with extended riches, (12)

and their children will witness. (13)

I have eased everything in front of them. (14)

Yet they continued to wish for more. (15)

Not only that, but they were stubborn in listening to our verses. (16)

I shall make it increasingly difficult for them. (17)

They thought and contemplated. (18)

Yet they erred the way they contemplated. (19)

And erred again when they contemplated. (20)

And so they did in the way they looked at things. (21)

Then they showed anger and frowned. (22)

Then they recoiled in arrogance. (23)

And said: "This is certainly an impressive magic." (24)

Then they said: "It is (*the Koran*) the sayings of humans." (25)

They shall be hit with a blast of heat. (26)

And how do you know what is a blast of heat? (27)

A blast that leaves nothing. (28)

Eats away the skin. (29)

Supervised by nineteen angel-keepers. (30)

We made all the keepers of hell angels, and the only reason We mentioned their number is to make it easy for people of the Book to see the truth, and make the believers even more sure of their faith, and to avoid letting doubt enter the heart of people of the Book, or the believers, and those who are lacking in faith, and the unbelievers, will say: "Why did God want to bring this up here?" That is how God misleads whomever He wants to, and guides whomever He wants. Only the Lord knows who His soldiers are, and it is a reminder to all humans. (31)

And so is the moon. (32)

And the night when it falls. (33)

And the morning as it brightens up. (34)

And there is also the big one (hell). (35)

A warning to humans. (36)

And to whomever among you who is still considering whether to go forward or backward. (37)

Every soul is held hostage by what it has done. (38)

Except for those on the right, (39)

In gardens questioning: (40)

"What happened to the transgressors?" (41)

Asking them: "How did you end up in hell?" (42)

They will answer: "We have not been among those who pray. (43)

Nor have we been among those who feed the poor. (44)

We used to talk about things we knew nothing of. (45)

And we denied the coming of the Day of Religion (*Day of Judgement*)." (46)

Until they realized it to be the truth after it was already too late. (47)

Then, no intercession by anyone will be helpful to them. (48)

For they have been shunning all reminders. (49)

As if they were wild asses, (50)

running away from predators. (51)

They behaved like each one of them was expecting a revelation of his own. (52)

They actually did not fear the Last Day. (53)

What they had was a reminder. (54)

Whoever wants to, can let himself be reminded. (55)

They will be reminded only when God wills. He is the One deserving of fear and worship, and He is the One who can forgive. (56)

THE LAST DAY (75)
(Day of Resurrection)

In the Name of God, Most Merciful, and Most Beneficent.

I swear by the Last Day, (1)

and the soul that blames itself first. (2)

Do humans think We are not going to get their bones together? (3)

Not only that, but We are even capable of making humans look as good as they have ever looked. (4)

Some humans think they can correct themselves sometime ahead, before the Last Day. (5)

Many ask: "When is that going to happen?" (6)

As the eyesight is dazzled, (7)

and the moon disappears, (8)

and the moon and the sun fuse together. (9)

On that day a human will say: "Where is the escape?" (10)

No, there is none. (11)

On that day all ends with your Lord. (12)

He shall tell, on that day, all humans what they have done previously, and recently. (13)

Humans actually know what they did. (14)

Even when they keep on making excuses. (15)

Do not try to move your tongue very fast as you read the Koran in an attempt to finish faster. (16)

It is our responsibility to bring it together, and establish how it is read. (17)

When We read it to you, just follow what you hear. (18)

Clarifying the meaning is Our responsibility. (19)

You like haste. (20)

Yet you seem not to worry much about the Last Day. (21)

Faces are reddened on that day, (22)

looking at its Lord. (23)

On that day there are also faces that are pale. (24)

suspecting that what will happen to them is unfavorable. (25)

As the soul is about to leave its owner, reaching the level of the clavicle (*the collar bone*), (26)

ready to depart. (27)

One thinks it is separation time. (28)

As the Last Day of life merges with the first Day of Resurrection, (29)

to your Lord, on that day, all are driven. (30)

What is going to happen to those who neither believed, nor prayed (31)

but rather denied and turned away, (32)

then went to their people boastful (33)

as if they did something to be proud of. (34)

Yes, they thought they did something to be proud of. (35)

Did humans really believe they are going to be left on their own (*dead or alive*)? (36)

Did they not all used to be sperms in semen ejected? (37)

Then from a clot they were created in the best form. (38)

From that creation He made the pairs, the males and the females. (39)

Is this creative ability not capable of resurrecting the dead? (40)

THE HUMAN (76)

In the Name of God, Most Merciful, and Most Beneficent.

Did not humans pass through a period of time in which they were nothing worth mentioning? (1)

We created the human from a mixture that included a sperm, and to test him we gave him hearing and eyesight senses. (2)

We showed him the way and he was either thankful or an unbeliever. (3)

We prepared for the unbelievers chains, cuffs, and fire. (4)

Those who did good works shall drink from a cup that is laced with the taste of camphor (*a good favorable taste*), (5)

a fountain from which the worshipers of God drink, and use it for whatever they want. (6)

They abide by promises of charity they made to God, and are afraid of a day that is full punishing evil. (7)

They feed others because of their love for God, including the wretched, the orphans and the prisoners. (8)

They will say: "We are feeding you to please God and we want from you neither pay nor thanks. (9)

We are afraid of God, for a day when the unbelievers shall be frowning with wrinkled foreheads." (10)

So God shall protect them from the punishing evil of that day, and make their faces happy and cheerful on that day, (11)

and shall reward them for their persistence with gardens and silk. (12)

They shall be reclining on couches and cushions protected from the sun and the cold (13)

in the shade of trees, the fruits of which hangs down enough to be easily reachable. (14)

They shall be served with cups and jugs of silver. (15)

The size of the jugs of silver shall be estimated to satisfy the person being served. (16)

Their drinks in the cups they are served with are either cold or warm depending on their preference. (17)

They shall drink from the Selsabeel fountain of heaven. (18)

They shall be served by young immortal lads, and when you see them they look like pearls. (19)

As you look, you shall see around you a blissful and huge kingdom. (20)

They shall be wearing robes of fine green silk and shining brocade, and bracelets of silver, and they shall have blessed drinks. (21)

This is your reward, and an act of thankfulness for your good works. (22)

We revealed the Koran to you gradually. (23)

So be patient with your God's will, and do not listen to their indecency or disbelief. (24)

Mention the name of your Lord, morning and evening. (25)

At night prostrate yourself for Him, and glorify Him most of the night. (26)

They (*unbelievers*) love what is coming soon, and pay little attention to a very heavy day (*Judgement Day*). (27)

We created them and gave them all their strengths, and if We choose to We can take them away and replace them with others like them. (28)

This is a reminder, and one who wants shall find his way to his Lord. (29)

You can will nothing unless God wills it for you. (30)

He enters whomever he wants under his mercy, and the transgressors shall find an excruciating torture awaiting them. (31)

THE SENDINGS (77)

In the Name of God, Most Merciful, and Most Beneficent.

In the name of these that are sent in succession. (1)

The winds that whistle. (2)

And the rains that come in dribbles. (3)

And the messages that separates right from wrong. (4)

And the messengers who serve as reminders, (5)

of what is excusable and what deserves a warning. (6)

What you are promised shall come to pass. (7)

when the stars shall be wiped out (8)

and the sky shall split open. (9)

When the mountains shall be wiped out (10)

and the apostles are convened. (11)

When has all of this been scheduled, (12)

the Day of the Decision. (13)

And how do you know what is the day of decision? (14)

On that day dire things await those who denied. (15)

Did we not annihilate their old forerunners? (16)

Then We followed them by their more recent ones. (17)

This is what We do to the transgressors. (18)

Their shall be no rescue on that day for those who denied. (19)

Did We not create you from worthless water? (20)

Then We gave them (*humans*) a solid place (21)

for a predefined period of time. (22)

We made all the decisions that no other can make. (23)

On that day those who denied shall see. (24)

Did We not make the earth the place (25)

where those who are alive go to when they die and those who are dead come when they are resurrected? (26)

We made on earth high mountains, and We provided you with fresh water to drink. (27)

On that day bad things await those who denied. (28)

Why do you not go and meet what you have been denying? (29)

Meet the shadow of the flames with the three peaks. (30)

The shadow provides no shade or protection from the heat. (31)

but it rather produces sparks the size of a palace, (32)

and columns of smoke the size of black camels. (33)

Bad things await those who denied. (34)

On that day they shall not speak. (35)

Nor shall they be given permission to apologize. (36)

It shall be a bad day for those who denied. (37)

On that day of decision We shall bring you together with those who came before you. (38)

If you thought before that you were smart enough to conspire, why do you not try it on that day? (39)

On that day bad things awaits those who denied. (40)

On that day, those who feared and worshiped shall be in blissful shades with fountains around them, (41)

with all of the fruits they may desire. (42)

Eat, drink, and enjoy, as a reward for what you were doing. (43)

This is the way We reward those who do good works. (44)

Bad days awaits those who denied. (45)

Eat and enjoy yourselves for a while, but you are transgressors. (46)

Bad things awaits those who denied. (47)

When they were asked to prostrate themselves, they would not. (48)

Bad things awaits those who denied. (49)

After this, what will they ever find appropriate to believe in? (50)

THE NEWS (78)

In the Name of God, Most Merciful, and Most Beneficent.

What are they asking about? (1)

The great news (2)

about which they are in disagreement. (3)

Yes, they shall find out. (4)

Certainly they shall find out. (5)

Did We not flatten the earth for them? (6)

And We raised the mountains like anchors. (7)

We created you in pairs. (8)

We made you sleep for comfort. (9)

And We made the night for rest and warmth. (10)

And the day for work and earning. (11)

We built over you seven great heavens. (12)

We also provided you with a shining light. (13)

And We brought down water from the clouds. (14)

To produce with it grain and other plants, (15)

and thick forestry. (16)

The day of decision (*Last Day*) has been predetermined. (17)

The day when the trumpet sounds, and you will all come in large crowds. (18)

The sky shall split in open doors. (19)

The mountains shall be moved until it looks like they were a mirage. (20)

Hell shall be a ready trap. (21)

A resort for the transgressors. (22)

They shall be in it for ages. (23)

They shall taste in it nothing cool or any drinks. (24)

Other than boiling liquids. (25)

A suitable punishment. (26)

They were convinced they shall not have an accounting. (27)

And they denied our verses and denied them repeatedly. (28)

Everything is kept and recorded. (29)

So taste what you shall get. For you shall get nothing but more torture. (30)

To the God-fearing worshipers there shall be a triumph. (31)

Gardens and grapes shall surround them. (32)

With the beautiful and the young. (33)

Their cups shall always be full in their hands. (34)

And they shall hear no inappropriate gossip or untruthful talk. (35)

A reward from your Lord, and from His ample bounty. (36)

Lord of the heavens and the earth, and what is in between them; the Merciful and no one is entitled to even address Him. (37)

The day the spirit and the angels shall stand in one line, and none shall say a word unless the Merciful permits and agrees. (38)

That will be the day of truth, and whoever wants, can find his way to his Lord. (39)

We have given you ample warning of a torture that will soon be coming. The day when a person will be faced with what his hands have done, and the unbelievers shall wish they were dust. (40)

THE SOUL TAKERS (79)

By those who take away the souls of humans, and extract it with difficulty. (1)

And by those who do it far more easily. (2)

Also by the ships that float and glide. (3)

And those that speed ahead. (4)

And by those who stay behind for a reason. (5)

The day the earth shakes, (6)

followed by the coming death. (7)

Hearts are then terrorized. (8)

And the eyes are looking down with fear. (9)

They ask: "Are we going to come back (10)

after our bones are hollowed?" (11)

If that happens it will certainly be no loss to us. (12)

It is going to take but a single angry shout, (13)

And they shall not have any sleep after that. (14)

Did you hear the story of Moses, (15)

as his Lord called upon him in the sacred valley of Towa? (16)

Go to the Pharaoh for his tyranny is out of control. (17)

Tell him: "It is time to purify yourself. (18)

I shall guide you to your Lord, so that you fear him." (19)

He showed him a great sign. (20)

He denied and rebelled. (21)

Then he turned and ran. (22)

And started getting his followers together. (23)

Then he said: "I am your highest Lord." (24)

So God took him and made an example of him for the Last Day and today. (25)

And in that there is an example for those who fear. (26)

Are you stronger or is He who raised the sky and built it? (27)

Decided on its height and size (28)

and made it dark at night and lit it up during the day. (29)

Then He straightened out the earth (30)

and brought out its water and grazing lands. (31)

He set the mountains as anchors (32)

for your enjoyment and as His blessing. (33)

As the worst of all events come, (34)

the Day humans shall remember what they have done. (35)

And hell becomes prominent enough for all to see. (36)

One who transgresses, (37)

and prefers this life. (38)

Hell becomes his or her permanent residence. (39)

But one who is afraid of the stature of his Lord, and forbids oneself from following his fancy. (40)

Paradise becomes his or her permanent residence. (41)

They ask you about the Hour (*Last Day*), "When is it going to occur?" (42)

You cannot answer that question. (43)

The timing is up to your Lord. (44)

You only deliver warning to those who should be afraid of it. (45)

When they are resurrected, on that day it will seem to them like they were away only one night and one day. (46)

FROWNED (80)

In the Name of God, Most Merciful, and Most Beneficent.

He (*Mohammed*) frowned and recoiled (1)

as the blind man came to him. (2)

How is it possible to know that he (*the blind man*) did not have something in his mind that he truly needed to clarify? (3)

Or he may have needed a reminder about something that may have been of great benefit to him. (4)

But to the rich man, (5)

you are more responsive. (6)

When it is not your responsibility that he converts (*the rich man*). (7)

Yet he who came seeking you, (8)

with fear in his heart, (9)

you turned away from him. (10)

No, it (*the Book*) is a reminder (11)

One who desires can get to it. (12)

It comes in sacred pages, (13)

exalted in value and accessible in meaning. (14)

Trusted to reliable hands (*the angels and the disciples of Mohammed*). (15)

All of them are honorable and righteous. (16)

Humans are terribly unbelieving (17)

in what created them. (18)

From a sperm He created them and gave them value. (19)

Then He showed them the way. (20)

He caused them to die and be buried. (21)

And if and when He wishes He will cause them to rise again, (22)

only when He wishes. (23)

Let the humans look at their food. (24)

We powered down the water. (25)

Then We split the earth. (26)

And caused the grain to grow from it (27)

in addition to grapes and grass, (28)

and olive and palm trees (29)

and thick and shade producing gardens. (30)

in addition to fruits and animal feed, (31)

for you and your animals to prosper. (32)

As the noisy day (*Last Day*) comes (33)

The day when one runs away from a brother; (34)

a mother or a father; (35)

friends or children. (36)

Each is concerned about himself. (37)

Some faces on that day are cheerful, (38)

smiling, and optimistic. (39)

Other faces on that day are unhappy; (40)

appearing exhausted and fearful. (41)

Those are the unbelieving transgressors. (42)

THE DISAPPEARANCE (81)

In the Name of God, Most Merciful, and Most Beneficent.

As the sun collapses on itself and disappears. (1)

And as the stars lose their brightness. (2)

As the mountains are made to move. (3)

And as camels stand unattended. (4)

As animals are driven together. (5)

And as the seas dry up. (6)

As souls are brought together, in righteousness or in sin. (7)

And as the female infant buried alive asks (8)

What did she do wrong to deserve being killed. (9)

As the records of behavior are published. (10)

And the sky is wiped bare. (11)

As hell is turned up to full blast, (12)

and as heaven is prepared to receive its blessed residents. (13)

Each soul shall know what it has done. (14)

I swear by the stars that shine at night (15)

and are screened out during the day, (16)

and by the night as its darkness supervenes, (17)

and the morning as it brings its first breezes in. (18)

It (*the Book*) is relayed by an honorable apostle, (19)

with the full authority for it coming from the owner of a powerful throne. (20)

Faithful and deserves (*the apostle*) to be obeyed. (21)

He is certainly not mad. (22)

The revelation was brought to him by what he saw clearly on the horizon (*Gabriel*). (23)

He will not hide anything he knows from anyone. (24)

This is not the sayings of a devil deserving of stoning. (25)

So where are you going? (26)

It is a reminder for the whole world. (27)

For whoever wants to straighten out. (28)

You cannot wish something to happen unless the Lord of the universe wills that it should. (29)

THE RESHAPING (82)

I In the Name of God, Most Merciful, and Most Beneficent.

As the sky is reshaped, (1)

and as the stars are scattered. (2)

As the oceans explode, (3)

and as the graves are disrupted. (4)

Each soul shall know what it had done, good or bad. (5)

O' human, what did mislead you about your gracious Lord (6)

who created you, straightened you and modified you? (7)

He could have made you in any shape He wanted, (8)

yet you deny the religion. (9)

We are watching you. (10)

By those with honor who write everything, (11)

they fully know what you are doing. (12)

The righteous are in a bliss, (13)

and the transgressors are in hell. (14)

Fueling it on the Day of Religion (*the Last Day*). (15)

And they shall never leave it. (16)

What do you know about the Day of Religion? (17)

And again. How much do you know about the Day of Religion? (18)

No soul can fend for or be responsible for another. Everything on that day belongs to God. (19)

THE CHEATERS (83)

In the Name of God, Most Merciful, and Most Beneficent.

Punishment awaits the cheaters. (1)

Those when they buy, they try to make sure that the measure is to their benefit. (2)

But when they sell to others, the buyers lose. (3)

Do they not think that they shall be resurrected (4)

on a great day? (5)

The Day the people rise for the Lord of the universe. (6)

The record of the transgressors shall lead them to confinement. (7)

How do you know what a confinement is? (8)

It is based on a record that is not alterable. (9)

On that Day, bad things await those who denied. (10)

Those who denied the coming of the Day of Religion. (11)

Only a determined transgressor will deny that. (12)

As our verses were recited to him he (*the transgressor*) called them legends from people of the old times. (13)

No, but it is their sins that put a screen on their hearts. (14)

And on that Day they are screened away from their Lord. (15)

Then they shall fuel hell. (16)

Then they shall be told: "That is what you were denying." (17)

But the record of the righteous leads to heights (*as contrasted to confinement*). (18)

Do you know what new heights are? (19)

An unalterable record, (20)

witnessed by those who remain close (*the angels*). (21)

The righteous shall be in bliss, (22)

watching on recliners. (23)

Their eyes show their blissful state of mind. (24)

They shall be served honey-like wine to drink from sealed containers. (25)

Sealed by musk, and for this, those who do good shall compete. (26)

The wine is mildly diluted by water from Tasneem (*a fountain in heaven*). (27)

A fountain from where those who are the closest (*to God*) drink. (28)

Those who were transgressors used to laugh at the believers. (29)

And if they passed by them they used to wink at each other. (30)

And as they get to their own people, they would seem like they have just entertained themselves. (31)

When they see them they (*the unbelievers*) say: "These are misguided." (32)

While those unbelievers were never given authority to watch over the believers. (33)

Today it is the turn of the believers to laugh, (34)

watching while relaxing on their recliners. (35)

Did they not receive the appropriate punishment for what they did? (36)

THE SPLITTING (84)

In the Name of God, Most Merciful, and Most Beneficent.

If the sky split. (1)

And obeyed its Lord's will as it should. (2)

When the earth is stretched straight. (3)

And threw out what it was holding inside it (*the buried corpses and bones*). (4)

And it obeyed its Lord's will as it should. (5)

You humans are working very hard to meet your Lord, and meet Him you shall. (6)

Those who receive their records in their right hand (7)

shall face an easy accounting. (8)

They shall return to their family happy. (9)

But those who are given their records to carry behind their backs, (10)

shall face a terrible ending; (11)

they shall fuel the fire of hell. (12)

He used to be happy with his family. (13)

He thought he will not be faced (*by God*). (14)

I swear by the red horizon just before sunrise (16)

and by the darkness of the night and what it brings (17)

and by the brightness of the full moon. (18)

You shall advance from one situation to a better one. (19)

What is wrong with them, why do they not believe? (20)

And when the Koran is recited to them, they do not prostrate themselves. (21)

The unbelievers even stubbornly deny. (22)

God is far more Knowledgeable with what they do. (23)

Predict for them an excruciating torture. (24)

Excluding those who believed and do good works; they shall have an unlimited reward. (25)

THE SKY TOWERS (85)

In the Name of God, Most Merciful, and Most Beneficent.

I swear by the sky and its towers (*star groupings*) (1)

and by the promised Day (*the Last Day*) (2)

I swear by the witness and what is witnessed. (3)

Doomed are those who dug the ditch. (4)

Ditches that were put on fire (5)

and they sat around them. (6)

They all witnessed what they were doing with the believers. (7)

They are only targeted because of their believing in God, the Exalted, and to whom thanks belong. (8)

He to whom the heavens and the earth belong, and God is a witness to all things. (9)

Those who try to forcibly convert, the believers, men or women, and then did not repent shall have the torture of hell, and it shall be torture by fire. (10)

Those who believed, and did good works, shall be rewarded with gardens, below which rivers flow, and that is the greatest triumph. (11)

Your Lord's crushing blows are severe indeed. (12)

He creates and resurrects. (13)

He is Forgiving, and Loving. (14)

He is the Owner of the Exalted throne. (15)

He does whatever He wishes. (16)

Have you not heard the story of what happened to the soldiers (17)

who belonged to the Pharaoh and Thamoud? (18)

They disbelieved and denied. (19)

And God was fully aware of all that is around them. (20)

It is an exalted Koran. (21)

Inscribed on an ever-preserved tablet. (22)

THE VISITING STAR (86)

In the Name of God, Most Merciful, and Most Beneficent.

I swear by the heaven and the visiting star. (1)

It is an exceedingly bright star. (3)

Each soul has a watcher. (4)

Let a human consider from what he or she were created. (5)

Each was created from a gushing liquid that comes out from between the lumbar spine and the pubis. (6)

God is certainly Capable of this (*a human*) recreation. (7)

The Day when what is invisible inside each soul shall be laid open (8)

And no one shall have power or assistance. (9)

I swear by the sky which returns to earth the water it receives in the form of rain (10)

and by the earth that shoots off the trees and the plants. (11)

This (*Koran*) is the final word (12)

and it is not a joke. (13)

They plot and plot against you (14)

and I plot against them. (15)

Give the unbelievers time, for I do sometime let them go for a while. (16)

THE MOST SUPREME (87)

In the Name of God, Most Merciful, and Most Beneficent.

Glorify the name of your most supreme Lord. (1)

Who created all, in the best way. (2)

He predetermined the destinies, and provided guidance. (3)

He is the One who creates the green grazing lands. (4)

And can turn them into a useless dried up lands. (5)

We shall make you recite the revelations, and not forget. (6)

Exactly as God wishes, for He knows what is hidden and what is revealed. (7)

We shall guide you through the most straightforward path. (8)

So do remind them, when a reminder is helpful. (9)

Those who fear shall be reminded. (10)

But the transgressors shall ignore the reminder. (11)

They shall be fuel for the great fire. (12)

And in it they shall neither die nor thrive. (13)

Happy shall be one who keeps to the side of purity (14)

and recites the name of the Lord and prays. (15)

You seem to give preference to this life (16)

while the next life is better and more lasting. (17)

This a repetition of what came in the early Scriptures, (18)

those of Abraham and Moses. (19)

THE HUGE OCCURANCE (88)

In the Name of God, Most Merciful, and Most Beneficent.

Have you heard of the huge event? (1)

Faces on that Day shall exhibit fear. (2)

Those faces belong to those who committed acts deserving of punishment. (3)

And punished they shall be in a huge fire. (4)

They shall be drinking scalding water. (5)

And eating food from hell (6)

which is neither nourishing, nor does it satisfy hunger. (7)

Other faces on that Day are softer, (8)

contented with the record of works they left behind. (9)

They shall be in elevated gardens (10)

where not a bad word is heard. (11)

It shall contain a fountain with running water (12)

and elevated recliners (13)

ready-for-use cups, (14)

luxurious cushions, (15)

and luscious carpeting all around. (16)

Do they not pay attention to how the camels were created (17)

and how the sky was raised (18)

and how the mountains were anchored (19)

and how the earth was flattened? (20)

Remind them, for you are a reminder. (21)

You have no control over them. (22)

Those who turn away and disbelieve, (23)

God shall torture them in the greatest of all tortures. (24)

They shall come back to us (25)

and We shall be the One to whom they will provide an accounting. (26)

THE DAWN (89)

In the Name of God, Most Merciful, and Most Beneficent.

I swear by the dawn (1)

and the Ten Nights (*the ten before the pilgrimage*) (2)

and by the even and the odd (3)

and the night when it departs. (4)

Who built structures that stood on Columns, (7)

an equal to which there was none in the land? (8)

And the tribe of Thamoud, who dug their dwellings inside the rocks. (9)

And the Pharaoh with his impalement rods. (10)

All of them ruled through tyranny in the land (11)

and by spreading corruption. (12)

Your Lord sent on them the sting of torture. (13)

Your Lord is ever watchful for those who are like that. (14)

When humans are blessed and given from your Lord's bounty, they will say their Lord honored them. (15)

But if they are tested, by tightening their means, they will claim that their Lord humiliated them. (16)

No, the problem is that you do not find your way to honor the orphan. (17)

And you do not encourage providing food to the wretched. (18)

You easily take inherited riches that do not belong to you (19)

and love money excessively. (20)

When the earth start being remade, piece by piece (21)

and your Lord comes with the angels behind him in row after row. (22)

As they see hell before them, humans start remembering, but what good does remembrance do then? (23)

They will say: "We wish we have lived our previous life differently." (24)

On that Day torture shall be delivered only to the ones intended. (25)

And incarceration shall be faced only by the ones it is intended for. (26)

The soul that is comfortable and contented (27)

shall return to its Lord contented and satisfied. (28)

Welcomed to join My worshipers (29)

and enter My paradise. (30)

THE TOWN (90)

In the Name of God, Most Merciful, and Most Beneficent.

I swear by this town, (1)

and by your rights as a resident of this town (2)

and the father and the one he fathered. (3)

We created humans capable of struggling through the difficulties of life. (4)

But do they think that no one can put them in their place? (5)

Some will say: "We have gone through a lot of riches." (6)

Do they think no one will see them? (7)

464

Did We not give them two eyes? (8)

Did We not give them a tongue and two lips? (9)

And did We not lead them to the bifurcation of the road to right and wrong? (10)

Humans rarely attempt to overcome the obstacle ahead of them. (11)

Do you know what is the obstacle? (12)

It may consist of freeing a slave. (13)

Or feed on a day of Hunger. (14)

A relative orphan. (15)

Or a wretched homeless. (16)

Then overcoming the obstacle is by ones who are among those who believed and exhorted each other to patience and to mercy. (17)

Those are the ones who shall be on the right. (18)

Those who disbelieved our verses, shall be on the left. (19)

And shall be targeted by the great fire. (20)

THE SUN (91)

In the Name of God, Most Merciful, and Most Beneficent.

I swear by the brightness of the sun during the day. (1)

Then it is followed by the moon. (2)

As the day clears all things. (3)

And the darkness of the night enshrouds everything. (4)

And the heavens and who raised it. (5)

And the earth and who stretched it. (6)

Also by the soul and who put it together. (7)

And instilled in it its potential for good and bad. (8)

Successful shall be those who purify it. (9)

And failures shall be those who desecrate it. (10)

Thamoud disbelieved and became transgressors. (11)

They became lead by their worst. (12)

God's apostle warned them about interfering with God's female camel and its access to drinking water. (13)

They disbelieved him and killed it, and God leveled the earth with them as punishment for their sins, (14)

and for not being afraid of the consequences of their actions. (15)

THE NIGHT (92)

In the Name of God, Most Merciful, and Most Beneficent.

I swear by the night as it enshrouds all things. (1)

And the day as it clears everything. (2)

And He who created the male and female. (3)

Your efforts frequently are contradictory. (4)

One who gave in charity, worshiped and feared God (5)

and believed in good works, (6)

We shall direct to the easy life. (7)

But one who is stingy and uncaring (8)

and does not believe in the value of charity, (9)

We shall direct to the hardest of lives. (10)

One's riches shall be of no use upon death. (11)

Responsibility for guidance is upon Us. (12)

We own this life and the one next. (13)

I have warned you of a devastating fire (14)

which shall be fueled by the worst among you. (15)

Those who denied and turned away. (16)

It shall be avoided by the God fearing and the worshipers. (17)

Those who purify their riches with charity. (18)

Those who spend in charity for the sake of charity. (19)

Only for the purpose of having the chance to see the face of their supreme Lord. (20)

They shall be made to feel contented. (21)

THE MID-DAY (93)

In the Name of God, Most Merciful, and Most Beneficent.

By the middle of the day (1)

and by the night as its silence sets in, (2)

Your Lord has not abandoned you, nor did He stop caring about you (*prompted by Gabriel transmitting no revelations to Mohammed for a while*). (3)

The next life is far better for you than the first. (4)

Your Lord shall provide for you until you are contented. (5)

Did He not find you an orphan and did he not provide a home for you? (6)

And did He not find you misguided and did he not provide you with guidance? (7)

And did He not find you poor and did he not enrich you? (8)

Never take an unfair advantage of the orphan. (9)

Do not rebuke the beggar. (10)

And always mention the bounty bestowed upon you by God. (11)

THE RELIEF (94)

In the Name of God, Most Merciful, and Most Beneficent.

Did We not provide you with relief from what is bothering you? (1)

Did We not relieve you from the huge weight? (2)

That was just about to break your back? (3)

Did We not elevate your stature? (4)

Ease comes after difficulties. (5)

And yes, there is ease after difficulties. (6)

After you are relieved of the load, go back (7)

and turn to your Lord. (8)

THE FIG TREE (95)

In the Name of God, Most Merciful, and Most Beneficent.

I swear by the fig and olive (1)

and the Sineen (*Sinai*) mountain (2)

and this safe town. (3)

We created humans in the best shape (4)

and shall be eventually returned to their worst (5)

except those who believed and did good works, for they shall be rewarded without limitations. (6)

Who dares to deny you after this religion? (7)

Is not God the best of all judges? (8)

THE CLOTS (96)

In the Name of God, Most Merciful, and Most Beneficent.

Read in the name of your Lord, the Creator. (1)

He created humans from clots. (2)

Read in the name of your Exalted Lord. (3)

He brought to humans what was transmitted using a pen. (4)

He taught humans what they did not know. (5)

But humans shall transgress (6)

when they find themselves becoming rich. (7)

All will return to God. (8)

Did you see him, he who forbids (9)

a slave from praying once he saw him doing so (*the person intended is an unbelieving uncle of the apostle*). (10)

Did you ever see him guided? (11)

Or instruct others to piety ? (12)

Did you see how he denied, and turned away? (13)

Did he not know that God sees everything? (14)

If he does not desist, we shall take him by the back of his neck, (15)

the back of the neck of a lying sinner. (16)

Let him call for help to any one he chooses. (17)

We shall, on Our part, call the attendants of hell. (18)

Do not ever relent to him, but prostrate yourself to Me and get closer. (19)

THE FATEFUL NIGHT (97)

In the Name of God, Most Merciful, and Most Beneficent.

We revealed it on the Fateful Night. (1)

Did you ever know what is the Fateful Night? (2)

It is a night better than a whole month. (3)

The angels and the spirit came down that night by permission of their Lord, with every detail. (4)

It is a night of peace until the sun rises. (5)

THE EVIDENCE (98)

In the Name of God, Most Merciful, and Most Beneficent.

Those unbelievers among the people of the Book seemed to be unwilling to desist, until they get the evidence. (1)

The evidence was an apostle of God reciting sacred pages. (2)

And in it there is information about valuable books. (3)

The split among people of the Book seem to have occurred after the evidence was provided. (4)

All they were asked to do was to worship God, and be faithful to Him in their religion, attend to their prayers, and pay the alms, which is the most valuable core of the religion. (5)

The unbelievers among people of the Book, and those who associate others with God, shall be immortalized in the fire of hell, and they are the worst. (6)

While those who believed and did good works are the best of all. (7)

The reward from their God shall be gardens of Eden, below which rivers flow, and in it they shall be immortalized. Their God shall be happy with them, and they shall be happy with Him, and those are the ones who fear their Lord. (8)

THE LAST QUAKE (99)

In the Name of God, Most Merciful, and Most Beneficent.

If the earth started shaking (1)

and it splits open to show its heavy insides (2)

and humans start asking what is going on, (3)

on that Day it (*the earth*) shall tell them (4)

that God has ordered her. (5)

On that Day people shall be moving in all directions trying to find out the record of their works. (6)

Those who did a small grain worth of good shall find it, (7)

and those who did a small grain worth of evil shall also find it. (8)

THE HORSES (100)

In the Name of God, Most Merciful, and Most Beneficent.

I swear by the horses as they snort (1)

and their horseshoed hoofs as they sparkle, hitting the rocks (2)

and the noise they make in raids early in the morning (3)

and the dust they raise (4)

as they cut through the enemy crowds. (5)

Humans are frequently ungrateful for their Lord's blessings, (6)

and their Lord is a witness to that. (7)

Humans also do not easily do what is good. (8)

Do they not know what is going to happen when the graves are disrupted, (9)

and what is inside the chests is exposed? (10)

That Day their Lord shall be the Expert on what they hide. (11)

THE OCCURRENCE (101)

In the Name of God, Most Merciful, and Most Beneficent.

The occurrence. (1)

What is the occurrence? (2)

And how would you know what is the occurrence? (3)

When people shall be spread like crowded butterflies (4)

and the mountains shall look like heaps of cotton, (5)

those whose scales weigh down with their good deeds (6)

shall find themselves enjoying the true good life. (7)

And those whose scales stay up (8)

shall find themselves going down head first. (9)

Do you know where? (10)

Into a hot fire. (11)

MULTIPLICATION (102)

In the Name of God, Most Merciful, and Most Beneficent.

Multiplying (*wealth and family*) has occupied your time (1)

until you are dead and buried. (2)

No, you shall find out. (3)

And most emphatically you shall find out. (4)

For if you knew for sure, (5)

you would know that you would see hell. (6)

And see it clearly you will. (7)

And then you will be interrogated about all the luxury. (8)

THE MID-AFTERNOON (103)

In the Name of God, Most Merciful, and Most Beneficent.

I swear by the middle of the afternoon. (1)

That humans are on a losing trend. (2)

Except those who believed, did good works, and exhorted each other to be righteous, and adhered to patience. (3)

THE INSULT (104)

In the Name of God, Most Merciful, and Most Beneficent.

Cursed are those who engage in insulting and backbiting behavior. (1)

Those who amass wealth and keep on counting it, (2)

they think their fortune will immortalize them. (3)

They shall be immortalized in the consuming fire. (4)

How do you know what is the consuming fire? (5)

It is God's own lit fire (6)

which sees inside the hearts. (7)

It is aimed at those hearts (8)

in very high flaming columns. (9)

THE ELEPHANT (105)

In the Name of God, Most Merciful, and Most Beneficent.

Did you not see what your God did with people of the elephant (*an army from Ethiopia that attacked Mecca with a large elephant intending to destroy the Kaabah – before the prophethood of Mohammed*). (1)

Did He not make their plot fail? (2)

He sent on them groups of special birds (3)

that threw on them sharp cutting stones (4)

that made them look like tall grass after it was fed upon by cattle. (5)

KOURAISH (106)

In the Name of God, Most Merciful, and Most Beneficent.

For the interest of Kouraish (1)

and the benefits they get from their two trips, in the winter and summer (*in the winter to Yemen in the south, and in the summer to Damascus in the north – Caravan trade trips*). (2)

Let them worship the Lord of this House (*the Kaabah*) (3)

Who fed them when they were hungry and kept them safe when they were threatened. (4)

THE UTENSILS (107)

In the Name of God, Most Merciful, and Most Beneficent.

Did you see the one who denies the religion? (1)

It is usually the same one who neglects the orphan (2)

and the one who does not exhort others to feed the poor. (3)

Unpleasant things await those who ought to pray (4)

but remain oblivious to the need for attending to their prayers. (5)

Those are also the ones who engage in hypocrisy (6)

and willfully discourage the exchange of utensils. (*The act of lending utensils that are not being used to those who do not have them is considered a significant act of charity*). (7)

THE GREAT GIFT (108)

In the Name of God, Most Merciful, and Most Beneficent.

We gave you the great gift (*the Arabic word is said by some to stand for a river in paradise*). (1)

So pray to your Lord, with your forehead touching the ground. (2)

Those who hate you shall always be failures. (3)

THE UNBELIEVERS (109)

In the Name of God, Most Merciful, and Most Beneficent.

Say you the unbelievers: (1)

"I do not worship what you worship. (2)

Nor do you worship what I worship. (3)

I do not worship the way you worship. (4)

Nor do you worship the way I do. (5)

I have my religion, and you have yours." (6)

SUCCESS AND VICTORY (110)

In the Name of God, Most Merciful, and Most Beneficent.

As God's victory and success come to be, (1)

and you see people joining God's religions in large groups, (2)

glorify the name of your Lord and ask for His forgiveness, for He is the Great Forgiver. (3)

THE ROPE (111)

In the Name of God, Most Merciful, and Most Beneficent.

Cursed be the hands of Abi Lahab (*one of Mohammed's Uncles*), and he himself. (1)

His wealth shall be of no use or help to him. (2)

He shall fuel a fire with big flames. (3)

His wife shall be carrying heaps of firewood (4)

with a thick rope around her neck. (5)

THE ONE GOD (112)

In the Name of God, Most Merciful, and Most Beneficent.

Say: He is God, the One God. (1)

The Everlasting God. (2)

He has never had a father, nor is He the father of anyone. (3)

He is the One who never had an equal. (4)

THE DAYBREAK (113)

In the Name of God, Most Merciful, and Most Beneficent.

Say: "I resort to the Lord of the daybreak. (1)

From the worst of what He created (2)

and from the evil that may come with darkness, (3)

from the harm of enemies as they convene and plot. (4)

and from the evil that may come from those who are envious." (5)

PEOPLE (114)

In the Name of God, Most Merciful, and Most Beneficent.

Say: "I resort to the Lord of the people. (1)

The Owner of all. (2)

The God of all. (3)

For protection from the evil that dwells in the chests of some people, (4)

Which may come from the nature of people or from madness." (5)

LIST OF CHAPTERS